Aztec: The Death of a Nation

As Told by the Conquerors and the Conquered

Translated and Edited by Kenneth Pearce

ISBN: 1-4107-8005-8 (e-book)
ISBN: 1-4107-8004-X (Paperback)

This book is printed on acid free paper.

Cover Illustration: The Serpent Mask of Quetzalcoatl. Presented to Hernando Cortés by the Emperor Moctezuma at Veracruz, 1519. © Copyright The British Museum

1stBooks - rev. 11/20/03

Contents

Illustrations

Maps

Introduction

The Aztecs, or Mexica, as they are more properly called, were the last of fourteen tribes to migrate into the Valley of Mexico. Their origins lay on an island called Aztlan, "the place of the white heron", on a lake far to the northwest, according to legend. They arrived in the valley sometime prior to A.D. 1325, shifting from one town to another as they scratched out a meager living working as menials or mercenaries for the established tribes in their constant wars with each other. They eventually found a home on a swampy island off the western shore of Lake Texcoco, the only uninhabited site in the valley. But this, according to their terrible war god Huitzilopochtli, was their Promised Land, and he predicted they would recognize it by an eagle perched upon a cactus.

In the fifteenth century, however, these barbarians, despised by all the other tribes, would overthrow the ruling powers of the valley and establish the foundations of a new civilization by enacting a legal code, appointing a judiciary, and establishing schools for the elite as well as the commoner. In a span of 34 years, their rulers would project Mexican power across the land from one ocean to the other and as far south as the Kingdom of Guatemala, creating an empire whose capital was more splendid than Constantinople.

Despite their high level of culture and political skills, however, the Mexicans possessed no alphabet or written language, relying instead upon oral tradition, songs, hymns, and poems to recall their history, and upon pictorial representations to portray their gods, religious ceremonies, social order, conquests, tribute lists, laws, events of note, daily life, and dates. Although they did develop a few phonetic signs, they were used primarily for the names of persons and places.

With the coming of the Spaniards, paintings, records, dates, and the codices of Mexico and other pre-conquest societies throughout the New World were destroyed by religious zealots or by edict from above as the political climate in Spain vacillated between their preservation for posterity or condemnation as heretical and detrimental for the conversion of the natives to Christianity. So complete was their destruction of the Maya codices that only four have survived.

What is known about the history of the Mexicans was developed in the post-conquest years by Spanish intellectuals and native scholars who persevered in their efforts to reconstruct their past. During the early post-conquest years, scholars such as Fray Bernardino de Sahagún, Ándres de Olmos, and Toribio de Benevente (Motolinia) perfected Nahuatl, the native Mexican tongue, as a written language. In 1536, the college of Santa Cruz was opened in Tlatelolco to instruct sons of the Mexican elite in Latin, logic, and philosophy. In time the Franciscans, most notably Sahagun, were able to develop a cadre of native scholars who set about to transform their oral history into Nahuatl and Spanish.

During the latter part of the sixteenth century, the writings of descendants of Mexican royalty and the royalty of other ruling groups in the Valley of Mexico, many of whom undoubtedly had access to documents that survived the Spanish purge, made major contributions to the history of their peoples. Among them were Hernando Alvarado Tezozomoc, a grandson of Moctezuma; Fernando de Ixtlilxochitl, a descendant of the Texcocan ruler Nezahualpilli; and Diego Munoz Camargo, a grandson of Maxixca, who governed the Republic of Tlaxcala at the time of the conquest. And to these writers, we must add the anonymous authors who produced such great aboriginal works as the *Anales de Tlatelolco* and the *Cronica X.*

A distinctive feature of these archival documents is the extensive use of monologues and dialogues between principal characters. The technique was, in all probability, introduced by Spanish intellectuals in the years immediately following the conquest, although the extent of their influence on the native writings is, in some instances, not evident, particularly those written within a few years after the conquest.

Cervantes de Salazar, the first historian in New Spain to write of the conquest, for example, made extensive use of dialogue as the ranking lords of Tlaxcala debated whether or not to receive the Spaniards, and later, when they defended their religion against Cortés efforts to convert them to Christianity.

In native documents the technique is used time and time again, often accompanied with allegorical tales, to depict critical events in Mexican history. The *Cronica X*, for example, uses dialogue to characterize the formalities observed between a Tepanec lord and a Mexican ambassador as their nations declare war upon each other. In another instance, the same document combines dialogue with allegory to describe the efforts of a lowly temple scribe as he persuades Moctezuma, driven to desperation by unfavorable omens, not to take his own life. Part history, part anthropology, and part sociology, these dialogues and monologues take the reader back in time to see life and culture in ancient Mexico.

The significance of the dialogues is not whether they were spoken as reported by the chronicler, or even whether they were delivered at all. The paramount issue is whether they are relevant to history. Some modern writers argue that the chroniclers placed these speeches in the mouths of public characters to emphasize the importance of critical moments in history and to dramatize noteworthy events.

The works of these native authors are presented as they were written, sometimes with a word or two added for clarity, occasional omissions of words or sentences that are redundant or add confusion, and at times, edited for continuity.

The conquest is well documented by eyewitnesses, the most prominent of which are Hernando Cortés and Bernal Diaz. Clergy and the laymen have also made significant contributions to the conquest, but a number have yet to be translated into English. Examples of these are such important chroniclers as Juan de Torquemada, Gonzalo Fernández de Oviedo y Valdez, and Francisco Cervantes de Salazar.

The work of Cervantes de Salazar, the first historian in New Spain to write of the conquest, has received little mention among contemporaries, even though some did not hesitate to copy his work. A master storyteller, he made extensive use of dialogue for discussion and debate between natives and Spaniards.

It is important to note, however, that the book is not presented as scholarly critique of either the Spanish or the native texts, although notes have been provided to qualify some of the material presented. The book is intended primarily for the general reader, but every effort has been made to preserve historical accuracy throughout. A reasonable amount of latitude has been taken to provide a readable version of the text rather than a literal translation, which can be labored and stilted. Sources translated into English by others is so noted. Other than that, the story is theirs, not mine.

1. The Priest:

Exodus[i]

Long before our people came to live in the Valley of Mexico, only the Chichimecs wandered across the northern tableland of Mexico, barbarous tribes that hunted small game such as rabbits, weasels, snakes, rats, and moles, and gathered locusts, worms, roots, and herbs for food. They had no gods, no chieftains, nor any other form of government, and they went about naked, without covering their private parts.

Beyond the realm of the Chichimecs, however, there were two provinces: Aztlán, the land of the white heron, and Teuculhuacán, the home of the tribe that worships ancestors. In this province there were seven caves, where dwelled the great tribes that would one day migrate to the Valley of Mexico.

These tribes were not cave dwellers; their people lived in houses and grew crops in cultivated fields. They had a civil government and their own gods, before which they performed sacred rites.

The first of these tribes to leave the caves was the Xochimilca, who settled on the shores of the fresh-water lakes. The second tribe to leave was the Chalca, who occupied the hills south of the great lake. Then came the Tepanecs, who would build great cities on the western shore of the lake. The fourth tribe to migrate was the Acolhuaque, who claimed the Eastern Shore of Lake Texcoco. The Tlalhuica, the fifth tribe, who were crude and coarse of speech, found the entire basin of the valley occupied by the other four, and the tribe moved on to the hot lands of Cuernavaca. The sixth of the tribes to migrate was the Tlaxcalteca, and its leaders chose to lead their people into the mountainous land west of the valley.

It is recorded in our paintings that three hundred and two years passed before our tribe, the Mexica, named after the chieftain Mexi, left the seven caves. For nearly a generation, the tribe wandered through the wilderness, meeting no resistance from the Chichimecs. Their weapons were simple clubs and spears, and they were backward people who were easily deceived.

My name is Cuauhtloquetzqui, and I was one of four priests charged with the care of our god Huitzilopochtli. Wherever the Mexica went, we carried the god in a coffer of rushes. In some places, the tribe stopped for ten or twenty years, building temples for the god, planting crops, and prospering in every way. When the crops died and the land grew barren, it was time to move on and seek the promised land, from which the Mexica would one day rule the world.

When the Mexica reached Michoacán, they settled on the shores of Lake Patzcuaro and found the land so bountiful they wished to claim it for their own. The people were well satisfied with this place, and they begged me to ask Huitzilopochtli if this was the land he had promised them. In a dream, he replied that this was not the place, but it would please him if some of the tribe were to remain here.

He ordered his priests to watch when certain groups went to bathe in the lake, and when they were out of sight, we were to take their clothes and lead the others away. When the bathers returned and found their clothes gone and the camp deserted, they knew that they had been tricked. Naked and ridiculed, not knowing where the others had gone, they decided to settle the land.

Malinalxochitl, a great sorcerer and a sister of Huizilopochtli, had gone on with the others, but they soon tired of her evil ways. She tried to make them worship her as a goddess, and when they refused, she terrified them with her trickery and her curses.

In desperation, the priests complained to Huitzilopochtli, and in our dreams he answered us, saying that he had not given her powers to abuse and cast spells over his people. That very night, after first sleep, he said, we must steal away with our leaders while she slept, and none must stay behind to tell her which road they had taken.

When Malinalxochitl awakened and found the people gone, she began to weep and complain to Huitzilopochtli, but there was no answer to her pleas. Not knowing which road they had taken, she left Michoacán with her attendants and founded a city called Malinalco.

The god directed us to follow the road to Tula, the city of the Toltecs. The great Toltecs, however, had abandoned the city more than 200 years before we arrived, leaving only the ruins of their magnificent temples and broken sculptures to mark their existence. The tribe settled on Coatepec, a nearby hill, and Huitzilopochtli ordered us to dam up the river so that his people might see what the promised land would look like. They built the dike, and water spread over the entire valley, creating a beautiful lagoon lined with poplars and willows and reeds. Soon the surface of the lagoon was covered with rushes, cattails, and water flowers of every color, and it abounded with fish and waterfowl, such as ducks, heron, and many other species of birds.

The land was so beautiful and plentiful that the leaders chose to settle here, saying that this was the promised land their god had given them.

But the god grew angry.

Who are they who transgress and defy my will? Are they perhaps greater than myself? Tell them that I will take my vengeance before tomorrow and none must ever again defy me.

In my dream I saw him, and his face was ugly and terrifying to behold.

On that very night a clamor arose from the center of the ruins, and in the morning, those who had spoken of remaining here were found dead alongside the skull rack of the Toltecs, their chests ripped open and their hearts torn out.

Huitzilopochtli ordered his priests to break open the dam, and the trees withered, the rushes dried up, the fish and the frogs perished, and the waterfowl flew away.

The Mexica resumed their march to the valley, using borrowed fields to seed and harvest their crops at towns along the way, but each time, the natives wearied of them and drove them away.

At Xaltocan, a city located on an island in the northern lakes of the valley, they were made welcome and permitted to sow their fields. Their harvests were bountiful, and provided them with sufficient provisions to move on to the territory of the Tepanecs, who ruled the western shore of the great lake.

They settled at Chapultepec, where they made camp and built huts, and they asked Huitzilopochtli for guidance, since there was no other place they could go. The god told them that this was not the place meant for them, and that he would give them his answer at the proper time. Meanwhile, they must now prepare to defend themselves, for enemies surrounded them.

The first enemy, however, came from within the tribe. Huitzilopochtli's sister Malinalxochitl, whom he abandoned in Michoacán, had given birth to a son named Copil. When Copil came of age, Malinalxochitl told him of the injury she had suffered at the hands of her brother, and in his rage, he set out to find Huitzilopochtli and kill him. He followed the Mexica to Chapultepec, and he warned the Tepanecs that they could not be trusted. He told them that they would regret every day they allowed them to remain at Chapultepec. Attack them now, he said, and be rid of them for good.

But the god was aware of his nephew's intentions, and he ordered his priests to seek out Copil and kill him. When we found him, we cut out his heart and presented it to Huitzilopochtli. He bade one of the priests to go into the marsh and cast it into the middle of the lake, and he told him that a cactus would rise from Copil's heart. When the Mexica found it, it would be the site where their city would rise.

But Copil had done his work. The Tepanecs sent their mercenaries from Chalco to attack the Mexica, and after a fierce battle, they retreated to Culhuacán and threw themselves upon the mercy of Achitometl, the lord of the city.

Then Huitzilopochtli spoke again.

Send your messengers to the lord of Culhuacán, and without prayers or compliments, ask him to designate a site and place where you can reside or rest. Do not fear to enter his presence boldly, for I will soften his heart so that he will receive you. Take whatever place he gives you, be it good or bad, and settle in this country until its purpose shall have been fulfilled.

4

Achitometl received the Mexica kindly, and treated them with consideration while he spoke of the matter with his council. After much discussion, they decided the Mexica could settle on a plain of volcanic lava, which was home to vipers, snakes, and poisonous insects.

Before long the Mexica multiplied and prospered, building homes and temples and growing crops in the hostile soil of the plain. Their gratitude to Achitometl was such that they asked him for permission to trade in Culhuacán and intermarry with his people.

But Huitzilopochtli was troubled that his people would choose to live among the Culhua. That night he spoke to me in a dream.

We must seek a woman, one whom we are going to call the woman-of-discord, and this one is to be called grandmother of the place where we are to go and remain. This is not the site where we are to make our home. That place is farther on, the place I have promised you, and a reason for leaving this place must be found, be it a war or a murder. Begin now to prepare the things necessary for your defense and give your enemy cause to attack you. Go immediately to the king of Culhuacán and ask him to give you a daughter for my service, and he will give her to you. She will be the woman-of-discord.

Achitometl loved his daughter very much, but he readily agreed to give her to the Mexica, considering it an honor that she was to be their queen and grandmother of their god. The Mexica carried her off in state with the well wishes of the Culhua, and both parties were well satisfied with the agreement.

That same night Huitzilopochtli spoke again.

This woman will be the cause of discord between you and the people of Culhuacán, as I have told you. Now you must discharge your duty to me. Kill this girl and sacrifice her in my name, and from this day on, I will take her as my mother. After that, flay her and let one of your nobles wear her skin and dress himslelf in her garments. Then invite the king, her father, to come and worship the goddess, his daughter, and offer her sacrifices.

This was done, and she now became the goddess who is called Toci in the book of sacrifices, which means our grandmother.

The Mexica called upon Achitometl to come and pay his homage to the queen of the Mexica and their new goddess. He gathered his nobles, and they brought offerings of incense, feathers, fine foods, and many fine gifts for Huitzilopochtli and the new goddess.

When the Culhua king and his nobles were rested, the Mexica placed the noble dressed in the skin of his daughter in front of Huitzilopochtli. Then the Mexica led Achitometl into the darkened temple, where he sacrificed quail and scattered their blood upon the altar, then laid incense, flowers, and food before the deities. As it was dark in the temple and he could not see the god before him, he took a lamp into his hand and raised it. There before him was the dread figure of Huitzilopochtli, and standing in front of the god was a man dressed in the skin of his daughter.

He covered his face in horror, then dropped the lamp and rushed outside the temple, shouting "They have murdered my daughter and dressed a youth in her skin! Kill these evil men! Destroy them so that no trace or memory of them will remain on the face of the land!"

They drove the Mexica into the waters as far as Ixtapalapa, then to Acatzintitlan, where they came to a river so deep they had to make rafts from their throwing sticks and reeds to carry their women and children to the opposite shore. The men hid in canebrakes, where they passed the entire night, listening to the women and children wailing on the other side of the river.

The following day the people went far out into the lagoon, seeking a place where they could settle. There was no place for them on land, because enemies surrounded the lake. They came upon a spring surrounded by white reeds and canes, and above the spring was a white juniper, and nowhere did they see a single green leaf. The water that issued between two rocks was clear and limpid, and in the water were fish, white frogs, and white snakes. The priests, remembering what their god told them, began to weep tears of joy, saying that they had at last found the place where their weary people could rest.

That night Huitzilopochtli once again came to the priests again in dreams.

Now you know that everything I have told you has come to pass, but there is yet more to be seen. When I told you to cast Copil's heart into the lagoon, it fell upon a rock, and from it sprang a cactus, and now a great eagle has made a nest upon it. Go there and you will find it, and this place will be called Tenochtitlán.

They returned to the spring they had found a day earlier, but now two streams flowed from it, one blood red and the other blue and thick. Beyond it they found the cactus, and an eagle with its wings spread out to catch the heat of the sun was perched on top of it. They knelt down before the eagle and wept tears of joy and happiness. "We have found our city, our abode. Let us give thanks to the god of creation and to our god Huitzilopochtli."[ii]

They went to the little island where the cactus stood and cut thick slices of mud from the lagoon and built a platform for Huitzilopochtli, and over it they built a roof made of straw. Carefully, they removed Huitzilopochtli from the coffer and placed him in the shrine.

Aware that they had settled in territory that was not theirs, some of the people wanted to go to Atzcapotzalco and offer to become vassals of the Tepanecs, and in that way, they might receive stone and wood to build their city. Others felt that this would only subject them to mistreatment from the Tepanecs. Better, they said, to go to the Tepanec towns of Atzcapotzalco, Tacuba, and Coyoacán with fish, frogs, and waterfowl on market day, where they could buy the stone and wood they needed.

They drove stakes around the tiny island and filled the gap with stones, and in time, a city began to rise above the lake. They erected a small temple of stone upon the platform, and although it was crude, Huizilopochtli was satisfied. When they finished laying the foundations of Tenochtitlán and raised a temple for Huitzilopochtli, the god spoke again.

Tell my people that their leaders must divide their city into four principal barrios, with each to be governed according to their friendships and alliances. My temple is to lie at the center of the barrios, and in each they must raise a shrine to me.

When the land had been divided, however, all were not pleased. Some of the elders and patriarchs felt that they had been slighted in the division of the lands. They took their friends and relatives and settled on a small island just north of Tenochtitlán, and they called their city Tlatelolco, the place-of-the-terrace. To secure their claim on the island city, they gained an alliance with Tezozómoc, the great lord of Atzcapotzalco, by taking his son Cuacuapitzhauac to be their king.

7

The leaders of Tenochtitlán, fearing that the alliance would tempt Tlatelolco to assume leadership of the Mexica, decided that it would be to their benefit to seek a king from Culhuacán, since that city held claim to as much of the island as Atzcapotzalco.

A Mexica warrior named Opochtzin had remained in Culhuacán when they fled the city, and he was now married to a woman of the royal family. A son named Acamapichtli was born of their union, and the leaders of Tenochtitlán felt it fitting that he be their king.

Nauhyotl, the lord of the Culhua, though aware of the fate of the daughter of Achitometl, was receptive to the proposal offered by the Mexica. He agreed to release Acamapichtli to be lord of Tenochtitlán, and to bind their people closer to Culhuacán, offered his daughter to be their queen.

Tezozómoc, the great lord of Atzcapotzalco, however, considered the marriage an affront to his sovereignty over Tenochtitlán. As punishment, he doubled their annual tribute and demanded that they plant juniper and willows, fully grown, in his city. Furthermore, they were to build a floating garden of chilis, maize, beans, and wild amaranth in the lagoon and bring it to Atzcapotzalco.

When the Mexica heard this, they began to weep and cry out against Tezozomoc's unreasonable demands. But that night Huitzilopochtli spoke again to his priests.

I have seen the suffering of my people and their tears. Let them not to be heavy of heart, for I will deliver them safely from all their troubles. Let them pay this tribute. To my son Acamapichtli, I say be of good heart. Take the junipers and willows to Atzcapotzalco, and build a raft in the lagoon to plant upon it all that Tezozómoc demands. They need not fear, for I shall make their task easy.

The tribute was paid just as Tezozómoc demanded, but he decided that the Mexica had not yet been sufficiently humbled. He now demanded that they build a floating garden with ripe and mature plants, and in their midst, there was to be a duck sitting upon her eggs and a heron hatching her eggs. Furthermore, the eggs must hatch the moment the raft reached Atzcapotzalco.

That night Huitzilopochtli came to me in a dream.

Tell my people to have no fear. Tell my son Acamapichtli that I know best what is to be done, and he must obey me. Pay the tribute that

Atzcapotzalco demands, and the day will come when it will be redeemed with the blood of his enemies. They will perish; they will become slaves within a few years. My children suffer and weep now, but their time will come!

The Mexica built a raft like the other, and planted flowers and ferns of every specie upon it. When all was ready, they set upon it a duck with her eggs and a heron with hers. To Tezozómoc's surprise, the eggs hatched the moment the raft reached Atzcapotzalco.

Tezozómoc now realized that the Mexica had a powerful god, and that they were to be feared. Determined to keep them under subjugation, he decreed that they must perform the same task each and every year.

Acamapichtli reigned over the Aztecs for nineteen years, during which time he fought Tezozómoc's wars as far away as the Valley of Toluca, and in his own right, extended Mexica hegemony over Xochimilco, a city located a short distance southeast of Tenochtitlán. He laid out houses and canals throughout the city, and his rule was one of peace and tranquillity.

On his deathbed, Acamapichtli refused to designate which of his many sons was to rule Tenochtitlán, but instead urged the people to select a lord of their own choosing. By doing so, he established a precedent for all the rulers who were to follow him: no son would ever inherit the turquoise diadem through primogeniture.

The lords of the four divisions of Tenochtitlán met to decide the succession, and they chose Huitzilíhuitl, a son of Acamapichtli, to lead the Mexica.

To improve relations with Atzcapotzalco, the lords approached Tezozómoc and sought a bride from his family to be Huitzilíhuitl's queen. Inasmuch as the lord of Tlatelolco was his son, Tezozómoc was pleased to offer a daughter to Tenochtitlán. The opportunity to exercise Tepanec influence over both island cities was too good to be ignored. The union was propitious for the Mexica as well, inasmuch as Tezozómoc relieved the Mexica of all tribute save for the annual gift of the floating gardens. His decision, however, was not popular with the lords of the Tepanec council.

Huitzilíhuitl ruled Tenochtitlán for 24 years in peace and wisdom, and was loved by noble and commoner alike. During his reign, he gave the Mexica their first laws, expanded the city farther out into the lake, built more temples, and set their religious ceremonies in order. He launched his principal military campaign against Cuernavaca, a fortified town 30 miles south of Tenochtitlán, where cotton, which provided Mexico with its first noble garments, was grown.

When Huitzilíhuitl died, Chimalpopoca, his son by Tezozómoc's daughter, was elected lord of the Mexica. He was only 18 years old, but he was the favorite of his grandfather. Tezozómoc now permitted the Mexica to visit Atzcapotzalco and trade in the city marketplace. The council of the Tepanec lords, however, resented Tezozómoc's favoritism for the Mexica lord, and they seethed under his relieving Tenochtitlán of all but nominal tribute. .

In view of their new relationship with the Tepanecs, the Mexica, in dire need for fresh water, urged Chimalpopoca to ask Tezozómoc's permission to bring the waters of Chapultepec to Tenochtitlán. The king readily gave his permission, and they built an earthen aqueduct across the lagoon.

Unfortunately, the walls of the aqueduct, being built of adobe, soon broke, and Chimalpopoca asked Tezozómoc if he and his people could provide them with stone, wood, lime, and stakes to build a new pipe.

Their request infuriated the Tepanec council. "Lord, they said, "do the Mexica think that we are their vassals and servants? We gave them our land and allowed them to build their city upon it, then we gave them our water! And now, disrespectful of our ruler, they dare ask us to build an aqueduct for them! Who do these people think they are to presume upon us in this manner?"

The Tepanec lords began to stir up the people, warning them that the Mexica were planning to enslave them and force them to pay tribute. They forbid Coyoacán and Tacuba, the Tepanec cities, to trade with the Mexica or give them any supplies upon penalty of death.

Tezozómoc, now on his deathbed, knew he could no longer forestall his lords from attacking Tenochtitlán, and he begged them to kidnap his grandson so that he could be spared the coming war. But the lords stood fast. Chimalpopoca, they said, was a Tepanec only through his mother; he was a Mexica on his father's side, and

10

therefore he was their enemy. The aged lord soon died, and the last obstacle to war had been removed.

---

[i] The journey of the Mexica from Aztlán to Tenochtitlán is described in a document written by an unknown native author sometime between AD 1537-1539. The document was last seen by native and Spanish chroniclers of the 16th century. Called the *Cronica X* for lack of a better name, the text appears in the works of three early writers-Hernando Alvarado Tezozomoc, Fray Diego Duran, and Juan de Tovar.

The location of Aztlán is unknown. Modern historians place it northwest of the Valley of Mexico, perhaps on the coast of Nayarit, but at an unknown distance from Mexico City. It is described only as being surrounded by water.

[ii] The Mexica left Aztlán AD 1111 (?), reached Tula in AD 1168, the Valley of Mexico in AD 1193, and settled in Tenochtitlán in AD 1345. The eagle perched upon a cactus is now the national symbol of Mexico.

2.Doña Isabel:

The Empire Builders

I was born in the eighth year of the reign of my father, Moctezuma Xocóyotl,[i] a royal princess of an empire in its golden age, an empire whose power and extent surpassed even that of our noble forbears, the great Toltecs.

In the Valley of Mexico, on the Western Shore of Lake Texcoco, the once-mighty Tepanec Empire and its sovereign capital, Atzcapotzalco, now served Mexico. On the Eastern Shore, Moctezuma's true and constant ally, Nezahualpilli, was supreme lord, and to the south, the cities along shores of the fresh-water lakes, Culhuacán, Cuitláhuac, Mixquic, and Xochimilco, were subject to Mexico. Beyond the valley, Moctezuma's empire reached from the eastern seacoast to the shores of the southern sea; to the north, as far as the Panuco River; and to the southeast, the distant lands of the Maya.

Yet the ascendancy of our people from a base vassalage to the most powerful nation in the world came about in less than seventy-five years; a momentous era that saw four gifted lords emerge. The first of these great lords would subjugate the Valley of Mexico, and his successors would project Mexican sovereignty beyond the sierra until it encompassed all of Anáhuac.[ii]

The empire was born when the Mexican people grew weary of serving as Tepanec mercenaries for the privilege of eking out a meager existence on the swampy, pestilent island a league from the western shore of the lake. For more than 50 years, Mexico served Tezozómoc, the mighty lord of Atzcapotzalco, in his wars to subjugate the Valley of Mexico and extend Tepanec hegemony beyond Toluca and Moreles. While he struggled for control of the valley, his levies were harsh and humiliating for our people, but as he aged, he tempered his demands, and when his favorite grandson, Chimalpopoca, was elected lord of Mexico, he all but eliminated them.

When the emperor's long reign ended, however, Maxtla, the lord of Coyoacán, eager to succeed his father and resentful of the many privileges granted to our people, persuaded the Tepanec nobles and the new lord of Atzcapotzalco to reinstate the old, unsparing levies.

The Mexicans were outraged, but Chimalpopoca chose to appease his Tepanec kinsmen rather than fight. When the Mexican nobles could no longer tolerate his continuing submission to the demands of Atzcapotzalco, they decided to eliminate him. Wisely, they hired assassins from Tacuba to kill Chimalpopoca, knowing the blame would fall upon Maxtla. With the death of the Mexican ruler, the Tepanecs blockaded the causeway to enforce their demands for tribute, and war seemed inevitable.

In 1426, Itzcóatl, the son of Acamapichtlí by an Atzcapotzalca slave girl, became our fourth *tlatoani*. Determined to resist Maxtla, he sought the support of Nezahualpilli, the lord of Texcoco, and that of his nephews, Moctezuma Ilhuicamina and Tlacaélel, in the event of war. Many of his nobles, however, feared the wrath of the Tepanecs more than the shame of bondage. They removed their god Huitzilopochtli from this temple and set out for Atzcapotzalco, intending to present their god to the new lord as a symbol of Mexico's enduring vassalage. But when they reached the causeway, they found Itzcóatl and Tlacaélel waiting for them.

"Mexicans," Tlacaélel said, "have you no shame? Have you become so craven as to throw yourselves at the feet of the Atzcapotzalca? Have you given no thought to how this contemptible act will reflect upon the honor of Mexico for generations to come?"

Turning to Itzcóatl, he said, "Lord, reason with your people. If they want only peace and security, prevail upon them to seek a more honorable course."

"Kinsmen," Itzcóatl said, "I know your fears are not unfounded, but do not deliver our god into the hands of the Atzcapotzalca. Let me instead offer you a compromise, a measure that should prove honorable and perhaps satisfy all.

"You are all celebrated lords; lords of unquestionable courage. Now I call upon one of you to go to the lord of Atzcapotzalco and remind him that we were once loyal servants of his father, and ask him why he is so bent upon destroying us. If there is one among you who can put aside his fears of Atzcapotzalco, go to him and petition him in my name for peace with honor between his people and mine."

The nobles fell silent. When Tlacaélel saw that none would step forward, he turned to his uncle and said, "Lord, do not let your spirit fail you for the lack of courage shown by our kinsmen. Let me go to the lord of Atzcapotzalco. If he refuses to hear me out and kills me, to what better end could I die than in the service of my country. Since I must die one day or another, it matters little if I die today or die tomorrow."

"Nephew," Itzcóatl replied, "I am deeply moved by your courage. Take my message, and if you succeed, I shall reward you as none has ever before been rewarded, and you will rank among our greatest lords. If you are killed by the Atzcapotzalca, these same rewards and honors will be bestowed upon your sons and your grandsons, and your sacrifice will live in our hearts forever."

Tlacaélel put on the time-honored robes of a royal emissary and crossed the causeway to Atzcapotzalco. When he reached the outskirts of the city, Tepanec sentries halted him.

"Are you not Tlacaélel, the nephew of the lord of Mexico?" they asked. "Do you know that we are forbidden to admit Mexicans, that we are ordered to kill them on sight?"

"Yes, I know your orders," Tlacaélel replied, "but I come as a royal ambassador, to whom all nations must grant an audience. I bring a message to your lord from Itzcóatl and the people of Mexico. Allow me to pass, and I promise no blame will fall upon you. I must come this way when I return, and I will place myself in your hands again."

14

The sentries let him pass, and when he was admitted to the royal palace, the lord of Atzcapotzalco was surprised to see a Mexican noble kneeling before him, and even more surprised that his warriors had not killed him on sight. Impressed by the young Mexican's courage, he bade him sit beside him and state his purpose.

Itzcóatl, Tlacaélel told the king, saw no purpose in a war between Mexico and the Tepanecs, since he and his people had no intent other than to serve him as they had served his father before him. This war that Maxtla and the Tepanec lords were determined to pursue, he said, would leave both cities devastated, bring about untold suffering among the common people, especially the elderly and the very young, and the people of one nation or the other would be slaves forever. If he and his nobles would accept Itzcóatl once again as their honored servant, he offered his solemn pledge that Mexico would do nothing to provoke the Tepanecs.

Moved by Tlacaélel's sincerity, the lord of Atzcapotzalco promised to present Itzcoatl's petition for peace before the Council of Tepanec Lords, but he warned him that his powers were limited. If the council refused to yield, war was inevitable. Their decision would be waiting for him when he returned in the morning.

Since Tlacaélel had entered the city without the benefit of a safe conduct, he was obliged to leave the same way. He reached the outskirts of the city without incident, but when he arrived at the causeway, he found a squad of armed warriors waiting for him.

"Comrades," he said, "I have presented Itzcóatl's proposal to your lord, and he has asked me to return in the morning for his answer. Let me leave now, and when I return, I will place myself in your hands again, just as I did today, when you gave me permission to enter the city. If it is still your will to kill me, what difference does it make if you kill me now or kill me tomorrow?"

The warriors, reassured by his return that he would keep his word, allowed him to pass.

Itzcóatl was pleased to hear that the lord of Atzcapotzalco would present his offer of peace before the Tepanec Council, but held out little hope that Maxtla and his supporters would offer any compromise or concession.

"Nephew," he said, "tomorrow we will know whether the Tepanecs will receive us as their friends and servants once more, or if they are still bent upon destroying our city and enslaving our people. If the lord of Atzcapotzalco fails to persuade his nobles to accept my offer, this is what you must do. Give him this shield and these golden arrows, then arm him with this *maquahuitl* so that he may defend himself. Then place these feathers upon his head and anoint his body with bitumen and pitch, just as we do with the dead, and tell him we must do now that which we must do."

Once again the Tepanec sentries allowed Tlacaélel to pass, and after he made his obeisance to the king, he rose and said. "Lord, your servant and vassal Itzcóatl, the lord of Mexico, awaits your decision. Will you, O Lord, raise your hand to protect your servants; will you favor us as your father did in the past, or have you forsaken us? Is it still the will of the Tepanecs to destroy our people?"

"Tlacaélel, my son," the king answered, "what am I to say? Though I am lord, it is the will of my people that we wage war upon you, and I am powerless to prevent them. They are angry with your people, and they are determined to kill them all. If I attempt to stop them, I shall forfeit my life and the lives of all my children."

"Then, O lord,"Tlacaélel said, "your servant the lord of Mexico stands in defiance of you. He advises you to gather up your courage and prepare for war, for now he is your mortal enemy. He sends you these arrows, this shield, and this *maquahuitl* so that may defend yourself, and he commands me to anoint you with this pitch, this unction of the dead, so that you may prepare yourself for death. Henceforth he will weep for you for taking this course from which no good can come; he will weep for your undertaking a war that can end only with many good warriors lying dead on the battlefield and the people of one of our nations enslaved forever."

The lord of Atzcapotzalco permitted Tlacaélel to arm him and anoint his body, and when he finished, he asked him to thank Itzcóatl for his offer of peace. Then he lowered his voice and said, "My son, do not leave by the palace gate. My nobles are waiting for you there. There is a secret opening behind the palace where you can leave without being seen. Go now my son, and for your courage, for your courtesy and friendship, take this shield and *maquahuitl* with you."

Tlacaélel left the palace without being discovered, and by avoiding the main road, he reached a point on the causeway well beyond the sentries.

16

"Tepanecs! Atzcapotzalcas!" he shouted, "How carelessly you watch over your city! Beware lest every man, woman, and child perish in blood and fire, for Itzcóatl, the lord of Mexico, is now your mortal enemy!"

The guards rushed toward him, but he stood his ground and killed the first to reach him. Then others arrived, and he turned and fled across the causeway.

War was only a matter of days away, and the common people began to panic. They gathered before the royal palace, threatening to abandon the city unless Itzcóatl submitted to the demands of the Tepanecs.

"Do not be afraid, my children," Itzcóatl said, "I give you my word that no harm will come to you, and when this war is over, you will be rid of the Tepanecs forever."

"But if you should fail," they replied, "what is to become of us?"

"If we do not succeed," Itzcóatl said, "My nobles and I will place ourselves in your hands to do as you please with us. You may sacrifice everyone of us and eat our flesh from cracked and dirty dishes."

"You have pronounced your own sentence," the people said, "and we accept your terms. For our part, if you succeed, we will work your lands, build your houses, and serve you as our sovereign lords. We will give you our daughters and our sisters, and they too will serve you. When you wage war, we will carry your arms, your provisions, and your baggage wherever you go. And lastly, we will pay you tribute from the fruits of our land forever."

The siege of Atzcapotzalco lasted nearly four months. Itzcóatl launched an attack against the eastern defenses of the city, Moctezuma Iluicamina attacked from the south, and Nezahualcóyotl, supported by the powerful lord of Huexotzingo, struck from the north. Our armies suffered heavy losses, but the Tepanecs were a house divided, without allies or mercenaries to fight beside them, and when their granaries were exhausted, they were forced to yield. The victorious allies swept into the city, sparing none as they fired the temples and sacked the palaces of Tezozomoc's empire.

But Itzcóatl had little time to relish his victory. Maxtla, who had survived the war by standing aside when Itzcóatl attacked Atzcapotzalco, now moved to claim the throne of Tezozomoc as lord of the Tepanecs. He would not realize his ambition, however, until Mexico was destroyed or subjugated, and the power vacuum created by the fall of Atzcapotzalco filled by Coyoacán. To do this, he had to seek allies among those cities surrounding the valley that had cause to fear or hate Mexico.

The Tepanecs still controlled the western shore of Lake Texcoco, and could be rallied to take a stand if Maxtla could gain sufficient support. On the Eastern Shore of the lake, a number of Acolhuaque towns subject to Texcoco still embraced Tepanec sympathies, but Nezahualcóyotl would have to be persuaded to renounce Itzcóatl. To the south, along the shores of the fresh-water lakes, Cuitláhuac was spoiling for a war with Itzcoatl, and the most powerful cities in the area, Xochimilco and Culhuacán, bore no love for Mexico.

Beyond the valley, the powerful Chalco confederacy situated along the southeastern approaches to Mexico had been enemies of our people even before Tenochtitlán was founded. Wars with Chalco had been bitter and incessant, and when Huitzilíhuitl, the second *tlatoani* of Mexico, captured Chalco in 1411, the Tepanecs, concerned with the rising aggressiveness of their mercenaries, turned against them and fought alongside the Chalca.

Maxtla's first overtures were to Atzcapotzalco, hoping to reunite the Tepanecs, but he received no encouragement from his kinsmen. The Atzcapotzalca were bitter because of his failure to come to their aid, and they had no desire to shed their blood again to further his ambitions.

Next he turned to the eastern shore, seeking to convince Nezahualcóyotl it was in his best interest to ally himself with Coyoacán. But he was on a fool's errand. After the death of Tezozomoc, he had appointed Nezahualcoyotl's half-brother to the throne of Texcoco, and twice sent assassins to kill him.

Failing to find allies along the eastern and western shores of the lake, Maxtla turned to the south. He proposed that the lords of Xochimilco, Mixquic, Culhuacán, and Cuitláhuac meet with him in Chalco to resolve the Mexican problem for once and all. Only the lord of Mixquic declined his invitation.

There was general agreement among the lords gathered in Chalco that Mexico should be destroyed, and that it be done as quickly as possible. When it came to working out the details of the alliance,

18

however, they could find no common ground. Who among them would lead the alliance? How would the spoils of war be shared? Which of them would the Mexicans serve as vassals when they were defeated? In the end, it was the lord of Amecameca, a Chalco ruler, who, convinced that their differences were irreconcilable, suggested that if the Tepanecs or any of the others were determined to wage war on Mexico, better they do so alone.

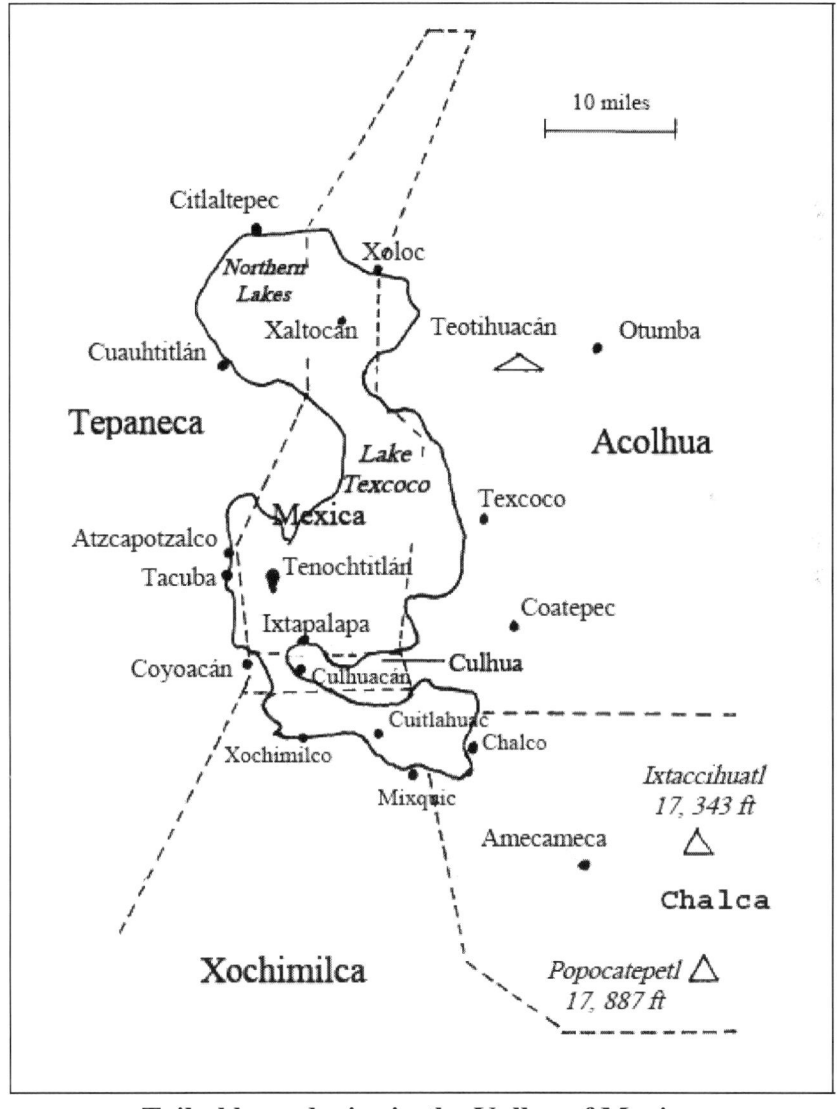

Tribal boundaries in the Valley of Mexico

With the collapse of the Chalco talks, Maxtla returned to Coyoacán, determined to stand alone against Mexico. He chose the feast of Xocotl Huetzi, the god of Coyoacán, to issue his crude but unequivocal declaration of war. He invited the principal lords of Mexico to the festival, and Itzcóatl obliged by sending Tlacaélel and a party of ranking nobles to honor their god. When the ceremony was over, Maxtla seized the Mexicans and dressed them in skirts and blouses. He then set them before the gates of Tenochtitlán, proclaiming that their dress was proper for men who could not be provoked into fighting.

Maxtla had no more success against the Mexicans that had the Atzcapotzalca. Itzcoatl met his squadrons head-on, while Tlacaélel circled the battlefield and attacked from the rear. Maxtla was forced to retreat to Coyoacán, but Tlacaélel reached the city before him and fired the temple. The war was over-Xocotl Huetzi had fallen before the power of Huitzilopochtli.

With the defeat of Maxtla, Itzcóatl set about establishing Mexican hegemony over the valley. The Tepanec towns of the western shore of the lake were quickly swallowed up, and the southern shore of the lake was secured by successive wars with Xochimilco and Cuitláhuac. In the Valley of Mexico, Itzcóatl was now supreme lord, and our young, vigorous nation looked forward to a future that lay beyond the sierra.

Itzcóatl died in 1440, and his nephew Moctezuma Ilhuicamina was chosen to succeed him to the jaguar and eagle throne.

Moctezuma's reign marked the beginning of a new order for Mexico. The simple laws that had sufficed for a migrant tribe of mercenaries were no longer adequate for a nation that now governed the older, more established and worldly cultures of the Valley of Mexico. To meet these newly acquired responsibilities of sovereignty, Moctezuma wrote the first legal code of Mexico and enacted the statues required to enforce it.

He established a judicial system whereby a high court sat in judgment of the nobles, and a lower court passed judgment on the common people. If the matter before the court was too complex or beyond the jurisdiction of either court, it was referred to a council of four princes, but neither the courts nor the royal council could impose the death penalty without first notifying the king.

The Coronation of Moctezuma I

The new emperor receives the turquoise crown from Nezahulcóyotl

Moctezuma decreed that his judges, who were appointed from the ranks of the commoners as well as the nobility, be men of good memory, that they rise early in the morning, avoid drunkenness, and honor their lineage. He demanded that they observe impartiality toward friend and enemy alike, and forbade them from hearing a case for a fee. Failure to enforce the law, regardless of the rank of the offending judge, was punishable by death.

He established a school for the sons of the elite, and another for the sons of the commoners, where they were taught religion and good manners. Under the watchful eyes of their teachers, they did penance, fasted, learned the art of warfare, and observed celibacy.

He determined when our religious rites were to be celebrated and how they were to be performed, and stipulated a dress code for all the people. Only the nobility and the great captains could wear gold, precious jewelry, and cotton clothing. Commoners could wear only coarse shifts woven from maguey fiber. In the royal court, only the *cihuacoatl*, the vice regent, could wear sandals. All others were to appear unshod, save for warriors who had performed a notable act of

21

valor, and were privileged to wear coarse sandals. Death was the penalty for violating the dress code, adultery, and breaking a vow of chastity.

The emergence of Mexico as the leading power in the valley established the supremacy of Huitzilopochtli over all other gods, and Moctezuma felt obliged to build a fitting home to pay him homage. He set about the monumental task of laying the foundation of a temple that would not be completed for 40 years, and bonded the mortar with the blood of 500 Chalca warriors and the precious jewels of his people.

Moctezuma's ambitions and the fate of his budding empire, however, hung in the balance when a series of disasters, one after another, struck the valley and the surrounding highlands.

In 1449, heavy rains raised the level of Lake Texcoco, inundating Tenochtitlán. Strong swells, driven by the winds that blow across the valley late in winter, destroyed so may houses and temples that it was feared the city would have to be abandoned. In desperation, Moctezuma turned to Nezahualcoyotl, who had designed and built the viaducts, dikes, and canals that fed the parks and fountains of Texcoco.

It was obvious that the city could be protected from unseasonable floods if a levee were to be built across the strait between Tenochtitlán and the peninsula that separates Lake Texcoco and the fresh-water lakes. But a permanent sea wall would have a disastrous impact upon the economy of the city, since it would isolate Tenochtitlán from the tens of thousands of canoes that supplied its markets every day.

Nezahualcoyotl's solution was to drive heavy wooden piles in parallel rows across the strait and fill the space between with rock and earth. To accommodate lake traffic, he devised a series of floodgates that could be opened to allow free passage of lake traffic during seasons of normal rainfall, yet sturdy enough to hold back the floodwaters when closed. Using forced labor from the towns surrounding the lake, Nezahualcoyotl built a massive dike ten paces across and three leagues in length across the strait.

The floodwaters abated, but within months, famine came to the land. The rains disappeared, the streams dried up, the rivers ceased to flow, and the land became barren. Moctezuma opened the royal granaries, but within a year they were empty, and he was forced to acknowledge that he could do no more for his starving people. With a heavy heart, he advised them to leave the city and survive as best they could in regions that had been spared the drought. For no more than a single basket of maize, parents sold their sons and daughters to foreign lords and merchants who could feed them. The Totonacs, whose fertile lands on the eastern seaboard never failed to provide them with abundant harvests, sent scores of merchants laden with baskets of maize and fruit to buy our children. Mothers and fathers wept to see their children wearing heavy yokes about their necks as they were led away to labor in the fields of the hot lands.

After four years of heavy drought, the rains returned, and the god Tlaloc poured forth his waters in such abundance that the crops flourished as never before. The harvests were so plentiful that many were able to ransom their children and reestablish their homes in the city and the surrounding valley.

Blessed once more by a bountiful land, sheltered from the floods by the great dike, Mexico embarked upon an unprecedented era of prosperity and expansion. As Tenochtitlán flourished, so did the merchants of neighboring Tlatelolco, who journeyed throughout Anahuac, extending Mexican commerce as far as distant Xicalango, the center of the vast trade network of the Maya. This newly acquired affluence did not come cheap, however. As Tlatelolco strove to reach the distant markets of Anahuac, its merchants found it necessary to enter hostile territories, where they were often tortured and put to death. To protect his profitable enterprise, Moctezuma was forced to maintain a standing army large enough to mount campaigns as far as the eastern seacoast, and deep into the home of the Cloud People[iii] in the southern sierra,

If Mexican commerce was to flourish, Moctezuma knew that it was vital that he open a route to the rich eastern seaboard. The most direct route lay to the southeast, where a pass crossed the sierra beneath the great volcano Citlaltepetl[iv]. Tepeaca, a small town some 30 leagues from Mexico, commanded the entry to the pass, and Moctezuma lost no time in overwhelming its defenses and establishing a garrison to secure the western approaches to the seacoast. From Tepeaca, he sent his warriors against the Totonacs at Ahuilizapan, and with his victory, all resistance to his intrusion collapsed. Moctezuma installed a Mexican governor at Cotastla, the principal town of the region, to enforce his levies on the Totonacs.

Moctezuma's farthest-reaching campaigns sent Mexican armies into Oaxaca, 90 leagues to the southwest, to seize control of Coaixtlahuaca, the great trading center of the Cloud People. But Moctezuma soon found he had reached the limit of his ability to maintain a Mexican presence so far from home. Neither the Cloud People nor the Totonacs were easily controlled, and other enemies, at home and abroad, demanded his full attention.

Although there were peaceful interludes between his campaigns, there was little time for his warriors to enjoy them, since an alert and ready military capability was essential to protect Mexican interests. To insure the combat readiness of his squadrons, Moctezuma established a series of incentives for status and rank that could be gained only in warfare. To provide his warriors with every opportunity to earn recognition, he arranged for a series of ceremonial wars to be fought at mutually convenient times with Tlaxcala, Huexotzingo, and Cholula, the independent provinces southwest of the valley. These wars, known as the Flowery Wars, would sustain Mexico's military supremacy throughout the great era of expansion the followed his reign.

The days of Moctezuma's reign were days of triumph and glory for the men of Tenochtitlan, but for the women, they were days of tears and heartache as they watched husbands, sons, and brothers leave for distant lands.

When her husband passed from sight down the long causeway, his wife turned back to a lifeless city to observe the nightly ritual expected of her, a ritual passed down to her by Coatlicue, the mother of Huitzilopochtli. Each night at midnight, she lit a fire in front of the door, and by its light, swept the threshold. Afterward she bathed, careful to avoid her face, since a soiled and grimy face was evidence of her virtue during her husband's absence. After bathing, she retired to the room where the household gods were kept, and wrapped the leg bones of the captives taken by her husband in paper and hung them above an incense burner. When the fragrance of sweet gum filled the room, she knelt before the gods and prayed into the late hours for the safe return of her warrior.

Moctezuma Ilhuicamina died in 1468, and my grandfather, Axayácatl, who was but nineteen years old, fell heir to an empire greater than Tezozomoc and the Tepanecs ever imagined.

His greatest achievements were along the eastern seaboard, where he established Mexican hegemony over more than 80 leagues of coastline, from the River Tuxpan in the north to the Papaloapan River in the south. The Totonacs and the Huastecs continued to harass Mexican merchants and tribute collectors in the region, but Axayácatl was able to maintain control by establishing garrisons at strategic points along the coast and in the sierra. During his 13-year reign, Axayácatl pushed the frontiers of the budding empire beyond the Valley of Toluca and the Valley of Oaxaca.

But his military successes were overshadowed by an ill-advised expedition into Michoacan. In a disastrous campaign, the well-trained Tarascans massacred his outnumbered squadrons, and for the first time in nearly 50 years, Mexico witnessed an emperor returning from war in disgrace.

Axayácatl's reign was also tarnished by a bloody civil war with Tlatelolco. The war opened a breach in the kinship between Tenochtitlan and Tlatelolco that never fully healed, leaving a bitterness in the hearts of the proud Tlatelolcans long after they reclaimed their rightful role in the affairs of Mexico,

Moquihuix, who ruled Tlatelolco for 20 years, resented Tenochtitlan's predominance in the affairs of state, and with the advent of a young, inexperienced lord to the jaguar and eagle throne, he sought to seize control of the empire. Believing that Axayácatl was unaware of his preparations for war, he launched a night attack against Tenochtitlán, but Tenochca warriors lay in ambush, waiting for him, and drove his squadrons back. Axayácatl gathered his squadrons on the outskirts of Tlatelolco, and sent the insignia of the dead to Moquihuix. After a furious battle, he gained the marketplace, where the Tlatelolcans milled about in confusion as their leader fled to the great temple.

Axayácatl found Moquihuix cowering at the foot of Huitzilopochtli, and he struck him down with a single blow of his *maquahuitl*. He dragged the body to the edge of the platform and threw it down the side of the temple into the crowd below, then fired the temple and put the city to the sack.

When peace was restored, the Tlatelolcans could no longer elect their lords, but were ruled instead by military governors appointed by Tenochtitlán. They were also compelled to worship the gods in Tenochtitlán, and as the years passed, their magnificent temple fell into ruin, and the plaza about it became overgrown with weeds and filled with garbage. It was not until many years later, shortly before the Spaniards came to the country, that Tenochtitlán allowed them to restore the temple to its former splendor.

After Axayácatl's death in 1481, his brother Tizoc was elected to the throne. Although Tizoc waged successful campaigns in the Valley of Toluca and crushed uprisings among the Huastecs and the Totonacs, he is remembered above all for his costly victory against Metztitlan, where he exchanged the lives of 300 good warriors for 40 captives.

For the greater part of his short reign, he spent his energies upon the construction of the great temple that Moctezuma had begun nearly 40 years earlier. The temple was within a year of completion when he died unexpectedly, in the fifth year of his reign. It was rumored that his council, who feared that his lack of military initiative threatened the security of the empire, poisoned him.

In 1486, Ahuitzotl, the younger brother of Tizoc and Axayácatl, was chosen to be the eighth *tlatoani* of Mexico, and in the young ruler, Mexico found an incomparable warrior, a lord worthy of the empire conceived by Moctezuma. Unlike the aging Moctezuma, who chose to direct his military campaigns from Tenochtitlán, Ahuitzotl led his squadrons into the field, inspiring them on the one hand by his example, and discouraging them from faint heart on the other with his uncompromising discipline. First and foremost, he was a soldier, sharing the hardships and discomforts of the road with the common warrior instead of exercising the privileges and prerogatives of a nobleman, much less those of an emperor. And in combat, no warrior or chieftain ever left his post, for Ahuitzotl's standing order to every man in the army was to kill his companion, whether he be noble or commoner, if he failed to fight.

Ruthless toward his foes, his campaigns were so devastating that he was often forced to repopulate conquered lands with people from the Valley of Mexico. Headstrong and unforgiving, Ahuitzotl was a difficult lord to serve, but this was the nature of the man who would conquer lands more than twice the extent of those subdued by Moctezuma and Axayácatl, lands that extended as far as the Southern Sea[v] and Guatemala.

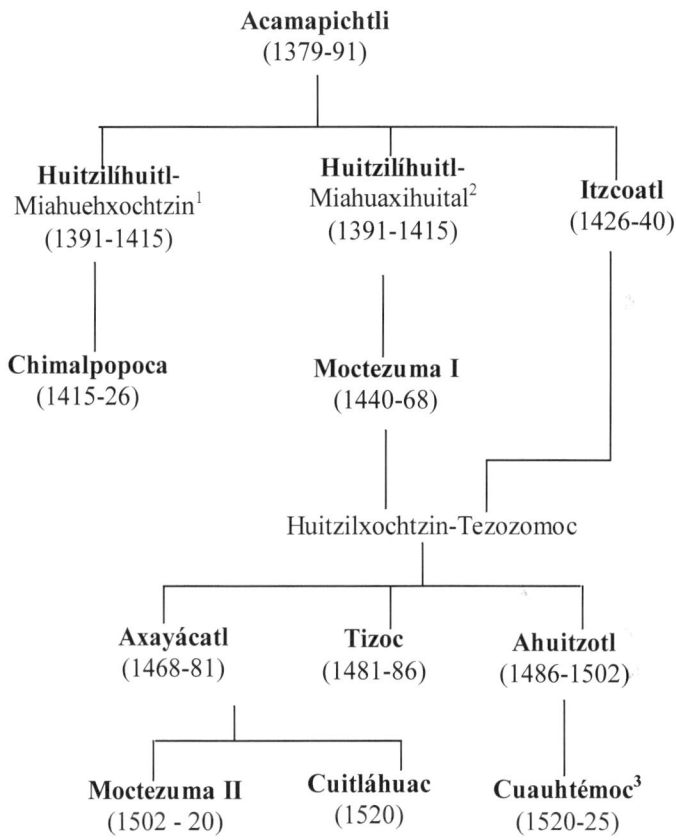

Acamapichtli
(1379-91)

Huitzilíhuitl-
Miahuehxochtzin[1]
(1391-1415)

Huitzilíhuitl-
Miahuaxihuital[2]
(1391-1415)

Itzcoatl
(1426-40)

Chimalpopoca
(1415-26)

Moctezuma I
(1440-68)

Huitzilxochtzin-Tezozomoc

Axayácatl
(1468-81)

Tizoc
(1481-86)

Ahuitzotl
(1486-1502)

Moctezuma II
(1502 - 20)

Cuitláhuac
(1520)

Cuauhtémoc[3]
(1520-25)

The Lineage of the kings of Mexico

1. First concubine
2. Second concubine
3. Served under Spanish rule from August 1521 until his execution in 1525.

Early in his reign, he crushed uprisings in the rugged terrain of the northwest, then faced about and undertook a forced march to the northeast, where the warlike Huastecs were ever-ready to test the will of a new emperor.

With the rebellious provinces contained, Ahuitzotl was ready to undertake new conquests. His first goal was Teloloapan, a town that commanded the pass across the southern sierra. When Teloloapan fell, the way was clear for a push to the Southern Sea, and in 1491, he led his armies across the sierra to attack Acapulco and other principal towns along the seacoast. Once he established a foothold, he pressed up the coast, and within four years, extended the empire as far as the River Balsas, outflanking Michoacan.

In 1496, Ahuitzotl marched against distant Tehuantepec, where the local ruler had broken off commerce with Mexico by butchering his merchants. No Mexican army had ever before attempted to launch an offensive against a city more than 130 leagues from home, but Ahuitzotl had paved the way by repopulating its ravaged cities with his own people by earlier forays into Oaxaca. Ahuitzotl's seasoned warriors easily routed the Tehuantepec squadrons, and after looting the surrounding towns, he incorporated the province into his empire.

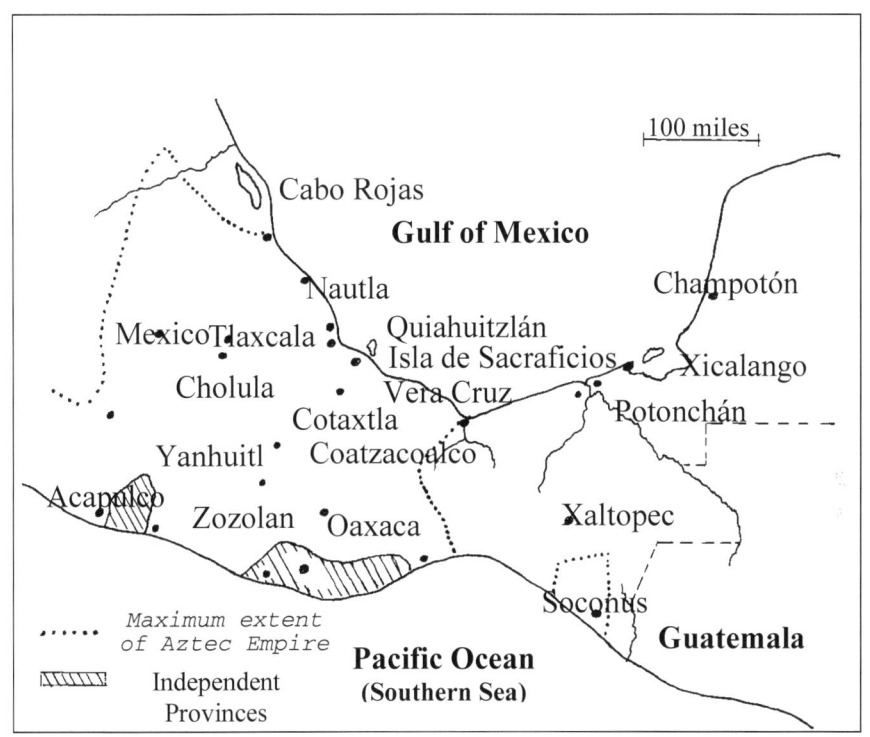

Anahuac. 1519

Ahuitzotl returned to Tenochtitlán, but he left Tehuantepec so weak and devastated that the province was unable to defend itself against the attacks of its neighbors. When raiding parties from Soconusco, a province on the border of Guatemala, began to pillage his towns, the ruler of Tehuantepec appealed to Mexico for aid, and Ahuitzotl marched more than 200 leagues to rescue his new vassals. When Soconusco was crushed, the lords of the province urged Ahuitzotl to press onward into Guatemala, hoping to share the wealth of this new land with Mexico. Ahuitzotl was tempted, but his warriors were weary; his control over these distant provinces was tenuous, and he had contacted an unknown ailment in the swamplands of Soconusco.

The war in Soconusco was to be Ahuitzotl's last campaign. When he returned to Tenochtitlán, he began to lose his strength and vitality. Each day he seemed to wither; his bones protruded through his sagging flesh, and in spite of the efforts of his physicians, he died in the sixteenth year of his reign, no more than a shadow of the fearless warrior Mexico had loved so well.

If Ahuitzotl's reign was the fulfillment of the promise made by Huitzilopochtli that our people would one day be masters of the world, it was also the fulfillment of a promise that the Mexican people made to their god 40 years earlier-that he would rule supreme over all the gods of Anahuac. In the second year of Ahuitzotl's reign, the great temple begun by Moctezuma Ilhuicamina was completed, and he consecrated it to Huitzilopochtli with a blood-letting more barbarous than ever experienced before or after. No prince or vassal who witnessed it would ever again dare deny the primacy of Mexico or its god above all nations.

Ahuitzotl demanded that every vassal lord bring his court of nobles to the ceremony, and he assessed each, according to his resources, the number of sacrifices he must offer to the god of Mexico. He also invited the lords of the independent states that lay within the borders of the empire to the ceremony, and even though they were often at war with Mexico, all considered it prudent not to offend the young emperor upon this occasion. And he decreed, under penalty of death, that every man, woman, and child in Tenochtitlán witness the spectacle.

On the week of the ceremony the vassal lords arrived, and as they led their captives onto the causeways, waiting priests censed them and pressed nosegays of flowers into their hands, and gave them bread consecrated in the temple. They comforted each in turn and encouraged them to take heart, for now they were the children of the sun, soon to realize eternal fame and glory. They led them to the temple and served them *octli,* then led them up the steps to the summit, where they paid homage to Huitzilopochtli. They escorted them past the palace gates for the emperor's inspection, then took them to the marketplace, where they were clothed, given sandals, feathers and flowers, and forced to perform the ritual dance of sacrifice. Afterward, they gave them tobacco and took them to the barrios, where they were lodged and treated as honored guests.

On the eve of the ceremony, the lords of the independent states gathered on the outskirts of the city, where Ahuitzotl's majordomos awaited them. Since Ahuitzotl had no mind to let his people know how he entertained their enemies, against whom they had sacrificed so many husbands, lovers, and brothers, the majordomos disguised them as Mexicans and smuggled them into the palace of the *Cihuacoatl*. There, in a secret room, they dined on the finest delicacies of Anahuac and received valuable gifts from the emperor. Later, as they prepared to retire, they were served raw mushrooms, and their magic brought them visions of the good and evil that would be their lot in life.

The following morning, long before first light, the captives were taken from the barrios and formed into four queues, each beginning at the foot of the temple and stretching out far down the causeways. Priests walk down the long lines of naked captives, painting each with a red dye and setting feathered plumes upon on their heads, while others adorned the steps leading to the summit of the temple with leafy branches and flowers.

By first light, the nobility of Tenochtitlán pushed and elbowed each other for choice locations in the plaza, while commoners and people from surrounding communities pressed into the center of the city and onto the roofs of the buildings surrounding the temple.

At sunrise a priest on the summit of the temple sounded a conch horn, and the crowd fell silent as black-robed priests formed and avenue between the royal palace and the courtyard. Ahuitzotl was the first to appear, followed by Nezahualpilli, the lord of Texcoco; Totoquihuaztli, the lord of Tlacopan; the *Cihuacoatl;* and a body of priests, each wearing the costume of a god. The procession passed between the rows of priests and up the temple steps. At the summit, they separated into four groups.

Ahuitzotl took his accustomed place before the altar of Huitzilopochtli, and four of the priests disguised as gods stood by his side. Nezahualpilli led two others to the Yopi altar, where Xipe Totec, the god of spring and the budding maize, was worshipped. The *Cihuacoatl* led his priestly gods to the altar of Tlaloc, the rain god, and Totoquihuaztli led his to the altar of Ometecuhtli, the father of the gods.

When the lords stood ready at their posts, the Tlalpanhuehuetl, the great temple drum, began its heart-stopping cadence, and with the first thundering boom, conch horns, bone whistles, wooden drums, tambourines, tortoise shell timbrels, and rattles sounded from every corner of Tenochtitlán.

Ahuitzotl stepped up to the altar, and standing before a stone deity, nodded to the priests. Four seized the first victim and dragged him to the altar, and when they spread him across the arched surface of the stone, Ahuitzotl turned to Huitzilopochtli and squatted as low as he could. He touched his middle finger to the floor, then pointed it at the god and licked the dirt of the temple floor from it. He rose and raised his knife first to the north, then to the east, the south, and the west.

Suddenly he turned and drove his knife into the victim's breast and ripped it open from one side to the other, exposing the still-beating heart. He slashed again at the gaping wound, and the heart seemed to leap into his hands as he raised it on high, offering it to the north, the east, the south, and the west. He handed the dripping heart to a priest, who took it to a brazier in the center of the jaguar stone as others tumbled the body down the side of the temple. Ahuitzotl turned back to the altar, where another victim awaited him, and he continued to make his sacrifices, working quickly to prevent the blood from cooling. As he tore out each heart, priests from the barrios stood by his side, waiting to take it from his hands and rush it to the local temples.

When Ahuitzotl tired, he gave his knife to a priest disguised as a god, and when that priest tired, another took up the frightful task, and when it was the turn of the priest disguised as Quetzalcoatl, he sacrificed more than any of the others. The *Cihuacoatl* and the other lords made their sacrifices as Ahuitzotl was performing his, and when they tired, they too passed their knives on to others.

Soon a steady stream flowed down the sides of the temple, and the priests were covered with so much blood that their bodies glistened as if they had been painted with the crimson dye of the cochineal. As quickly as the wash of blood spilled over the rim of the lowest platform, priests scooped it into buckets and set out to smear the doorways, the lintels, and the walls of the lesser temples, then on the heads of the tutelary gods.

The carnage continued for four days, and by the second day, the air was foul with the stench of drying blood, excrement, and flesh decaying in the afternoon sun. At night, fires glowed throughout the city as the bodies of the victims were dismembered. Their thighs and arms were boiled in steaming cauldrons for the feast that followed, and their heads were rendered into skulls and mounted on the commemorative rack in the plaza to whiten in the sun. The torsos were thrown into the lake behind Tepepolco, a rock outcropping just off the south shore, and the entrails were thrown into a deep well that runs into the bowels of the earth, where they cast albinos, two-headed babies, and other deformed creatures during times of drought or famine.

Only Ahuitzotl's enemies were spared the smell of the city and the unsightly disposal of the remains of the captives. They saw only the spectacle taking place on the temple, hidden from sight in a retreat covered with leafy branches and fragrant flowers on the roof of the *Cihuacoatl's* palace. When the ceremony was over, they left with precious jewels, gold shields, luxurious feathers, and elegant mantles as keepsakes of the wholesale slaughter of 4,000 men.[vi]

In the year 10 Rabbit, the year of our lord 1502, my father became the ninth *tlatoani* of Mexico. He was 34 years old, a lord whose eloquence and courtly manners were befitting a noble prince, and respected by all as a wise and devoted man who observed his priestly duties as well as his secular obligations. On the day of his election to the throne, a majordomo found Moctezuma at his devotions in the Temple of the Eagle Knight, and informed him that the lords of Texcoco, Tlacopan, and the *Cihuacoatl* awaited him in the council chamber.

When he stood before them, priests removed his clothing and dressed him with the vestments of purification and fasting. They placed a green robe about his shoulders, covered his head and face with a green hood, and shod his feet with green-toed sandals. They tied a tobacco gourd on his back, gave him a censer and a bag of incense, then led him to the house of fasting, where he would do penance for four days. Each day, before eating the single meal that was allowed him, he went to the temple and prayed before Huitzilopochtli. At midnight, he returned to the temple and drew blood from his earlobes and offered it to the god. Afterward, he was permitted to bathe.

On the fourth day he was led back to the council chamber, where, standing in a circle of eagle and jaguar bones, priests removed the garments of fasting and invested him with the robes and royal devices of the emperor. He knelt before the *Cihuacoatl* and Nezahualpilli and listened as each in turn recited the homilies that bound a newly elected emperor to his people.

They warned him of the great labors that lay ahead, of the self-restraint he must exercise if he was to rule wisely, and of the demanding studies he must pursue if he was to recognize and interpret the signs and omens manifest in the motions of the stars. They spoke of the emperor's binding duty to their religion, of his duty to honor the priesthood, and of his obligation to satisfy the unending needs of the gods for the blood of man. When they finished, Nezahualpilli pierced the cartilage of Moctezuma's nose with a sharp bone, and thrust a jade rod through the incision. He then set the turquoise diadem on his head and proclaimed him Lord of Mexico and sovereign ruler of all its provinces.

Unlike Ahuitzotl, Moctezuma believed that only those of noble birth were fit to govern. His first edict purged the army and the royal household of commoners that Ahuitzotl, in recognition of honors earned, had elevated to high office. In their stead, he appointed sons of the royal families of Tenochtitlán, Texcoco, and Tlacopan. Under his guidance and tutelage, the young nobles of learned the art of government and the ways of the royal court, the required protocol due the emperor and his vassal lords, and the courtesy and respect due the wives and concubines of the emperor. He restored the titles of the Tlatelolca nobility and allowed them to rebuild their temple, but he reinstated the heavy tribute levied upon them by Axayácatl, which had long since been forgiven by Tizoc and Ahuitzotl.

If my father was a severe man, he was also a just man. None, no matter what his station in life, was exempted from the harsh and unsparing punishments prescribed by the laws and statutes he had inherited from his ancestors. He demanded the same exacting interpretation of the law from his judges as his own, and he often wore disguises in the courts to judge for himself the soundness of their verdicts. As insistent as Moctezuma was in enforcing the laws of Mexico in the community at large, he was even more intolerant of wrongdoing in the palace, for he considered the palace to be the house of god. Often, for offenses no more than irreverence or some foolish oversight, the punishment was death.

But if history would condemn Moctezuma Xocóyotl for his cruelty, let it also be recorded that compassion on the part of a

Mexican ruler was unthinkable. His enemies looked upon clemency as a sign of weakness and lack of resolution, and his court as a threat to the security of the empire. And Moctezuma was all too well aware of the untimely deaths of Tizoc and Chimalpopoca.

Although Moctezuma exercised his command of the armies of Mexico in a manner different from that of Ahuitzotl, he was no less a courageous and skilled general in the field. The vast and rapid expansion of the empire under Ahuitzotl had stretched Mexico to its utmost ability to control its 38 provinces, leaving the difficult task of maintaining Mexican hegemony over these troublesome regions to his successor. In particular, uprisings in Oaxaca, one of the richest provinces of Anahuac, plagued Moctezuma from the moment he assumed the throne until the arrival of the Spaniards. Revolts in the Southern Sierra forced him to undertake one campaign after another to protect his merchants and maintain his lines of communication to the Southern Sea, and each time, whether he chose to lead his warriors or not, his armies returned in triumph.

Unlike his predecessor, Moctezuma chose not to wage his inaugural campaign close to home, but instead chose to lead his army to Nopallan, a town on the shores of the Southern Sea, more than 100 leagues from Tenochtitlán. Heavy fortifications surrounded the city, and when the Mexicans attacked, the emperor, wearing his battle dress of red spoonbill feathers, was the first to cross the ramparts.

His most distant campaign was against Xaltepec, a town on the border of Guatemala, where the inhabitants butchered Mexican merchants, fortified the town, cut the roads to the province, and defied Moctezuma to attack. They did not have long to wait. Moctezuma arrived with a host of warriors from Mexico and his allies, Tlaxcala, Huexotzingo, and Cholula, all eager to sharpen their skills in combat and to share in the spoils. When the defenses of the city crumbled under Moctezuma's onslaught, he ordered every man and woman over 50 put to death, for he held them responsible for the uprising.

Although Moctezuma was hard-pressed to preserve and maintain the empire of his forebears, he did not relish the role of custodian. His ambition to expand the empire lay on the shores of the Southern Sea, where he could claim the riches of the province of Tototepec. The gateway to the capital was Quetzaltepec, a fortified town on the far bank of the River Quetzal.

When Moctezuma reached the river, however, it was in a flood stage, swollen by recent heavy rains. The enemy was out in force on the far bank, challenging his army to cross, but the emperor chose to withdraw, pretending not to hear the jeers and whistles from the other side. Once out of sight, he felled balsa trees and gathered reeds to build rafts, and under cover of darkness, his warriors launched their fragile craft into the raging current. They crossed without mishap, and the sleeping city, secure in the belief that the river was impassable, offered little resistance as his warriors fired the temples and palaces, looting and killing until daylight.

As was the custom in campaigns that were fought in distant provinces, Moctezuma returned with few captives to shed their blood before Huitzilopochtli. Those who survived the attack were put to the knife.

The rare interludes of peace between Moctezuma's campaigns, however, brought little time for his warriors to enjoy the fruits of victory and the tranquillity of family life. An idle and complacent army could neither keep the peace within the provinces nor safeguard Mexico's flourishing commerce. But no emperor since the time of Moctzuma Ilhuicamina lacked for enemies ready to test the will of his armies. Just beyond the rim of the Valley of Mexico, wars with Tlaxcala, or Huexotzingo, or Cholula, were a recurring ritual, fought for no purpose other than acquiring sacrifices for the gods and the realization of glory. For those who fell in battle, there was an afterlife as companions of the sun, where they sang war songs and fought heavenly battles for four years, after which they returned to earth as hummingbirds.

When Moctezuma felt that his warriors had rested long enough from their victorious campaign in Tototepec, he challenged the lord of Huexotzingo to meet his army three days hence on the plains of Atlixco. Huexotzingo accepted the challenge, and Tlacahueypan, the emperor's brother, led an army of 100,000 warriors into the field of battle. But Moctezuma had waited too long to exercise his warriors. The Huexotzincas were well prepared, and at the end of the day, Tlacahueypan and two more of Moctezuma's brothers lay dead on the battlefield.

When the broken army returned to Tenochtitlán, priests and elders, wearing the insignia of mourning, met the wounded and the weary on the causeway to comfort and console them. The army straggled into a city silent but for the weeping of women. Stilled were the conch horns, the flutes, and the drums of victory. When the warriors filed past the great temple, they cried out against the gods, and refused to offer them sacrifices for having failed to favor them against their enemy.

The following day the grieving city prepared for the funeral rites of its fallen warriors. Wooden statues of the emperor's brothers were dressed in elegant robes and adorned with jeweled nose plugs, ear pendants, and labrets, and painted with their insignia of rank. Then they were taken to the great temple to stand before the altar of Huizilopochtli.

On the day of the funeral, lords and nobles from every province in the land came to offer their condolences to Moctezuma, and they brought him many slaves to be sacrificed before the images of his brothers. After the last noble paid his respects and departed, the statues were fired, and as the flames consumed them, the slaves were killed and cast into the fire. When nothing but ashes remained, they were gathered and buried beneath the altar in the Temple of the Eagle Knights.

With the news of the Mexican defeat at Atlixco, Yanhuitlan and Zozolan, towns that lay across the strategic route to Tehuantepec, began killing our merchants and blockading the roads, daring Moctezuma to send his humbled army into Oaxaca. Mexico's losses at Huexotzingo, however, had not been in vain. Moctezuma's warriors, seeking to reclaim their honor and dignity, struck Yanhuitlan with a fury that sent the people of Zozolan fleeing for their lives into the sierra.

As 1507, the year 2 Reed approached, the empire prospered as never before. Peace prevailed throughout the provinces, and the tribute that flowed into Mexico every 80 days exceeded that ever imagined by Moctezuma's predecessors. Yet there was little joy in Tenochtitlán. Instead, an atmosphere of dread and apprehension settled over the people, a sense of foreboding for the future, a fear that had existed since time immemorial, long before our forebears left their ancestral home in Aztlán.

Our people were the people of the sun, who lived in a shifting, unstable world, a world that would endure only as long as the sun rose in the morning and the blood of their sacrifices fueled its journey across the heavens each day. But now the year 2 Reed was nearly upon them, and with its arrival came the fateful night when the very existence of the sun was threatened by a cataclysm that neither the gods nor all their sacrifices could forestall.

The passing of the year 1 Rabbit into 2 Reed marked the end of a cycle that repeated itself after 52 years, and between the final moments of the old year and the first of the new, there was a gap in the flow of time. Should this gap fail to close, the sun would vanish, leaving the world in a void of everlasting night.

The sages told of the first sun that had survived 13 cycles before the years failed to bind, leaving it to be eaten by the jaguars; of the second sun that had been swept away by the winds after but six; of the fire that rained down from the heavens and consumed the third after seven; and of the flood that swallowed the fourth after thirteen.

When the fourth sun perished and the world lay shrouded in darkness, the gods gathered at Teotihuacán[vii] to seek a way to bring light into the world once more. Who among them, they asked, would offer himself for mankind and be reborn as the sun? Who would cast himself into the eternal flames and be reborn as the moon? But only the least of the gods, only Nanahuatzin, the scabby god of lesions, and Tecciztecatl, the god of snails stepped forward.

They prayed and did penance for four days; Nanahuatzin on the hill where the Temple of the Sun now stands, and Tecciztecatl on the hill where the Temple of the Moon would be built. On the fifth day they descended from the hills and offered themselves to the flames. Four times Tecciztecatl approached the fire, but each time the searing heat drove him back. Then the gods bade Nanahuatzin to step forward. The little god stood for a moment before the fire, then shut his eyes and leaped into midst of the flames. In an instant he was devoured, and Tecciztecatl, taking heart, leaped in after him.

The fire dwindled into glowing embers, then into ashes as the gods waited for Nanahuatzin to appear. Hour upon hour they waited in the endless night, watching for the first blush of morning. Just when it seemed that the lightless canopy above would never be broken, a feeble glow appeared in the east, then blossomed into a radiant disk that grew ever larger until it burst into a light so bright that it blinded those who looked upon it. Slowly the light climbed into the morning sky, but when it stood midway between the horizon and the zenith, it faltered and fell back, growing dimmer as it slid toward the horizon. Quickly the gods drew their blood and offered it to the dying sun, and once again it rose, only to stop again. Then Ehecatl, the Wind God, stepped forward and sent it into endless motion across the heavens.

Thus, the sages said, was the fifth sun born, but it would be the last sun of all, and when it failed to cross the threshold of the last 52 year cycle, the world would lie in darkness and its people left to the mercy of the demons of the night.

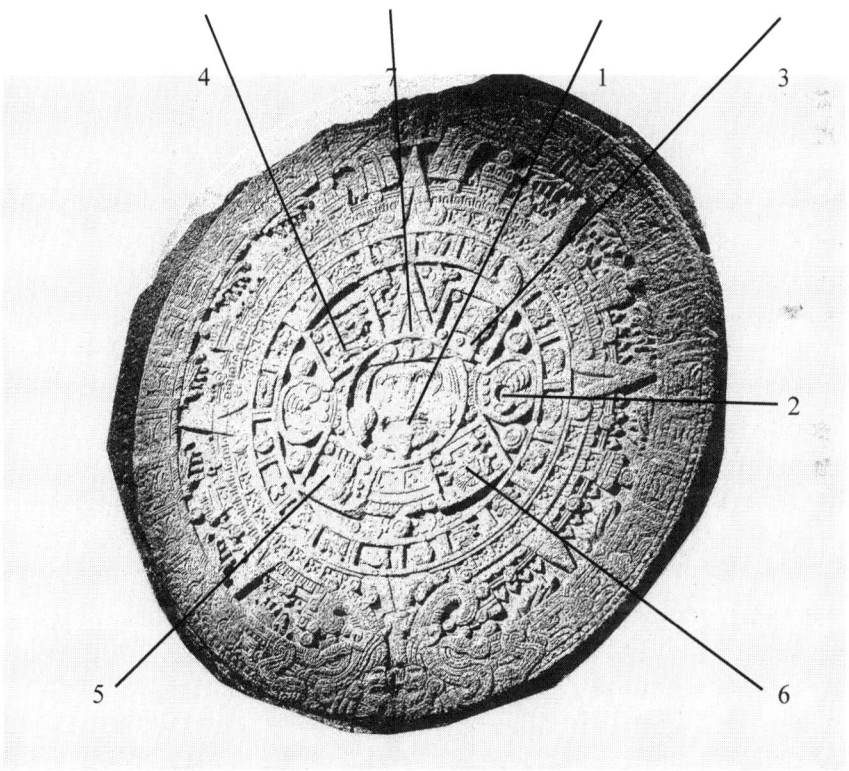

Stone of the Fifth Sun

Mexican National Museum of Anthropology

The stone, unearthed in the Zocalo in 1790, was carved during the reign of Axayácatl (1469-1481). The olivine basalt monolith is 3.6 meters in diameter, 0.72 meters thick, and weighs 24 metric tons.

The central figure is Tonatiuh, the Fifth Sun, pictured with a flint sacrificial knife hanging from his mouth (1). On either side are two claws clutching human hearts (2). The four square glyphs represent the dates that the four previous suns were destroyed by the jaguars (3), the winds (4), the fiery rains (5), and the great flood (6).

The Fifth Sun was created by the gods at Teotihuacán on AD 1011. The predicted date of the destruction of the Fifth Sun is given by the "ollin" glyph (7), which occurs every 52 years. Two fire serpents, their tails at the top and the heads at the bottom, form the outer ring of the monolith. The heads are those of the Fire God and Tonatiuh.

The binding of the years last took place in 1455, during the reign of Moctezuma Ilhuicamina. The preceding year was one of promising auguries, and when 2 Reed came to pass, the emperor embarked upon conquests that would one day make Mexico master of the world. But now, as 2 Reed approached once again, there was an ominous shift in the omens.

When the *nemontemi,*[viii] the five days that mark the closing of the old year arrived, the fire priests gathered on the hilltop temple at Uixachlan to rehearse the ritual that symbolized Nanahuatzin's sacrifice and his resurrection as the sun. Throughout the city, people emptied the rubbish from their homes, scrubbed the walls and floors, and threw their hearthstones and figures of the household gods into the canals. Pregnant women were locked up in the granaries lest they become animals that feed upon the flesh of men and turn children into mice, and women and children prepared masks from agave fronds.

On the eve of 2 Reed, every man, woman, and child in the city gathered on the rooftops and looked to the south, toward Uixachlan, waiting for the signal that would tell them that Nanahuatzin had survived the junction of the years. On the temple, fire priests observed the stars as they rose in the night sky, and when they reached their proper alignment, the high priest spun his fire drill into a wooden block set upon the breast of a highborn captive. With the first flicker of flame, he thrust the smoldering tinder into a brazier and fed it until it blossomed into beacon that could be seen from one end of the valley to the other. Then with a quick thrust of his knife, he ripped open the captive's breast and cast his heart into the fire.

A soon as the people saw the burst of fire on the temple, they drew blood from their ears and sprinkled it toward the east to set the sun in motion, then watched for the sign that would tell them that the sun had survived. It appeared first as a point of light moving down the hillside, then toward the city along the pitch-dark causeway as a runner brought the new fire into the city. He carried his torch up the steps of the temple of Huitzilopochtli and cast it into a pile of fagots, and immediately a towering blaze lit the plaza below. Drums, conch horns, and whistles sounded throughout the city as waiting priests carried firebrands from the temple to every barrio in the city. When Tenochtitlán was bathed in the light of a thousand fires, the people left the rooftops and rekindled their hearths from the new fire.

For the people, the crisis had passed and was all but forgotten as they returned to the commonplace tasks of daily life. They spread new mats throughout the household, replaced old clothing with new mantles, new shifts and blouses, and returned newly fired clay images of the tutelary gods to their customary place alongside the hearth.

For Moctezuma, his universe was again secure, but the unfavorable omens and sinister prophecies that threatened his future and that of the empire continued. From the day he assumed the throne, diviners foretold that he would be the last of his lineage to rule Mexico, that in the eighth year of his reign, a more powerful lord would take his place.

There was an ancient legend, handed down from generations past, of a lord who brought his people to our land when the Otomies ruled it. The Otomies allowed his people to settle in the valley, but they refused to accept their lord, and set their own chieftains to rule over them. The lord was exiled to his native land, but as he departed, he promised that one day his sons would return to take the land by force and claim their heritage.

Now the omens seemed to bear out the prophecy. The first omen appeared on the day Thirteen Death-the sun vanished at midday, casting a pall of mortal fear over the city. This, the diviners said, was a sign from the heavens that the days of Mexico were numbered, that soon our great city would disappear from the face of the earth as if it had never been.

Next a mysterious fire erupted in the Temple of Huitzilopochtli. The fire seemed to issue from within the roof beams of the shrine, but when priests threw water on them, the fire burned more fiercely than ever, leaving nothing but a heap of ashes. Was the god of the

Mexicans threatening to abandon them, the people asked? Had their emperor failed in his duty to the gods?[ix]

Recalling how Huitzilopochtli had favored Mexico after Moctezuma Ilhuicamina laid the foundation of his great temple, and how the god of Mexico had raised his people above all others after Ahuitzotl consecrated his temple with the blood of thousands, Moctezuma felt it wise to please his god in some like manner.

The destruction of Huitzilopochtli's shrine offered him an opportunity. Since it must be rebuilt in any event, he resolved to build a shrine that would truly reflect his glory, a shrine so splendid that Huitzilopochtli would cherish and safeguard him and his descendants for generations to come. From the floor to the ceiling, he would cover the walls with layer upon layer of gold foil, and inlay them with thousands of turquoise gems to reflect the glory of the heavens. Then, when the shrine was ready, Huitzilopochtli's garments would be removed and his body covered from head to foot with the exquisite feathers of the quetzal. The project, however, would require a considerable share of tribute from every province in Anahuac, and before he proceeded, he felt it wise to seek the counsel of Tzompanteuctli, the lord of Cuitláhuac.

Tzompanteuctli was a descendant of the great Toltecs, a learned man who had mastered the six hundred and ten sciences of the world, and his opinion was sought for all matters of consequence. He listened attentively as Moctezuma spoke of his fears that he had provoked the gods, and his conviction that they would abandon him and his people unless he could temper their anger with some noble gesture. He described the shrine he proposed to build for Huitzilopochtli, and when he finished, the sage spoke.

"Lord," he said, "do not undertake this task. If you persist, you will only offend the heavens above us and hasten the downfall of your city. I say this to you because he who is now our god will not be our god in times to come. The day approaches when a new god, a god who created man and all the creatures of the earth, will overthrow him."

For this dark revelation, this unwelcome counsel, Moctezuma ordered the people of Cuitláhuac to put their lord and all his children to death.

The Angry Lord, the emperor who created a court more noble than that of the great Toltecs, the warrior who led one army after another across the sierra to make war on the most distant provinces of the land, now spent his days and nights searching for dreams and divinations that would prove Tzompanteuctli wrong, only to learn that the worst was yet to come.

---

[i] Literally, "he who speaks." Moctezuma would be known as the *Ueyetlatoani,* "he who speaks for all."

[ii] Anahuac covers approximately 90,000 square miles of southern Mexico between the Gulf of Mexico and the Pacific Ocean. Its northernmost point reached as far as Tampico, and its southernmost boundary lay near Coatzacoalcos.

[iii] The Mixtec people of Oaxaca

[iv] Orizaba, the fourth largest mountain on the North American Continent at 18,696 feet.

[v] The Pacific Ocean

[vi] The number of sacrifices made by Ahuitzotl varies widely from one source to another. Duran states that 80,400 captives were killed, and Torquemada sets the number at 72,344. Some historians accept 20,000 as the most likely number, since it is inscribed on a tablet commemorating the ceremony. Nigel Davis suggests that the number may have been no more than 2,000 if the number of units on the tablet were misread. If one considers how many minutes the priests needed for one sacrifice and the logistics of disposing of the bodies, 4.000 appears to be a reasonable upper limit.

[vii] The ancient city that lies 27 miles northwest of Mexico City. Founded about 200 BC, Teotihuacán grew to a metropolis of 150,000 people by AD 600. The Pyramid of the Sun and the Pyramid of the Moon were built about AD 100 The city was destroyed sometime between AD 600 and AD 650. Neither the origins of the the people who founded the city nor their fate is known. They left no hieroglyphics to record their history.

[viii] The Aztec Solar Year is made up of 18 months of 20 days each. The nemontemi is the five day period needed to make up the 365 day year.

[ix] There are numerous legends, prophecies, omens, and dreams attributed to native sources that spelled the end of the empire in the time of Moctezuma. The basis of many lie in myth, allegorical tales, fear of natural phenomena such as earthquakes, volcanic eruptions, solar and lunar eclipses, and comets. Some, however derive from the post conquest era, and

although many of them seem to be pure invention, all cannot be summarily dismissed.r

3. Juan Díaz:

The Log of the San Sebastián

The Discovery of Mexico[i]

Francisco Fernández de Córdoba was dead, as were 50 good Christians he left on the beach of a new land he discovered 40 leagues west of Cuba. Although his enterprise with Cristóbal de Morante ended in disaster, those who survived brought news of a country where the riches dreamed of by the Admiral Cristóbal Colón might at last be realized.

Francisco Fernández provisioned two ships for a voyage to the islands off the coast of Honduras, where he hoped to realize a handsome profit by transporting Indians for service in the *encomiendas* of Cuba. A third vessel, a brigantine with a cargo of tools and equipment for mining gold, was purchased on credit from Diego Velásquez, the Governor of Cuba.

The fleet departed Santiago on February 8, 1517, and rounded the Cape of San Antón on the western tip of Cuba 12 days later. Two days out to sea, a heavy storm drove the ships far north of their course. When the storm abated, the pilot-major came about to southwesterly course, and seven days later, land was sighted.

From a distance, the crew could see large towns and tall buildings made of stone, and as they drew nearer, they saw natives wearing clothing finer that anything ever seen in the islands. Because of the shallows and salt marshes that extended far out to sea, Francisco Fernández made his first landfall on a small island a league offshore. Here he found stone temples and numerous female figurines, which led him to believe that the island was occupied by a race of women, although he saw no natives.

The following day the pilot-major brought the ships as close to the mainland as he dared, and the company went ashore. Their objective was to inspect a town two leagues inland, but before they reached it, a shower of stones and arrows fell upon the vanguard, and a squadron of warriors rushed at them from a thicket. A single volley from the muskets and crossbows felled nearly a score, and the others panicked and fled into the bush.

The Christians found the town deserted, and while some stood guard, others searched the temples and the houses. The most significant discovery was that of the priest Alonso González, who found gold medals and pendants, jeweled diadems, gold figurines, and some excellent earthenware pottery in an oratory. The gold in the artifacts was an alloy of low-grade ore and copper, but the workmanship was that of a culture far higher than any encountered in the New World. When Francisco Fernández was satisfied that nothing more of value would be found that day, he ordered the company back to the ships, taking two Indian captives with him to learn more of the country and its language.

The ships followed the coast on a westerly course for more than 70 leagues, where it turned sharply to the south. Thirty leagues down the coast, a large town was sighted. Judging that he might find a source of fresh water there, Francisco Fernández anchored offshore and ordered the boats lowered.

The Christians found the chieftain and his people well disposed toward them, and after they filled their casks, they bartered with the Indians for game, tortillas, and fruit. When they were sufficiently provisioned, they traded a few trinkets for richly colored mantles, elegant featherwork, and necklaces of iridescent seashells mounted on gold and silver chains. Francisco Fernández named the town Lázaro[ii] in remembrance of the saint we honor on the day he discovered it.

Francisco Fernández resumed a southerly course along the coast, but a heavy norther nearly foundered the ships and fouled his casks with salt water. Hard pressed for fresh water, the ships coasted along the barren shore until they came upon a small inlet, where a river fed into the sea. When the men went ashore, several squadrons from a large town a league south of the river arrived, but they kept their distance and withdrew at sunset. During the night the Spaniards could hear trumpets and drumbeats on both sides of the river, and they feared that a large force was gathering about them.

The attack came at first light, and although the Christians were able to hold off the Indians for a time with muskets, crossbows, and swords, they kept arriving in such numbers that the captain, fearing to be cut off, ordered the men back to the boats. The boats were so waterlogged from storms that they began to sink before they crossed the breakers, and many of the men were forced to cling to the sides, half swimming to keep afloat, as they moved away from the beach under a heavy barrage of stones and arrows.

Nearly every man who reached the safety of the ships suffered one or more wounds. Some were dying, the captain was bleeding freely from an unsightly wound, and fifty men were missing. The Indians had taken some alive, but most were left dead or dying on the beach. So few mariners survived the attack that the pilot major could man no more than two ships. He ordered the brigantine stripped of cables, anchors, sails, and anything else useful, then fired it. The following morning the survivors, weak and disabled, lacking fresh water and food, gathered their courage for the long voyage back to Cuba.

The Grijalva Expedition[iii]

The first news of their fate came from Sancti Spiritus, where Francisco Fernández lay recuperating from his wounds. In a letter to Diego Velásquez, he described an unknown land that lay less that 59 leagues from Cuba, where people built great stone temples, wore rich clothing of many colors, cultivated maize, and, most of all, possessed gold. He sent the governor artifacts he brought from the new land, and promised him a full report of his findings when he was well enough to travel.

Diego Velásquez lost no time in readying another fleet. He requested that Francisco Fernández send his ships to Santiago as soon as possible, purchased two others, and set about organizing a company to lay claim to the new land. Francisco Fernández was named captain-general, and Pedro de Alvarado, Alonso de Ávila, and Francisco de Montejo were chosen as his commanders. Anton de Alaminos, now recovering from his wounds, was to be pilot-major, Bernardino Vázquez de Tapia was appointed *alferez-general*, Fulano de Villafaña was designated as the crown's representative, and I was selected to attend to the spiritual needs of the company. In order to establish a legitimate title to the new land, Diego Velásquez wrote to the *Audiencia* in Santo Domingo to solicit a warrant from the king.

Long before the company was ready to sail, however, a letter arrived from Sancti Spiritus with news that Francisco Fernández had died of his wounds. On his deathbed he had bequeathed his share of any profits from the undertaking to Diego Velásquez. In his place, the governor gave the command to Juan de Grijalva, one of his kinsmen.

The first destination of the fleet was Havana, where additional provisions and weapons were taken aboard, and a large complement of men we recruited on the western part of the island joined the expedition. On the day of departure for the new land, the entire company came ashore where mass was said, and each man made his confession before God. When the ships were safely out of port, the men cut off their braided queues and swore to take their revenge upon the Indians for our comrades.

We doubled the Cape of San Antón on Saturday, the first day of May, in the year 1518. Three days later we sighted land, and as we approached, we could make out a white building on the headland. We found an inlet from the sea, which was no more than a small lagoon, but sand banks and shallows prevented us from entering, and we moved to the other side of the headland for a closer look at the building. It appeared to be a temple, a pyramid set upon a broad platform about the height of a man and square in form. Beside it stood a thatch-roofed hut. We could go no further that day, since the sun was about to set, and we moved offshore to seek a safe anchorage. The day upon which we discovered this land was the day we celebrate the Mass of Santa Cruz, and we called it by that name.

The following morning two canoes came out to inspect us, but the Indians kept a good cannon shot from the ships. The captain ordered Julian, one of the Indians captured by Francisco Fernández, on deck, and he called out to them that we meant no harm, that we had come only to trade with them. There was a brief exchange among the Indians, and one canoe began to move toward the ships. When it halted alongside the *San Sebastián,* the captain tied a few shirts and a bottle of wine to the end of a pole and lowered them into the canoe. Through Julian, he asked them what this land was called, and they replied that it was called Cozumel, and the land to the west was called Yucatán.

The next morning their chieftain ventured to come aboard the flagship, and the captain asked him if he knew anything of two Christians who, according to Julian, were reported lost in Yucatán[iv]. The chieftain replied that one was still alive, but the other was dead. The captain gave him some shirts and other gifts, and before he departed, he invited us to come to his village, where we would be welcome.

We made sail along the East Coast of Cozumel, where the sea is deep enough to sail within a stone's throw of the shore. We counted 14 temples along the coast like the one we had seen on the headland, and just before sunset, we came upon a crowd of men and women gathered about a large temple. We anchored not more than a crossbow shot from the shore, and after dark the island began to echo with drumbeats from the surrounding bush.

On Thursday, the sixth day of May, the captain took a hundred armed men ashore. The *alferez* and I were privileged to accompany them. We proceeded with caution, fearing an imminent attack by hostiles, but we reached the temple without incident. The surrounding area was deserted, and after setting the watch, the captain and the *alferez* climbed the temple. They raised the flag of Castile on the summit to claim the island in the name of the Catholic king, and the *alferez* bore witness as the captain posted a writ of possession.

The base of the temple was massive, 45 feet on each side, with 18 steps that led to a broad terrace. Another staircase led up one side of the temple to an oratory. The oratory was square, with a doorway on each side that led to the interior. Inside, we found bones, ashes, and sculptures of grotesque creatures, and we knew that the people who lived here were idolaters.

As we were inspecting the temple, four Indians approached and climbed the steps to the oratory. While three stood guard, the fourth, an old man whose toes had been cut off, carried a smoldering pot inside, and within moments the oratory was filled with a fragrant odor, much like that of sweet gum. He censed the idols while chanting an offertory in a high-pitched monotone to invoke his gods. When he finished, he lighted some reeds about the length of a man's hand and offered one to each of us. As they burned, they gave off a delicate aroma. After the Indians left, we said mass in the oratory, but not before we removed the bones and idols and scrubbed the interior.

That afternoon the priest returned with eight Indians, and they led us to a stone building where they prepared a meal for us consisting of fowl, honey, and roots they call maize, from which they make bread. In exchange, the captain gave them a few strands of beads. He showed them a few articles of gold, which is called *taquin* in their language, and gave them knives, scissors, and other trinkets for gold, but all they brought him in exchange was a pair of earrings and a few medals made from low-grade ore.

At nine the following morning there was not an Indian in sight, and the captain took ten of us ashore to explore the interior. We found several villages surrounded by well-cultivated fields of maize, carefully measured out and neatly set off from each other. We learned that the natives cultivate bees, and although their hives are somewhat smaller than those in Spain, they yield an abundance of choice honey and fine wax. The land abounds with rabbit and hare, and later we learned that there were deer, peccaries, and a number of other indigenous animals. In all, we found Cozumel to be a delightful island. From three leagues offshore, we could catch the scent of exotic aromas that pleased and mystified us.

We moved on to a town that we had sighted from the temple, and found it as deserted as the countryside. In the central plaza there were five massive pyramids that rose steeply from a broad base to a small platform, and on each platform there was an oratory for the heathen idolaters. The streets were paved with cobblestones, and thatch-roofed houses with stone foundations and adobe walls lined both sides of the streets. Judging from the construction of their homes and temples, these people are obviously very ingenious, and of it were not for the fact that their buildings bore little resemblance to ours, one would be inclined to think that they had been built by Spaniards.

On Friday, the seventh day of May, we left Cozumel and set sail for Yucatán, but heavy weather and a critical shortage of fresh water forced the captain to return to Cozumel. We filled our casks from cisterns the Indians dig in the ground and line with flagstones to collect rainwater, and provisioned ourselves with the fruit of the *mameye* tree, which are about the size of melons; with tubers that taste somewhat like carrots; and with *ungias*, a species of small rodent.

The fleet weighed anchor again on Tuesday, the 11th day of May. Our first landfall on Yucatán was a span of coastline where three towns[v] lay, separated from each other by less than a league. We approached the shore as closely as we dared, and we could see temples and palaces within walled enclosures and countless thatch-roof dwellings. The men asked to go ashore, but the captain refused, and we continued our voyage along the coast all that day and well into the night.

The next day, just before sunset, we saw a large temple towering above a town as splendid as Seville, and as we passed by, a crowd of Indians kept pace with us along the shore. The Indians signaled us to come ashore by raising and lowering banners, but the captain ordered the pilot to keep to his course.

On Thursday, the 13th day of May, the fleet arrived at the mouth of a large bay. Shallows and reefs prevented us from sailing inside, but hoping to find an outlet, boats were lowered to tow the ships beyond the reefs. We made way slowly and cautiously, until soundings indicated that we were in danger of running aground. The pilot-major set out in a boat to find a channel, but when he returned, he reported that there were shallows everywhere, and in some places the bottom lay at less than a fathom. It was his opinion that we had reached the southernmost tip of Yucatán, and that the reefs marked the northern end of the continent Tierra Firma[vi]. With the concurrence of the pilots, the captain decided to turn back and set a course for the northern coast of Yucatán. We named this body of water the Bahía de la Ascensión, because we discovered it on the day commemorating the heavenly ascension of Our Lord.

On Sunday, the 16th day of May, we cleared the reefs and sailed northward. On the third day we came upon a small island, where a small temple lay perched on a promontory high above a turquoise sea. It is said that the island is occupied by women like the Amazons, who live without men.

Later that day we turned westward and began following the north coast of Yucatán, seeking the lord of Lázaro, the chieftain who had welcomed Francisco Fernández. Columns of smoke, one rising behind the other, preceded us as we sailed along the coast, bringing Indians to the shore in great numbers.

We reached Lázaro at sunset on the 25th day of May, and the shore was alive with Indians. We anchored two miles out to sea, waiting for daylight to land, and all through the night, the sound of drums and trumpets filled the air, warning the surrounding countryside of our presence.

Two hours before dawn, the captain took 100 men ashore, and sent the boats back to the ships for the remainder of the company. The shore party moved up the beach to a small temple and positioned the cannons aimed in the direction of the town.

At daybreak hundreds of Indians appeared on the beach, threatening to attack us if we moved any closer to the town. The captain summoned Julian, who was a native of Lázaro, and the interpreter told them that the Christians would not harm them or steal from them. They had come only to barter for water, and would leave when their casks were filled. The clamor of the Indians subsided, and the captain passed a few trinkets among them. They pointed to a well beside the rock, but it contained so little water that we could barely ladle it into the casks. We knew, however, that there was a deeper well nearer the town where Francisco Fernández had filled his casks.

The captain ordered the company to move forward as slowly as possible, but with the first step, the Indians raised their weapons and motioned us to turn back. The men continued to advance, always moving toward the well, and the Indians backed off, giving ground reluctantly. We reached the well without incident, and the captain signaled the gunners to bring up the cannon.

There was a heavy wooden palisade in front of the town, and scores of Indians wearing quilted armor waited for us in a dense grove before it. From time to time they approached Julian, demanding that we leave immediately, and each time the captain replied that we would leave as soon as we had sufficient water. He showed them gifts that he had brought for their chieftain, and asked them to bring him to the well so he could offer him our friendship. The Indians left, and when they returned, they brought us fruit, fowl, and tortillas. They told us the chieftain had given us permission to take water, and that he would arrive shortly.

Soon a festive mood prevailed in the camp as we handed out our trinkets. One of our men began to play a flute while another beat time on a tambourine, and although the strange sounds frightened the Indians at first, in time they began to enjoy the music, and their children came out to dance.

Later that day the chieftain's brother came to see us, and the captain gave him some beads and a linen shirt. The captain told him that the lord of Cuba, who would offer his protection to his people if the chieftain agreed to become his vassal, had sent him here. Then he asked him if he had any gold, pearls, or jewels he would like to trade with him. The Indian returned with a few gilt copper medals and one large medal of low-grade ore.

Toward evening the Indians began to show hostility again, but when the captain promised we would depart by noon the following day, they withdrew to the town.

The next morning, shortly after daybreak, a large force of heavily armed Indians manned the palisade and gathered in the grove. As they shouted threats and insults at us, an unarmed Indian approached the camp with a smoking brazier. He set it on a stone before us, and after speaking with Julian, turned and walked back toward the grove. Julian told the captain that it was an offering to the gods for victory, and when the smoke died out, the Indians would attack.

The crossbowmen readied their weapons, the muskets and the cannons were primed, and the company was drawn up in battle order. The moment the brazier stopped smoking, the Indians showered us with arrows and stones amid a chorus of shouts and whistles. The company held fast until the cannons fired, then rushed the terrified Indians, driving them back into the grove. Some overeager soldiers pursued them into the trees and immediately fell into an ambush. Before the captain could rescue them, one Christian was dead, forty others wounded, and he had lost two teeth.

The wounded were taken aboard the ships while a shore party, working under the protection of the artillery, began hauling water casks to the boats. Near sunset, a few unarmed Indians approached the camp and made signs that their chieftain wanted peace. As a token of his good intentions, he sent the captain a wooden mask covered with a veneer of gold leaf.

As the boats were pulling away from shore, an Indian begged the captain to take him with us. By signs, he told us that he knew of a province where there were ships like ours and men who resembled us, save that they had large ears. All were disappointed when the captain left him on the beach.

On Friday, the 27th day of May, the fleet left Lázaro on a southwesterly course, seeking an inlet where one of the ships that was taking on water could be repaired. After sailing 12 leagues along a barren, uninviting course, we came upon Champotón, where the Indians had killed so many of our comrades. A fleet of canoes came out to attack us, but two artillery rounds sent them fleeing for the shore.

On the 30th day of May, we found our first good port in a large bay sheltered from the sea by two islands. We careened the weatherworn ship, and while it was being repaired, the men lived ashore, sleeping in shelters built of branches and palm leaves. We named the inlet the Puerto Deseado, for it provided us with an abundance of good fish called *jurel*, as well as rabbit, deer, and an ample source of fresh water.

During our stay, Antón de Alaminos brought his charts up to date, and from his computations, he confirmed that Yucatán was an island that we had almost circumnavigated. He estimated that only 20 leagues remained between our present position at Puerto Deseado and the Bahía de la Ascensión. The strait, however, was too shallow for the ships; only a small brigantine could pass through it. The land that we could see west of Yucatán, however, was unknown, and it was rightfully the captain's to claim.

On Saturday, the fifth day of May, the fleet left Puerto Deseado for the new land, and on the following Monday, we arrived at the mouth of a great river. The river sends a current of fresh water nearly two leagues out to sea, so powerful that we could not make headway to move upstream. We anchored as close to the mouth of the river as we dared, and waited for the current to slacken.

That night an Indian we seized at Puerto Deseado, whom I had baptized Pero Barba, told Julian that the Indians here gathered gold from a river three days journey inland. In the interior, he said, there were high sierras, broad savannas, great forests, and cities where the inhabitants scarified their ears and made sacrifices to their gods. It was a journey of 160 days, he claimed, to travel to the great sea beyond the sierra. These were the first tidings we received of the whereabouts of the Southern Sea.

The next morning a host of Indians followed the ships upstream as far as the current would permit. When we anchored, a large canoe manned with armed warriors came alongside the flagship. The Indian standing in the bow held a magnificent gold shield fringed with featherwork on high.

Julian neither spoke nor understood the language of the region, but Pero Barba knew it well, and he told the Indian that we came in friendship, and wanted only to barter our goods with them. The Indians climbed aboard the flagship, and the captain exchanged beads, scissors, knives, and a wool cap with them for a large wooden mask covered with a veneer of fine gold leaf, and a panache of parrot feathers with a small bird perched upon a human bone.

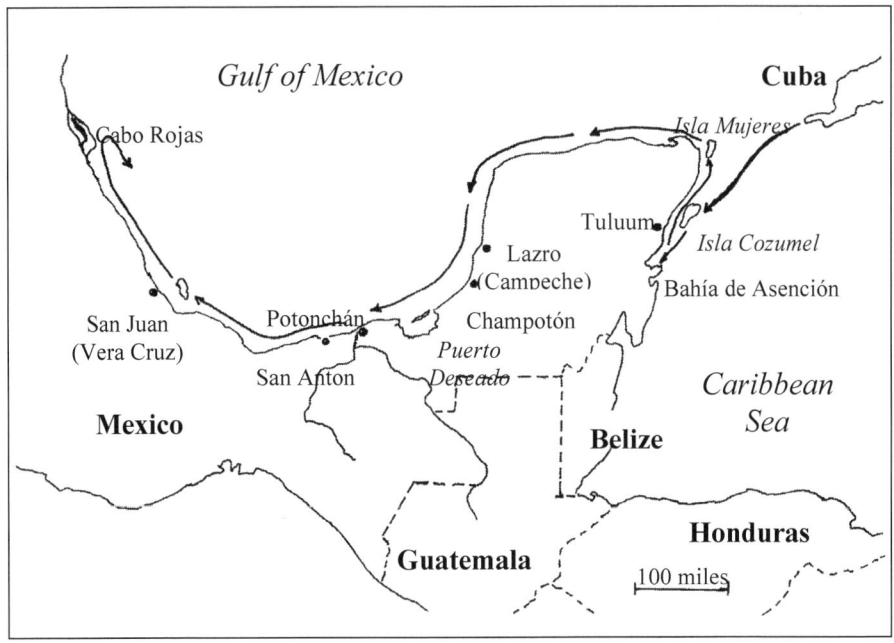

Grijalva Expedition

The next day the chieftain arrived with artifacts of gold and precious stones that bespoke of an order of civilization we had lost all hope of finding in the New World. He gave the captain three masks covered with gold and turquoise mosaics, a gilded helmet with curved horns, a black wig made of human hair, a gilt medal inlaid with a turquoise demon, leg armor covered with gold leaf, and a number of small gold artifacts.[vii]

In exchange, the captain offered him a green velvet doublet, a velvet nightcap, two linen shirts, a pair of linen breeches, and several other items of little value.

We dressed the chieftain in the green velvet doublet, put crimson stockings and hemp sandals on his legs and feet, and set the velvet nightcap on his head. This so delighted the Indians that they dressed the captain in a corselet of bright-colored feathers, put gold armlets on his biceps, shod him with half-boots decorated with gold ornaments, and set a crown made of fine gold leaf on his head.

When it was time for him to leave, the chieftain asked the captain to give him our Indian interpreter. The captain refused, but the chieftain persisted, offering to bring him the Indian's weight in gold the following day.

We named the river the Rio Grijalva in honor of the captain. Its source lies in the high sierra, and the land about it seems to be the best under the sun. The province is called Potonchán, and its people are cultured and knowledgeable. They possess bows and arrows, swords and shields, and fashion beautiful artifacts from gold and precious stones. The men had their hearts set upon entering the territory, for they believed each would realize more than a thousand gold pesos in trade, but the captain ordered them to keep to the ships.

On Friday, the 11th day of June, we left Potonchán and followed the coast on a westerly heading. We passed a number of towns and buildings along the coastal plain, and beyond, far into the interior, we could see high mountain ranges. The brigantine that the captain had sent ahead to survey the coast reported that Indians were following them along the shore, carrying shields that glistened like gold, and women wearing gold necklaces and armbands accompanied them.

On Saturday, the 12th day of June, we came upon several canoes fishing off the coast. They fled when they saw the ships, but we managed to cut one off before it reached the shore. A boat was lowered, and as it neared the canoe, the Indians began slashing at their bodies, drawing blood from their ears, their tongues, and other parts of their bodies in what seemed to be some kind of ritual. When they were brought aboard the flagship, we found that neither of our interpreters could speak their language. We gave them food and drink, and when they had eaten, we gave them gifts and made them understand by signs that we would not harm them. Later, the captain showed them some gold, and by signs they told him that it came from the riverbeds, and they offered to bring some to him if he set them free. The captain released two, and promised them he would set the others free when they returned.

The following day a party of Indians signaled us from the shore, and the captain, assuming the Indians had returned with gold, ordered a boat lowered. A heavy surf was running that day, however, and the mariners refused to attempt a landing. The captain signaled the Indians to row out beyond the breakers, but they kept to the shore, and he returned to the flagship.

The fleet resumed its course, and later that day we anchored in the lee of a small island at the mouth of a bay, about a league from the shore. When the ships were secured and the watch posted, the captain summoned the principals of the company to the flagship for a conference. He informed us that the pilot-major, after consulting with his pilots and other learned members of the expedition, had concluded that the land that lay before us was not an island, but an unknown continent. Their finding, he said, was supported by the mountainous terrain and the towering peaks we had seen in the interior, the strength and volume of fresh water that flowed from its rivers, and the 130 leagues of unbroken coastline that lay between Puerto Deseado and our present position. The continent, he announced, was ours to claim.

Early the next morning we set out to explore the island, which was no more than six miles in circumference. Not far from the beach, we found a path that passed through a grove of fig trees and into a clearing, where broken-down walls surrounded the ruins of stone buildings and a structure that resembled an ancient arch in Mérida.

Beyond the walls we came upon a circular tower about 15 paces in diameter. A grotesque beast, resembling a lion, stood upon an altar at the summit. The beast's tongue hung loosely from its mouth, and there was a hole in its forehead where incense was burned. A stone trough alongside the altar ran the length of the platform, and a row of stakes, set at an angle above it, extended from one end of the trough to the other. Skulls and human bones were heaped at the foot of each stake, and the trough was black with dried blood. An idol with a feathered plume stood to one side, its head twisted sharply to the rear, looking down at the trough.

Between two pillars we found the decaying bodies of two young Indians wrapped in a painted mantle, who had been dead for about 20 days. Nearby were two more bodies, not more than three days old. Their throats had been cut on a broad sacrificial stone near the altar, and their blood drained into the trough.

When we finished inspecting this loathsome scene before us, the captain sent for an Indian who was a native of the province to find out what manner of heathen ceremony had taken place here. When the Indian saw where the Spaniards were taking him, he fell to the ground in a swoon, convinced that he was about to be sacrificed. When the captain made him understand by signs what he wanted, the Indian told him that it was their practice to sacrifice those captured in warfare. They tore out their hearts and offered them to the idol, then roasted and ate the fleshy parts of the arms and legs. We named this place the Isla de Sacrificios.

In the afternoon, Indians on shore signaled us with white banners, and Francisco de Montejo went ashore to see what they wanted. He returned shortly with several beautifully painted mantles and a promise from the Indians that they would return later to barter with gold.

The following morning there were more signals from the mainland, and when we went ashore, we found a meal set out for us on a cloth spread beneath a shelter of branches. There were several varieties of fruit wrapped in corn tortillas, tender ears of roasted maize, and small bowls filled with a spicy chicken stew. Unfortunately, it was Friday, and we had to forego the stew. We traded a few glass beads, some combs, caps, and a mirror for a few mantles and headdresses that day, but the Indians promised to bring gold the next time we came ashore.

That afternoon the captain convened a meeting among the captains and other ranking members of the company to decide the future of the enterprise. It was his intent, he said, to take possession of the continent for His Majesty and Castile in the name of Diego Velásquez. After the writs of possession were executed, we had to decide whether to map the coast to confirm that the new land was truly a continent, or alter our course and seek out other undiscovered lands.

The *Trinidad,* he continued, was in dire need of repairs to stay afloat, but since there was no need for the entire company to carry out our mission, we could send her back to Cuba with whatever men were not needed. This would give us more provisions and allow us more time at sea, and we would make better time without the *Trinidad.* Furthermore, it would please Diego Velásquez to receive a report of what we had accomplished.

Since we could take no course of action without the consent of the pilot-major, we looked to Anton de Alaminos for his opinion.

The fleet, Alaminos said, came here in quest of a new land: we had no warrant to waste time and consume precious provisions by sailing about blindly for other islands that may or may not lie about us. The land before us was without question a continent. With our own eyes we had seen its snow-capped sierras and its broad, fresh-water rivers pouring far out to sea, and with our own ears we had heard the natives speaking different languages from on end of the land to the other. We must take possession of it now and draw up our maps, Alaminos said, then if time and provisions permit, we could move on to seek other lands. As for the Trinidad, he agreed that it was a hindrance to the enterprise, and he would send it back to Cuba a soon as he could make it seaworthy for the voyage.

The following morning we went ashore and the captain took formal possession of all the land between Puerto Deseado and the Bahía de Sacrificios. He named the site San Juan, in honor of the apostle who baptized Our Lord.

Soon after the ceremony, a party of unarmed Indians approached us. The chieftain bowed low and placed his hands on the ground, then rose and kissed his palms and held them out to us in an unmistakable sign of peace. He embraced the captain as if they were dear friends, then spoke to him, but none of us understood a word he said. The chieftain ordered his men to set up shelters to protect us from the sun, and when this was done, they spread plantain leaves beneath them. He beckoned the captain to be seated, and motioned the rest of us to gather around.

An Indian handed each of us a black reed and carefully touched an end with a smoldering twig. These reeds are made in such a manner that they consume themselves without ever bursting into flame, much like the fuses that are made in Valencia. The smoke that rose from them had a most pleasant aroma, and by their gestures, the Indians indicated that we should inhale it and not allow any of it to be wasted. As we smoked the reeds, Indians came in and out of the encampment continuously without showing any fear or suspicion of the Christians. It was as if they had lived among us for many years.

They laughed constantly as they used their fingers and hands to communicate with us, and never seemed to doubt that we understood every gesture. In exchange for a few strands of glass beads and a pair of thin-soled women's shoes, they brought us mantles, masks inlaid with turquoise stones, and a few small items of gold. When the captain pointed to the gold and made the chieftain understand that this was what we wanted more than anything else, he sent his son for more.

Each morning the Indians brought us tortillas, corn biscuits, and tortilla pastries filled with meat and chili sauce. If we were late in coming ashore, they were annoyed with us. If we arrived before they had set up our shelters, the chieftain, whom we had named Ovando, caned them, but they never failed to please us in every way they could.

During our stay in San Juan, the Indians brought many beautiful artifacts crafted from gold and jewelry. The finest specimens were a figurine of a man wearing a gold half-mask, a crown inlaid with gold beads and turquoise jewels, a gold bracelet four fingers in width, several pairs of gold earrings inlaid with turquoise, and a figurine of a demon wearing gold earrings and horns. In exchange, the captain gave them an assortment of beads, combs, mirrors, cheap hats and coats, linen shirts, knives, scissors, and women's shoes, all of which were worth less than two gold ducats.

What excited us more than the artifacts, however, were the nuggets of raw gold, each worth more than seven gold pesos. The chieftain told us that the source of the gold lay not more than half-day's journey into the interior. There, in the rivers that are born in the high sierra, an Indian had only to dive to the bottom and sift nuggets out of the sand. In a matter of a few hours, he could fill a reed as thick as a finger with pure gold. To smelt the gold nuggets into ingots, they placed the reeds on an earthen dish and heated it with a fire fanned by a bellows made from a hollow cane.

The quantity of gold and precious jewels the Indians brought to San Juan convinced us that this was the richest land in the world. We believed that if we were to colonize it, none would fail to realize less than 2,000 castellanos. We proposed to take the country by force, but the captain refused to establish an outpost until he could send to Cuba for enough men and supplies to support a colony. Instead, he ordered the fleet ready for departure.

As we prepared to board the ships, the Indians wept and embraced us, and as a parting gift, the chieftain gave the captain a comely woman, so finely dressed that she could not have been more elegant had she worn gold and silver brocade.

On Thursday, the 24th day of June, Pedro de Alvarado set sail for Cuba in the Trinidad with 50 men and all the gold and jewels we had acquired from the Indians. We left San Juan that same day, following the coast on a northwesterly heading, since the captain was determined to establish if the end of the sierra marked the northernmost point of the continent. The strong offshore currents drove us toward a town surrounded by heavy foliage, which we named Almeria[viii], a city in Spain that it brought to mind. Later that day we saw a town as large as Seville, and as we came abreast of it, 15 war canoes came out to intercept us. We signaled that we came in peace, but when they came within bowshot, they showered us with arrows, but few rounds of artillery sent them flying. The men called upon the captain to let them go ashore and take the town, but he kept to his course.

That evening we witnessed a great miracle. A comet with two tails appeared above the flagship shortly after sunset, and as it passed westward, it emitted a continuous stream of light until it disappeared beyond the city. By this sign, and by others we had seen so clearly, we knew that it was God's will that we colonize this land.

On Monday, the 28th day of June, Alaminos felt that there was no reason to continue with our mission. We were wasting time and the ship's stores, he said, and the currents were running against us. Furthermore, winter, which was not far off, would make these waters dangerous. There was no point in our pursuing this course, because the new land was clearly a continent. Now was the time to turn back to seek other lands to claim, in keeping with our charter.

The captain yielded, and the pilot-major set a course for San Juan, but the currents were so strong that he was forced to head into the open sea. When we came about, a lateen yard broke, and we could do no more than run before the wind, hoping to find a safe inlet where it could be repaired.

On Friday, the ninth day of July, after 11 days at sea, we found and inlet about 10 leagues west of the Rio Grijalva. We stayed there until the following Sunday trying to move up the river, but the currents and foul weather prevented us from moving a safe distance upstream. Lack of fresh water finally forced us to turn back up the coast. Fifteen leagues to the west, we came upon a river, and on

Monday, the 12th day of July, we crossed the sandy shoals at the mouth of the inlet.

Upriver we found a sheltered anchorage that we named San Antón, and we remained there for three days while we repaired the lateen yard. We found a good source of fresh water and several varieties of fruit along the riverbanks. Upon two occasions, unarmed Indians came to barter hatchets made of an alloy of copper and low grade gold for mirrors and glass beads.

On Friday, the 16th day of July, the weather broke and the fleet prepared to leave San Antón. The brigantine led the way across the shoals, but the flagship missed the channel and struck bottom several times. When we reached the open sea, it began taking on so much water that we were forced to turn back. The ship was so flooded by the time we reached the mouth of the river that the men had to be taken ashore to lighten ship enough for the boats to tow it upstream.

While the mariners were struggling to berth the flagship, the men noticed a group of about 20 Indians gathered on the opposite bank a small distance upriver. Francisco de Peñalosa took three men to find out what they were doing, and when they came abreast of the Indians, four crossed over to them in a canoe. They drew blood from their tongues and spat it on the ground as a sign of greeting, and gestured that they came in peace. They gave the Christians 32 hatchets, much like the others we had bartered for, some coarse cotton mantles, a small gold cup, and a metal knob shaped like and apple.

When the Indians returned to the opposite bank, they moved upstream and halted at a sandy spot. One came to the river's edge and spread his arms out toward us, then gestured with his fists to the Indians behind him, then toward our ships. He put his hands palm-down into the sand, then walked back to the others, whereupon they all sat. In a few moments, they rose again and brought a bulky object wrapped in a mantle from the brush. They buried it in the sand, then brought out two more bundles and buried then beside the first. Our men had no idea what they were doing and returned to the ships.

That same day Julian and Pero Barba disappeared.

We set up camp on the riverbank, leaving only the watch and those needed to make repairs aboard the ships. That night the captain prepared another set of ordinances, for now he was aware of the bitterness and resentment among the men for his refusal to establish a colony. The ordinances were posted and read to the men immediately after mass on Sunday. They forbade any discussion of founding a colony, prohibited the men from gathering in groups, which he would interpret as unlawful and mutinous, and demanded that they obey his every order without question or comment.

The following day more Indians came into camp to barter with us, and as always, they were a fearsome sight as blood streamed down their faces and necks from newly slashed earlobes. In exchange for cheap clothing, they gave us pineapples, mameyes, fowl, more hatchets, some violet jewels, and hollow gold beads.

That afternoon a fishing party returned to camp with gold artifacts worth at least 100 castellanos. They showed us two necklaces with pear-shaped pendants; a pair of tiny pincers, much like those that ladies used to pluck their eyebrows; a bell with wings mounted on it; an idol's head; and two ornamented eagles.

The men found them in a pit covered with freshly turned earth and a few cactus plants on a sandy beach upriver. They opened the pit and found the bodies of three children whose throats had been cut and their hearts removed. One of the children was 13 or 14 years old, but the other two were no more than five or six. From the condition of the bodies, they could not have been dead for more than a few days. The gold artifacts were found in the folds of the children's mantles. The men took the gold and buried the bodies again.

The graves were on the same plot of land where Francisco de Penalosa observed the Indians burying three bulky objects. We judged that the children had been sacrificed on Friday, when we were forced to come back upriver, and it disturbed us greatly that our coming might have been the cause of this cruel act.

We spent 15 days in San Antón repairing the flagship, and when it was seaworthy, we departed and set a course for Cuba. Heavy weather kept us from making much headway, and on the 16th day of August, we were forced to turn shoreward to seek water. Midway between the Rio Grijalva and Puerto Deseado, we found an inlet that opened into a wide body of water, where we saw a continuous procession of native canoes crossing from Yucatán to the mainland. Fish were so plentiful that we were able to salt a great number for the voyage home, and the *aguadas*, the stone cisterns in which the Indians gather rain, were full of fresh water. The captain named the inlet Puerto de Terminos, since the pilot-major calculated that it lay at the southern tip of Yucatán.

No more than a league from where we anchored, we found 14 or 15 clay idols between two large pillars, separated from each other by about 12 paces. In front of each idol there were potsherds and clay pots with feet, which were obviously used to cense the idols, since they contained the ashes and residue of some incense. Between two idols were the figures of two men engaged in the abominable and unnatural act of sodomy. Next to them a man sculptured in clay held his erect member in both hands, and it appeared to have been circumcised. When the fleet was provisioned and ready to depart, the captain buoyed the men's spirits by proposing that we stop at Champotón to take revenge upon the Indians who had killed our countrymen. After so many months of inactivity, the prospect of battle so delighted the men that they turned to readying their weapons as soon as we left port.

The fleet reached Champotón late in the afternoon of the first day of September. The flagship anchored two leagues offshore, and the entire company boarded the smaller ships and moved as close to the shore as they dared. The men aboard the brigantine, which lay only a half-league from shore, were to land as quietly as possible before daybreak.

An island with a fortress at its highest point lay between the brigantine and the shore. That night the men aboard the brigantine thought they heard drums on the island, and fearing that the ship was about to be attacked, sent for the captain. He came with reinforcements, but with first light we could see that the island was deserted. He sent the company to occupy the island, and from the fortress they could see that heavy barricades and deep ditches defended the town, and that any number of warriors could be waiting for them in the trees between the shore and the town. Below the town was a river where war canoes could circle behind us and cut us off from the beach. As the day grew brighter, trumpets and drums began to sound, and a host of Indians gathered along the shore, shouting their defiance of us.

As it was evident to every man on the island that any attempt to take the town would cost us dearly, the captain asked them if they were still willing to proceed. Some felt that it would not go well for us if we attempted a landing, and urged him to return to the ships. Others were eager to go ashore and fight, and some were willing to leave the decision up to the captain.

The captain said that he was willing to lead them ashore, but it must be done according to the ordinances he had published at Puerto Deseado, which prohibited them from seizing property from the Indians against their will and provoking them in any manner. He read the ordinances again, emphasizing the grave penalties for disobeying them. When he finished, every man in the company voted to return to the ships. The ordinances were at odds with their eagerness to punish the Indians and the profit they would gain from sacking the town.

The captain felt that they had made a wise decision, and gave the order to return to the ships. When the Indians saw them leaving the island, they waded out into the sea as far as they could, shouting threats and insults after them.

The fleet left Champotón in Friday, the third day of September, and the following Sunday we arrived off the shores of Lázaro. Since we knew of no source of fresh water beyond the town, we went ashore to take on enough water and provisions for the voyage to Cuba. The Indians attempted to lead us into an ambush, but we were well prepared, and with the support of our artillery, we drove them back into the bush.

On Wednesday, the eighth day of September, we left Lázaro and set a course for Cuba, but heavy weather forced us to stay close to shore. On Saturday, the 11th day of September, we came upon a chain of sandbanks lying across our course, and once again we were forced to turn back toward Yucatán. On Tuesday, the 21st day of September, we placed ourselves in the hands of God and set our course for Cuba, even though we had little water and faced unfavorable weather.

On the morning of September the 29th, the day of the Archangel San Miguel, we came in sight of Cuba. Our journey of 152 days had come to an end. The following day we entered the port of Cárdenas, where we learned that Pedro de Alvarado and the *Trinidad* had arrived safely after a difficult voyage.

The fleet moved on to Matanzas, where we met Cristóbal de Olid, whom Diego Velásquez had sent in search of our ships. Olid first sailed to Cozumel, where, presuming he was the first to discover the island, took possession of it in the name of the governor. From

Cozumel, he sailed around the north coast of Yucatán until he reached an inlet three leagues north of Puerto Deseado. A storm swept away his anchors and cables, and since he failed to find any sign of our ships, he returned to Cuba, arriving in Matanzas eight days before we entered port.

We had not been in Matanzas long before the captain received an order from Diego Velásquez to bring his ships to Santiago as soon as possible. A soon as the ships were repaired and provisioned, they would join another fleet that was making ready to sail to the new land. Any man in his company who wanted to join the expedition was to wait in Matanzas for the fleet, and the magistrate of San Cristóbal would provide for him at the governor's expense.

When the captain arrived in Santiago, he learned that Diego Velásquez had chosen another to be captain-general of the new fleet. His failure to colonize the new land had not only cost him the favor of the governor, but the confidence of the men who had sailed with him. Instead of participating in the momentous events that were to follow on the heels of his historic voyage, he would meet with violent death in Nicaragua. Only the mighty river that bears his name was left for posterity to recall his discovery of a great continent.

Here ends the *Itinerary* of its discoverer, Juan Grijalva, written by his chaplain.

---

[i] The brief account of the Córdoba expedition is composed from the accounts of Torquemada and that of Bernal Díaz del Castillo, a member of the company.

[ii] Campeche

[iii] The account of the Grijalva expedition is based upon the eyewitness account of Juan Díaz, the chaplain of the expedition. Unfortunately, his original manuscript is lost, and the only copy available is an inferior one written in Italian.

The Italian version often exhibits confusion with regard to the Mexican coast and the chronology of the expedition, and in a number of cases, descriptions of events that took place during the voyage are too sketchy to be of value.

Gonzalo Fernández de Oviedo y Valdez, however, possessed a *cedula* requiring all governors in the Indies to provide him with whatever he required for his *Historia*, and Diego Velásquez gave him a certified account of the expedition. His descriptions of the Mexican coast show good correlation with modern charts, and his chronology is consistent throughout Grijalva's journey. Oviedo's references to the navigational data that convinced Grijalva that Yucatán was an island indicate strongly that he had access to the pilot Anton de Alamino's log.

Both accounts have been used to reconstruct the narrative, however, since Díaz relates events not cited by Oviedo, and he provides the reader with the priest's enchantment with the land and his admiration of the civilization of the inhabitants.

[iv] Julian was undoubtedly referring to Jerónimo de Aguilar and Gonzalo Guerrero, who had been cast ashore on Yucatán six years earlier.

[v] The three towns are Xel-Ha, Tancah, and Tulum, which were founded during the Maya Late Postclassic Period, A.D. 1200-1519. Ceramic evidence indicates that they were occupied as late as 1618.

[vi] Tierra Firma refers to South America, which Columbus discovered in 1498. During his fourth voyage in 1502, he determined that the continent extended beyond the northern coast of Honduras, some 350 miles southeast of the Bahía de Asención.

[vii] For a complete inventory of the articles taken from Mexico by Grijalva, see Gomara, Simpson ed., 15-17.

[viii] Nautla, on modern maps.

4. The Acolyte's Tale:

Journey to the Underworld

The *Tzoncoztli*, the scribe responsible for the night watch in the Temple of Tezcatlipoca, was careful not to wake the apprentices, dreaming the uneasy dreams brought about by their yearlong fast, when he rose to make his rounds. The hour was rapidly approaching midnight, and as he looked to the east, he saw a light on the distant horizon. As he watched, the light began to rise in the night sky, and as it rose, it grew larger and larger until it blossomed into a glowing white cloud, so bright that it lit up the city as if it were midday. He roused the apprentices, and they watched the specter as it spread across the sky like a shimmering curtain, then diminished in intensity until it was lost in the light of early dawn.

Moctezuma watches the apparition cross the skies from the top of his palace

When they told Moctezuma what they had seen, he questioned each of the apprentices in turn, then dismissed their tale as no more than a bad dream.

"Lord," the *Tzoncoztli* said, "Why would we tell the greatest ruler in the world that we had seen something that lies beyond all reason? If you doubt us, watch the heavens tonight and you will see it for yourself."

The following night Moctezuma climbed to the roof of the palace and spent the night watching the apparition, which was whiter than the snows of the sierra, cross the heavens of Mexico. At daybreak he sent his hunchbacks to fetch the *Tzoncoztli,* and when he arrived, Moctezuma said, "What you have told me is true. Last night I saw the cloud rise and cross the sky, just as you described it. But what must I do? Who can I call upon to tell me its meaning?"[i]

The scribe replied, "Lord, Mexico is the center of the world, and you are a sovereign who knows no peer. Who am I to tell you the significance of the cloud? Surely there are necromancers and diviners who can explain it to you."

But when he summoned the sorcerers and diviners to the palace, they could tell him nothing about the apparition, for none had ever seen anything like it. In frustration, he ordered them taken to Cuauhcalco and sealed into the walls.

Next he sent his nobles to Texcoco to invite the lord Nezahualpilli to Tenochtitlán, and when he arrived, Moctezuma took him to his private quarters.

"Most honored lord, as a man of great learning, a man who understands the motions of the heavens, what can you tell me of this apparition that has appeared in our skies? Is it of worldly origin, or is it an omen sent by the gods?"

Nezahualpilli replied, "Surely lord, those who watch over the city have told you of its meaning. Have they no reckoning of the sky and the stars? The apparition has appeared in our skies for many nights, but as I believed that its meaning had been revealed to you, I did not speak of it.

If it is a sign that all will come to an end, what can I say to you other than as a man of spirit, gather your courage and brace yourself for the blows of misfortune, for as I once told you, a great disaster will come in your time. As for me, my beloved son, I have but one consolation-I shall not witness the end, for my remaining days are few."

Moctezuma wept, and through his tears he said, "My lord, what will become of me? Where will I go, what will I do? Must I now become a bird to fly away and hide, or must I wait here for whatever the heavens have in store for me?"

The death of Nezahualpilli left Moctezuma in a deep melancholia. Although Nezahualpilli had condemned the son of Moctezuma's eldest sister to death for a notorious affair with one of his wives, the lord of Acolhuacán nevertheless remained his closest friend and the only man he looked upon as his peer.

Moctezuma's thoughts now turned to his own mortality, and convinced that death was not far off, he ordered the stonecutters to carve his image, which would be placed beside those of the dead kings of Mexico at Chapultepec.

The stonecutters sought out a suitable block of stone, and carved out the figure of the emperor seated upon the jaguar and eagle throne with a tigerskin tapestry in the background. He held a shield on his left arm and a small timbrel in his right, and tigerskin cuffs were wrapped about his wrist and ankle. The features of the emperor were somber. His hair was braided into a queue intertwined with flamingo feathers, a golden rod pierced his nose, a jeweled bezote his lower lip, and turquoise earflaps covered his ears.

Moctezuma wept when he saw the finished work. Each feature had been carved with painstaking detail, and painted with such living colors that the figure before him seemed about to rise and speak.

"You have done your work well," he told the stonecutters. "The great lord Nezahualpilli, who knew and understood the six hundred magic arts is dead, but he left behind no such monument to recall his accomplishments. Nor did Tzompanteuctli, who knew and understood six hundred more arts of necromancy, leave a memorial beside his house. Now he too is dead and his remembrance lost forever. Soon I shall die and leave this world, but my image will endure the ages in this stone, and my glory and fame will be everlasting."[ii]

In the weeks that followed, Moctezuma looked upon the sculpture, and each time he was taken with such sadness that he wept as thoughts of death overwhelmed him. In time his fear of life became as great as his fear of death. In death there was a place for him in the thirteen horizons of heaven and the nine depths of the underworld, where he would realize an idyllic eternity among the immortals. This blissful sanctuary was the abode of Tlaloc, the rain god, which was reserved for those who had taken their own lives rather than endure the sorrows of the world. To reach this paradise, however, he must first pass through the gates of the dread Mictlan, where the bitter winds of heaven never ceased to rage. Beyond Mictlan, he would find Huemac, the last lord of the Toltecs, who had hanged himself on Chapultepec hill, waiting for him.[iii]

Moctezuma gathered his dwarfs and hunchbacks about him and said, "My children, I know of a place where we can live forever and enjoy all the pleasures of the world, a place where food and drink and fruit is plentiful, a place where there is joy and contentment, and a greater peace than we have ever known. Together we will go to Chapultepec and seek Huemac, the lord of the Toltecs, and he will open the gates of his kingdom for us."

The dwarfs and hunchbacks frolicked and tumbled about the throne with delight, then took Moctezuma by the arms and led him to the temple, where they gave thanks to Huitzilopochtli for their deliverance to a better world.

Next he summoned his necromancers, and together they drank *octli*. When the cup had passed its rounds, they took four slaves to the temple and sacrificed them, then flayed their bodies. He gave the skins of the flayed men to the necromancers and said. "Go to Chapultepec, to Huemac's palace, and say to him, 'Your vassal Moctezuma sends these gifts, and he asks that you allow him to sweep your palace or perform any other task in your house, no matter how low or menial."

At Chapultepec the necromancers found the entry to the cave that led to the underworld, and inside the cave, they came upon four gates. They chose the lower gate, but before they had gone very far, Totecchicahua, the drummer god, halted them.

"Who are you? Where are you going?" he said.

"Lord," they answered, "we are ambassadors, come to see the king."

"Which king do you seek?"

"Moctezuma has sent us to speak with the lord Huemac."

"Very well. Follow me and I will take you to him."

When the drummer god led them before Huemac, he said, "My lord, Moctezuma has sent commoners from the world above to speak with you."

"What does Moctezuma want?" asked Huemac.

The necromancers answered, "Lord, he sends you the skins of four men, and he asks you to receive him into your royal household, where he will sweep your floors and do anything else you demand of him."

"The lord who bestowed this domain upon me, Huemac replied," is a very great lord. Tell that poor wretch Moctezuma that I can relieve him of his troubles only if my lord orders me to do so. Go now, and give him my answer."

Huemac's refusal to admit him into his house so infuriated Moctezuma that he ordered the necromancers stoned to death. Determined to pursue his quest for immortality, he summoned his slaves and once again sent an appeal for sanctuary to Huemac.

A blind man called Ixtepetla met the slaves in the underworld, and although his eyes were no larger than the tip of a blade of grass, he led them to Huemac,

"One night at midnight," the slaves told Huemac, "Moctezuma saw a great white cloud rise above the horizon in the eastern sky. The cloud grew ever larger as it rose into the heavens, and it gave off glowing vapors until it vanished with the dawn. When this apparition appeared in the sky, Nezahualpilli knew the time had come for him to die, and he told Moctezuma of certain events that were to come to pass, things that caused Moctezuma much grief. Now Moctezuma wishes to known what is to become of him, because Tzompanteuctli, the lord of Cuitláhuac, told him these same things. Moctezuma wishes now that he had never seen the cloud, and if Huemac knows its meaning, surely he will grant him sanctuary.

"Does Moctezuma imagine that this place is no different from the earth above, where he rules?" Huemac replied. "Does he think that I and those who dwell here with me do not know what the underworld is like? Does he not know that we are not the same as we were when we lived on earth; that here we are of another form, another manifestation? When we lived upon earth, we were happy, contented, and lived in peace, but here we have nothing to look forward to but everlasting anguish and torment.

"Tell this to Moctezuma! If ever he should see this place, he would flee in sheer fright, he would flee until he found a stone big enough to hide behind forever. Tell him he could not bear it here for a single hour, much less a day. Tell him to enjoy the pleasures of earth while he can. Let him enjoy his precious jewels, his gold, his elegant feathers, and all his splendid robes and rich food. Go now, and tell this to him."

The slaves returned to earth with Huemac's warning, but Moctezuma refused to accept it. He was so angered that he ordered them taken to the stockade and stoned to death.

Moctezuma now chose two nobles from Texcoco to ask Huemac for asylum in the underworld. A steward called Acuacuauh met them at the entry of the cave and took them to Huemac.

"Lord," they said, "your vassal Moctezuma has sent us to you again, hoping that you will relent and admit him to your household, where he can serve you for all time. He can no longer suffer the shame, the dishonor, and the stigma that is to be his lot in life."

"I would have him know," Huemac replied, that he is wretched among all men, that his troubles are of his own doing, brought upon him in his ruthless pursuit of power. I would have him know that whenever his name is spoken, he will remembered only for his bold pride, his excessive cruelty, and for the way he took the lives of his fellow creatures in every inhumane manner known to mankind.

"If he is to come here, he must forsake the stewardship of his dominion and begin a penitence. He must abstain from rich foods and observe a strict fast, eating nothing but biscuits made from *michihuautli* and no more than a spoonful of beans each day. Tell him that beautiful flowers and heady perfumes are forbidden him, and most of all, he must be celibate, he must not go to his wives. If he observes this penitence for 80 days, the gods will lift the sentence they have prescribed for him, and he may come to me.

"Tell him that if he does as I say, he is to go to the hill at Chapultepec on the morning of the fourth day following his penitence and wait for me. I will come for him that night and take him to *Tlachtonco,* where I dwell with my people."

Moctezuma rewarded the Texcocans and immediately set about the observance of his penitence. In the weeks that followed, he distanced himself from his court and ignored the duties of his office. He took no pride in his appearance, forsaking his royal robes in favor of a coarse loincloth and a cloak made of henequen. For 80 days he kept to himself in a small room, observing the simple diet proscribed by Huemac.

As the 80 days of the penitence drew to a close, he sent his dwarfs and hunchbacks to Chapultepec, and on the fourth day following the penitence, they saw a white stone atop the hill. They ran to the palace to tell Moctezuma, and when he saw the stone, he said, "It is time. Cover the ground with sapote leaves, and use the stalks to make a seat for me. We will wait for him here."

The dwarfs and hunchbacks began to weep, and he said to them, "Do not cry, my children, for soon we shall live in a place where there is peace and contentment, where there is no remembrance of death."

Moctezuma tied leather thongs, gilded and painted red, around his wrists and ankles, and slipped a gold band onto his arm. He hung several strands of turquoise beads about his neck, set an emerald bezote in his lower lip, and wove a queue of flamingo feathers into his hair. Then he pulled the flayed skin of a sacrificed noble over his head and, surrounded by his dwarfs and hunchbacks, sat down and waited for Huemac.

As the hour approached midnight, a shimmering light appeared in the distance. As it approached, it grew ever brighter until it reached *Tlenamacacoyan*, where it halted. It began to pulsate, first growing bright then diminishing, and each time it grew bright, Moctezuma and his dwarfs saw the houses of the city and the mountains about them as if it were midday.

The *Tzoncoztli* thought it was a dream at first, but when he heard his name spoken again, he became aware of a presence in the shadows of the temple.

"How can you sleep when your are responsible for the watch?" a voice said. "Look at your apprentices." The scribe looked about and saw that all wcrc fast asleep and snoring.

"Rise," the voice said, "and look now upon the one who calls himself Moctezuma. See how his pride has led him to shame and infamy! What will the empire say about him now? What will our enemies say now? By this shameful act he brings only dishonor upon his people, for the fate that has been prophesied for him must come to pass, It cannot be set aside." The lord of the air, the land, the sea, the rivers, and the mountains has sent me here to warn him that he cannot go where he wants to go. You must take the word of the god who sustains the heavens, the earth, and all its people, and tell Moctezuma that what he seeks is impossible, that he must not continue to seek asylum with Huemac. I have been sent here to stay the hand of Huemac, to keep him away from Moctezuma, and when he sees me, he will go back to the underworld where he belongs."

The voice fell silent, and the scribe knew that the presence was gone. He left the temple and went to the lakeshore, where he found a canoe waiting to take him to Chapultepec. He found Moctezuma waiting on the hill, surrounded by his dwarfs and hunchbacks. He approached the emperor warily, summoning his courage to speak.

"Lord," he said, "I am but a lowly scribe, and I know that it is beneath the emperor of the Mexicans to speak with a person such as me, but I bring you a message from the heavens above.

"As I lay sleeping in the temple of Tezcatlipoca, a voice awakened me, calling me by name. The voice first scolded me for sleeping on watch, then it told me that the lord Moctezuma was intent upon doing that which he should not attempt, and that Huemac had come to take him to his domain in the netherworld. Then Huemac passed by the temple, and the one who woke me stood before him and said, 'Go back from whence you came, for it is not within your power to carry off Moctezuma.' Huemac turned away, and the one who spoke to me said to him, 'If you seek him again, I will turn you back again, and if you persist, I will put you in chains.' Then he prepared a canoe for me, and ordered me to seek you out and warn you. After that, I saw and heard nothing more. Thus was the command of the lord of the lords, the lord of the mountains, the rivers, the air, and the deep waters. You must turn away from this path that will bring dishonor upon the empire.

"Lord," the scribe continued, "why is it your wish to descend into the underworld? Why would you give strangers the will to destroy our kingdom, the center of the world, for what is no more than self-pity? What will the great lords say if you disappear without a single clue? The shame and disgrace will not be yours alone, for it will be passed down to all your descendants. What must come to pass cannot be changed, no matter what. The gods have sealed your fate themselves.

"But do not grieve, my lord. this inevitability is not for the present but for the future. Remember what was said of the noble Ceteuctli, and of Matlacxochitl, Ozmatli, and Timal, the greatest necromancers of Tula, whom Quetzalcoatl took through the sea of heaven to Tlapalán, where they were ordained to die together. Has it not been revealed that although they are no longer of this world, they did not die there, but were carried off to a better place by Quetzalcoatl? Put aside your fear, O lord, and let your people stand by your side, for fear is the companion of the lonely man.

"Now we must leave, for daybreak is upon us. As for what the voice revealed to me in the temple, rest assured that none will ever hear of it, for have I not been fast asleep with all my brothers this entire night?"

Moctezuma was silent, lost in thought for some time before he spoke. Finally he turned to the scribe and said, "Yes, my son, let us leave now. You have counseled me well and you have given me comfort in my hour of need. In the days to come, stay by my side and help me endure my fears for the future and the future of my children now that my fate is sealed. You will come live with me in the palace, and together we will walk in the gardens of Cuaunahuac and hunt game in the forests of Oaxtepec."[iv]

---

[i] The Florentine Codex sets the date of the appearance of the comet in the year 12 House. (1517). This date agrees with the sighting on June 24, 1517, documented by the chaplain, Juan Díaz, of what is evidently a comet passing westward over Mexico. A painting made 60 years after the conquest shows Moctezuma watching the comet from the roof of his palace.

[ii] No such stone has ever been found, but Moctezuma's image can be seen on the hillside at Chapultepec.

[iii] Huemac, the last ruler of the Toltecs, left Tula in 1156 or 1168 and established his capital in Chapultepec.

The afterworld of the Mexicans, like that of the Maya, was made up of 13 levels of heaven and nine levels of the underworld. The sixth level of heaven, which was ruled by the rain gods, was a special abode for suicides, particularly for those who had hanged themselves.

[iv] The Huemac allegory is one of several tales that demonstrate Moctezuma's paranoia prior to the conquest.

5. Tlilancalqui[i]:

The Mask of Quetzalcoatl

A native of the town Mictlanquauhtla, a priest who had no big toes, no thumbs, nor any ears appeared one day before the gates of the royal palace. He had traveled night and day from the land of the fiery mountain to warn Moctezuma that a strange craft, a vessel as big as the surrounding hills, was moving about in the great sea.

I was in the dark house, the temple of the goddess of Coatlique, where the emperors of Mexico come to pray to the mother of our god Huitzilopochtli, when I received Moctezuma's summons.

"Tllilancalqui," he said, "you must go at once to Cuetlaxtlan and ask the governor what these craft in the sea of heaven seek. Take the slave Cuitlalpitoc with you and return as soon as possible."

I sent for the slave and we departed immediately for the seacoast, resting only briefly before we reached Cotastla, the principal town of Cuetlaxtlán. There the governor received us, and he told us that his spies had watched two enormous towers that lay off the coast for many days. The natives of the region had bartered food and cotton with the men who lived aboard them for jewels and odd articles for which he had no name.

The following day he led me to a cove where the strange craft lay at rest, not far from shore. Eight men were fishing from a small boat near the beach, and Cuitlalpitoc and I hid in the foliage of a nearby tree while we watched them. At sundown they pulled in their lines and nets and rowed to the nearest tower. When I was satisfied that I would learn no more that day, we climbed down from the tree and took our leave of the governor.

I found an impatient emperor waiting for me in Tenochtitlán. "O lord," I told him, "it is true that strange craft are now lying off the shores of the great sea, and they have brought men of an unknown race who trade with the natives. I saw them fishing from a small boat with canes and nets that they cast upon the water. They fished until late afternoon, then rowed to the nearest craft and joined the others who live aboard it. Their skins are white, and they have long beards and hair that hangs below their ears. They wear clothing of many different colors; blue, gray, green, and one that can only be described as dirty and ugly. a few wear loose red coats, and others walk about barechested. Some wear hats made of fine red cloth, and others shield their heads from the sun with round hats that look much like shiny earthenware pots."

I gave the emperor strings of crystal, colored beads, a sweet fruit confection, and a heady drink they call wine that they had bartered with the natives. When I gave him one of their biscuits, he remarked that it resembled the tufa stone found in the springs. He ordered a steward to fetch him a piece of tufa, and when he compared one with the other, it seemed to him that the stone weighed less than the biscuit.

He called for his hunchbacks and dwarfs, and gave a biscuit to each. "Eat this," he said, "and tell me what you think of it." When they had eaten the biscuits, they said, "Lord, they are sweet and have a good flavor, but they are very hard." Moctezuma broke a piece from one of the biscuits and tasted it warily. "It is indeed sweet," he remarked, "but it seems to have been preserved in smoke, as if it came from the infernal regions. We must be careful, however, as it may be a gift from the god who once lived in Tula, and we must consecrate it in his temple."

Priests put the biscuits in a blue cup and placed it in the eagle vessel at the foot of Huitzilopochtli. They censed the biscuits and blessed them, then took the cup to Tula and set it in a stone casket. They beheaded a bevy of quail and sprinkled their blood upon the casket, then gave it to the priests at Tula, who, accompanied by the trumpeting of conch horns, buried it in the temple of Quetzalcoatl.

If the arrival of the strangers heralded the return of a god and the fulfillment of an ancient prophecy, his homecoming could neither be ignored nor ill rewarded by the throne of Mexico. Moctezuma sent for the most gifted goldsmiths, lapidaries, and featherworkers in the city, and when they stood before him, he said, "Fathers, I have brought you here for a most important task. The goldsmiths are to make a necklace with links four fingers long, with a cluster of emeralds as a centerpiece. Then you must make bracelets with gold chains pendant, and the lapidaries will grind and polish them. The featherworkers will make fly flaps from the most luxuriant feathers in the land, and each will have a half-moon centerpiece on one face and a golden sun on the other.

"You are to work here in the palace, where I can observe your progress, and if you reveal what I have asked of you to the son of any woman, I will level your homes until the waters rise above the foundations and put every member of your family to death."

When the artisans were finished, they laid out their work before him, and after he expressed his satisfaction and rewarded them, he summoned me to his side.

"Tlilancalqui," he said, "the ancient ones of Tula tell us that when Quetzalcoatl crossed the sea of heaven to Tlapalán, he foretold that he or his sons would return one day to rule all the provinces of this land. When he left, he possessed all the treasures of the world-even this throne, this seat of majesty and power, is his, and I only hold it in trust until his return. Now I have been led to believe that the one who has come to our shores is he, and that he has returned to claim what is rightfully his.

"You are to take these gifts you see before you and present them to him. You are also to order the governor of Cuetlaxtlán to prepare a feast of tamales, tortillas, roast fowl, barbecued venison, rabbit, ground chilis, and baskets of fruit for our visitor. If he eats these foods, it will tell us that he is familiar with our food, and that he is truly the one we await.

"If, however, he refuses our food and demands human flesh, we will know that he is not our god. If he should eat you, have no fear for your family. I will protect your wife and children for as long as they may live, and I will appoint each of your sons a majordomo of one of my towns, and they will enjoy a generous income for as long as they live. Take Cuitlalpitoc with you, and if he is eaten, he is only a slave I bought for such a purpose.

"If indeed it is Quetzalcoatl who has come, welcome him to his kingdom, and assure him that it was left in the hands of my ancestors only for safekeeping until he returned. Ask him, however, to permit me to end my days here in Mexico; beseech him to let me die before he reclaims his throne."

Fortunately, neither Cuitilalpitoc nor I were faced with the prospect of being devoured by the strangers. When we reached Cuetlaxtlan, they had spread their sails and disappeared.[ii]

When we returned to Tenochtitlán, Cuitlalpitoc was given his freedom, and a relieved emperor rewarded me with riches worthy of a prince. He granted me houses in the barrios of Tonantitlán and Moyotlán, with male and female slaves to serve each household. He sent me jewels, gold, fine featherwork, and bales of cotton, and he decreed that the yearly tribute from two towns in the provinces was to be mine for as long as I lived.

The strange men were gone, but their departure brought little comfort to an emperor who had been driven to near-suicide by cosmic displays and the doomsday prophecies of his soothsayers.

"Tlilancalqui," he said, "we must learn everything we can about the men who came here. We must know who they are and where they came from. Send for Tocual the painter and describe exactly what you saw in Cuetlaxtlán to him. Describe their ships, their weapons, the food they ate, and all their customs. Be exacting in your descriptions, but give him a free hand in his portrayal of them."

As I described what I had seen, Tocual's brush brought the strange men to life before my very eyes. I saw the same white faces, the heavy beards, thick manes, and long queues; I saw the same odd clothing of many colors, and the same glazed pans they wore upon their heads.

We took the painting to Moctezuma, and he stared at it as if he were in a trance. When he looked up, he asked Tocual if he or his ancestors knew of any prophecy that those in his painting would rule Mexico one day. Tocual replied that he knew of no such prophecy, nor was he aware of any painter in Mexico who had ever produced a work bearing the mark of such a prophecy.

Moctezuma summoned artists from Malinalco, Chalco, and the hot lands of the coastal provinces, but their work portrayed only grotesque creatures born of overactive imaginations. The painters of Cuitláhuac and Mixquic, who were descendants of the Toltecs, knew the prophecy of Quetzalcoatl's return quite well, but the creatures they painted were unlike the men painted by Tocual.

When Moctezuma called for the painters of Xochimilco, I said, "Lord, there is an aged priest there, a great learned man called Quilaztli.[iii] It is said that his gods, the *Teomamaque*, left such a prophecy to all the priests who served them. Let me bring him to you."

When the ancient seer was led before Moctezuma, the emperor put the same questions to him as he had to the others. "How will we know the men who are to rule our land? Will they come from the east, the west, or will they descend upon us from heaven?"

"My lord," Quilaztli replied, "there are those who have prophesied that *coayxeeques*, creatures with the faces of snakes and fish, or creatures with the feet of caterpillars, will come to rule our land. Others have foretold of warriors who will come mounted upon eagles and snakes. But I can only offer you the truths that have been written by my ancestors. They have proclaimed that noblemen will come to our land from Tzonanpan, from the top of the great sea. They will eat and sleep in their craft as if they were in their own homes. Their faces and bodies will be white, they will have long beards, and they will wear clothing of many colors. These are the men who are to be our masters, lord, and they will come very soon."

He unrolled a timeworn and faded painting and spread it before the emperor. Moctezuma looked at it for a few moments, then beckoned me to his side. "Look at this painting," he said, "and tell me if they resemble those you saw in Cuetlaxtlán."

The resemblance of the men in Quilaztli's painting was unmistakable. "Lord, they are the same men who came to our shores." I showed Tocual's painting to Quilaztli, and the old Xochimlcan agreed. The bearded men were the same men as his ancestors had painted.

"The great wise men of Xochimilco have indeed bequeathed their legacy in the magic arts to you, Quilaztli," Moctezuma said. "the men you see in this painting came to our shores in Cuetlaxtlan, and have only recently departed. Your knowing of them, however, means you can never return to Xochimilco-what you have seen here today must forever be kept secret. I will provide lodgings for you and your family, and I will give you lands so that you can feed them. You will enjoy all the privileges of my nobles, and you will sit in judgment with them in the royal council."

Moctezuma studied both paintings for a few moments, then turned once again to the ancient seer. "Tell me, Quilaztli, will these men return?"

"My lord," Quilaztli replied, "the road from the sea will be as broad tomorrow as it is today. Have no doubt, they will return. They will return this year or the next, and if the gods do not grant me enough days to see it come to pass, the lives of my wife and my children will be forfeit."

"Only the gods of the air, the sun, the waters, and the mountains know what the future holds," Moctezuma said. "Let us pray that they never return."

But the gods failed to heed Moctezuma's prayers. Within the year reports reached Mexico of a great battle fought between the Maya and an army of bearded men at Potonchán. Mochocoboc, the lord of Champotón, had shamed his brother Tabzcoob, the lord of Potonchán,.for failing to take a stand against the foreigners when they first arrived in his province, Humiliated by his brother's contempt, he fell upon their army in the marshlands, and for a time it appeared that the Maya would carry the day. Their will to fight, however, was shattered when monstrous demons, half beast, half man, rose from the swamps like evil spirits and charged through his squadrons, leaving a trail of crushed and broken bodies in their wake.

Tabzcoob surrendered the following morning. Among his peace offerings to the captain of the foreigners were twenty handsome women, one of who was to play an influential role in the downfall of Moctezuma's empire.

When the coast watchers alerted the governor of Cuetlaxtlán that eleven ships lay off the shores of his province, he sent two nobles to greet the captain and offer him the friendship of Moctezuma. Coastal fishermen rowed them out to the flagship, and they kissed the prow reverently before boarding the vessel.[iv]

They gave the captain a gold rattle and five silver medallions, and told him that Teuhtlitl, who governed the province in the name of the great lord Moctezuma, had sent them. The governor, they said, welcomed him and his men, and offered his hospitality for as long as they cared to remain in Cuetlaxtlan. If, however, they chose to move onward, he would provide them with whatever they needed. To the nobles surprise, the gifts were accepted by a native woman, who spoke to a foreigner darkened by long days in the sun, and he in turn gave their message to the captain.[v]

Through his interpreters, the captain thanked them for the presents and motioned them to be seated beside him. He told them that he was the ambassador of a great emperor who lived in a faraway land, and that he had been sent here to offer the friendship of his lord to the celebrated Moctezuma, of whom he had many good things. He had also come to speak to Moctezuma on behalf of his god, who would grant the emperor and his people undreamed of blessings and benefits. He would remain in Cuetlaxtlán, therefore, until the lord Moctezuma was ready to receive him.

Before the nobles left, he served them a small repast of conserves, fruit, and wine, and gave them a red hat, scissors, knives, and few strings of colored beads.

When Teuhtliltl heard that the foreigners planned to stay, he sent 500 natives to the seashore to set up shelters for them along the dunes, and sent 4,000 porters bringing chickens, hen turkeys roasted in chilis, tamales, tortillas, beans, and several varieties of fruit. The following day he set out from Cotastla with a retinue of nobles and porters to welcome them to his province.

The captain received him beneath an arch of leafy boughs, and as he rose to greet him, Teuhtliltl touched his forehead to the ground, then rose and took a reed from his mantle. He thrust it into his tongue, piercing it so deeply that it came out the other side, then offered the bloody reed to the captain. Among our people, this is a most devout ritual, used only when speaking to the gods.

The governor then beckoned to the porters, and one by one they offered the captain gold jewelry, precious stones, richly embroidered mantles, and elegant featherwork.

"Lord, valiant captain," Teuhtliltl spoke, "my nobles tell me that you have come to see the emperor Moctezuma, whose slave I am, on behalf of your great king. He bids me to offer you these gifts in his name, and to tell you that he is truly honored that such a great prince as your emperor sends him his greetings. It is also his command that I welcome you and your men, and serve you in any way I can for as long as you remain in my province."

The native woman translated his words, and the captain rose and embraced Teuhtliltl. "I am honored," he said, "that you have seen fit to greet me in the name of the lord Moctezuma. You must tell him that I kiss his hands, and that I shall send his gifts to my emperor as pledges of his love and friendship."

The captain gave him a silk coat, an ornate armchair inlaid with pearls, a red cap with an engraved medallion, several strands of colored beads, spectacles, and scissors. The governor accepted the gifts in the name of Moctezuma, then pointed to a half-rusted helmet lying on the ground, and asked him if he could send it to the emperor.

Later that day foot soldiers, with pikes and armor glittering in the afternoon sun, marched smartly along the beach to the stirring accompaniment of fifes and drums. After the foot passed in review, men armed with long pikes mounted upon the four-legged brutes that had routed the Maya at Potonchán raced along the shore and through the breaking surf. After the parade, a series of blinding flashes and deafening thunderclaps erupted from heavy tubes, and as the governor watched in horror, a stone wall shattered and vanished in a cloud of smoke.

In the privacy of his pavilion, the captain explained the purpose of his visit to the governor. "Teuhtliltl, faithful servant of Moctezuma," he began, "when you send your account to Moctezuma of what you have seen here today, it is most important that you tell him who I am and why I have come here."

My name is Hernando Cortés, and I am a vassal of the most powerful lord in the world. When he heard of your land and the fame of the emperor Moctezuma, he sent me here to offer his friendship and to speak with him of our god, who is the creator of everything we can and cannot see. It is my sworn duty to my god and emperor that I warn Moctezuma that he and his people, who worship idols and false gods and sacrifice innocent men, are living degenerate, unclean lives,

lives that conflict with the nature of all mankind. I must make him understand that our god does not demand the blood of his people, but only their confessions for having offended him. I must make him realize that no man may know salvation unless he accepts this almighty god as his own, for only he can take the soul and give it everlasting life; only he can redeem man from eternal damnation and raise him to the state of blessedness for which he was created.

"Tell Moctezuma that I will visit him soon and speak with him about our religion, but warn him that I must have sufficient time to do this properly, otherwise neither he nor you will be able to comprehend it. Tell him also that when he learns of the great kings and lords who obey and serve my emperor, whose only wish is to save him and his people from their sins, he too will serve him, and, by his own free will, acknowledge him."

The notion of Moctezuma willfully becoming the vassal of another lord amused Teuhtliltl, but the captain's audacity was disturbing, for he knew it would trouble the emperor. "Cortés, son of the sun," he replied, "I am certain that my lord Moctezuma will be pleased to receive you as his friend. He will be delighted to see things which he has never before seen, and he will rest easy when his is free of these sins in which you say he lives. But I do not know how Moctezuma can acknowledge your emperor as his sovereign, for my lord reigns over many kingdoms and dominions. Great provinces lie within his empire, and many powerful vassals are subject to him. Nevertheless, I shall send messengers who will tell him everything you have told me, and before many days have passed, you will have his answer."

Teuhtliltl took his leave and withdrew to Cotastla, leaving a thousand natives to construct additional shelters for the foreigners and provide them with fish and game.

Teuhtliltl's message upset and confused Moctezuma. When the first bearded men appeared upon our shores, there had been little time to observe them, and no opportunity for any noble of the court to communicate with them. The coastal natives who traded with them were no help, since neither spoke a language the other could understand. Teuhtliltl, lacking instructions from Tenochtitlán, did no more than keep track of their movements until they left as mysteriously as they appeared. Moreover, they left nothing behind them to bear out whether they were mortals, supernatural beings bent on evil, or the men the prophets foretold would rule Mexico.

Now, according to Teuhtliltl, a native woman who spoke our language came with these men, and through her, he learned that their captain was intent upon bringing a new religion to Mexico, a religion that was to replace that of our ancestors. More important, this new religion, like that of Quetzalcoatl, renounced human sacrifice. If they spoke our language, one could easily believe that the captain or his emperor was Quetzalcoatl incarnate.

What then, was to be Moctezuma's course of action? Should he acknowledge the captain as Quetzalcoatl and bow to the inevitable, or should he accept him as an ambassador of a foreign prince and receive him in Tenochtitlán? The latter course, however, seemed unwise. If he was truly and ambassador, why had he come with an army and an arsenal of the most powerful weapons Mexico had ever seen?

After discussions with the royal council, Moctezuma decided that it was best to welcome the captain as if he were a god, but to keep him on the seacoast until he proved to be either divine or mortal.

To the gifts that he had prepared for the first foreigners, Moctezuma added the emblem of the sun, a disk ten palms across cast from pure gold, and the emblem of the moon, a larger disk cast from pure silver.

If Quetzalcoatl had indeed returned, then best he also send him the vestments he had worn when he lived among our ancestors. From the temple came the nine strands of turquoise gems that covered his chest and shoulders, the crown of raven feathers trimmed with a jaguar pelt, his shield faced with bands of gold and golden toads, his serpent-head scepter, his golden staff, and his mask.

The mask was a masterpiece of the jeweler's art. The grotesque body of a double-serpent formed the face of the mask: One serpent's body was fashioned from blue turquoise, and the other from green turquoise. The heads of the serpents hung below the chin of the mask, and their bodies coiled about each other as they spiraled upward from the mouth and nose. Above the bridge of the nose, the bodies looped around to form the eyes of the mask, then crossed the forehead to form eyebrows with the tails. The mask was affixed to a plumed crown, made in such a way that when the crown was placed upon the head, the mask covered the god's face.[vi]

When all was ready and carefully wrapped in cotton mantles to protect them from the hazards of the journey, Moctezuma summoned me to his side.

"Word has reached me," he said, "that our lord Quetzalcoatl is now in Cuetlaxtlan. Go to him, listen carefully to what he has to say, and see that you forget nothing. Give him the priestly garments he wore in ancient times, and give him these gifts in my name. Go quickly now, and when you pay homage to the god, say to him, "these gifts have been sent by your servant Moctezuma, who welcomes you back to Mexico."

When we arrived in Cuetlaxtlan, an honor guard was waiting to receive us and escort us to the captain's pavilion.

The one who greeted us did not much resemble the god that Moctezuma feared so greatly. He appeared to be a man of some 30 odd years, slightly taller than his companions. Although he was slender, his muscular and broad-shouldered upper body gave the impression that he was a man of exceptional physical vitality. His face was pale, his beard fair, and his eyes dark and owlish, giving him a look of deep solemnity. His dress was simple but elegant, adorned only with a single medallion about his neck.

We prostrated ourselves before him and kissed the ground, then we rose and censed him with copal. "Lord and god," I said, "your return to Mexico is most welcome, for we, your loyal servants and vassals, have awaited you for many generations. Moctezuma, your surrogate and loyal servant, has sent us to greet you in his name, and he asks that you accept these most precious and sacred vestments you wore when you lived among us."

He rose and stepped forward when I held up Quetzalcoatl's habit, and allowed me to drape the nine strands of jewels and the gold medallion about his neck and shoulders. Then I tied the golden shield to his left arm and placed the crown and serpent mask of Quetzalcoatl upon his head.

He returned to his seat, and I could feel the ripples of excitement running through the men crowding about us as we presented Moctezuma's gifts. As each precious article, more splendid than the one before it, was laid at the captain's feet, they murmured their approval. When I offered the rusty helmet to him, now filled to the brim with gold nuggets, they could hardly control themselves, and when they saw the golden sun and the silver moon, their cheers echoed from the dunes.

After the presentation, the captain invited us to his pavilion to hear Moctezuma's answer to his message.

"The great lord Moctezuma, whose slaves we are for as long as we live in this land," I began, "bids me to tell you that he is pleased with the tidings you bring him of your one and only god, in whom you urge that he place his trust and accept as his own. He is impressed with what he has been told of the great emperor of the Christians, because if he is the lord of men like yourself, whom we hold and venerate as a god, he has no doubt that he is a powerful prince, and he will accept him as a friend and serve him in every possible way. As his servant and ambassador, he commands that his vassals are to serve you as they would serve him for as long as you remain with us.

"He regrets, however, that he cannot meet with you at this time, since an illness has left him in such a weakened condition that he cannot travel to the seacoast. As for your coming to Tenochtitlán, he strongly advises against it, since the journey is long and difficult. Many high sierras lie between the seacoast and Tenochtitlán, and beyond them are vast deserts where you will suffer unbearable hardships. Furthermore, hostile natives will attack you at every step along the way."

The captain listened carefully to all that I had to say, and when I was finished, he made no immediate response. He offered me a few jewels and some silk garments, which he requested I give to Moctezuma. Then he stood and said, "You may tell your master Moctezuma that at the bidding of my king, my men and I have crossed 2,000 leagues of ocean for no other purpose than to visit him, and it is most important that he hear me out. If I were to die a thousand deaths, I would not turn back without doing my duty, because we Christians look upon death as a reward if we die for god and our king in a righteous cause. I will not be disgraced now by turning back without ever meeting the great Moctezuma."

We could say no more; the captain was steadfast in his resolve to meet Moctezuma. The matter would have to be referred back to Tenochtitlán.

Teuhtliltl spoke for the first time. "You must do that which you must do in the service of your lord," he said. "Since you are resolved to meet with the emperor in spite of the dangers of the journey, I will send messengers once again to Tenochtitlán. If Moctezuma agrees to meet with you, however, you may live to regret your decision. In the meantime, while we await the emperor's decision, I suggest that you move to a village five leagues inland, where you will be more comfortable than in these pestilent dunes."

The captain thanked him for his consideration, but he replied that he would prefer to remain on the beach until he received his answer from Moctezuma.

The response from Tenochtitlán was less politic than Moctezuma's message of welcome. He replied that princes were not in the habit of receiving ambassadors accompanied by heavily armed troops. He was, however, welcome to come to Tenochtitlán with a few companions, and an armed escort of Mexican warriors would be provided for his protection.

"Teuhtliltl," the captain said, "you must tell Moctezuma that neither fear nor threats can stay a Spaniard from his sworn duty. My emperor has ordered me not to return until I speak to Moctezuma, even though it may cost me my life. I would go to Tenochtitlán with only a few companions rather than cause Moctezuma to fear that my intent is hostile, and I would have no fear, since any of my men would venture the journey alone. But I know that Moctezuma's enemies are numerous and powerful, and I will take enough men with me to strike them from the face of the earth if they attempt to stop me."

Teuhtliltl was visibly angered by the captain's answer, and he withdrew in ill humor, knowing full well that Moctezuma would be displeased with the outcome of the meeting. Upon his return to Cotastla, he ordered that no more provisions were to be given to the Christians, and he withdrew all the native workers from their camp. The following morning the dunes were deserted; only their abandoned shelters remained.

I gathered my porters and left for Tenochtitlán before first light. We rested only long enough to ease the fatigue of the previous day's journey, and arrived in the city late at night, long after Moctezuma had retired. Nevertheless, I went to the palace and asked the guards to summon the royal chamberlain. When he appeared I told him it was urgent that the emperor be advised that his ambassador to Cuetlaxtlán had returned. He nodded and disappeared in the direction of the emperor's quarters, and upon his return, he directed me to go to the House of Judgment, where the emperor received all communications dealing with affairs of state.

At the House of Judgment a priest led me into the dim interior and bade me to wait. To the left of the emperor's chair, several priests were holding the arms and legs of a captive stretched across the sacrificial stone while two others rubbed his body with blue chalk. They had scarcely finished when Moctezuma appeared and took his seat. He nodded to the priests, and in an instant they slit the captive's breast and caught the sudden rush of blood in a bowl. The high priest dipped his fingers into the bowl and sprinkled blood on my face and clothing, then stepped back into the shadows.

When I finished my account of the events that had taken place on the seacoast, Moctezuma sat in silence, melancholy and lost in thought. Finally he lifted his head and dismissed the priests, then spoke to me with a troubled voice.

"Our gods, the Weather, the Night, and the unknown god who is the creator of all things, have grown weary of us. The Air, whose slaves we are, has left us to its caprice. Now they favor those who have come to our land. What are we to do? Where are we to go?"

There was another deep and prolonged silence before Moctezuma spoke again.

"This has long been foretold: Nezahualpilli's prophecy has come to pass. Many lives will be lost when others take over my kingdom; my people will be their slaves and vassals, and never again will they be free. Even though the gods allow me to live, there will be no other lord in this land save for the one who comes from the sea. He will strip Mexico of its throne and humble our nobility, and our courts, which the ancient rulers abided by, will cease to exist. When I no longer rule this land, all will come to an end.

"Tlilancalqui," he said, "you have realized wealth and high office because of my affection for you. Now I must ask a favor of you in return. In the days to come, look to the welfare of all my sons. Watch over Ilhuiltemoc, Chimalpopoca, Acatlxoxouqui, Acamapich, Nezahualtecólotl, Axayácatl, and Tlacahueypan as you would your own sons, for when I am dead by the hands of those who have come to our land, the wrath of the Mexicans will turn against them. You must hide them, shelter and protect them, because when I am dead, there will be no mercy for them. From this day forward, I place them in your hands. If they are to survive this crisis we face, it will be because you cherish them as I have cherished you."

Then Moctezuma's voice broke and he wept softly.

---

[i] An Aztec priest, a confidant of Moctezuma

[ii] Juan de Grijalva left Cuba on May 4, 1518, and sailed along the east coast of Mexico as far north as Cabo Rojo before bad weather turned him back. He returned to Cuba on September 29, 1518.

[iii] Quilaztli is another name for Coatlique, the mother of Huitzliopochtli and patron goddess of Xochimilco.

[iv] Hernando Cortés left Cuba on February 18, 1519, with a force of Cortés 11 ships, 553 soldiers, 110 mariners, 200 Cuban porters, and a few women. His armament included 16 horse, 10 heavy guns, 4 falconets, 13 muskets, and 32 crossbows.

The accounts of both the Grijalva expedition and that of Cortés were derived from the *Cronica X* by Hernando Alvarado Tezozomc and Diego Duran. Considerable editing is required to separate the expeditions, however, since both are intermingled in the texts.

[v] The Spaniard Jerónimo de Aguilar, who spoke Chontal Maya, was shipwrecked off the coast of Yucatán in 1511 while traveling from Darien to Hispaniola. The woman, whom the Spaniards called Marina, was raised in a Nahuatl-speaking village and subsequently sold to the Chontal Maya, where she learned their language.

[vi] The mask of Quetzalcoatl is on display in the Museum of Mankind Collection in the British Museum. Although the mask fits the description given by Sahagun in every detail, it is not recorded in the manifest of the treasure ship that Cortes sent to Charles V on 16 July, 1519.

6. Hernando Cortés:

The Turning Point

Nothing that Grijalva had seen or experienced on his newly discovered continent prepared us for the imperial reception we were accorded when we reached the shores of Cuetlaxtlán. Grijalva, for want of an able interpreter, over-eager to return to Cuba with the profits of his enterprise, failed to learn that the petty coastal chieftains he had bartered with were no more than minor vassals of a supreme lord who controlled all the wealth of the land. By his failure, he presented us with an opportunity seldom realized in the course of history.[i]

For reasons we could not fathom, our arrival was the occasion for a royal celebration, an affair of state that kings reserve for other kings. Montezuma's nobles welcomed us as if we were gods, yet we frightened him, leaving him guarded and wary of admitting us to the interior. When I pressed him for a meeting, he left us in limbo, stranded on the beaches, neither aiding us nor attempting to cast us from his shores. We could not go forward, and retreat was unthinkable-the opportunity granted us by fate must not be squandered, no matter what the consequences.

But until our ships were protected from the raging north winds that struck without warning, until we found relief from the oppressive heat of the dunes and the sand flies that tortured us day and night, until we found an adequate supply of fresh water, Montezuma and his empire would have to wait.

I sent Francisco de Montejo and Antón de Alaminos north to seek a suitable harbor, and Pedro de Alvarado inland for provisions and water. More than a week passed without word from them, and tempers grew short as malcontents in the company began to press for a return to the comforts of Cuba.

Shortly after Teutliltl's people abandoned us, five odd-looking Indians appeared on a nearby dune, and after observing us for several days, they ventured into camp. All were hideously disfigured. Their lower lips, weighted down by large jewels set into deep incisions, gave them a witless, slack-jawed appearance, and their earlobes, stretched into long strands by heavy stones, sagged almost to their shoulders. The woman from Potonchán did not understand their language, but two spoke the language of Mexico, and from them we learned that they were Totonacs, who lived in a large town called Cempoala, not more than eight leagues north. Their lord, they told us, had heard of our great victory at Potonchán, and he was most anxious that we visit him.

I told them to thank their lord for his kind invitation, and promised that I would visit him when my affairs here in Cuetlaxtlán were concluded. Before they departed, I invited them to join me in a light lunch of fruit and wine. As we ate, I learned that unlike Cuetlaxtlán, where authority was invested in a Mexican territorial governor, their own lords governed the Totonacs, even though they were tributaries of Mexico. They complained endlessly of Montezuma's outrageous levies, and gave me to understand that his ruthless enforcement of them had caused a number of revolts, particularly in the highlands, where the natives were difficult to control. At the present time, however, Mexican garrisons maintained and uneasy peace throughout the territory.

The Totonacs could not have come to us at a more opportune time. We were not, as I feared, isolated on the shores of an empire whose provinces were united to a central power by close political ties, but in a land of bitter and resentful tributaries. Montezuma ruled not by diplomacy, but by virtue of his powerful military. Furthermore, it was obvious that the Totonac nobles had not come to pay a courtesy call-they were seeking an ally for their chieftain.

Montejo and Alaminos returned at the end of 12 days. They had surveyed the coast as far north as the Panuco River, but the only satisfactory anchorage they found was in the lee of a rocky prominence that lay 13 leagues from our present position. This seemed to be ideal for a permanent base, since a broad stretch of grasslands, fresh-water streams, and large stands of timber lay just beyond the beach. Furthermore, the site was defensible and in Totonac territory, just five leagues north of Cempoala.

My decision to move the company northward, however, was ill received by those who had wearied of the hardships of the campaign. Deaf to my reminding them of all we had accomplished in four short months, they pressed for a return to their haciendas in Cuba. If we returned to Cuba with Montezuma's treasure, I warned them, every fortune hunter in the Old World as well as the New would descend upon us like flies upon a dunghill. Better to go forward, I argued, and trust to our good fortune rather than abandon our just rewards to others.

They responded that we had neither enough men nor sufficient resources to gain a foothold on the continent. The fighting at Potonchán had cost the lives of 40 men, and if our cavalry had been held up much longer in the marshes, the entire army might have been lost. Montezuma, who could field an army as great as that of Spain, had made it clear that he no longer tolerated our presence in his country, and we could not hope to survive if we provoked him by trying to establish a colony. Furthermore, only a fool could possibly imagine that a few hundred adventurers from all walks of life, led by a planter with no more military experience that suppressing Arawak uprisings in Cuba, would dream of confronting Montezuma's army. Better to return to Cuba now and let Diego Velásquez organize an army capable of mounting an effective campaign in the interior. Better to settle for a lesser share of the huge profits that would come then rather than throw away everything now on some ill-conceived endeavor that would only antagonize Montezuma.

Others, however, were determined to stay in Mexico regardless of the hazards and uncertainties facing us. Some were penniless adventurers with nothing more to lose than their lives; others were minor landholders from Cuba, who, lacking the patronage of Diego Velásquez, risked little more than a small parcel of land and a few

Indians. Many had sailed with Grijalva, and they made no secret of their resentment for the lost opportunities that his failure to colonize the land had cost them. My closest friends, who had incurred heavy debts and the wrath of the governor for the enterprise, would suffer financial ruin and arrest if we returned to Cuba. The future would not wait for them-nothing less than a permanent settlement in Mexico would satisfy them.

But Diego Velásquez's followers were quick to point out that we were not empowered to colonize the country. Since the governor had no warrant from the Crown to establish a settlement, his instructions to us were to chart the ports along the coast of the new continent, locate sources of fresh water, take soundings of off-shore depths, and determine the resources of the country. We had done all he demanded of us, save for sending him reports, samples of the flora and fauna of the land, and Montezuma's treasure. If we failed to return now, they said, we risked everything we had gained and were neglect in our duty to the governor.

Their arrogance infuriated those who wanted to colonize the country. They were promised a settlement when they were recruited, they said, and notices to this effect had been posted throughout Cuba. If the governor had no warrant for a colony, he had deceived them and they were no longer bound by his orders. They were free to stay or return to Cuba as they pleased.

In the end, those whom I count as my friends prevailed. They drew up a charter for a Crown colony, and prepared to submit it to Their Majesties for approval and recognition. The king's notary duly recorded the colony as the Villa Rica de la Vera Cruz, and I appointed Alonso de Puertocarrero, one of my closest friends, and Francisco de Montejo, a friend of Diego Velásquez, as *alcaldes*. I handed them my instructions from Diego Velásquez and my resignation as captain-general, and left them to their deliberations.

Their meeting did not last long. When I returned, they informed me that my commission and my instructions from Diego Velásquez were no longer valid, since the governor's authority was not recognized in Vera Cruz. It was their intent to write to Their Majesties for advice as to their future course of action, but until they received instructions from the Crown, they would be pleased if I would serve as chief justice of the colony and captain-general of the armed forces.

I was honored, I told them, that they had placed their confidence in me, but I pointed out that the responsibility they were asking me to assume must be commensurate with the risk involved. I reminded them that I had invested 5,000 castellanos and purchased three ships for the venture; that I was indebted to Diego Velásquez for an additional sum of 2,000 castellanos; and that I had assumed a note to buy enough salt pork to feed the entire company for five months. Moreover, my friends and I had secured loans for four additional ships and financed every man in the company who could ill-afford to join the enterprise.

Diego Velásquez, on the other hand, had provided three weatherworn ships, and had paid 1,800 castellanos for supplies that his agent sold to the company at an unreasonable profit. At 100 castellanos for each cask of wine, six castellanos for each *arroba* of oil and vinegar, and one castellano for a pair of sandals and two for each bundle of beads, our principal trade item, there would be little enough profit left for the common soldier. For my investment, I had asked nothing in return from the company, nor was there any guarantee that I would profit or recover my investment if Their Majesties issued a warrant in my favor, for they could replace me with an officer of their choosing at any time.[ii]

When the bargaining was done, it was agreed that I was to be awarded one fifth of all future profits after the king's fifth had been set aside.

As I expected, our change of allegiance and disavowal of Diego Velásquez did not sit well with his friends. They accused us of plotting against them in secret, and one faction, led by Diego Ordaz and Juan Velásquez de Leon, a kinsman of the governor, refused to accept my authority as chief justice of the colony. To avoid an open rebellion, I sent both to the ships in irons. There were no more challenges to my authority, and when I announced that no man would be held in Mexico against his will, an uneasy calm settled over the ranks.

We broke camp and followed the ships northward, traveling as light as possible. The first day's march saw the dunes gradually give way to broad savannas, then to green meadows and dense forests. On the second day we came upon a labyrinth of fresh-water streams that flowed through cultivated fields of maize as rich and productive as those of the finest farmholds in Spain. Five leagues further, we saw a mighty peak rising far above the sierra, its snow-capped crest often hidden in the clouds. At night, we made camp on one or another of the small towns we encountered along the route. None of the towns were occupied, but from the fresh blood we saw on the walls of the temples, we knew that men had been sacrificed a short time before we arrived.

On the morning of the fourth day we halted on the outskirts of Cempoala. Musketeers and crossbowmen moved out ahead of the foot, but as they approached the town, 20 Indian nobles came out to greet us. They censed us with braziers that gave off sweet-smelling vapors and handed us nosegays of roses, then led us down a road bordered on either side by orchards and gardens. As we approached the plaza, the reflection of the morning sun from the whitewashed buildings and the burnished walls of the town gave us the impression they were made of silver.

The chieftain of Cempoala was a grossly fat Totonac whose massive bulk had to be supported by two men when he stood. We found his welcome as generous as his flesh, however, and during our two-week stay in Cempoala, we could not have been more comfortably quartered and better fed. I found him to be shrewd and well informed, and I spent every possible moment listening to what he had to say about the political climate of the land.

From him I learned that 38 provinces recognized the imperial eagle of Mexico, but other than a select few, none profited from their allegiance to the empire. Nothing more than tributaries, Montezuma systematically stripped them of their resources, leaving behind only enough to sustain the natives as they struggled to meet his levies.

Other than a few fortified towns, there were no Mexican garrisons in the provinces. The principal towns were governed by a variety of political systems. Native chieftains ruled some, and natives appointed by Mexico others, but in every case, the cities retained their political and administrative autonomy. The only restraint placed on the chieftains was that they paid Montezuma's tribute every 80 days, provided conscripts to his army, and sent slaves to be sacrificed on Mexico's altars.

There had been periodic revolts against Mexico, some as distant as the Southern Sea, but each time, the armies of Mexico crushed them with a bloodletting that left the population weak and impotent into the following generation.

Oddly enough, while Montezuma's control over his most distant provinces was absolute, he tolerated states within a few leagues of Tenochtitlán that openly defied him. Three independent states, Tlaxcala, Huexotzingo, and Cholula, warred incessantly with him, and Acolhuacán rebels, who were determined to overthrow him, occupied the northeastern sector of his valley. Together, they could flank Mexico to the east, but their alliances were too fragile and short-lived to form a united front.

The chieftain of Cempoala had a heart as great as his overfed body. Willing to risk the displeasure of a Caesar, he provided us with a foothold in Mexico, and granted us a sanctuary where we could keep our company intact and build a colony. If we dared defy Montezuma and march inland, he promised to furnish guides who knew the roads and the location of the strongest Mexican garrisons. But most important of all, in his determination to find an ally, he had opened the door that showed me wherein Montezuma's greatest weakness lay.

As we prepared to leave Cempoala, the chieftain sealed our alliance by giving me his niece, who, although of noble lineage and quite wealthy, was unforgivably ugly. With her came seven maidens for my commanders. The prettiest I gave to Puertocarreo in exchange for the woman interpreter from Potonchán, whom I took into my quarters.

We continued our journey northward to Quiahuitzlán, a town built upon the heights of an outcropping overlooking the anchorage discovered by Montejo and Alaminos. I established my headquarters in the town, and sent the company a half league inland to stake out the buildings that were to be the seat of government for Villa Rica de la Vera Cruz. With the help of the Indians who dug foundations and hauled timber from the foothills, construction began on the townhouse, the church, and the arsenal of the fledgling colony.

We had not been in Quiahuitzlán many days when five nobles led a train of porters into town. By their dress, I knew that they were Mexicans, and by the deference paid them by the Totonacs, I had no doubt that they were Montezuma's tax collectors. They looked neither right nor left as they strode by Spaniards gathered in the plaza, fanning themselves against the noonday heat with jeweled flyflaps. The Totonac nobles fawned upon the Mexicans like lackeys. They took them into their homes to feed and entertain them, but when it was time to read the tribute list, the Mexicans added ten men and ten women for sheltering us without the express permission of Montezuma.

I realized that if I allowed Montezuma's officers to exact his tribute after promising the Totonacs my protection, the result would be an irreparable loss of confidence with my only allies in Mexico. Worse, if I permitted the Mexicans to leave the town with a train of Totonac slaves for sheltering us, they would turn against us as sure as night follows day. Yet I could make no hostile move against the Mexicans if I hoped to gain favor with Montezuma.

That evening, after the Mexicans retired, I summoned the Totonacs to my quarters and urged them not to yield to the demands of Montezuma. They were now vassals of the most powerful king on earth, and as such, they were obliged to pay tribute to no other lord. Their enemies were now his enemies, and by his orders, I must defend them against all who would make war upon them. If they were ever to shed the yoke of Mexico, now was the time. Montezuma would think twice before he risked his squadrons against men who had routed a powerful Maya army at Potonchán.

The Totonacs needed no further encouragement. They fell upon the Mexicans and dragged them into the plaza, where they beat them with heavy canes. When the tax collectors were nearly senseless, they bound them hand and foot and left them on the cold flagstones to reflect upon their fate.

Late that night, when the plaza was deserted, I ordered two of the Mexicans brought to my quarters without alerting the Totonacs. I asked them who they were and why they were prisoners of the Totonacs. They replied that they were servants of the great lord Montezuma, and they were charged with collecting his tribute throughout the coastal regions. In the past, they had always been received favorably by the Totonacs, and they were at a loss to understand why they had been seized and beaten now. Perhaps our presence had inspired the Totonacs to turn against them, but whatever the reason, morning would see them stretched across the sacrificial stone.

I reassured them that they need have no fear of being sacrificed, for I had given my word to Montezuma that as long as I was a guest in his country, I would serve him and watch over his interests. I promised them that I would release them before daybreak, and I would see to it that their companions were released within a few days. I summoned the surgeon, and when their wounds had been treated, I gave them a message for Montezuma and sent them to the anchorage, where a ship would take them beyond Totonac territory and put them ashore.

The Totonacs were terrified when they discovered that the Mexicans were missing. Within days, they said, Montezuma would know what had taken place, and his wrath would be quick to follow. They shunned my company and met in secret, trying to decide whether to appease Montezuma or trust in my word to stand by them and the strength of Spanish arms. Some urged that they tell Montezuma that we had forced them to seize his tax collectors and beg him for clemency. Others argued that there would be no compassion for them in Montezuma's heart no matter how they groveled before him, for no Mexican emperor had ever been known to show mercy toward those had risen against him. What was done was done. Better to take a stand against Montezuma now while they had a powerful ally to fight alongside them, and if Montezuma prevailed, better they die fighting than live in servitude any longer.

When they were agreed upon their decision, they came to me. "Lord," they said, "Last night you persuaded us to lay hands upon Montezuma's tax collectors, but during the night two escaped and fled to Mexico. Before many days have passed, you will see the plain below us filled with Mexican warriors. Now we must ask you to honor your pledge to stand with us, for the time has come when we must rid our people of Montezuma's tyranny or die fighting him."

Instead of sending an army to the seacoast, however, Montezuma sent his nephews with gold and jewels and a pardon for the Totonacs. He expressed his deep-felt gratitude and his indebtedness for releasing his servants, and appealed to me to do everything in my power to safeguard those still held prisoner. He sent his regrets that for the present his commitments prevented him for his meeting with me, but he promised to look to the future for a more suitable time.

My little artifice paid greater dividends than I could hope for. Within days, word spread throughout the territory that Montezuma feared to send an army against the Totonacs while the Christians were in the area. Totonac warriors began attacking his garrisons in the sierra, driving one detachment after another into mountains, yet Montezuma failed to react. This was the moment I had waited and prayed for-fate would grant us no better opportunity to march to Mexico.

Before we left the seacoast, however, we had to justify our establishing a colony to the Crown in spite of Diego Velázquez's instructions to the contrary. It would not be easy.

Francisco de Saucedo, a cavalier who had followed our track from Cuba, brought word that the king had appointed Diego Velásquez governor-for-life of Yucatán and all the lands he discovered in the area. As a reward for his initiative on Their Majesties behalf, and for the expenses he had assumed for the expedition, he was to receive a fixed percentage of all profits for his lifetime and that of his chosen heir. Furthermore, if he should discover and settle four islands, one 20th of the profits was to be his, and all such profits could be passed on to his heirs in perpetuity. If by chance he should discover gold, the crown would demand no more than one-tenth for the first two years, and wait until the fifth year before demanding the customary royal fifth. For three worm-ridden ships and the supplies he sold so dearly to the company, Diego Velásquez was to realize the wealth of Montezuma's empire.[iii]

If those who had suffered the hardships of the journey, if those who had risked their lives and fortunes in the venture, were to realize their just reward, I would have to convince the Crown of their right to the fruits of their labor.

The normal channel of communication between the New World and the Crown was through Juan Rodriguez de Fonseca, the Bishop of Burgos. The Bishop held some of the richest lands in Cuba, and was the governor's staunchest ally in Spain, and we had no doubts whatsoever that he would dismiss us as rebellious malcontents seeking to break a lawful contract with our benefactor.

There was, however, a legal instrument that would allow us to circumvent the Bishop and send our appeal for recognition directly to the Crown. In the 13th century, Alfonso X wrote the *Siete Partidas,* a covenant between the king and his subjects that upheld the right of all men to act in the public interest whenever such interest conflicted with self-serving private enterprise.[iv]

Two letters were prepared for the king. The first letter bore the signatures of Francisco de Montejo and Alonso de Puertocarrero, who, as *alcaldes* of Vera Cruz, appealed to His Majesty not to grant judicial authority in Mexico to Diego Velásquez. The corruption of his government and his favoritism, they wrote, was evidenced by his granting *repartimientos*, allocations of Indian labor, to his friends, and bribes he offered to Crown officers to insure their silence about his activities. They urged the king to appoint a *residencia*, a judicial review, to investigate complaints about his conduct in Cuba, and requested that he be removed from office if such complaints were found to be justified.

For such time as the country was conquered and pacified, they requested that the king to issue a warrant in my favor as captain-general and chief justice of Mexico. Their recommendation was based upon my experience in the islands, my devotion to Their Majesties interest, and my considerable expenses for this undertaking. As for Diego Velásquez's contribution, they pointed out that he had paid for little more than supplies and barter goods, which we were obliged to buy from him at an outrageous profit.

My letter to the king was brief. I described the invaluable resources of the land and told of the fabulous empire hidden in the interior, whose lord would soon become a vassal of Spain. I gave the king a frank account of my difficulties with Diego Velásquez, details of the costs I had borne for the venture, and closed with a plea for the funds I would need to accomplish the crown's objectives in Mexico.[v]

Montejo and Puertocarrero would present our claim to the Spanish Court. Montejo, a friend of Velásquez, would bear us out that the company had acted in accord, that the colony was not divided into one faction loyal to the governor and another that supported me. Puertocarrero, a kinsman of the Count of Medellin, would muster all the influence he could among the nobility to promote our interests in Spain. To insure that we would receive a favorable hearing before the capital-hungry court, I asked every man in the company to forego his share of Montezuma's treasure and send it to the king. Only enough gold was set aside to cover the expenses of the voyage to Spain and for those of my father, Martin Cortés, who would represent us in court.

The *alcaldes* set sail for Spain in the 16th day of July 1519, bound for the port of Palos. Alaminos's orders were to sail well north of Cuba, keeping to the hazardous Bahama channel, where he would be less likely to be intercepted by one of the governor's ships. Under no circumstance was he to stop at any port in Cuba.

The tidings of the king's grant to Diego Velásquez, however, had the effect I feared upon those who remained loyal to the governor. Juan Díaz, the priest who had sailed with Grijalva, in an attempt to further his career and fortune in the New World, prevailed upon Pedro Escudero, Juan Cermeno, and a few mariners to seize a ship and make sail for Cuba. If they reached Santiago in good time, the governor would be able to intercept the treasure ship north of Hispaniola, or failing that, send word to have it impounded when it reached Palos. The plot had been organized so quickly and with such secrecy that it surely would have succeeded if Bernardino de Coria had not betrayed his fellow conspirators.

Against my will, and with a heavy heart, I ordered Escudero and Cermeno hanged. Cermeno, who had often broken the monotony of the dunes with his soaring vaults over a beam held on high, would be sorely missed, but I had little choice in the business of mutiny. As was the custom in Spain, each was offered a few moments of privacy with a public woman before the sentence was carried out.

The pilot, Gonzalo de Umbria, was sentenced to have both feet cut off, and each of the mariners was given 200 lashes. But the priest Juan Díaz, protected by his holy orders, was beyond my authority and escaped justice.

The incident was sufficient to convince me that I could not leave 150 men in garrison at Vera Cruz and march off to Mexico while a single ship remained in port to tempt others to reach the outside world. Because of the shipworms that prevail in these warm waters, some of our ships were unseaworthy, and it was a matter of little concern when I ordered them stripped of chains and rigging and ordered them scuttled. But when the remaining four were holed and sunk, those who had agreed to remain on the condition that they were free to return to Cuba whenever they chose, cried out that I had betrayed them, that by cutting off our only avenue of retreat, I had led them into a slaughterhouse. Only with time and patience, and with the support of those who understood that what was done was unavoidable if we were to succeed, was I able to restore a degree of harmony in our ranks.

The fleet was out of reach, ten fathoms below the surface, but if we were secure in the belief that our secret was safe from the outside world, we were quickly disillusioned when four ships appeared off the coast. Three kept a safe distance from the shore, while a fourth, a brigantine of shallow draft, anchored in the mouth of a nearby river. I set out immediately with four horse and 50 foot, but before we had gone half a league, we met three Spaniards on the road. One identified himself as a notary, and said they had come to claim the land in the name of Francisco de Garay, the governor of Jamaica.

Garay had heard of Grijalva's discovery, and through the good offices of his friends in the Spanish Court, secured a warrant granting him to settle along the northernmost latitudes reached by Grijalva. He outfitted a fleet of four ships and recruited a company of 270 men under the command of Alonso Álvarez Piñeda, and directed him to establish a colony at Almeria, a town the Indians call Nautla, some 25 leagues north of Vera Cruz. I asked the notary to show me the king's warrant, but when he failed to produce it, I asked him to invite Piñeda ashore so that we might reach an understanding. I assured him that if Piñeda produced a warrant, I would do everything in my power to assist him. Garay, however, had issued strict orders to Piñeda to stay away from my company, and the notary convinced me that nothing would induce him to come ashore or bring his fleet into port.

Without ships, there was little I could do to prevent Piñeda from going wherever he pleased, and in good time, he would learn of Montezuma's empire and send word to Garay. The ship anchored in the river was an inviting target. We changed clothing with the notary and his men in an attempt to lure the crew ashore. Twelve men set out in a small boat and approached the riverbank cautiously, keeping the boat at a safe distance while four waded ashore for a better look at us. When they saw our unfamiliar faces they turned and fled, but we overtook them before they reached the boat. By this time the others were well beyond the shallows, and when they came alongside the ship, the pilot weighed anchor. That was the last we saw of Garay's fleet.

The march inland could be delayed no longer. On the 16th day of August 1519, we left Cempoala and set out for Mexico. Our army, reinforced by the mariners, who had no ships to concern them, numbered some 450 foot, 300 Cempoalan warriors, 15 horse, six canon, 200 Indian porters, and 40 Cempoalan nobles, hostages to guarantee the lives of 150 men we left behind.[vi]

---

[i] The Spaniards landed at Cuetlaxtlan on Good Friday, April 21, 1519.

[ii] The specifics of Cortés's investment in the expedition and that of Diego Velásquez are found in the sworn depositions of Montejo and Puertocarrero before Lorenzo Galindez de Carabajal, a member of the Council of the Indies, in Coruna, Spain, on 29-30 April, 1520. Both witnesses, however, state that the figures cited were obtained through hearsay in Cuba, before Cortés departed for Mexico.

[iii] The full text of the rights and privileges granted to Diego Velásquez in Mexico by the Crown is found in CDIAI, v22, 38-46. The grant is dated 13 November, 1518, in Zaragoza, Spain, and signed by Juan Rodriquez de Fonseca, the Bishop of Burgos. When Cortés founded Vera Cruz in the summer of 1519, Fonseca and Lope de Conchillos, the secretary of the Council of Castile, were responsible for all administrative matters dealing with the New World. Shortly afterward, in the cedula of September 14, 1519, the Crown announced the formation of the Council of the Indies and appointed Fonseca its first president.

[iv] For a discussion of the Siete Partidas, see J.H. Elliot, in *Hernan Cortes, Letters from Mexico*, trans. and ed. A.R. Pagden, (New York, 1971), xviii-xx.

[v] See *Carta de la Justicia*, in *Cortes, Letters*, Pagden, ed. 3-46, for an English translation of the petition from the municipal council of Vera Cruz to the Crown for permission to establish a colony.

Cortes's letter to the Crown, known as the First Letter, has never been found despite exhaustive searches in the libraries of Europe for more than a century. Gomara is the only chronicler known to have seen the letter, and for its contents, we must depend upon the brief summary in his *Historia*. Gomara, Simpson ed. 87-88.

[vi] The size of the army that set out for Mexico varies somewhat among chroniclers. Cortés, states that he took 300 foot and 15 horse, and left 150 men in garrison at Quiahuitzlan. Gomara, Torquemada, and Cervantes, set his force at 400 foot and 15 horse, disagreeing only upon whether Cortés took three or six cannon.

Beranal Diaz tells us that more than 40 men were lost in the fighting at Potonchán. If we subtract these losses from the 553 soldiers and 110 mariners that answered muster at Cozumel, and the 150 men left in garrison at Quiahuitzlan, and add Saucedo's 11 men, then no more than 484 men were available for the march inland.

Gomara states that the Indian force that accompanied the Spaniards consisted of 300 warriors, nobles, porters, and Cubans. Bernal Diaz states that the Spaniards took 40 chieftains and 200 porters to transport the artillery

7. Ecatl[i]:

The Totonac Rebellion

The Totonacs became vassals of Mexico when Moctezuma Ilhuicamina resolved that his people would never again suffer the disastrous famine that took place in the early years of his reign, and looked to the fertile lands of the eastern seaboard to provision the granaries of Tenochtitlán. Control of this bountiful region, however, would never be realized until Mexican hegemony was first established over the heavily populated provinces of Cuetlaxtla and Cuauhtochco.

Moctezuma chose his grandsons, Tizoc, Axayácatl, and Ahuítzotl, who, with Moquihuix, the lord of Tlatelolco, would lead his armies across the eastern sierra. When they reached the slopes of the great volcano Citlaltepetl they were within striking distance of the Totonac army, but before they could advance, runners from Tenochtitlán brought orders to withdraw as quickly as possible. Huexotzingo, Tlaxcala, and Cholula had formed an alliance with Cuetlaxtlán, and the squadrons of four provinces awaited them at the foot of the volcano. Moctezuma had no desire to risk his army against a superior force.

That should have been the end of the campaign, but Moquihuix chose to defy the emperor and ordered his squadrons to hold fast. The Tenochca, shamed by his example, could do no more than fight alongside him. Spurred on by Moquihuix, Moctezuma's army carried the day and returned to Tenochtitlán with more than 6,000 captives, whose heads would consecrate the newly erected *tzompantli* in the ceremonial plaza.[ii]

Now Moctezuma Xocóyotl prepared to send another army across sierra and into Totonac territory. Three days had not passed before Moctezuma learned that the captain had seized his tax collectors, and his hand was forced. If he failed to deal with the captain and the Totonacs at once, he risked the loss of the entire region east of the sierra.

Only the unexpected arrival of two of the tax collectors imprisoned by the Totonacs prevented him from giving the order to march. Their story tempered Moctezuma's anger, and offered him an opportunity to test the strength of the captain's commitment to the Totonacs before risking a costly and potentially disastrous war.

Moctezuma's agents told him that they observed nothing unusual in the behavior of the Totonacs when they arrived in Quiahuitzlán, and there was no outcry from them when they added 20 slaves to his tribute.

The beating they suffered that night was so severe that they were barely conscious when shadowy figures lifted them from the ground and carried them into a dimly lighted building. They cut their bonds and took them to the captain, who seemed troubled when he learned that they were servants of the lord Moctezuma. He apologized for the beating they had suffered, and said he was embarrassed that it had occurred here where he was quartered. Had he known of the intent of the Totonacs, he would have done everything in his power to prevent it, since he was obliged to earn the trust and friendship of their master.

His men would take them from the city at once, before the Totonacs realized that they were missing. He assured them that he would release their companions when he could, but for now, he could ill-afford to antagonize the Totonacs. He gave them food, and, as they were about to depart, he gave them a message for Moctezuma.

He welcomed the opportunity, he wrote, to prevent a breakdown of Mexican authority in the provinces. Furthermore, by taking his vassals out of the hands of the Totonacs, Moctezuma must surely know by now what was in his heart. Even though Moctezuma had yet to acknowledge his friendship, he bore him no ill will, for he knew this was the doing of his servants, who believed that they were acting in the best interest of their lord. This, he knew, was not the wish of a great prince-a great lord would never refuse to receive an ambassador who had come on behalf of his emperor and his god to reveal divine secrets to him. There was no doubt in his mind that in time, he would accept the friendship of the emperor of the Christians as his friend and offer him his allegiance. Until that time, he would seek every opportunity to serve him.[iii]

Not withstanding the conciliatory tone of the captain's message, Moctezuma was not so naive as to believe that he had not instigated the uprising. But it was just as obvious that he was not committed to the Totonacs, for why else would he risk their anger by releasing the Mexicans while he was building a settlement in their territory? The affront to Mexican sovereignty could not be overlooked, but in light of this new development, he considered it prudent to acknowledge the captain's gesture to him, but to keep him at arm's length until the situation was better resolved. The fat chieftain of Cempoala would be taken care of at the appropriate time.

The course Moctezuma chose was to buy the captain's loyalty. He sent two nephews of the royal house with gold medallions, gold and silver ornaments inlaid with precious jewels, cotton mantles, feathered plumes, and another helmet filled with gold nuggets, gifts the Totonacs could never match. They found the captain at his newly constructed garrison, and when they were escorted to his pavilion, they knelt and touched their hands to the ground before him, then kissed their palms, just as they did when they approached the emperor. They rose, and the eldest held out the helmet to the captain. His uncle, he said, had heard that he and his companions suffered from a disease that could be cured only by gold, and if these gifts eased their illness, he would send more.

The lord Moctezuma, he said, was indebted to him for setting the servants of his house free, and if he could bring about the release of the three still held captive, he would be forever grateful. His uncle, however, was deeply offended, for he failed to understand why the Christians, who were of his own lineage and whose coming had long been predicted by his ancestors, had chosen to live in the houses of the Totonac traitors. Furthermore, he knew that the Totonacs would never have dared rebel against him and refuse to pay his tribute without his encouraging them. Nevertheless, he was pleased that the

Totonacs had received the captain and his companions so hospitably, and for this he saw fit to pardon them. If they acknowledged their offense and laid down their arms, he would not punish them, but he warned them that if they ever rose against him again, their punishment would serve as an example to others.

As for his wish to speak with Moctezuma, however, his uncle regretted that this would not be possible at this time. He was currently occupied with a war and other government matters that demanded his attention, but if an opportunity should arise in the future, he would arrange for a time and place where they could meet.

The captain listened carefully as the interpreters translated Moctezuma's message, and when they finished, he replied, choosing his words carefully. He suggested that Moctezuma's nephews remind their uncle that he was forced to seek shelter with the Totonacs when his vassal Teuhtliltl left him and his men to starve on the dunes of Cuetlaxtlán. Although he chose not to fault Moctezuma for the actions of his governor, the emperor must understand the position in which he had been placed. Alone and deserted in an unfriendly world, the Totonacs had shown them such kindness and goodwill that he was obliged to offer them the patronage of the emperor of the Christians. Since they could not serve two masters, he had relieved them of their obligation to pay tribute to Moctezuma. But this was a matter he preferred to resolve when he came to Tenochtitlán.

Other than bringing about the release of his tax collectors, Moctezuma's latest design had accomplished nothing. Mexican authority in the province crumbled as the Totonacs, emboldened by Moctezuma's inaction and the captain's strength of purpose, fell upon our garrisons and scattered our squadrons into the sierra. As for the words of the captain who had promised to serve Moctezuma, the captain who said he had come only to speak to us of his god, they now rang hollow as he led a Cempoalan army against our garrison at Tzapantzingo. If Moctezuma still had any hope that he would be satisfied with the precious gifts he had lavished upon him and leave the country, it foundered in the harbor at Quiahuitzlán when he sent his fleet to the bottom and led his army into the sierra.

Leaving a strong detachment behind to protect his rear, the captain set out with an army of Spaniards and Cempoalans 800 strong. Guided by three Totonac nobles, he chose the difficult northern route to the tableland rather than risk Mexico's principal artery from the coastal lands through Tepeaca, where a large Mexican army was garrisoned.

The route climbs to a height of 10,000 feet before it reaches the pass between Citlaltepetl to the south and Nauhcampatepetl, the massive granite block that rises in the north. The heavy layer of ash that covers the slopes of Nauhcampatepetl provides precarious footing at best, and the raw, piercing winds that blow unceasingly from its broad crest make the descent of its western slopes wearying to the very soul. Beyond the pass lies a barren desert, a vast area of salt lakes and marshes interrupted only by desolate stretches of sand as far as the eye can see. This remote and uninhabited wasteland cannot be crossed in less that three days, and there is no water. During the rainy season, the route is all but impassable.

After a steady climb of two days, the small army reached Jalapa, a town situated nearly 5,000 feet above the seacoast. At the end of the third day, the army arrived in Socochima, a fortified town that clings to a precipitous incline. The only entrance passes through a narrow defile and up a staircase carved from solid stone, so narrow that only two men abreast can squeeze by. The terrain about Socochima is so formidable that a single squadron of well-armed warriors can hold off an army indefinitely.

Beyond Socochima the Christians climbed the arduous grade to the pass between Nauhcampatepetl and Citlaltepetl, and before nightfall caught them on the mountainside, they were fortunate enough to reach Texutla, where they found shelter from the penetrating cold. The next day they began the long journey across the dry wasteland, but before they reached the other side, their porters, accustomed to the warm climate of their native island, perished from exposure to the bitter cold.

On the ninth day of their journey, the Spaniards reached the Zacatami Valley, where they found the climate more to their liking. As they approached Xocotlan, the largest city in the valley, the townspeople came out to greet them, and they lifted the footsore and the weary onto litters and carried them into town.[iv]

Xocotlan was a prosperous town; its temples and homes were well constructed and plastered with white stucco, and Olintetl, the lord of Xocotlan, was one of Moctezuma's wealthiest vassals. He in turn ruled over more than 20,000 other vassals, and 2,000 retainers served his household, where he maintained 30 wives and many concubines. His sacrifices were in keeping with his wealth, for more than 100,000 skulls were on display in the plaza, and on the day the Christians arrived, he sacrificed 50 men to celebrate their coming.[v]

That evening Olintetl called upon his guest, and after the customary amenities were observed, the captain, unsure of the relationship between Xocotlan and Mexico, asked him if he was a friend, and ally, or a vassal of Moctezuma. Olintetl looked at him in surprise, and said, "In this land there are none who are not either slaves or vassals of Moctezuma. He is lord of many kings, a sovereign who has no rival in the world. Thirty of his vassals can field more than 100,000 warriors each, and every year he sacrifices at least 20,000 men; sometimes as many as 50,000. His authority is so absolute that great lords wear the threadbare clothing of a commoner and go barefoot in his presence, and none dare look directly into his face.

"His city is the greatest and most beautiful city in all of Anahauc, and it lies in the middle of a vast lake with 40,000 canoes ready to defend it. His palaces are incomparably elegant; his court is both cultured and enlightened, and princes from every province in the land are obliged to render their services to it.

"The expenses of his household and his court are outrageous, and the expenditures for his army are staggering, for he wages war continuously and maintains garrisons throughout every province. But his revenues are more than adequate, for there is none, however a great lord he may be, who does not pay tribute to him, nor any so poor who does not pay tribute in some form, although it may be no more than a token amount of blood drawn from his arm."

With this Olintetl clapped his hands, and four lovely slave girls wearing golden collars and anklets, were led into the room and presented to the captain.

The Christians remained in Xocotlan four days, enjoying the mild climate of the valley and the warm hospitality of Olintetl before they moved on to Ixtacamaxtitlan, a fortified town on the border of Tlaxcala. Upon their arrival, four Cempoalan nobles were observed leaving in the direction of Tlaxcala.

Tlaxcala and Mexico were old and bitter enemies. Their abiding hatred dated from the reign of Moctezuma Ilhuicamina, when Mexicans tortured one of Tlaxcala's most celebrated nobles until he died. His body was embalmed and seated upon a stool, then placed in the hot sun with his right arm upraised. When it was judged that his body was sufficiently preserved, they took the Tlaxcalan to the emperor's living quarters, where, to the everlasting shame of the republic, a majordomo placed a lighted candle in his hand each evening to brighten Moctezuma's supper table. To add insult to injury, this disgraceful spectacle was painted on henequen cloth and sent to Tlaxcala.

The lords of the republic kept the painting, and before every battle, paraded it around the plaza to warm the appetites of their warriors for combat.

In the years that followed the reign of Moctezuma Ilhuicamina, the sovereignty of Mexico spread far beyond the mountainous terrain of Tlaxcala, and the republic became isolated in its barren province. Although Mexico had the power to overrun Tlaxcala whenever it chose, the republic was never invaded. Like Huexotzingo, it was a convenient and economical battlefield for Mexico to exercise its warriors before committing them to wars in distant lands, and served as a source of heart's blood to meet the insatiable demands of Huitzilopochtli. And so an impasse was created; a field of honor for our warriors, but for the people of the republic, a precarious existence that endured from one generation to the next.

The Cempoalan mission to Tlaxcala troubled Moctezuma, but other urgent matters had to be dealt with first. A message arrived from Quauhpopoca, the governor of Tuxpan, the northernmost province on the eastern seaboard. With the message came a litter covered with a bloodstained mantle, rank with the stench of putrefaction. Beneath the mantle was the body of a man who had been dead for several days. His enormous head was covered with a great mass of tangled hair, filthy and caked with dried blood, but the pale skin beneath the dirt was like the skin of no man Moctezuma had ever seen.

With the main body of the Christian army far off in the sierra, Quauhpopoca began to press the Totonacs for tribute, and when they refused, he fell upon their towns. The Christian commander at Quiahuitzlán warned him that the Totonacs were now under his protection, and if the attacks continued, he would march against his capital at Nautla. Quauhpopoca's response was that if he wanted war, he would find him ready and willing.

Forty Christians and 2,000 Totonac warriors met with 4,000 Mexicans on the outskirts of Nautla, but with the first volley of stones, the Totonacs turned and fled, leaving the field to their allies. The Mexicans, however, fared poorly against repeated charges of the horses and the devastating fire of cannon, muskets, and crossbows, and fled in disorder into the hills. The Christians entered Nautla and fired the town, then withdrew to the south before Quauhpopoca could regroup his scattered forces.

When the Mexicans returned to Nautla, they found only a gutted horse and a gravely wounded Christian who had been left for dead by his companions. They bound his wounds and sent him to Tenochtitlán on a litter, but he failed to survive the rigors of the journey to the tableland. By the time his body reached the city, it was in an unsightly condition to present before the emperor.[vi]

Quauhpopoca's messenger beheaded the Christian with a single blow of his *maquahuitl* and he raised the head by its heavy mane where all could see it. Moctezuma stared at it for a long time before he spoke. Finally he turned away and said that he knew now that the Christians were not immortals, but the face of the dead man convinced him that they were very brave.

With the Christians now within 30 leagues of Mexico, the moment of decision had arrived for Moctezuma. If the lords of Tlaxcala should choose to welcome the Christians, the captain would gain another powerful ally and cause more unrest in the provinces. Many members of the royal council, however, believed that the proud Tlaxcalans would never permit the Christians to enter the province. The captain had made no secret that he sought Moctezuma's friendship, and Xicoténcatl, the captain-general of the republic, who despised foreigners as much as he hated Mexicans, would never tolerate one who openly sought Moctezuma's favor.

It was the consensus of the council that the captain would avoid a confrontation with the powerful Tlaxcalan army in the mountainous terrain of the province. Instead, he would most likely pass north of Tlaxcala and approach the Valley of Mexico through territories under Mexican control. This being the case, should Moctezuma send an army to halt his advance, or should he choose to receive him in Tenochtitlán?

The first to voice his opinion was Cuitláhuac, the lord of Ixtapalapa. Offer a gift for the emperor of the Christians, he said, but make it conditional upon their leaving the country at once. Make it a gift so grand that it cannot be refused, and with it, offer a pledge to pay tribute to the emperor each and every year. And to be sure that the captain agrees to these terms, offer him a bribe of gold and jewelry that will make him wealthy for the rest of his years.

Moctezuma's nephew Cacama, the lord of Texcoco, disagreed. "Most high lord," he said," inasmuch as I dislike having to contradict my noble uncle, I urge you instead to receive the Christians and honor their captain as you would the ambassador of any other great lord. Send word to the governors and chieftains through whose lands they will pass to welcome them, and assure them that they will be just as welcome in your court.

"They say that they have not come to our country with hostile intent, but to bring greetings from their emperor and to reveal the secrets of their religion to us. Hear them out. When they see the majesty of your court and realize the extent of your power, they will do no more than pay you homage. If, however, they should be foolish enough to attempt to harm you, we, your vassals, who are pledged to die in your defense, are here to protect you."

Many agreed with Cuitláhuac that every attempt short of warfare should be made to keep the Christians out of the country. But others, those who saw an opportunity to ambush the Christians on the causeways, supported Cacama. When he saw that no consensus was forthcoming, Moctezuma made his decision.

He saw no purpose, he said, in allowing the captain to come to his court with an army and a host of warriors from a rebellious province. Furthermore, Ixtlilxóchitl, the renegade prince of Acolhuacán, was actively seeking allies to move against Texcoco and Mexico. If bribes and promises were sufficient to prompt the captain to leave the country, well and good. With him gone, the provinces would be far easier to control.

Six nobles, accompanied by 200 porters bearing the greatest treasure ever offered by a Mexican emperor, departed for

117

Ixtacamaxtitlan, where they would present Cuitláhuac's proposal to the captain.

---

[i] Ecatl was second in command of the army of Tlatilolco. During the conquest, he routed a superior Spanish force attempting to enter the city, and came within minutes of capturing Cortés. He also accompanied Cortés on his ill-fated expedition to Honduras.

[ii] The account of Moctezuma Ulhuicamina's campaign against Cuetlaxtlan presented here is that of Torquemada. A different version of the campaign, one which omits Moquihuix's role in the Mexican victory, is found in Duran, HH ed.

[iii] The seizure of the Mexican tax collectors by the Totonacs is found in a number of sources. See Bernal Díaz, Gomara, and Andres de Tapia.

[iv] Bernal Díaz gives the names of the towns that lay along Cortés's route. Several variations exist in the spelling of the names of the towns, and name changes have occurred over the centuries. Modern maps identify the towns as follows: Jalapa-unchnged: Socochima-Xico; Tejutla-Ixuacan; Xocotlan-Zautla; Ixtacamaxtitlan-unchanged.

[v] Bernal Diaz's count of more than 100,000 skulls mounted on the rack in Xocotlan may have been a typical Spanish exaggeration, but he contends that his estimate was aided by their orderly arrangement.

[vi] Seven Spaniards died from wounds suffered at Nautla, including Juan de Escalante, the commander of the garrison at Quiahuitzlan. The Mexicans, however, found only Arguello, whose head was taken to Moctezuma, lying mortally wounded on the battlefield.

8. Maxixca:

The Compromise

When a messenger announced that the council of governors was ready to hear out some ambassadors from Cempoala, I was certain that they had been sent by their new ally, a foreign captain whose army was poised less than a day's march from the western border of Tlaxcala. As I dressed, I could not help recalling the prophecies of the ancients, who foretold that one day men from unknown lands across the sea would rule our land. These prophecies, our diviners said, were now confirmed by signs from the gods. First a powerful whirlwind of dust rose from the crest of the sierra, and like a raging tempest, it soared into the heavens. Then a great curtain of light rose in the east three hours after sunset and spread across the night sky, sending our people into the sierra to await the end of the world.

When I reached the council hall, Tlehuexotlotl, the lord of Tepeticpac, and Citlalpopocatl, the lord of Quiahuiztlán, were seated at their accustomed places, but I waited until Xicoténcatl the Elder, the blind and aged lord of Tizatlán, was led to his seat on the platform before I joined them. The last to arrive was Xicoténcatl the Younger, the captain-general of the armies of Tlaxcala. The young general was an impressive figure, tall, broad shouldered, his handsome face long, coarse, and pockmarked. Unlike his modest and unassuming father, however, he was filled with overbearing arrogance and pride.

As the lord of Ocotelulco, the central district of the Republic, it was my place to receive the Cempoalans. Led by a majordomo, they entered the council hall, walking slowly, carefully placing one foot before the other. Each carried a single rose, and kept his head bent and his eyes upon the ground until they stood before the platform. The eldest looked up to us and extended his hand in greeting, then brought it back to his mouth, indicating that he was ready to speak.

"Great and valiant lords, illustrious nobles," he began, "the lord of Cempoala and the Totonac lords send their greetings to you. They pray that the gods keep you and grant you victory over all your enemies. They would have you know that men who have come from a faraway land to the east have freed them from the yoke of Mexico. These men are as powerful as the gods, and their captain says that they are vassals of a great emperor who has sent him here to greet Moctezuma.

"He asks that you grant him safe passage through your territory, even though we have told him that Moctezuma is your capital enemy, and that you have sustained many injuries and much damage from his tyranny and oppression. He also knows that you have defended your country well against him, and have inflicted heavy losses upon his armies. If you grant him permission to enter Tlaxcala, he promises to aid you in your struggle against Mexico. The lord of Cempoala and the Totonac lords urge you to accept these men as friends, for although they are few, they are the equals of many Mexicans. Their friendship, they say, will be of great advantage in your war against Mexico."

The ambassador stepped back and lowered his eyes, waiting for me to speak.

"We are pleased," I said, "to welcome the honored ambassadors of the lord of Cempoala, and to hear that the Totonacs have been set free from the tyranny of Moctezuma. We thank them in the name of the Republic of Tlaxcala for their counsel, and we will take the request of the foreign captain under consideration at once. Since our deliberations will take some time, let me suggest that you make Tlaxcala your home until we reach our decision."

After the Cempoalans were escorted to their quarters, I stood and addressed the council.

"Lords and nobles," I began, "our friends the Totonacs, the enemies of our enemy, say that these powerful foreigners will join us in our war against Moctezuma if we grant them safe passage through the Republic. This offer, I believe, cannot be lightly dismissed. Moctezuma has kept us confined in these mountains from one generation to the next, and has denied us all but the basic necessities of life.

"Furthermore, the gods themselves demand that we offer our hospitality to all travelers. If we refuse to admit these foreigners, we will show our lack of compassion for our fellow man, and worse, appear to be cowards, afraid to admit them for fear they will do us harm. Such is not the nature of Tlaxcala.

"Let us now turn to the prophecies that our ancestors left us in their paintings and manuscripts. They foretold how a great lord in a faraway land, who is protected by a powerful god, would one day send his sons to our land, and although they would be few in number, each would be more powerful than a thousand warriors.

"The ancients predicted that they would overthrow our gods and introduce a new religion. They would bring us new customs and new laws, forbid sacrifice of men, and abolish sodomy and other abominable sins that prevail in our land. It is said that these men will establish the seat of government in our nation, and that Moctezuma's empire will come to an end.

"Let us receive these men with joyful hearts, for their coming may well be the fulfillment of the prophecy of our ancestors. If we do otherwise, we may perish, for human forces cannot resist divine power and decrees that come from heaven itself. This is my council to you-let those who think otherwise speak now."

Xicoténcatl the Younger rose slowly to his feet and faced the assembly, speaking in a voice charged with emotion.

"Brave warriors, valiant chieftains, you who are the strength and rampart of Tlaxcala! Did I not suspect that Maxixca desires peace and comfort more than the glory of battle, more than the fame you have won on the field against Moctezuma, his eloquence could easily sway me to his way of thinking. If, however, we allow ourselves to be deceived by his words, we will lose the best opportunity ever to bring us fame that will endure for generations to come.

"Maxixca tell us that it is the commandment of the gods to welcome strangers to our land. This decree of the gods, however, applies only to those who mean us no harm, not those who come to us under the guise of friendship to measure the strength and size of our forces. To do so would threaten the very security of our nation, for the enemy familiar with our weaknesses is twice armed.

"Maxixca also says that these foreigners-whom he likens to gods for no apparent reason-are the ones who, according to our prophecies, are to rule our land. I have two things to say about this. First, for the greater part, our prophecies have always proved to be ambiguous, and second, how can we be sure that these men are the ones we await? Are there others yet to come who will fulfill the prophecies? If we do not make certain who these foreigners are and why they have come here, we shrink from the duty our country demands of us. If we find that they are immortals, we have no choice but to offer them our friendship. If, however, we find that they are only men, no different from us, then let us not deceive ourselves and act the fool.

"To me, these men do not appear to be gods, but monsters cast upon the shores by the spume of the sea. From our merchants, I have learned that they came to this land mounted upon great deer, and that wherever they go, they bring about devastation and ruin. They love gold, silver, and precious tones to excess, and their greed is never satisfied. They are no better than beggars, given to sleeping in their clothes and shunning the hoe in search of pleasure.

"I believe that the sea, unable to suffer them any longer, has cast them out, and if this is as I say, what greater evil can befall our country than to receive these monsters as friends? All the rabbits, hares, and chickens in the land will not suffice to feed them, and they will strip our fields bare to feed the shorn deer they ride.

"Our people must make do without salt, without cotton clothing, and without any vegetables more palatable than maize and herbs. What extremity must they suffer if they have to provide for these foreigners as well? And most important of all, why should we who have shed our blood to live in freedom subject ourselves to those who would make us their vassals?

"Tlaxcala has no riches other than its bows and arrows, its maquahuitl and shield, and its fire-hardened javelin and dart. We need not depend upon foreigners for our protection. You are many in number, no less courageous than the foreigners, and you live in rugged and formidable mountains where they know neither the land nor the passes. If they attempt to enter Tlaxcala by force, we will drive them back, and by all that is in me, I promise that I shall not fail you.

"If you are the same warriors who have defeated Moctezuma's armies time and time again, if you believe in freedom above all else, and if you are resolved to fight for our gods and the honored name of Tlaxcala, follow me! Die with me! Better we die for all we hold dear than forfeit them to the enemy without raising a hand in their defense!"

Xicoténcatl's fiery speech brought the chieftains to their feet with a chorus of cheers. The lords and nobles of the Republic did however, not share their enthusiasm for a war with the foreigners. Arguments between the two factions broke out immediately, and voices rose as the arguments grew more heated. It seemed that the assembly had reached an impasse, since it was equally divided between my position and that of Xicoténcatl until Temilotecutl, the chief magistrate, rose to his feet.

"My friends," he began, "there is always controversy in matters of great moment, for there is nothing in human affairs so evident that does not have two sides. If, however, such affairs are handled in a prudent manner, and each point of view carefully considered, they can be resolved. In the affair that is now before us, two opinions have been presented. The lord Maxixca proposes that the foreigners be welcomed as friends, and the lord Xicoténcatl insists that they are bent upon doing us harm. Although they are in disagreement, each is to be praised for his counsel. In my opinion, however, each viewpoint has its merits, and each can be exploited to our advantage. Let us then consider a stratagem that should satisfy all, especially the wise Xicoténcatl, the father of our captain-general.

"It is my proposal that we send a message of welcome to the foreign captain, and tell him that his visit will bring great honor to Tlaxcala. In the meantime, the lord Xicoténcatl will form a pact with the Otomies,[i] and when the captain enters the Republic, his warriors and the Otmies will fall upon his army. If Xicoténcatl prevails, we will know that the foreigners are men, not gods, and our Republic will gain everlasting glory. If, however, the strangers should prove to be immortals, too powerful for our warriors, we will blame the attack upon the Otomies, saying that they are a barbarous people over whom we have no control. This plan, I believe, incurs no risk for us, and should be acceptable to both Maxixca and Xicoténcatl."

As neither Xicoténcatl nor I were able to rebut Temilotecutl's logic, the council unanimously adopted his plan. The Cempoalan ambassadors were summoned and informed that we would send our ambassadors to welcome the captain as a friend. Meanwhile, they would remain here as hostages until the assurances of the Totonacs were confirmed.

The assembly was adjourned, and as the nobles and the lords made their way out of the council hall, each embraced Temilotecutl in turn, telling him that he was the voice of the Republic, and that the gods truly lived in his heart and spoke through his mouth. They praised him not only for his statesmanship, but also for the solemnity and humility with which he began and ended his speech.

---

[1] The Otomies were a warlike race originally from the tableland north of the Valley of Mexico. Some migrant Otomí groups found their way into the valley and beyond to Tlaxcala. Their courage and loyalty speedily found them a place in the armies of Tlaxcala, and they were assigned to protect the frontiers of the Republic. The Otomies had their own religion, culture, and language.

9.Xicotencatl:

War, Bread, and Turkeys

A great rampart stretches across the valley in which Ixtacamaxtitlan lies, a massive wall built many years ago by the people of that city to protect them from Tlaxcalan and Otomie armies. This formidable barrier, built at great expense, stands in testimony to the military might of Tlaxcala. The only opening in the wall lies at its midpoint, a narrow corridor more than 60 paces in length and no more than ten paces wide, formed by apposing segments of the wall that overlap each other in a great arc. The wall is nine feet high and 20 feet thick, and a parapet a foot and a half wide for its defenders runs along its entire length.[i]

When the captain led his army through this confined passage way into Tlaxcala, we knew that there would be no turning back, not for the captain, not for the Republic.

A league beyond the wall, the foreigners passed through a dense pine grove, where our sorcerers had woven grass ropes and colored paper ribbons strewn across the road to strip them of their powers. Beyond the grove they came upon a party of Otomies, who fled when they saw mounted men in the fore of the army. Two horsemen galloped after the Otomies, but before they could overtake them, warriors sprang from the brush alongside the road. One, with a single stroke of his *maquahuitl*, nearly decapitated the first horse, leaving its head dangling from the reins. The second horse reared in fright, then stumbled when another warrior slashed at its foreleg, blood gushing from its severed leg as it spilled the rider to the ground. Before the Otomies could fall upon the horsemen, however, other mounted men over took them and ran them through with their lances.

The horsemen gave chase to the others, but they pulled up when a thousand warriors rose upon the crest of a ridge and showered them with stones and arrows. They closed in upon the horsemen, but others came to their rescue and swept through their ranks, spearing and trampling them. The Otomies scattered, but before they could regroup, the main body of the Christian army moved forward in support of their horsemen, and they fled, dragging their dead with them.

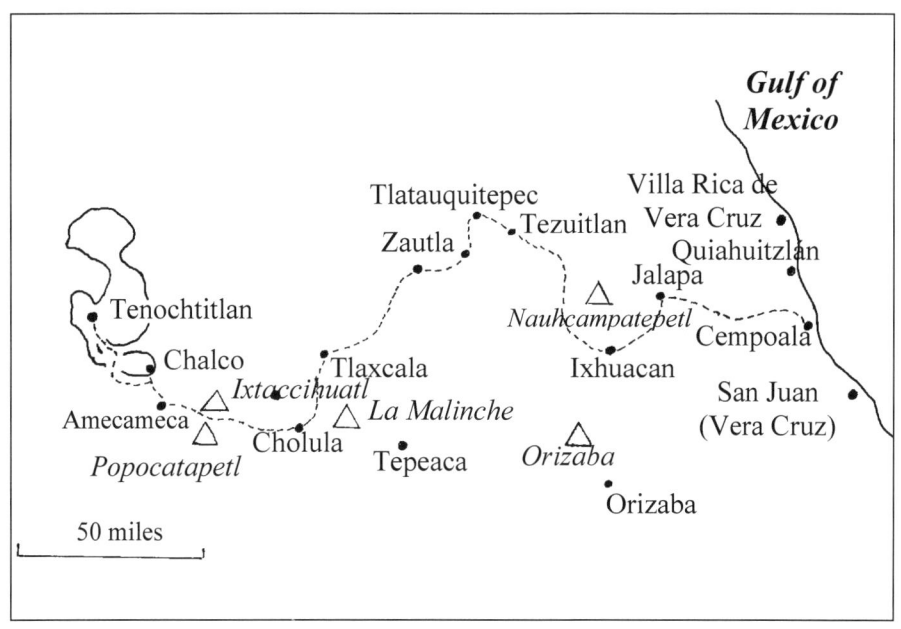

Cortés March to Mexico

News of the encounter left no doubt in our minds that the foreigners were powerful, but they were by no means as invincible as the Totonacs claimed. Their horses were devastating at full gallop, but in close combat they were vulnerable to a *maquahuitl* in the hands of a skilled warrior. We knew also that their god could not protect them from our stones and arrows, for that night we could hear them cry out in pain as they dressed their wounds with the grease of a fat Otomie they had cut open.

The following day we sent a party of nobles, accompanied by two Cempoalan ambassadors, to the camp of the foreigners. They told the captain that the lords of the Republic had sent them to welcome him to Tlaxcala and to offer him free passage through their territory. They also hoped that he and his men would come to the city, where they would be welcomed as honored guests.

They apologized for the attack on his men and assured him that it was not of their doing, but that of the Otomies. They were a barbarous people, they said, whom they had never been able to subjugate. Nevertheless, the lords of the Republic assumed full responsibility for the attack since it had taken place in their territory, and they would pay the captain for the horses he had lost.

The captain asked the nobles to thank the lords of Tlaxcala for their warming him of the Otomies, and promised that he would visit their city soon. He appreciated their offer to pay for the horses, but declined the gold and jewels they had sent to him, saying that he expected many more horses to arrive in the near future.

That night our priests prepared a ritual offering to the gods, asking them to allow us to dine on the flesh of our enemies. We seized the two Cempoalan ambassadors still held hostage and prepared them for sacrifice, but in an unguarded moment, they escaped and fled to the foreigner's camp. Men or immortals, now Tlaxcala would have to stand against them.

At first light I sent a force of a thousand warriors to attack their column, but they met with no more success than the Otomies. They fought bravely against the repeated charges of the mounted men and the withering fire of the crossbows, but they were driven back into a narrow ravine, where they broke and fled.

The foreigners, their blood raised in the heat of battle, plunged in after them, But this time it was not undisciplined Otomies who lay in wait for them, it was my elite squadrons from Tizatlán, and I had chosen my ground well.

Once the foreigners and their Cempoalan allies were well inside the ravine, we fell upon them from both sides, showering them with arrows, stones, and darts. Then we closed in with our *maquahuitls*, spears, and tridents. Handpicked warriors concentrated their attack

127

against the mounted men, who were caught between their foot and our squadrons, and in moments, a horse was down, its neck neatly severed and its rider lying wounded on the ground.

Spurred on by their captain as he moved up and down the ravine shouting encouragement, the foreigners crept forward despite our attack on both flanks and a steady barrage of missiles from above. At times they seemed on the verge of collapse, but their discipline served them well as they pressed onward and upward. Try as we may, we could not contain them, and they fought their way to level ground on the far side of the ravine. When they reached it, the mounted men were able to scatter our squadrons long enough to give the foot time to bring their heavy cannon into play. The effect was devastating. Our warriors watched in horror as the bodies of their comrades were torn apart by thunder and lightning.

Our losses that day were staggering. Scores of the finest warriors in Tlaxcala were left dead or dying on the battlefield. Some were missing arms and legs, and eight chieftains, all sons of prominent nobles, perished that day. The only trophy gained that day was the body of the horse that had fallen in battle. Its iron shoes were taken to the temple and offered to the gods, then priests cut up its body and sent pieces of it throughout the Republic to show the people that the beasts were neither gods nor immortals.

The foreigners move on to Teocacingo, a small town of the rim of a ravine seven leagues from Tlaxcala, the capital of the Republic. To prevent them from moving closer to the city, I posted my army on the opposite side of the ravine.

There followed a heated debate in the council about the failure of the ambush. I placed the blame upon the son of one of our ruling lords, who fell back when the fighting was heaviest. He immediately challenged me to a duel, but this was no time for personal feuds. Failing to find satisfaction, he withdrew his warriors and those of his Huexotzingo allies from my camp.

Our disastrous experience in the ravine taught us not to underestimate these foreigners-they were indeed as powerful as the Totonacs said they were. Now they were entrenched in a strong position, and the only way to dislodge them was to attack them with every warrior in the Republic. We must not fail again.

That night the captain sent me a proposal for a truce. His offer stated that he would leave immediately and peacefully if we granted him safe passage through the Republic. My reply to him was that he would find the peace he sought in Tizatlán, where my father was lord. There we would dine upon his flesh and offer his blood to the gods.

At daybreak, the plain before us was a sea of noise as the throbbing of drumbeats, the blare of conch horns, and the whistles and shouts of 8,000 Tlaxcalan warriors filled the morning air. Thousands of gold and silver devices sewn into the cotton armor of our warriors reflected the rising sun, and the plumed helmets of the chieftains rose and fell in the shifting breeze. In the midst of this host, our standard bearers held the golden eagle of Tlaxcala and the white heron of Tizatlán on high.

I summoned my captains. "The time has come," I said, "for these foreigners to learn what Tlaxcala is capable of in battle. They are tired and hungry, but I take no advantage of a weary enemy. Tlaxcala destroys its enemies by force of arms, not by starvation. Take enough hen turkeys, tortillas, and tamales to feed a thousand men to them, and allow them to eat in peace."

When they had eaten, I summoned the chieftain who was to lead the first attack. "Go to them now," I said, "for they have eaten and they must pay us for our bread and turkeys. Today we will learn why they have come here, and if Moctezuma sent them, let him rescue them. Take them alive if you can, for then we shall appease our gods with their blood. See that you fight wisely and bravely, because you are the flower of our army, and you do battle for our gods and our nation."

The chieftain only grunted that he was offended to take so many good warriors into battle against so few men.

An eerie silence fell over the plain. The shouting stopped, the conchs and the whistles stood mute, and the drums were stilled. The feathered panaches of the chieftains fell in the dying breeze, and 8,000 faces, now painted blood red, stared at the enemy over bamboo shields.

The forward ranks parted and two warriors dashed to the rim of the ravine. Arching their bodies backward, they swept their *atlatls* in a great arc and launched the magic darts of our ancestors at the enemy.

129

One struck a Cempoalan warrior, and a rousing shout rose from the army as he fell. The gods would grant us victory!

Two thousand warriors, the elite of Tlaxcala, crossed the ravine and moved upon the foreigners. Mounted men posted in front of the town waited until our men were beyond the rim, then charged at full gallop. Their momentum split the force in two, and our forces withdrew to regroup. When order was restored, they rushed the enemy again, only to see the forward ranks cut down by a thunderous cannonade. Nevertheless, our squadrons pushed on to the town, but a well-disciplined unit of veteran soldiers waited for them with crossbows, muskets, and swords. Our warriors died by the score, their wounds hideous to behold, and the few survivors fled in panic across the ravine.

When the Tlaxcalans saw their comrades put to flight in disgrace, the entire army charged across the ravine. Their rush carried them into the plaza, but they found themselves caught between the defenders and the heavy press from those behind. Our superior numbers proved to be of no advantage, since in the close confines of the town, only a few were able to engage the enemy. Losses mounted steadily before the well-entrenched defenders, and the confusion grew as our warriors tried to retreat through the press of their comrades behind them. The battle lasted four hours, but the foreigners held fast, and our squadrons withdrew when they saw the day was lost.

The following day I sent food to the foreigners again, and when they finished, I sent fresh squadrons across the ravine. The battle lasted five hours, but we were no more successful than the day before, and once again we withdrew in disgrace.

Too many good warriors were now dead, and unless we adopted a better plan of attack, many more would follow. Since the narrow confines of the town worked to the advantage of the enemy, it seemed better to wear down the foreigners by committing only as many warriors as could fight effectively, and rotate fresh squadrons into action each day. Furthermore, by committing squadrons from only one district of Tlaxcala at a time, squadrons from other districts would make every effort to outdo the others.

The fighting the next day was as fierce as ever, but now there was no compulsion to overwhelm the enemy in a single, decisive battle. When the chieftains felt that they had fought well enough to satisfy their honor, they withdrew in pride, challenging the next squadron to do as well.

I continued to send turkeys and tamales to the foreigners, but now warriors disguised as porters carried the food across the ravine. The warriors reported that they never saw a dead soldier, but there were at least 40 fewer soldiers in camp than when they first arrived. They also said that they saw many lying ill and trembling with chills and fever.

By now our warriors were gaining confidence in contending with the deadly weapons they faced each day. They found that they could avoid cannon fire by falling down when they saw the gunner lower a brand to the breech, and they were proving to be more of a match for the swords of the enemy. One of our warriors isolated two soldiers from their companions, and he nearly cut them to pieces before a horseman rode to their rescue.

The war was also a private affair between Tlaxcala and Cempoala, and it was fought according to time-honored conventions throughout Anahuac. Whenever a warrior sought honor in single combat, the enemy was obliged to cease hostilities to accommodate him. Thus both sides lay aside their weapons when an Otomie sent a challenge to the Cempoalan camp.

A Cempoalan noble met the Otomie on the rim of the ravine, and when they were less than a spear-length from each other, they raised their shields and circled each other warily, watching for an opening. The Otomie lunged, swinging his *maquahuitl* at the legs of his adversary, hoping for a crippling blow, but the Cempoalan was quick and leaped back in time to catch the blow on his shield. The Otomie spun away to avoid his counterstroke, and both became more cautious, feinting and trading blows that were readily deflected with their shields, with neither being able to gain any advantage. Suddenly the Cempoalan stood erect and lowered his shield and *maquahuitl*. For a moment his breast was exposed, and the Otomie lunged at him, momentarily lowering his shield. The Cempoalan raised his shield in time to ward off the blow and struck the exposed shoulder of his opponent, opening a frightful wound. He delivered several blows in quick succession and the Otomie dropped to the ground. Another stroke took off the Otomie's head, and he raised it high for all to see.

Whistles and cheers from the Cempoalans filled the air, but the Otomies turned their backs and walked away, leaving the headless body of their comrade soaking the ground with his blood.

By now our daily attacks against the foreigners produced little evidence of progress. Our warriors took no captives to gain glory or earn promotions, and the Republic still awaited the promised sacrifices to appease the gods. This prolonged and difficult war began to weigh heavily upon Tlaxcala, for never before had our wars lasted more than one or two days. A single battle usually decided the outcome, and friend and foe alike observed a ritual that never varied. Every passing day saw more and more sons of prominent nobles lying dead before an enemy that sometimes bent but never broke. Those who opposed the war were gaining strength, and Maxixca was preparing to sue for peace. Victory, at any cost, could wait no longer.

Our diviners and necromancers had advised us that the foreigners were invincible by day, but at night, when their strength left them, they were vulnerable. For a night attack to succeed, they said, we must kill the foreigners and their horses while they slept. Although it was not our custom to fight after dark, it seemed that we had little choice but to accept their counsel.

I moved a large force as close as I dared to Teocacingo, and sent 50 warriors into town, disguised as porters bringing food. Their mission was locating the sleeping quarters of the soldiers and horses, and to take stock of the defenses. They wandered about the camp, acting the fool as they touched the beards and clothing of the foreigners, and feigned fright at the sight of the horses. But like the fools they were, they lingered overlong and aroused the suspicions of the Cempoalans.

The captain, who until now had never concerned himself with the comings and goings of our porters, quietly seized 17 and began to question them. The foreigners stripped the first and fastened a heavy clamp to his testicles, and while his companions watched in horror, they turned the screw tighter and tighter until nothing was left but a bloody pulp. To the warrior's credit, he never revealed the plot, but the others, terrified by his screams and the sight of his bloody groins, broke down and told the captain everything. The foreigners took the others back to the plaza, where they cut off their hands and drove them out of town.

They ran screaming to the place where our army was hidden, and when our warriors saw their bloody stumps, they panicked, certain that the captain had a secret spirit who told him their very thoughts. As they milled about in confusion, mounted men burst out of the dusk of twilight and charged into their midst. In the rush to escape, they threw away their weapons and fled into the safety of the cornfields.[ii]

Now in disgrace, the lords of the Republic ordered me to return to Tlaxcala. I stood alone before the council; all those who had once supported me were silent, waiting for Maxixca to pass judgment.

"Did we not tell you," he began, "that the god of these foreigners has invested them with such powers that neither 10,000 arrows nor all the *maquahitls* in Tlaxcala will suffice to defeat them? Yet you, in your foolish audacity and insufferable arrogance, persisted in fighting until they drove you back home with your warriors at your heels.

"You are a disgrace to the glory and the honor of our celebrated Republic. You have not dealt with this affair as our defender, but as an aggressive fool; not as a citizen of the Republic, but as a self-serving warlord; not as the father you should be to your country, but as a contemptible stepfather. Were it not for the honor of your father and the respect we hold for his venerable gray head, we would reduce you to the ranks of the commoners, and none of your descendants would ever be entitled to eat salt, wear a cotton mantle, or attain the insignia of a nobleman."

Maxixca's words could not be denied-I had failed my country and my comrades. Concealing my shame as best I could, struggling to control the tears swelling in my eyes, I replied, "Lords, you may never know how deeply my disgrace pains me, nor how I suffer in my heart.

"It was, however, with your approval and your confidence in the army that I attacked the foreigners, and if I am to blame, it is for my persistence in continuing this war beyond any hope of victory. I would be sacrificed a thousand times over rather than pursue this futile war, but I will return to Teocacingo and fight to the death if it is your wish."

Before I could say more, Maxixca rose and dismissed the council, postponing their decision to the following day.

When the grand council of the Republic reconvened and the priests finished an invocation for a favorable peace, Maxixca rose and pronounced judgment upon me.

"Valiant lords, he began, "courageous captains to whom we entrust the fortunes of war, and you, wise and judicious men who are charged with governing our Republic, as the gods are my witness, I would offer my life and thrust my children upon the swords of the enemy to bring about victory for our people. But we know that this cannot be, for the god of these foreigners has another design for us. He has proved himself far more powerful than our gods, who have failed us despite all the sacrifices we made to them.

"The foreigners tell us that they solicit the friendship of Moctezuma, our age-long enemy. If we permit them to ally themselves with him, what then will Moctezuma be capable of when he chooses to make war upon us? If this should come to pass, the day will come when there will be none to recall the memory of our great nation.

"But these men who call themselves Christians say they are honorable men, and they have asked us for peace many times. It is not unreasonable, therefore, to assume that they will still accept us as friends if we ask their forgiveness. Once we make peace with them, our precious resources will no longer be wasted in a war that we cannot win. Our young men will no longer die in a hopeless cause, and the honor of Tlaxcala will live on.

"If the Christians accept our offer of peace, we must convince their captain that the Mexicans are evil, perverse men whose friendship cannot be depended upon. Then, with him as our ally, we can avenge the many wrongs that Mexico has inflicted upon us.

"Now, since Xicotencatl is so experienced in dealing with the Christians, let us offer him the opportunity to undo his mistakes. Let him be the ambassador we send to them in the name of the Republic. Let him take them a gift, which always mellows the spirit of those offended, and let him offer the allegiance of our Republic to the great lord who sent them to our land."

This, then, the ultimate humiliation for a warrior, was to be the price of my failure. Maxixca now spoke for the Republic, and unless I took his offer of peace to the enemy I hated to the depths of my soul, I would become an outcast in my own land. Furthermore, to my

134

everlasting shame, I knew that my father had agreed that I undertake this mission.

Feigning a composure that was not in my heart, I said, "Never would the gods want me to act against the will of my country. I shall carry your message to the captain, and by all that is within me, I shall do my very best to convince him of our peaceful' intent and to persuade him to join us in everlasting friendship."

---

[i] A sketch of the great wall of Ixtacamaxtitlan can be found in Cortez, MaNutt ed, which the editor has reproduced from Clavigero.

[ii] The siege of Teocacingo lasted 12 to 14 days. The size of the Tlaxcalan forces is overstated by eyewitnesses and early historians. The author has chosen Alfonso Chavero's estimate of 8,000 warriors, based upon his study of 16th century Tlaxcala. (See Diego Munoz Camargo, *Historia de Tlaxcala,* 186-87n).

According to Bernal Díaz, more than 45 Spaniards died in battle or succumbed to disease at Teocacingo.

10. Alonso de Grado:

Journey into Darkness

There had been no sign of the enemy since the cavalry drove them into the maize fields, and Cortés, no longer pressed by daily attacks on the company, took advantage of the break in hostilities to survey the surrounding area from the top of the temple. The only evidence he saw of habitation, however, was several columns of blue smoke four leagues to the west, rising from the foot of a mountain ridge formed by a chain of massive boulders. Later that day he summoned the principals of the company to his quarters.

"Senors," he said, "our enemy seems to be unwilling to continue his attacks, yet he is indisposed to make peace with us. But we can no longer stay here and allow him to attack us at will, since the men are nearly spent and our food supply is precariously low. I see evidence, however, of a large town some distance to the west, where I am sure we will find all the provisions we need, provided we take the offensive. I ask each of you to give me your thoughts about a night attack against the town, but before you speak, keep in mind that if we succeed, the enemy will now have to defend himself, and the advantage will be ours.

Cortés, we knew by now, always sought the counsel of his captains whenever he proposed some new course of action; not for our opinions, but only to create the impression that all had a voice in the plan that he was fully determined to pursue.

Finding little opposition to his proposal, we set forth with 200 foot and six horse late that night along a road that led toward the columns of smoke. The night was so dark that we could barely make out the direction of the ridge, and a cold wind blew steadily from the snow-capped sierra. The surrounding territory was unfamiliar, and the darkness was disquieting, since the enemy could be upon us at any moment.

From the very beginning, everything that was humanly possible to discourage us from continuing our journey happened that night. We had traveled no more than a league from camp when one of the horses fell to the ground with colic. Cortés ordered the rider to return to camp with his mount, but no sooner than he left, another horse fell. Moments later, four more were down.

This ominous sign unnerved every man in the company, and they called for Cortés to turn back immediately.

"Senor," they said, "why are we still going forward when it is obvious that we should turn back? Let us return to camp and resume our journey by day, for if we continue now in the dead of night, we tempt God himself."

Cortés only scoffed at their fears. "In times such as this," he said, "one must have courage, for good fortune is the fruit of courage. Omens and signs of evil are brought about by the devil himself, but it is God's affairs that we attend to here, and He is above all. The horsemen will return to camp with their mounts, and we shall go on. My heart tells me that this night we shall accomplish more than ever before toward gaining the good will of the Tlaxcalans."

Cortés had no sooner said this than his mount fell beneath him. This was more than the company could tolerate. He would be the ruin of all, they said, if he insisted upon continuing, because he would be setting himself above divine will.

Cortés, as usual, was unruffled and calm. He replied that great affairs are never free of danger and adversity. "Let us take the horses by the reins and continue our journey," he said, "for I assure you that this night will turn out well for us."

The horses recovered before we had traveled a league, and we never did find out what had caused them to fall. Upon our return, we examined the road for burrows and found none; instead, we found it wide and well packed.

We soon lost our bearings in the dark, and we could no longer make out the boulders that marked the ridge. We encountered rocky terrain where the road ended, and in a few moments, we found ourselves on the edge of a series of steep ravines. The crossing was so perilous that our hair stood on end before we reached the other side.

We could see small fire in the distance, and we moved in that direction. As we drew nearer, we saw two women tending the hearth inside a small house. When we passed by, we chanced upon two Indians, whom we persuaded to guide us to the boulders where Cortés had seen the smoke.

In the lightless hour that comes before dawn, we arrived on the outskirts of a small settlement, and our raid caught the sleeping villagers by surprise. A few Indians were killed, and the rest fled from us in terror. For fear of being detected, we did not linger to fire the houses, and our unwilling guides led us to a large town of some 20,000 people that they call Tzompantzingo.

We charged into the city just before sunrise, and the attack caught the people just as they were rising from their beds. The men, roused by the screams of the women, rushed out of the houses naked or wrapped in blankets, but only a handful carried weapons. In the panic, husbands abandoned their wives, and friend left friend to our mercy. A score or more were killed in the charge, but when Cortés realized that there was no resistance, he ordered the killing and looting stopped, and prevented the men from dragging off the native women. His orders were obeyed promptly, and we began making signs of peace. We gave a few small gifts to the children, then sent the women back to their husbands. Some of the men asked the Indians for food, and reassured them that we had not come to make war upon them.

By sunrise the town was under control, and Cortés climbed a nearby hill to survey our surroundings. Three leagues to the southwest he saw a city so large that it took his breath away. He asked the Indians what the town was called, and they told him it was Tlaxcala. He summoned us to join him on the hilltop, and he asked us what we had accomplished by killing Indians here when there were so many more over there.

We were unnerved and demoralized when we looked upon that great city. Cortés, sensing our fear, turned to me and said, "Look at the multitude that lies before us. What do you think we should do?"

"Senor," I answered, "I feel it unwise to tempt God by staying here. We are too few to oppose so many. I suggest that we return to the seacoast, where we are less vulnerable, and send a message for help to Diego Velásquez. If we stay here we will lose more and more men. If the enemy does not eat us, illness will finish us, and we will have gained nothing-not a single crumb of spoils to divide among us."

Cortés was visibly angered with my answer. "What kind of man are you, Alonso de Grado, to counsel me thus," he said. "If we turn back, the very stones will rise up against us. Fate pursues fugitives until neither bones nor hair remain of them. Onward! Onward, Alonso de Grado! If death does not stay us, better we die in pursuit of our goals facing the enemy, not showing them our backsides."

I could say nothing more. He was determined to stay to the very end. I turned away and walked down the hill.

The nobles of Tzompantzingo were waiting for us in the plaza when we returned. With tears in their eyes, they begged Cortés not to kill any more of their people, and they promised to do everything in their power to prevail upon the Tlaxcalans to accept us as friends.

Cortés told them that they must not deceive him, since he knew that they had made war on us as allies of the Tlaxcalans. If they swore to become loyal vassals of His Majesty, however, he would forgive them.

The journey back to Teocacingo was unbearable. At every step of the way, Cortés crowed in triumph.

"Hereafter you will learn never to speak ill of any day until it has ended."

"You must remember that the sun always rises after the storm, and although the day may dawn gloomy and oppressive, the afternoon usually brings sunshine and good fortune."

"Before many days have passed, you will see the Tlaxcalans accept us as friends, because they will realize that our coming will bring them prosperity and blessings many times over."

When the first mount that had fallen the night before returned to Teocacingo, the entire company feared that Cortés had met with disaster. Their fears, however, were washed away in a flood of relief

139

when he rode into town at the head of the column, with a train of porters bearing provisions behind him. Before he could dismount, his captains surrounded him and lifted him from the saddle, and he embraced each in turn.

"Senors," he said, "what we have done this day will make us lords of Tlaxcala, and this is but the beginning of our quest. Before us lies the richest prize of all-Mexico!"

That day an air of festivity and good cheer prevailed in the camp, but the euphoria was short-lived. By the next day, the company came to realize that Tlaxcala was a city as large as any in Spain, and fear and apprehension spread throughout the camp. They knew now that we were isolated in the midst of great urban centers inhabited by a hostile population.

The men began to meet secretly in groups of three or four to talk about returning to Vera Cruz. Once there they could wait for the ships that Diego Velásquez would surely send in search of them. And when word of our discovery reached Cuba, there would be men and arms enough to march against Tlaxcala, Mexico, and all the great cities of the tableland.

Cortés, smug and confident with the success of his night march, paid little attention to the rumors spreading in the camp. I found his attitude disquieting, as did many of his officers, and we met with him to discuss the situation among the men. We told Cortés of our concerns, and we warned him that the morale of the company was crumbling, and that the men were threatening to turn back. If he did not give the order to retreat to Vera Cruz soon, we feared that the entire army would desert and leave him in Teocacingo.

Cortés only scoffed at us. He was aware, he said, that some would like nothing more than to return to the estates they loved so well in Cuba, but there was no reason for the company to fear for our future. We should not come to him with stories like this, he said, because he could never believe that Spaniards were faint of heart, especially now, when they were so close to their goal.

But Cortés's lack of concern was rudely dispelled when by chance he overheard a conversation while inspecting the night watch. He stopped to listen, and he heard a voice inside one of the huts say, "If the captain is crazy enough to take us to a place from which there can be no retreat, to a place where we will be cut to pieces, then it's up to us to see that he doesn't sacrifice us for his own selfish goals. Let's all just tell him that we're going to turn back. He can do as he pleases-he can come with us or stay here!"

The talk continued, and among the voices were two he recognized as those of his officers. He sent for two friends to act as witnesses, and together they moved among the huts, listening carefully to what the men were saying.

"Our captain is just like Pedro Carbonero," one of the voices said, "who was foolish enough to attack the Moors in their own country, and all the men who followed him there died with him. Best we learn from the experience of others, for he who follows a captain who is lost is lost himself. One cannot avoid ruin if he follows a blind man. We must do something while we still have time; the captain can't hang us all, and he can't go to war without us."[i]

Cortés would have preferred to punish the agitators, but he was a prudent man, and he knew that this was not the time for the pillory and the gallows. Instead, he resolved to first win over the common soldier with consideration and concern for his well being. In the days that followed, he could not have been more solicitous of the men, and when he felt the time was right, he ordered the army assembled at the foot of the temple.

"Gallant captains, valiant soldiers," he began, "I know that there are those among you who would like me to withdraw to the seacoast. Some of you would like nothing more than to return to Cuba, where you can once again enjoy the peace of your haciendas. Others, I know, have grown weary of the difficulties and the dangers you have encountered in this enterprise. If the risk of facing danger, thirst, hunger, and perhaps death outweigh the fortune we seek, then you must turn back. If this is what seems best to all, I will not deny your leaving. I am a man no different from you, and I wish for peace and quiet no less than you. I too fear death and danger, and I weary of hunger and fatigue just as you do.

"But you have elected me as your captain and father, and a good father does not give his son all that he asks for, even when he is ailing, for that would do him more harm than good. I have always treated you as sons and as soldiers worth every honor, and I have always considered your safety before all else in the risks and difficulties we have faced. You and I have shared equally the hardships of this venture-this you cannot deny-and I am entitled to your hearing me out in this matter.

"We are all Spaniards, vassals of an emperor who is served by the armies of many nations, but when he speaks of us, he smiles and says, 'Ea, my lions of Spain!' We have crossed a sea that, until now, no other man has sailed. Together we have journeyed across a vast country, a great land with many people that no Christian, Moor, or heathen has ever set foot upon. We have come here to distinguish ourselves and to glorify the name of Spain. We have come to claim the empire of a Caesar, so that common soldiers and poor gentlemen, by virtueof their courage and strength, can prevail upon him to make them lords and grant them the right of inheritance for generations to come.

"More important, however, is that which we must be prompt in doing. We must set right these idolaters and uproot Satan from this barbarous land. We must unseat the Prince of Darkness, who has maintained his sordid tyranny over them for so many generations, and we must eradicate the unnatural and abominable depravities that he has sown in the breasts of these wretched people.

"We have come to preach the Holy Gospel, to bring it to these chosen sheep who are far beyond its pale. This is a divine mission, one that every Christian is obliged to undertake, and one can never do better in the service of God. The crown and the triumph of the martyrs are greater than the orders of all other saints, since by dedicating our lives to God whom we love, we prove our perfect love. Consider then, if the least of these goals is worthy of pursuing, would we not undertake every obstacle to reach it? Why then, with so many more worthwhile goals before us, would we not do everything in our power to overcome the same difficulties?

"Until now we have had nothing to complain about: rather, we should thank God for the miraculous victories over our enemies that He has granted us. If we place our trust in God alone, who has given us the strength to prevail in all our battles so far, He will grant us the strength and will to finish what we have begun.

"The army that lies before us is infinite in number and well armed, but they are convinced that we are immortals, and they fear us as they fear lightening from the heavens. Although they outnumber us many times, they are disorganized and easily confused in battle; if one is killed, the others flee behind him like dogs. You have all witnessed this. If we retreat before them, we will forfeit the good fortune that has been ours in every difficulty we have faced. We will be retreating before God, who has protected us at all times.

"But what account will we give of ourselves if, at the most opportune moment, we abandon our venture? How will we judge ourselves if, by our fears, we let the chance of a lifetime pass by, only to learn later that our fears were unjustified? If by retreating you seek peace and tranquillity-truly a shameful thing for men like you-let me assure you that you will find it more readily by challenging what lies ahead of us, no matter what the danger. The hare dies by fleeing, for in its impulsive flight, it invites and excites the dogs. Now a great distance lies between the sea, and us, and all those we meet along the path of our retreat will fall upon us, because none is friend to the vanquished. All shun the falling wall.

"If we die while striving for our goal, better we die for God and honor rather than abandon this great adventure, for by doing so, we will die at the hands of enemies we have already defeated, enemies who revere and fear us as gods.

"This is no time to give way to fear. The Tlaxcalans, the most powerful of our enemies, are ready to yield, and the Mexicans have done nothing to stand in our way. Fortune smiles upon us! Follow it, do not flee from it! Follow it! Fortune favors only those who pursue it, and it will be ours if we do not lack courage. God is with us, and none can stand in our way![ii]

"I have said what I came to say, and now each of you must decide what he is to do. As for me, I am determined to pursue the destiny that God has set before me, even though I must do it alone."

We would never know if Cortes's rousing speech won over any of the malcontents, because his timing could not have been more opportune. The following day a large party of Indians approached Teocacingo, and even from a distance, we could see that they were not Tlaxcalans, but Mexican nobles leading a long train of porters.

They had set out from Mexico several weeks earlier, hoping to find us in Ixtacamaxtitlan or in other territories subject to Mexico. As they skirted the sierra in Huexotzingo, they received word that we had entered Tlaxcala, and to avoid being attacked by the Otomies, they circled the Valley of Zacatami and approached us from the northeast.

The nobles paid their respects to Cortés and presented him with quills filled with gold nuggets, cotton garments, elegant feathers, and gold artifacts inlaid with jewels. When the last gift had been set before him, a noble stepped forward and raised his hand to his mouth, then extended it to Cortés, requesting his permission to speak.

"The great lord Montezuma, your good friend and my master," he began, "sends you his greetings and wishes you every success in your endeavor. He asks that you accept this small gift as a token of his esteem, and later, at a more suitable time, he will send other gifts more appropriate to a captain of your rank and to others who are more ennobled that we. He wants to know if you and your men are well, and if you have any needs that are in his power to grant, you have only to ask and he will send you whatever you require. He bids me also to tell you that he is pleased with your many victories over his capital enemies, the Tlaxcalans.

"Montezuma, however, asks that you not attempt to come to Mexico, because the road is difficult and very rough, and many dangers lie along the way. He would regret it all of his days if any misfortune should befall men of such valor, whom he loves very much.

"If it is your wish that he accept the emperor of the Christians as his sovereign, he will serve him until the day he dies, as will all his descendants. As proof of his homage, each year he will send him as many of our noble young men and women as he desires, which, among our people, is the greatest gift we can offer to any prince. In addition, he will send gold, silver, feathers, precious jewels, and the finest clothing in the land to him each and every year."

With this the Mexican bowed his head and extended his arms, one hand placed over the other, waiting for Cortés to reply.

Cortés said he kissed the hand of Montezuma for his gifts and for his recognizing the emperor of the Christians as his sovereign. He promised to heed Montezuma's warning about the dangers of the road, and that he would inform him of his future plans as soon as possible. In the meantime, he suggested that the Mexicans rest from their journey with us for a few days, since they must be tired from having to travel so far.

It was as if the arrival of the Mexicans was an omen that changed the tides of fortune for us. The following day, just past the meridian hour, the sentries reported a large group of Indians approaching us from the direction of Tzompantzingo. As they came nearer, we could make out a procession of 50 Indians wearing red and white robes, leading a train of porters behind them. While they were yet a distance from the camp, runners arrived, announcing that the lord Xicotencatl sought an audience with the captain.

Cortés was in bed recovering from a fever when he was notified that the Tlaxcalans were coming. He dressed quickly, and managed to be presentable by the time they reached the camp. He stepped forward and braced Xicotencatl, for although he had never seen him up close, there was no mistaking him for other than a great lord. He took the Tlaxcalan by the arm and led him to a seat in front of his pavilion, and as we gathered about them, the porters laid featherwork, cotton mantles, and a few gold artifacts at Córtes's feet. None of their gifts, however, were comparable to those the Mexicans had given us.

After the presentation, Xicotencatl turned to Cortés and began to speak with a voice that was scarcely audible.

"Wise and powerful captain," he said," I am Xicotencatl, captain-general of the armies of Tlaxcala, and I have come in the name of the Republic to greet you and to seek peace between our people and yours. As I welcome you, so do Maxixca and the other lords of Tlaxcala, and they have empowered me to solicit your friendship and wish you success and prosperity in all your endeavors. We beseech your pardon for waging war against you, and if you accept our offer of peace, we promise to be your faithful friends and loyal allies.

"With clear minds and of our own free will, we offer our vassalage, which has never before been offered to any prince, to the great emperor in whose name you have come. We know that he is as good as he is powerful, since men such as you serve him.

"If we fought a bitter and uncompromising war against you, it was because we feared that you were a friend of Moctezuma, who, like all his ancestors before him, is our capital enemy. We had good cause, however, to believe that you were his friend, since we have seen his vassals by your side many times, and therefore, we did not trust your word that you wanted peace.

"We have preserved the freedom that our ancestors passed down to us since time immemorial by shedding our blood, enduring hunger and going naked, and by suffering other untold hardships. Until we

145

could be certain of your intentions, we had no choice but to defend our people, for there is no man in this world who would not die before he surrendered the freedoms for which his father died.

"We have lived for generations upon the meager resources of these mountains, where even the barest of necessities are scarce. We lack fruit, salt that gives flavor to all food, adequate clothing, and all the luxuries that our neighbors enjoy. We continue to suffer the lack of these basic needs because we will never subject ourselves to Moctezuma. The tyrant has subjected many nations and committed unheard-of atrocities in the course of his conquests, which he has undertaken only for the sake of his unbridled ambition. Before we yield to his yoke, we will die, because our noble forbears were his equals in every respect.

"We know now that you and your men are invincible by day and by night, and that is fruitless for us to continue to fight against the will of your great god. The Cempoalans tell us that you are good and merciful men, and that you will help us in our fight against Moctezuma. We therefore offer you our friendship and our pledge of everlasting peace. As a guarantee of our word, I give you these youths, sons of our leading nobles, as hostages."

The Tlaxcalan's eyes filled with tears, and he halted until he recovered his composure before proceeding.

"Remember, valiant captain," he said, "Tlaxcala has recognized neither king nor lord, nor has any man entered our Republic without first being invited or summoned. Treat us as you would your own, for we deliver our wives, our children, and our homes into your care."

Cortés reached out and took him by his hands, then embraced him.

"Valiant Xicotencatl," he said, "do not despair, for my people will be as your people, and you will never regret taking us into your homes. It has ever been our nature to repay our friends as well as our enemies with kindness, because the greatest virtue of all is to make friends with a fallen enemy. It is my deepest wish to show your people the love I hold for them, and to show them the good works that our coming will bring to Tlaxcala.

"If you abide by this peace and trust in me, you will come to realize in time that your lives will be so much the better for it. But if I suspect treachery, I will shower death and destruction upon you, for the God in whom we believe and whose power brings us victory does not tolerate deception and wickedness. There were times in the past when you fought us disguised as Otomies, and times when you waylaid us on the road like cowards instead of challenging us openly and boldly. I have forgiven you for these base schemes that failed you time and time again, and I urge you to reflect upon the past before you break the peace with us.

"You may tell Maxixca and the other lords of the Republic that I am grateful for their offer of friendship and good will, and you may assure them that there will be no deceit upon my part. As evidence of my good faith in this truce, I shall dismiss the Mexican ambassadors who have offered Montezuma's friendship to me before I enter Tlaxcala."

The meeting was over. The generals embraced once more, then Xicotencatl and his party departed.

In less than a week, everything that Cortés said on that dark night on the road to Tzompantzingo had been borne out. It was as if he had been blessed with divine foresight.

---

[i] Bernal Diaz suggests that Alonso de Grado was one of the agitators against Cortes, but does not name him. Although Alonso de Grado's disloyalty is well documented, Cortés continually supported him and rewarded him

[ii] Cervantes is the author of Cortés's speech.

11. Bernardino Vázquez de Tapia:

The Mission to Montezuma[i]

Xicotencatl's unexpected surrender stunned the Mexican ambassadors. Knowing that Montezuma would not be pleased when he learned that the Tlaxcalans, his most troublesome enemy, were now our allies, they requested an immediate audience with Cortés.

The Tlaxcalans, they claimed, were a treacherous people, and their offer of peace was only a trap to lure the Christians inside the city. They begged Cortés to stay out of Tlaxcala until they could inform Montezuma of Xicotencatl's surrender, and they assured him that the emperor would invite him to come to Mexico instead.

Cortés heard them out, and he told them that he too had misgivings about the good faith and honorable intentions of the Tlaxcalans. He agreed with them that it was quite possible that an ambush awaited him inside the city, because they had attacked him repeatedly, all the time claiming to be his friends. He was confident, however, that he and his men were ready for them, since the Spaniards were always prepared for a surprise attack. In any event, he said, preferred to deal with the Tlaxalans in the confines of their city rather than in the open field, where they could use their superior numbers to better advantage. But to accommodate Montezuma, he agreed to wait in Teocacingo until they informed the emperor of his

148

situation. This pleased the ambassadors, and they promised him an answer from their master at the end of six days.

Cortés had no intention of sitting by idly until the messenger returned with Montezuma's answer. It would be best for us, he said, if a senior officer accompanied the messenger, and if Montezuma granted him an audience, he might persuade the emperor to allow us to come to Mexico. In any event, the officer would gain valuable information about the road, the terrain, and the towns along the route to the city.

Rather than ask for a volunteer, Cortés let it be known about the camp that he would prefer someone of rank, someone he regarded as a son or brother, to represent him before the emperor.

As a regidor of the colony and the king's factor in New Spain, I felt I would be the best choice to represent His Majesty. I spoke with Cortés, and he seemed pleased with my offer. Pedro de Alvarado also had volunteered, and the captain decided it would be best if both went to Mexico. He gave us our instructions and provided us with whatever gifts we could carry for Montezuma, which was little enough, since we had to travel by foot. The risk of losing a horse was too great.

Guided by the Mexicans, we left Teocacingo along the road that passes by Tlaxcala, confident that we could travel in safety now that there was peace. When the Tlaxcalans saw us traveling in the company of Montezuma's noble, however, they may have suspected a plot. Perhaps it was Xicotencatl's plan to ambush us on the road, perhaps not, but the attack occurred well beyond Tlaxcalan territory, where no blame could fall upon him.

We had not traveled far when we came to a river that flows from the mountainous country between Tlaxcala and Cholula. Late summer rains had swollen the river to overflowing, and when we reached the crossing, we found that the bridge had been removed. It seemed that we had no choice but to risk a crossing against the heavy current, but our guide convinced us that it was a trap set by the Tlaxcalans to drown us, and they led us to a safe ford upstream.

We were well inside the territory of Cholula when several squadrons of warriors appeared on either side of the road, and as they closed in upon us, they brandished weapons and made threatening gestures. Their shouts, however, aroused people from villages and the fields along the road, and they came to our assistance with whatever weapons they had on hand.

The Mexican sent runners to alert the city that we were under attack, and soon a party of warriors appeared on the road ahead of us. Our guides pressed us to hurry, and when we fell behind, they grasped our wrists and pull us along as fast as they could. The enemy was nearly upon us, but it pleased God that two squadrons of Cholulan warriors arrived at that moment. One squadron held off the warriors, while the other closed ranks about us and escorted us to the city.

In Cholula, the lords of the city quartered us in a fine palace, and they provided us with everything we could want, but the urgency of our mission prevented us from remaining as long as we would have liked.

From Cholula the Mexicans led us in a southwesterly direction, avoiding roads for the entire journey. We circled the mountains along footpaths until we reached the other side of the sierra, and we reached Huaquechula, an ally of the Tlaxcalans, without incident.

From Huaquechula we traveled north to Tochimilco, then took a westerly course around the foot of a great volcano. We passed through Tetla and Tenantepeque, and on to Ocuituco, a town granted to the Bishop of Mexico after the conquest. From Ocuituco we turned north until we reached Amecameca, a town situated in the pass between two towering volcanoes. Beyond Amecameca, we descended the western slope of the sierra into the Valley of Mexico, then traveled nearly three leagues along the shores of a great lake until we reached Texcoco.

The city was magnificent, the greatest city we had seen in all our travels in New Spain. A great wall nine feet high encircled a complex of palaces, temples, public buildings, and a busy marketplace. The palace of the ruler was built upon a hill covered with hanging gardens, and water cascaded down terraces through a series of pools until it flowed to the ground level, where a statue of a winged lion rose from the surface of a large pond.[ii]

We were greeted there by seven Mexican lords led by Chimalpopoca, the eldest son of Montezuma, and among them was a lord called Cuitláhuac, who was brother to the emperor. They made us understand that Montezuma was too ill to meet with us, and they discouraged us from proceeding any further. We could not enter

Tenochtitlán without great risk, they said, because the city was surrounded on all sides by water. We knew that it was useless to insist any further upon an audience with the emperor, and we returned to Teocacingo with an escort of three Mexican nobles. Notwithstanding Cuitláhuac's insistence that Montezuma was ill, however, I had a strong feeling that he was there in Texcoco, watching our every move.

Although we failed to see Montezuma after such a difficult and hazardous journey, the venture proved to be worthwhile. Our guides insisted that there was no road to Mexico other than that which we followed, but had Cortés taken this route with the army, all might have been lost. The road was the most difficult and dangerous route that led to Mexico. Dry washes and broken ravines lay along the way, with walls so steep that we were forced to use ladders to descend one side and climb up the other. Worse, some of the passes in the mountains were so narrow that 20 Indians could hold off an army.

Cortés was disappointed that we had failed to see Montezuma and gain passage to his city. The Mexican nobles told him that Montezuma wanted his friendship very much, and he regretted that he was too ill to receive him. His city, he said, was surrounded on all sides by water, and he would not be able to enter. Furthermore, the land was barren, and he would find nothing to eat if he came.

---

[i] The journey of Vázquez de Tapia and Alvarado is one of the least known exploits of the conquest. Until the publication of Vázquez de Tapia's manuscript by Manuel Romero de Terreros in 1939, only partial records of the journey were recorded. Bernal Diaz states that Cortés ordered them back before they reached Tenochtitlan. Díaz does not say how far they travelled, but implies that it was not a considerable distance. Cervantes states that their journey ended at Ixtapalapa, not Texcoco.

[ii] The most magnificent examples of Mexican architecture were designed and built by Nezahualcóyotl, the great lord of Texcoco. His complex of royal residences, public offices, and estates for his nobles, more than 400 buildings in all, covered more than 250 acres. Around the marketplace, council chambers, halls of justice, embassies, accommodations for scientists and artists, and the great library of Texcoco, there was a brick wall six feet wide and nine feet high.

Nezahualcóyotl's favorite residence lay on a hill about six miles from Texcoco. The palace was built upon terraces covered with hanging gardens, and a flight of 250 steps rose from the base of the hill to the summit. In a garden at the top of the hill, in the middle of a reservoir, there was a large boulder carved with the years of Nezahaulcoyotl's reign and his principal achievements. On the lower terraces, three reservoirs contained statues of women, and at the ground level, a winged lion holding a picture of Nezahualcoyotl in its mouth rose from a fourth reservoir. From these basins, water flowed into spacious gardens, where baths and pavilions were available for the household.

See Prescott, 101-103

12. Maxixca:

A Fight for the Gods

A period of festivity and rejoicing was proclaimed throughout the Republic when the Christians accepted our offer of peace. More than 20,000 people gathered in the plaza to dance and sing, while priests sent clouds of incense rolling into the sky and children laid flowers at the gates of the city. But the day ended with no sign of them, as did the next day and the day after that. We sent majordomos to arrange suitable quarters for the men and the officers, but each time the captain put us off with a promise-he would come soon. We had good reason to worry. Despite his promise to send the Mexican ambassadors home, they remained in camp and were seen constantly by his side.

When we saw two of his officers and a Mexican noble traveling the road to Mexico, we began to suspect that the captain might have had a change of heart. Was he about to enter an alliance with Moctezuma, one that would bring a Mexican army to Tlaxcala? Could we be sure that he would not elect to join forces with the most powerful nation in the world?

Once again we were divided as to our course of action, but even as we debated, the chieftains sent warriors to stop the Christians from reaching Mexico. Fortunately, they were able to reach Cholula safely, but it would only be a matter of time before the captain learned of the ambush. It was imperative that the lords of the Republic meet with the captain at once to convince him that our offer of lasting friendship was sincere

Preceded by a standard bearer carrying the golden eagle of the Republic, we entered Teocacingo, and when we were led to the captain's pavilion, we knelt three times before him and touched our hands to the ground. We rose, and I led the blind Xicotencatl, lord of Tizatlán, to his side.

The aged lord touched the captain's face and his beard, then ran a hand over his clothing. "Never in my life have I regretted being blind as much as this moment," he said, "for I cannot to see these valiant men whom our ancestors foretold would come to us."

"Lord," he said to the captain, "we ask your forgiveness for the war we waged against you. Had we known who you were, we would have gone to the sea and swept every step of the road to Tlaxcala. Now you say that you have forgiven us for our offenses against you and your men, yet you refuse to honor us by allowing us to share our homes with you. We are deeply hurt that you distrust us and lack confidence in our word. Our pledge of friendship to you is the pledge of our honored Republic, and the very gods would disown us if we were to violate it.

"If, O lord, you still fear for your safety, ask for as many hostages you wish, and we will send you the sons of the greatest families in the Republic. Ask for whatever else you feel necessary to guarantee the safety of your men, and we will grant it before you ever set foot inside our walls. But permit us the honor of offering you the comfort of our homes, because it pains us to see such men as you living in the hovels of Teocacingo."

The captain was visibly moved by the sincerity of the patriarch, and after speaking with the Cempoalans, he agreed to bring his men to Tlaxcala.

On the day of his arrival, the entire population of the city was outside the gates, waiting for his arrival. When they saw the first Christians appear, they rushed into the road, pressing nosegays of fragrant flowers into their hands and placing garlands upon their heads. The column tried to push them aside, but the press of the crowd was so great that three hours passed before the rear guard reached the gates of Tlaxcala.

Once inside the city, the captain was quick to move his men into the plaza about the main temple. He posted sentries armed with crossbows at the gates, surrounded the plaza with his Cempoalan allies, and imposed a 24-hour curfew on the army. No Christian was permitted beyond the gates unless accompanied by an armed squad, and then only when is business was necessary. Security was so tight that the men had to ask permission to relieve themselves in a gutter behind the temple.

As the days passed, however, Christians and Tlaxcalans began to form casual relationships with each other despite the heavy security in the compound, and an efficient system of barter was established with the soldiers. Whenever a Christian wanted something, he had only to tear a piece of cloth from his coat and give it to a Tlaxcalan and, by signs, tell him what he wanted. When the Tlaxcalan returned with the article requested, he had only to present the piece of cloth to a sentry to be admitted into the compound.

The greatest difficulty for our people was their terror of the horses. During the war, many of our warriors were convinced that the horses were demonic beasts that ate men. In the heat of battle, they often saw blood dripping from their mouths, and not knowing that an over-heavy bit could draw blood, they believed that the horse had eaten a warrior. There was no porter in all of Tlaxcala brave enough to bring them fodder.

Life within the compound, however, continued to be austere and sober under the strict discipline of the captain. More than 400 battle-weary men were doing nothing beyond eating, sleeping, and performing routine tasks. Their only diversion was gambling, which led to one fight after another every day. The pent-up frustration of this heavily armed force milling about in the center of our city, we felt, could turn against us at any moment.

Since there were but a few native women among them to ease the unrelieved heat of the flesh, we dressed 300 young women in seductive robes and took them to the compound. Most were slaves, or captives taken as spoils of war. Others were daughters, granddaughters, and even great grand daughters of slaves, as slavery in our society is passed down from one generation to the next. There were also a few women awaiting sacrifice, condemned to death for violating our laws.

155

As they were led into the plaza, they wept for the fate that lay beyond the gate, certain that they were being given to evil gods who tortured their victims before eating them. Even those condemned to die drew back, convinced that they faced a death far more cruel than the sacrificial knife.

The captain surprised us when he refused to accept the women. Their religion, he said, forbade them from consorting with women unless they had been baptized as Christians. Furthermore, many of his men had wives, and the law prohibited them from taking another woman to his bed.

His refusal to take the women upset and humiliated us, and we failed to understand why his men could not take the slaves to do as they pleased with them. We tried to reason with him, but he would not listen until we told him that our people considered the refusal of a gift, even though it be a single rose, to be an act of hostility.

He would not, however, accept them for his men. Instead, he placed the women in the service of his interpreter, the woman they called Malintzin. Among the Christians, he said, it was customary for a great lady to be served by many retainers, and by their serving Malintzin, she could serve him and his men so much the better. The pretext satisfied all, and we took the women into the compound.[i]

The women were quickly absorbed into the daily routine of the army, and, as we had hoped, tensions in the compound eased. We watched closely to see how they treated the women, and by their unmistakable contentment, we felt that we could now offer our daughters to the Christian leadership. Four noblewomen, including the daughter of Xicotencatl the Elder, and my eldest daughter, whom their priest baptized as Doña Maria Luisa, and Doña Elvira were given to the commanders.

In the days that followed, we became more accustomed to the ways of the Christians and they to ours. The captain, however, never relaxed the watch in the plaza, and he continued to send patrols throughout the city by day and by night. His only concession was to release the hostages, but only after I told him how hurt we were because of his distrust of our people.

His remoteness and lack of communication with us were disturbing, since we knew nothing of his intentions or of his plans for the future. We reminded him that the Cempoalans had told us that he would help us in our war against Mexico, but he offered us no assurance and gave no indication that he would keep his promise. There was also the matter of the Christians he had sent to Mexico. Had they returned with some message from Moctezuma that caused him to change his mind? Furthermore, we were not yet certain that the Christians were men and not immortals who had been sent to us for reasons we had yet to learn.

Resolved to settle these issues and ease our minds, we invited the captain to address the assembly of nobles. We gathered in the council hall, and when he was seated, I rose and turned to him.

"Valiant captain, lord of the bearded white men whom we have received as our friends and brothers," I began, "now that you live with us in peace, now that you are favored with a covenant that will never be broken by our people or their sons, we ask that you tell us, with an open heart and in simple words, what you seek in this land. We ask if you are truly gods, or if you are mortal men like us, but with powers that spring from a mighty deity. If you have come with a message from the sovereign gods of heaven, to whose will we are all subject, tell us what they demand of us, so that we, their servants, can do our duty to them.

"If you wish to live in Tlaxcala, you may build your homes wherever you please, and select whatever of our lands you want. We will grant you forests and fertile lands, and we will build your houses so you can live among us in peace and prosperity forever. If, however, it is the will of your gods that you move onward, we will support you and provide for you, whether in peace or in war, and we will offer your gods as many sacrifices as they demand of us."

The captain rose, and a hush fell over the assembly as he began to speak.

"I am deeply grateful, my noble friends, for your good will and for the hospitality of your esteemed Republic. What you have asked of me is appropriate, and I shall answer as best I can to relieve you of your doubts and fears.

"I have been sent here by the Emperor of the Christians to bring you tidings of the one true God, the God who created heaven and earth and all its creatures. As a son of this great God, I have come here to rid you of your idols and of the false gods you worship. I have come to cast out these silent and unfeeling gods who force an unbearable existence upon you; gods that have no substance, no vitality, and no meaning for you. I have come to put an end to your monstrous sacrifices and to those demonic rites that Satan, with his evil and cunning ways, has inspired you to practice. I have come to deliver a death blow to this demon who binds you and chains you with evil illusions that have been passed down from one generation to the next.

"In the name of our friendship, I appeal to you to cast down these idols you worship as gods. Root this great deceit out of your hearts and forget your ungodliness and heresy, forswear the infamy of men who sacrifice other men, and renounce all those who eat their own flesh and blood. These are the most abdominal and loathsome of all sins, and they are infernal deeds condemned by all civilized men and by every law of nature. Not since the days when wild animals, which are ruled only by their bestial instincts, ceased eating their own kind, has any nation upon this earth tolerated such monstrous practices.

"Now you know, my lords, why I have come here. Tell your people what I have told you today. Tell all who wish my friendship and that of my emperor that they must attain the perfect love found in our Holy Lady, the Church of Rome, and that they must receive the sacrament of baptism to free them from the devil. By doing so, I will be assured of your love for me, and by our bond of love, our friendship will endure forever. Then you too will be called Christians, which is the most exalted title of all, for it is taken from the name of the Son of the True God, Jesus Christ, the Lord and Redeemer of all mankind. When this is done, we shall become as one, incorporate in one body. As Christians, we shall march together against Moctezuma to avenge the wrongs he has done you.

"In closing, let me assure you that we are not gods, but mortals no different from you, save for the great powers that the True God we serve so faithfully has bestowed upon us."

He looked out over the assembly, seeking some reaction, but there was none. The passion in his voice as he threatened our gods stunned us all, and more than one noble was reduced to tears. Then he turned to me, waiting for my response.

"Great captain," I said, "you who are the most powerful prince in the land, the most venerated man in the world, if you are indeed a son of the gods, why must you set such little value upon our gods? How can you deny the sanctity and glorification of those who rule us from the heavens? You say that our idols are no more than statues without feeling, statues that neither speak nor move, and that they have not been created by god but by the hand of man. We acknowledge this, noble captain, but know that these silent images we worship are the likeness of men who once trod upon the earth, men whose deeds were once so celebrated that they ascended into heaven and became gods. There they live in eternal peace, and when they see us worshipping their images, they, with their divine powers, send their bounty to us who live upon the earth. Someday, invincible captain, you too will dwell with them in their abodes of pleasure, and when you leave us, you too will leave your image here below for us to worship.

"You admonish us that there is only one god who is the creator of heaven and earth, and if we believe in him and allow you to sprinkle water on our brows, we will be cleansed of our sins and we will become his children and be called Christians. But, you say, this cannot be until we permit you to cast down the images of our gods, gods whom we have worshipped and revered for ages, long before our time and the time of our ancestors. How can you think that we would forsake them so easily? Why do you want to burden our hearts by forcing us to break their sacred laws? How can you think that we would let you profane them with your violent and sacrilegious hands? Why do you even want to embark upon an affair as troublesome as this?

"I must warn you that if you attempt to overthrow them, they will destroy us all to protect their divine rights. When they see that we despise them, they will pour hunger, pestilence, and other calamities upon us; they will cast us out as men who are damned, and they will forbid us to speak with them forever more. Then the sun and the moon and all the stars that shed their gentle light across the heavens will be angry with us, and never again will we see their splendor.

"Lord, we love you very much, and we pray that you give up this resolve to overthrow the gods lest some disaster befall you. We know from experience that whenever we approach their shrines with irreverent hands, lightning flashes across the sky and thunderbolts from the heavens crash upon us.

"Now let us put aside this affair of the gods and turn to the other matter you spoke of-the war against Mexico. If you join us in our

159

campaign to lay waste to Moctezuma's empire, our army will be yours to command, which is the greatest honor the Republic can confer upon any man. If you accept this command, we will acknowledge the Emperor of the Christians as our sovereign lord, and we will serve you, his loyal vassal, for as long as you may live."

But it was as if I had not spoken. He continued to lecture us upon the evils of our religion.

"Honored lords," he said, "in the brief time I have known you, I have found you to be true friends, friends whose loyalty allows neither artfulness or deception. Because of our friendship, however, I must insist upon doing that which you would prevent me from doing. I must save your immortal souls from damnation! Your salvation, your redemption from the sins in which you live, is far more important than laying waste to any nation in the world, now matter how well-deserved.

"It is a most grievous thing for me, my lords, that I as a Christian and a son of the True God, must live among men who worship gods whose very substance is based upon lies and deceit. The notion that they can send hunger, fire, and pestilence from the heavens is no more than a creation of your imagination. They are neither gods nor anything else that belongs to this world, and they have no power whatsoever. As a faithful friend, I ask you not to believe in these abominable idols. Let us cast them down, let their names and the memory of them vanish from the earth forever. Give up your illusions, cast them out of your hearts and become sons of a God who will instill his divine grace within your hearts and enlighten you with His truth!"[ii]

He stepped down from the platform and strode out of the council hall.

What could we say to the people now? How could we tell them that after sacrificing their sons, husbands, and lovers in this cruel war, we had gained a peace with men whose only aim was to overthrow their immortal gods? Which of us would tell them that, contrary to our promises, the captain would not make war against Mexico with us unless we served his god and only his god?

Word of what the captain said that day was not long in reaching the farthest corners of Tlaxcala. Throughout the Republic, people wept and begged their chieftains to speak to the captain.

"Ask the bearded lord," they said, "ask him why he must cast out the gods we and our ancestors have worshipped for generation upon generation. Tell him he can place his god alongside our gods, and we will worship him and serve him as we do our own. Tell him we will build temples and shrines for his god, where he can dwell among us for eternity; tell him we will honor and revere his god no less than our own, and give him our pledge that we will obey his laws as we do for other gods who have been brought to us from distant lands."

Many said nothing at all. They took their gods from the temples and hid them in the mountains, where they ate herbs and drank holy brews that brought them divine visions from heaven.

Had it not been for the Christian priest, there might have been an open revolt. He cautioned the captain that we were not yet ready to forsake our gods, but given time and the opportunity to observe the workings of their god, we would come to realize the way of truth. The captain yielded, albeit reluctantly, and we offered him our shrine on the great temple for his god. The Christians replaced our god with a cross and adorned the walls of the shrine with leafy boughs, and when they were finished, they invited all of Tlaxcala to celebrate the first Christian rites in the Republic.

With the matter of the gods now set aside, the captain turned his attention to our war. Nearly 10,000 warriors, commanded by the most able chieftains in the army, were readied for the march to Mexico, but the captain, unsure of his ability to manage a force so large, reduced the number by half.

As we gathered our forces, Moctezuma's enemies began to gather before the gates of Tlaxcala, eager for an audience with the captain. Ixtlilxochitl, the rebel prince of Texcoco, was the first to offer his services. Ixtlilxochitl was the heir apparent to the throne of Nezahualpilli, but when the great lord of the Acolhuaque died, his brother Coanococh contested his right of accession. The nation was split in two by the brothers, and civil war threatened until Moctezuma intervened and decided the succession by placing Cacama, a son of Nezahaulpilli by Moctezuma's eldest sister, on the throne. Ixtlilxochitl fled from Texcoco and sought sanctuary in the northern regions of the kingdom, where a number of towns supported him. He established the seat of his fledgling principality at Otumba, and set about building fortified garrisons throughout the territory.

Acolhuacán, once Mexico's principal ally, was now a nation divided, leaving a gap in the northern approaches to the Valley of Mexico.[iii]

Ixtlilxochitl proposed to the captain that he would march south from Otumba, and join forces with the Christians at Cuauhtlalpa, a town a league west of Lake Chalco. With their combined forces, they could enlist allies from Chalco and other provinces hostile to Mexico.

Ixtlilxochitl's offer pleased the captain, and he agreed to meet him at Cuauhtlalpa unless events dictated otherwise. Ixtlilxochitl's cause was just, he said, and he would do everything possible in his behalf.

The captain, however, chose instead a route that would take him south, through Cholula.

I feared for the safety of the captain and his men when he informed me of his decision. The leadership of the Republic of Cholula was unstable and unpredictable, and their alliances shifted with the winds of opportunity and fortune. There was a time when we fought side by side against Mexico, but during one of our bloodiest battles, the Cholulans, seduced by Moctezuma's bribes, turned against us and destroyed our unsuspecting army.

Since that time we kept our distance from the Cholulans, and there have been no further hostilities. Our armies are strong again, and their god, the mighty Quetzalcoatl, against whom no human power can prevail, protects their city. On top of his great temple, priests stand ready to call lightning from the heavens and send water from the depths of the pyramid pouring down upon the invader.

But nothing we could say would turn the captain aside from his decision: with or without our support, he would go to Cholula.

The lords of Cholula had sent no ambassadors to welcome the captain, nor had they offered him their hospitality. We sent messengers to Cholula informing them of the captain's desire to come to their city, but their warriors insulted and mocked our couriers.

"Look at these witless Tlaxcalans!" they shouted, "look at these cowards who use foreigners to fight their battles! Where did you find foreigners willing to fight your battles for you? Why did you submit to them so meekly? Your warriors are nothing more than whores of the bearded men, who have castrated you with fright! What will become of Tlaxcala now that your warriors have disgraced your pure-blooded ancestors, the great Teochichimecas?"

"Let your mercenaries come here! Their only reward will be death by the hand of Quetzalcoatl! And let those fools who trust them share their fate."

Notwithstanding the insults, however, the Cholulans sent four minor chieftains to greet the captain. The lords of the Republic, they said, were too ill to meet with him.

I refused to take this insult to the captain, and I sent the veteran ambassador Patlahuatl to Cholula. He was to inform their lords, ill or not, that the Christians intended to pass through their city en route to Mexico. He was also to assure them that the Christians were noble men, who would offer them their hand in peace and friendship. They had done no harm to any of the peoples of Anahuac except when forced to defend themselves against unprovoked attacks. If they chose to receive them, they would find, as had the Republic of Tlaxcala, that the Christians would honor them always as valued friends.

Patlahuatl, however, was to caution them that if they angered the Christians, they would find themselves defenseless against their powers. Their soldiers rode great beasts that crushed all who stood before them, their constant companions were large dogs that could tear a warrior to bits, and their weapons belched fire and thunder that left the battlefield strewn with bloody flesh from one end to the other. Furthermore, the Christians feared neither Quetzalcoatl nor the armies of the mightiest nations of Anahuac.

The lords of Cholula chose to ignore Patlahuatl's sound advice. "Return to your lords," they said, "with this answer for these gods or foreigners, whoever they may be."

They flayed Patlahuatl's face, then his hands and arms to the elbows. They slashed his wrists, leaving his hands dangling by no more than a strip of bloody flesh, and sent him back to us.

Thus died the most genteel and noble man of our Republic, and we immortalized him from that day forward in our songs and poems.

The people clamored for revenge. They pressed the captain to fight with them against Cholula and put the entire population of the city to the sword, but the captain held back. Instead, he sent one of the chieftains back to Cholula with an ultimatum. If the governing lords failed to appear before him within three days, he would march against the city.

The lords of Cholula chose not to wait for the Christians. They came to Tlaxcala with a large escort, and when they met with the captain, their spokesman said, "Valiant captain, we your servants kiss your hands and ask what you demand of us. First, however, we ask that you forgive us from failing to greet you when those from other towns welcomed you to our land. Moreover, know that we chose not to come here when you summoned us, because the Tlaxcalans are our capital enemies, and only a fool would enter the house of those who would drink his blood.

"We know that the Tlaxcalans have told you many bad things about us, but we are confident that you will place little credit upon what they say, since they are our sworn enemies. We invite you to come to Cholula, and you will see for yourself that what they have told you is false. Come with us and we will lodge you in our homes and serve you loyally and faithfully, and you will see that the Tlaxcalans do not love you as much as they would have you believe"

---

[i] Bernal Díaz states that Cortés and Father Olmedo agreed that this was an opportunity to press the issue of conversion to the Tlaxcalans, but when Maxixca resisted, Olmedo convinced Cortés to yield. Cortés then accepted the women to serve Marina to appease the Tlaxcalans and save face.

[ii] Following the debate, Camargo states that the Tlaxcalans allowed Cortes to throw down their idols and accepted Christianity, but this is not corroborated by any other chronicler or the eyewitness Bernal Díaz.

[iii] For an excellent summary of the dynastic conflict among the sons of Nezahualpilli, see Charles Gibson, *The Aztecs Under Spanish Rule.*

13. Ecatl:

The Fallen Idol

Cholula lies on a broad and fertile plain at the foot of Popocatepetl, not more than 30 leagues southeast of Tenochtitlán. More than 20,000 houses and 400 temples are inside the city walls, and on the outskirts, another 30,000 houses are scattered about the countryside. A large and prosperous city, Cholula thrives upon the products of skilled artisans who work gold, silver, and turquoise into artifacts that rival those of Atzcapotzalco, and pottery so exquisite that Moctezuma will use no other in his household.

Cholula is a holy place, a sanctuary that draws pilgrims from every corner of Anahuac to visit the city where Quetzalcoatl once lived among men. His temple lies in the very heart of Cholula, a great pyramid that rises from a base more than 300 paces along each side to a broad platform on the crest, an enormous structure that more resembles a mountain than a creation of man. The temple on the summit is very old, built long before the Toltecs ruled at Tula, and countless centuries before our people came to the Valley of Mexico. Evidence of its great age is the heavy vegetation that covers the sides as high as the summit, where only the shrine of Quetzalcoatl breaks the vast expanse of greenery.[i]

Inside the shrine, the incarnation of Quetzalcoatl as the wind god stands on top of an altar inlaid with gold, silver, and jeweled ornaments decorated with the beautiful feathers of the quetzal bird.[ii]

Although Quetzalcoatl left Cholula many generations before our time, his cult in Cholula is as strong and active now as it was in his day. His priests, who wear white mantles embroidered with red crosses, are everywhere, and each day they pray before a monkey's head carved from turquoise. The relic is said to have belonged to the god himself.

The faith of the people in Quetzalcoatl's powers is steadfast and unshakable. They believe that he can strike their foes with bolts of lightning, and that his priests can call forth floodwaters from his temple. In the distant past, ancient priests stopped up springs that rise from deep inside the temple with mortar bonded by the blood of children sacrificed to the god. When the invader came, they broke open the spills and drowned their enemies with torrents of water racing down the sides of the temple.

Like Tlaxcala, Cholula is a republic, governed by the lords of six districts and the captain-general of the army. Like Huexotzingo and Tlaxcala, Cholula was once an enemy of Tenochtitlán, and we fought endless wars with all for no purpose other than glory and sacrifices for the gods. After Moctezuma offered them bribes, however, they became his allies and fell upon the Tlaxcalans from the rear. But Cholula was a house divided. Only three lords of the Republic favored Tenochtitlán; the others favored their long-standing bond of friendship with Tlaxcala. Thus Moctezuma's alliance with the Cholulans was fragile, but it offered him an opportunity to prevent the Christians from reaching his city.

At Tepeaca, not more than nine leagues east of Cholula, a strong Mexican garrison guarded the approaches to the seacoast, and an order from Moctezuma would bring 20,000 warriors to the city in less than a day's march. If there was to be war, what better choice of a battleground than a city whose loyalty could be bought and sold? Moctezuma risked nothing: if the attack failed against the powerful Christians, he could blame the Cholulans.

Moctezuma retreated to the temple, and after praying and fasting for three days, he proclaimed that Huitzilopochtli and Tezcatlipoca had decreed that the Christians were to be killed. He sent his agents to

Cholula with gifts for the lords favoring him, and instructed them to seize the lords who favored Tlaxcala. The Tepeaca garrison was alerted to be ready to march to Cholula the moment Moctezuma gave the order.

The Cholulans, however, were unwilling to bring Mexican troops inside the city. Moctezuma had a habit of leaving his squadrons behind when the fighting was done, and they had no mind to become another of his tributaries. As a compromise, when the Christians left, they would lead them to a place in the mountains where the earth was soft and sandy and the canyons flooded with seasonal rains. Their horses would be of little use, and they would be trapped between the impassable ravines and our warriors. The pact was sealed with the blood of ten children sacrificed to Quetzalcoatl, each no more than four years old.

When the Christians left Tlaxcala, they found the fields on both sides of the road alive with men, women, and children shouting encouragement and warning them to beware of the Cholulans. The press of the crowd was so heavy that the captain called a halt until the road could be cleared. The delay, however, prevented him from reaching Cholula before nightfall, and instead of entering the city after dark, he chose to set up camp on the banks of a nearby river and wait for daylight. That same night the lords of Cholula who favored Tlaxcala escaped and sought refuge with the Christian army.

The following morning the nobles of Cholula, accompanied by a band playing flutes, trumpets, and atabals, led a procession of 10,000 people to greet the Christians. Quetzalcoatl's priests, dressed in sleeveless robes, censed them with copal and gave them flowers, while the commoners sang songs of joy and gave them bread, fruit, and fowl. They entered the city to the cheers of the entire population, and found the narrow streets so crowded with well wishers that they could scarcely move. That night and the next day, the Cholulans made them welcome and set down banquets before them.

Moctezuma's plan might have succeeded had the Cholulans not been so careless in the days that followed. Their first mistake was quartering the Christians in a run-down palace that was far beneath the dignity of their guests. Four days passed, and not once did the ruling lords pay their respects to the captain, nor did they send the men any provisions. Soon the townspeople, following the example of their rulers, gathered about the palace shouting insults and threats at the Christians. Although the Cholulans had taken the precaution of keeping the Tlaxcalan warriors outside the city, they foolishly allowed the Cempoalans to wander freely through the streets, where they had set up barricades, dug pitfalls, and piled stones on the rooftops. By the end of the fourth day, neither women nor children could be seen in the city.

The captain did not wait for the Cholulans to act. His men laid hands on a priest and a noble, and within the hour, they revealed the plot. He summoned the ruling lords, and after complaining about the outrageous treatment his men had been subjected to, accused them of plotting to attack him. If they preferred him as an enemy, he said, well and good; let them challenge him openly, as brave men should; not lie to him then plot against him when his back was turned.

The Cholulans denied everything, insisting that they were his true friends and servants, and had neither lied to him nor attempted to deceive him. It was true, however, that they had avoided the Christians and withheld food from them, but only because they feared the wrath of Moctezuma. For as long as he chose to remain in Cholula, however, they would provide his men with food and anything else they needed, no matter how offended Moctezuma might be.

The captain ignored their pleas. He informed them that the Christians would leave Cholula the following morning, and he demanded porters for his baggage and 2,000 warriors to protect him from the Mexicans,

Early the following morning, warriors, nobles, porters, and townspeople gathered in the plaza, and by midmorning, the captain had assembled his army, and was prepared to depart. The captain asked the lords of the Republic to join him so that he could take his leave properly, but when they stood before him, Tlaquiach, the ranking lord, was not among them. When the captain inquired about him, they replied that the governor was too ill to leave home, but he wished him a safe and uneventful journey. The captain was not pleased. As the ambassador of a great prince, he said, he could not depart without a formal and proper leave-taking of the head of the Republic.

When the aged lord appeared, the nobles gathered about the captain, waiting for him to speak.

"From the very first day I entered your city," he began, "I dealt with you in good faith. I loved you as I would a brother, yet you despised me as if I was your enemy, and you told me nothing but lies. You asked me to dismiss the Tlaxcalans before I entered your city, and although they warned me of treachery, I did so willingly. I ordered my companions not to molest you or anger you in any way, no matter what the provocation, and this they have done. Even when you refused to provide us with food, I forbade them to take as much as a single fowl from your people. Many times have I asked you to deal honestly and openly with me so that I might set your minds at ease about my intent, but you shunned me and plotted among yourselves.

"As a reward for my forbearance, you conspired to kill me and my men. You barricaded the streets and heaped stones on the rooftops, then you sent your women and children from the city. Even as you stand before me now, twenty thousand Mexican warriors lie not two leagues distant, waiting for us, so that if you fail to kill us here, we will not escape them. Do not deny this, for I know it to be so! Your treachery is beyond contempt, beyond all mercy!

The Cholulans were thunderstruck. They blamed the Mexicans for everything, even though Moctezuma's ambassadors stood by his side, listening to them. The captain took five Cempoalan nobles beyond the hearing of the Mexicans, and began to question them.

When he finished, he summoned the Mexicans to appear before him. The Cholulans, he said, insisted that they had prepared to attack him by orders of Moctezuma to prevent him from reaching Mexico. This, however, he knew to be false-it was not the doing of a great prince, but the act of traitors and liars, and he would punish them for their treachery. They need not fear for themselves, he said, since as ambassadors, their safety was guaranteed by all nations. Furthermore, he would never harm any of Moctezuma's servants, because he had come to this land to serve him, not to anger him.

The captain ordered the Cholulans seized, then signaled to a sentry. The sentry raised his hand, and a single shot rang out in the courtyard. In an instant, the hiss of crossbows and the thunder of muskets broke the silence of the plaza. Before the crowd realized what was happening, the horsemen charged into their midst. The crowd began to scream and rush for the gates, but swordsmen were there, waiting to cut them down. When the carnage was over and the flagstones covered with blood from the dead and the dying, the Christians rushed into the streets. With the Tlaxcalans, they swept through the city, firing temples and houses.

Within two hours, more than 3,000 Cholulans were dead, and by the end of five, all resistance ceased. The Cholulans made their last stand upon the temple of Quetzalcoatl, where more than 40 warriors and priests showered the Christians with arrows and stones. The captain sent a captive to the summit of the temple with his ring and a pledge that they would not be harmed if they surrendered, but only one defender set aside his arms and left the temple. His companions jeered as he descended the steps, and shouted insults to the crowd below, then renewed the rain of stones and arrows to the crowd below. The captain, realizing that further appeals were pointless, ordered the temple fired.

The priests began to vilify the gods and curse Quetzalcoatl for forsaking his people, and the warriors, bound by an ancient and honored tradition, hurled themselves headlong from the summit. When the chieftain stood alone, he stepped to the brink of the platform and shouted, "Tlaxcala! Tlaxcala! Today is your day for revenge, but soon the day will come when Moctezuma will avenge us for the blood we have shed for him this day!" He stepped to the edge and hurled himself down the side of the temple.

The city was put to the sack. The Christians ransacked every house and temple left standing for gold and silver while the Tlaxcalans searched for salt, cotton garments, and prisoners to sacrifice to their gods. Other Tlaxcalan towns in the vicinity converged upon the city to share in the spoils, and before long, the captain lost control of his allies. Two days passed before he could persuade the Tlaxcalans to move their warriors outside the city walls. When order was at last restored, he placed control of the city in the hands of the lords who had defied Moctezuma, and once again there was peace between Cholula and Tlaxcala.

The captain summoned the Mexican ambassadors to his quarters, but this time he was blunt and outspoken. What kind of prince, he said, would profess love and friendship for him, then set a trap for him when he found him vulnerable? What manner of emperor would be so cowardly as to use others to do his bidding so that no blame would fall upon him? He wanted to come to Tenochtitlán in peace, but now that Moctezuma had shown himself to be his enemy, he had no choice but to wage war upon him and his people.

The ambassadors were stunned. Caught off-guard by the captain's accusations, they could only swear that the emperor had no part in a plot conceived by the Cholulans. But the captain refused to listen to them, and ordered all but one taken into custody. This one he sent to Tenochtitlán to give Moctezuma an opportunity to respond to his charges.

The ambassador returned in a few days with ten gold plates, 1500 cotton garments, and palace servants to serve the Christians warm chocolate, a drink they had never tasted before.

Moctezuma denied everything: he had neither conspired to kill the Christians nor had he ordered Mexican troops into the Republic. He did, however, acknowledge that he bore a measure of responsibility for the actions of the Cholulans. There was pact, he said, between Cholula and the Mexican garrison at Tepeaca, and this may have led some of his squadrons to believe they were acting in his behalf. This would not happen again. He had ordered the governor of Tepeaca to appear before the captain and offer him and apology.

Moctezuma concluded his message by once again asking the captain not come to Tenochtitlán. In exchange, he offered to provide his men with everything they might need while in his country.

The captain accepted Moctezuma's apology, but he replied that could not turn back without the consent of the Emperor of the Christians. He hoped that Moctezuma would receive him in peace and friendship when he arrived, but if there were any more attacks, he was prepared to take the city by force, even though he would regret having to do so.

When Moctezuma received the captain's reply, he withdrew to the temple with his priests, and he remained there for 80 days, making sacrifices to Huitzilopochtli and Tezcatlipoca. On the 80th day the gods spoke to him, and they told him that he need not fear the foreigners. They were few in number, and his warriors were the finest in all Anahuac. If they came to Tenochtitlán, he would have them at his mercy, provided that he made daily sacrifices to the gods and performed them properly. The Cholulans, they said, had failed to kill them because Quetzalcoatl was angry for begrudging him the sacrifices due him.

Moctezuma left the temple and sent a message to the captain. He would be pleased to receive him in Tenochtitlán when it was convenient for him to leave Cholula.

---

[i] The base of the great temple of Quetzalcoatl measures 300 meters on each side, and a broad platform on the summit once contained a number of buildings that served as temples and housing for the priests. The temple, superimposed upon two temples built at an earlier date, was built circa AD 400.

The oldest and smallest temple was built circa AD 300. Architectural motifs and artifacts found in its interior indicate a strong Teotihuacan influence. The second pyramid is larger than the Pyramid of the Moon at Tenochtitlan, Its base measures 170 meters on each side, and its height is 45 meters. In the interior, channels from the base to the summit may have led the Cholulans to believe that the temple contained springs.

The temple and the surrounding structures were abandoned at the end of AD 800, and lay in ruins until small buildings and tombs were built on the platform during the Late Post-Classic period (AD 1200-1520)

[ii] The vitality and longevity of the cult of Quetzalcoatl in Cholula undoubtedly rose from the influence of Teotihuacan in the fourth and fifth centuries, and the subsequent southward migration of the Toltecs from Tula in AD 1200, when Topiltzin-Quetzalcoatl took up residence there.

14. Tlilancalqui:

The Vision of Tezcatlipoca

The crest of Popocatepetl is the gathering place for swollen rain clouds that feed the rivers and streams that flow down the sides of the volcano and onto the broad tableland below. These are the waters that irrigate orchards that cling to its lower slopes, where the sweetest fruit in the land grows, and fields of maize that reach from its base to the horizon.

To the people, Popocatepetl symbolizes the bounty bestowed upon them by the Lord of All Things, who created the high sierra and all the lesser mountains. Each year they gather on the southern slope of the volcano, where the rumble of thunder echoes from the storms at the summit. There, on the Hill of the Divine Singer, they lay their offerings of incense, food, and feathers at the feet of the jade god who lives in the Temple of the Mist.

Popocatepetl stands between heaven and the underworld, and its dark side appears when pillars of fire roar from its crown and clouds of billowing smoke turn day into night. This, the people say, is the stirring of evil kings and governors who have passed through the Gate of Hell deep inside the mountain, seeking the path to eternal peace.[i]

During the early years of his reign, Moctezuma was more fascinated than frightened by the volcano's fiery displays of raw power, and he set about the task of discovering its source. He waited until one of its periodic eruption abated, then selected ten of his strongest nobles to scale the mountain and enter the vent.

The chosen ten hardly relished the task, but fearing the certain wrath of the emperor more than the capricious eruptions of the volcano, they began the ascent. The climb was relatively easy until they reached the level where heavy layers of ash began to slide beneath their feet, and as they worked their way upward, breathing became more and more difficult with the evil-smelling gases that contaminate the thin air.

Two men died before they reached the summit. The others explored the vent for as long as they dared, and on the third day, they began their descent of the mountain. On the fourth day, six men perished on the slopes, and the two survivors were more dead than alive when they reached the foot of the mountain. Under the care of Moctezuma's physicians, however, they recovered enough to describe what they had seen.

The smoke, they said, did not issue from a great mouth as the emperor had assumed, but from a lattice work of wide fissures that honeycombed the crater. The vent was much like a vast grating, with some fissures set at angle to the others. Although large boulders made the footing hazardous, two men could easily walk abreast between the fissures if they were careful not to breathe the thick and deadly smoke rising from the depths.

Moctezuma's nobles never fully regained their health, but until the day they died, they never ceased telling any who would listen to what they had seen on the summit of Popocatepetl.

Now the Christians were nearly upon us. The mountain began to grumble and shake the earth, and every house and temple in Tenochtitlán rocked and shuddered with its thunderous booms. By day, vast clouds of smoke pouring from its crest cast a shadow over the land, and as night fell, a blood-red incandescence blossomed in the southeast and grew until it spread from one horizon to the other. Then a day came when black smoke boiled from its vent until it blocked out the light of the sun, and the heavens were split with bolts of lightning and the crash of thunderclaps. It was as if the evil spirits penned up in the mountain were trying to break out and join the Christians.

Moctezuma retired to the temple in fear. He drew blood from his arms, his legs, and his ears, and offered it to the gods with his prayers. He prayed for them to protect and care for widows and children, and for the aged. Why had they allowed this sorrow fall upon my people, he asked. Had he not served them well? Had he not pleased them with his sacrifices? Had he not raised them above all the gods of Anahuac?

He summoned the lords of Texcoco and Tlacopan to his palace. "How little time we have been granted to enjoy the kingdoms that our ancestors bequeathed us," he said, "they suffered no grief, no sorrows, and when their time came, they left this life in harmony with heaven and earth. Ay, what have we done to deserve this? How have we offended our gods that we must suffer this calamity, that we must endure this burden? Who are these men who have come to our land? Who led them across the great sea to our land? O, lords, we must take courage and gather our strength, for they are at our very gates."

The Christians had already reached Amecameca, the Chalco stronghold in the high pass between Popocatepetl and Iztaccihuatl, the mountain we call the Sleeping Woman. The Chalca lords welcomed them not as strangers, but as brothers. They brought the captain gold, cotton mantles, and 40 slave women for his men to bed, and although they were vassals of Mexico, they warned him that Moctezuma could not be trusted.

Moctezuma sent his half-brother, Tzihuacpopoca, to Amecameca to reassure the captain that he would be welcome when he reached Tenochtitlán. Tzihuacpopoca bore a striking resemblance to the emperor himself, and word spread quickly that Moctezuma himself had come to greet the Christians. The Mexicans did nothing to discourage the rumor, hoping to learn more of the captain's intentions.

The Mexican prince knelt and laid gold and jewels at the captain's feet, but when he rose to speak, the captain stopped him. He spoke to his interpreter, and the woman turned to Tzihuacpopoca and said, "This captain wishes to know if you are indeed the lord Moctezuma." Before the Mexican could reply, however, a Tlaxcalan noble stepped forward and said, "No, lord, this one is not he, for I know Moctezuma well. I know this noble also, and he is a chieftain called Tzihuacpopoca."

The captain heard no more. He dismissed the Mexican and retired to his quarters.

Moctezuma next sent his sorcerers to stop the Christians. He chose the greatest necromancers in the land; wizards who were known to cast spells of profound sleep upon their victims, warlocks who could turn themselves into carnivorous beasts, and conjurers who caused poisonous snakes and scorpions to rain from the heavens.

As the sorcerers approached Amecameca, they met a man walking toward them. By his dress, he appeared to be a native of Chalco. Save for eight strands of feathergrass that girdled his chest, he was bare above the waist. He appeared to be drunk, but as he drew closer, they saw that he was neither drunk nor witless; instead, he seemed to be infuriated with them.

The stranger stopped and began to laugh in a voice bitter with irony. "Why have you come again?" he said. "What does Moctezuma hope to accomplish against the Christians by your futile efforts? Has his fears finally driven him to this?

"Only now has he reflected upon changing his ways, but the time is long past for him. He has misjudged-he cannot be absolved from the sins of his past. He has destroyed many people, he has killed without reason, and he has committed every possible offense against mankind. He has ruled not as a righteous lord, but as a cruel tyrant, and his fate has been decided. His kingdoms, his possessions, and his glory will soon be things of the past because of the injustices he has inflicted upon mankind.

His words terrified the sorcerers. They threw themselves on the ground before him and begged him to take them with him. They dug up the earth and made an altar before him, they made a seat for him with foliage and grass, and they offered up a sacrifice to him. But the stranger laughed at them, and as he laughed, he grew even more furious.

"Why have you come here, false ones!" he shouted. "You can do nothing!" Now leave me, for I can no longer protect your people. Turn around and look back upon Tenochtitlán, and behold what is to become of your city before many days have passed."

The sorcerers looked back, and they saw the city in flames. As they watched, they saw a great fire consuming temples, schools, and the houses of nobles and commoner alike. This, the stranger said, was to be the fruit of their war with the Sons of the Sun. The sorcerers stood transfixed by the sight, and their throats grew dry with fear.

The vision faded, and they turned to the stranger, but he had vanished. They knew now that he was not a mortal, but the god Tezcatlipoca himself who had spoken to them. They turned back to Tenochtitlán to warn Moctezuma of the danger that threatened him and his kingdom.

Moctezuma listened in silence as the sorcerers told him of their encounter with Tezcatlipoca, and when they finished, he lowered his head. At length he looked up at the sorcerers and said, "We can do nothing about the inevitable. The gods who once protected us have abandoned us, and now they stand against us." He drew a deep breath and rose slowly. "Now we are lost," he said. "We have eaten death. But come what may, we are men, and the glory that is Mexico must not perish with us."

---

[i] Francis A. MacNutt, *The Letters of Cortez*, cites the known dates of Popocatepetl's eruptions, and gives the years 1519-1528 as a period of near-continuous activity. In the post-conquest years, the Spaniards mined sulfur from the crater for gunpowder.

15. Hernando Cortés:

The Emperor Speaks

For the moment, Cholula was secure. We had little reason to fear an immediate attack from any quarter, and Montezuma's permission to visit Tenochtitlán led me to believe that his warriors would not trouble us. Nevertheless, I felt it imperative to keep the army at full alert. We had not yet accounted for the Mexican squadrons said to be in the area, and worse, bad news arrived from Vera Cruz. Juan de Escalante, the company commander, had been forced to lead a punitive expedition against Nautla, a fortified Mexican town on the north coast. Escalante routed the Indians and fired the town, but a Spaniard was missing and a horse had been lost. The fate of the Spaniard was not known, but dead or alive, he was in the hands of the Indians, and their perception of our invulnerability was now damaged. The loss of the horse would be felt even more than the loss of the man should there be trouble at Vera Cruz.

We had been in Cholula 14 days now, and we could delay our journey to Tenochtitlán no longer lest Montezuma have a change of heart and withdraw his invitation. I inquired of our Mexican ambassadors the best route to take to Tenochtitlán, and they drew a map on a paper that they make from the agave plant. The route they drew would take us on a southwesterly course around the base of a volcano, then north until we reached Tenochtitlán. Since the route they proposed did not seem much different from the one reported by Vázquez de Tapia and Alvarado as being hazardous, I sent a party to reconnoiter the terrain.

While I waited for our scouts to return, I sent a second party to explore the great mountain the Indians call Popocatepetl. This towering peak seemed a paradox. Its crest was snow-covered even in mid-summer, but from a vent near the summit, turbulent clouds of black smoke boiled into the sky with an updraft so powerful that even the strongest winds could not shift them from their course. His Majesty, I knew, would be delighted to read about this remarkable volcano we had discovered in his new realm.

Diego Ordaz led ten men along a road that his native guides said would take him to a pass between Popocatepetl and another snow-capped peak four leagues to the north.[i] When they reached the pass, they saw a vast lake with cities and towns in the valley below, and far out in the lake, a city larger and more splendid than the others, a city with towers that seemed to rise out of the lake. The city, their guides told them, was Tenochtitlán, and if they continued along the road that crossed the pass, they would reach it in a day's journey.

Ordaz's attempt to climb Popocatepetl was less gratifying than his first sight of Tenochtitlán. Heavy snow and the intense cold of the upper reaches made the climb difficult and exhausting, and clouds of ashes blown about them by the unceasing winds blinded them. Nevertheless, they might have reached the summit if the volcano had not chosen that moment to erupt. A column of fire burst from the vent, and the ground shook so violently that they scrambled to descend before they were buried under a blanket of ashes.

Meanwhile, the scouts I had sent to reconnoiter the route proposed by the Mexican ambassadors returned, and their report was not encouraging. The army would have to cross any number of bridges that spanned deep ravines, and we would have to pass through narrow defiles, ideal places for the enemy to lie in ambush.

When Ordaz returned with word that he had found a good road that led directly to Tenochtitlán, I summoned the ambassadors and asked them why they had chosen the more difficult route. They were aware, they said, of the road that led to the pass, but it passed through Huexotzingo, a province that was now at war with Mexico. The route they had recommended posed less danger, they felt, than an attack by

Huexotingo warriors. If I chose the mountain road, however, they would so advise Montezuma, and he would send a party to meet us on the other side of the pass. I accepted their explanation, keeping in mind, however, that Ordaz had noted heavy barricades blocking the road.

We traveled no more than four leagues the day we left Cholula, and we spent the night in a Huexotzingo village called Yscalpan. The Indians afforded us a warm welcome, and although they were as poor as the Tlaxcalans, they gave us a few gold artifacts and some female slaves.

At first light we began the climb that led to the pass. The grade became very steep when we were still two leagues from the top, and the arduous march and the bitter cold were wearying to our very bones. Had the Mexicans chosen to defend the pass, we could not have survived.

When we reached the pass, I caught sight of Tenochtitlán for the first time. It was as much and more than I had hoped for. Even from this distance, I could make out the towers that seemed to float above the mirrored surface of the lake, and the long, slender causeways that moored the city to the shore. The cities and towns along the lakeshore were as large and larger than any we had seen before, and they bore witness to the immense population of the Valley of Mexico.

Yet the splendor of the sight below us did not please all— there were many who trembled at the thought of descending into this densely populated valley. It would do no good to tempt God any further, they argued, for there were more than a thousand Indians for every man in the company, and if they took up arms against us, we were lost. With the help of those who knew that their fortune lay before us, those who saw the promise of our enterprise fulfilled, however, we began our descent into the valley.

We had not gone far when heavy barricades set across the trail brought us to a halt. The Indians had felled the great pines that grow in the sierra, and they had stacked them so closely that neither horse nor foot could pass. But with the help of our allies, who sought out footpaths wide enough for our baggage to pass, we moved safely beyond the barriers.

Late that afternoon we came upon a cave so deep that any number of warriors could have hidden inside, waiting to pounce on us. We halted and made camp, and as night descended, we could hear Indians all about us, shouting threats and insults at us from the forest.

The watch was guarded and uneasy that night, and I nearly lost my life while making my rounds. In the darkness, I came upon Martín López so suddenly that I scarcely had time to shout "Hallo the watch!" before catching a bolt in my chest. López could make out no more than a shadow in the moonless night, and his finger was on the trigger of his crossbow when I shouted. He was angry and upset with me, and he warned me to keep farther back from the perimeter and challenge the sentries promptly lest I meet with an accident that all would regret. I returned to my tent shaken, but I was comforted in knowing that the watch was vigilant and wide-awake.

The next morning we reached an open plain where we found a lodgehouse that was used by traders. The lodge was large enough to accommodate the entire company, and the Tlaxcalans set about erecting their huts of branches and leaves in a nearby clearing. That night we ate a good supper, and the Tlaxcalans gathered enough firewood to ward off the cold that crept down from the snow-covered peaks towering above us. Only Montezuma's ambassadors, who were obliged to sleep with the porters, suffered the bitter chill of night.

The following day we reached Amecameca, a large Chalco town. During our stay there, Indians from Chalco Atenco, Chimalhuacan, Ayotzingo, and a number of other Chalco towns came to pay their respects to me.

Like Cempoala, Chalco was a vassal state of Mexico, and as the fat Totonac chieftain had done, the lords of Chalco spent many hours complaining about the tyranny of Montezuma and the hardships they had suffered at his hands. Unlike Cempoala, however, Chalco lies on the very threshold of Montezuma's empire, and I could ill-afford to provoke the Emperor now. I sympathized with the Chalco lords and asked them to consider me a friend, but to bear with me until I could help them gain their independence from Mexico.

As we prepared to leave Amecameca, a large party of Mexicans approached, and word reached my ears that Montezuma himself had come to greet me. When their leader came before me, however, I learned that he was only a brother who closely resembled the Emperor. He offered me a liberal quantity of gold and some fine cotton mantles, then, as I had anticipated, he withdrew Montezuma's invitation to Tenochtitlán. By now I had lost patience with this nonsense, and repeated what I had said to his ambassadors: my emperor had given me no choice but to visit Montezuma. I gave him a few articles from Spain and dismissed him.

Montezuma's brother departed, but he left several nobles, majordomos, and porters to see to all our needs. There had been some hostile activity in the woods surrounding our camp, and I felt it necessary to warn them that it would be wise if they kept well away from us at night, since our sentries were under strict orders to kill anyone they failed to recognize. In spite of my warning, however, a number of Indians attempted to cross our lines that night, and they suffered the consequences. The next morning Montezuma's nobles strode by their bodies without so much as a glance.

We resumed our march to Ayotzingo, a port city built half upon the lake and half upon the shore. As we entered the city, we found the streets heavy with human excrement, which we took as a sign that several squadrons of warriors had passed through earlier in the day. We spent the night here, although I did not care much for our position between the lake and the hills behind us. My misgivings were realized not long after dark. War canoes closed in upon us from the lake, and a party of warriors approached from the hills. A brief skirmish followed, and the Indians soon retreated, leaving some 20 dead behind them.

As we prepared to depart the next morning, a large party of Indians approached us from the west. From the display of green featherwork and silver ornaments that graced a litter at the head of the procession, it seemed that we were about to receive a royal visitor.

Eight nobles set the litter down before my tent, and more than a dozen porters swept a path clear of every stone and sliver of straw between the litter and the tent. The curtains parted, and a youth of some 25 years stepped out and knelt before me.

By his dress, I knew that he was a great lord, and from my interpreters, I learned that he was Cacama, the lord of Texcoco and the most favored of Montezuma's nephews.

I thanked Cacama for coming so far to greet us, and I told him how pleased I was that I would soon be able to deliver the message of my emperor to Montezuma.

He rose, however, and surprised me with an outburst that stunned even the lords with him. He spoke so passionately of the difficulties we would face if I persisted in coming to Tenochtitlán that I believed he was prepared to defend the road before us. I calmed the young lord as best I could, and I promised him that our coming would bring no harm to his Emperor and his people. My words seemed to put him at ease, and after I gave him a few gifts, he summoned his nobles and left.

We departed Ayotzingo shortly after Cacama left, and followed the shore of the lake that they call Chalco. The shore is heavily populated, and before long the road and the surrounding area were so congested with Indians that I called a halt. I sent the Tlaxcalans ahead to keep them from the road, and I instructed them to warn the crowd that we would kill any who refused to stand clear of the army. A league further down the road we came upon Mixquic, a city of some 2,000 inhabitants that was built entirely on the lake. Beyond Mixquic, we turned north on a causeway that divides the lake of Chalco from the Lake of Xochimilco. Lake Chalco lies somewhat higher than Lake Xochimilco, and the causeway, about the width of a lance, serves as a levee to divide the waters.

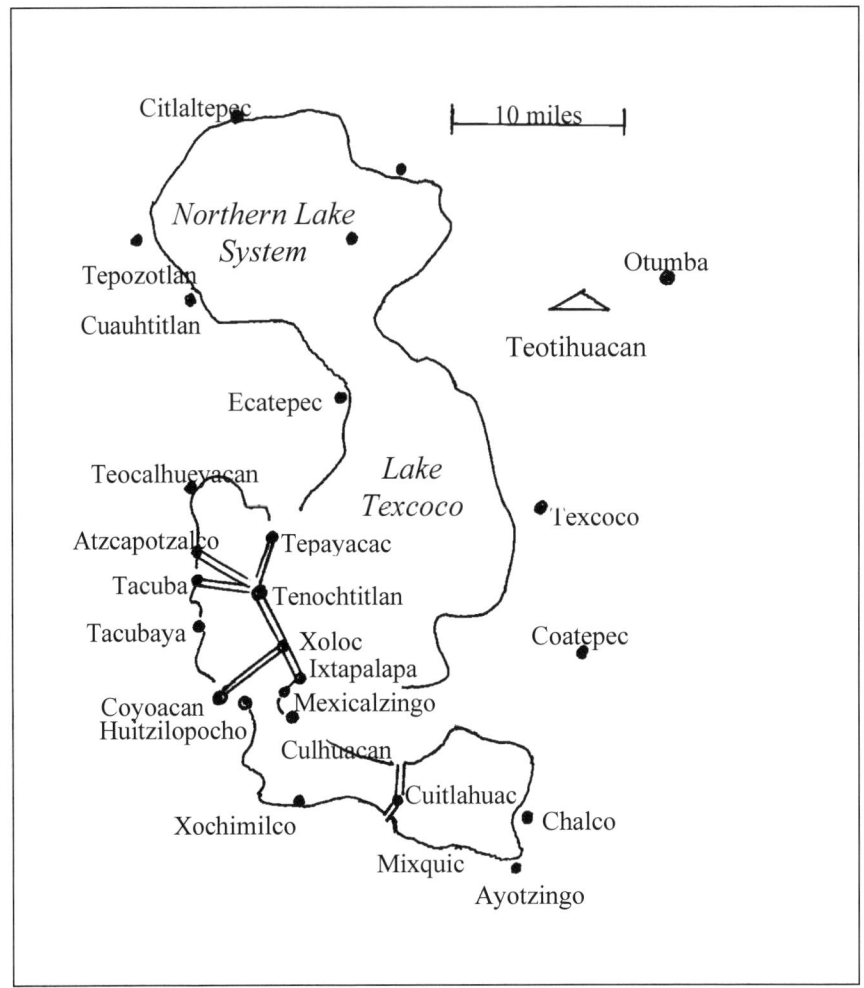

Citlaltepec

10 miles

Northern Lake System

Otumba

Tepozotlan

Cuauhtitlan

Teotihuacan

Ecatepec

Lake Texcoco

Teocalhueyacan

Texcoco

Atzcapotzalco Tepayacac

Tacuba

Tenochtitlan

Tacubaya Xoloc

Ixtapalapa

Coatepec

Coyoacan Mexicalzingo
Huitzilopocho

Culhuacan

Cuitlahuac Chalco

Xochimilco

Mixquic

Ayotzingo

Northern and Southern Lake Systems in the Valley of Mexico

Midway across the causeway we entered Cuitláhuac, a city whose houses and temples appeared to ride upon the waters. Although the day was hot, the city was pleasingly cool due to a steady breeze that sweeps across the lake during the day. This delightful city pleased us so much that we named it New Venice.

We found the lord of the city to be friendly and hospitable, and after providing a pleasant meal for us, he urged us to spend the night. Montezuma's ambassadors however, insisted that we move on to

184

Ixtapalapa, where the emperor's brother, also called Cuitláhuac, would be our host for the night.

Cuitláhuac proved to be a gracious host, and upon our arrival, he gave us gold artifacts, finely worked cotton mantles, and a number of female slaves.

Cuitláhuac's estate was by far the finest we had seen in Mexico. The large, open-aired palace was constructed of cut stone, cedar, and other sweet-smelling woods. Spacious rooms, with finely embroidered drapes that hung from ceiling to floor, looked out in every direction upon gardens and orchards. Along the promenades, roses and other exotic flowers, imported from every corner of the land, blossomed upon lattices, and walkways from every room of the palace led to hidden pools where members of the royal house bathed every day.

A canal connects the great lake with a small lagoon, 400 paces in length, where canoes can enter the palace grounds. All the waterfowl of the lake; herons, wild duck, and cranes, nest along the shore to feed upon the fish that spawn there.

We left Ixtapalapa at mid-morning the following day, and after marching no more that half a league, we reached the causeway that joins Tenochtitlán to the mainland. This broad thoroughfare stretches across Lake Texcoco like an unbroken ribbon, two leagues in length, before it vanishes into the heart of the city. The causeway is so wide that horsemen can ride eight abreast all the way from Ixtpalapa to Tenochtitlán.

As we marched along the causeway, we passed between Mexicalzingo and Huitzilopochco, two cities with some 10,000 houses that thrive on the salt trade. All about us we saw Indians skimming it from the briny marshlands along the shore and casting it into light brown loaves.

As we proceeded, we crossed a number of bridges that spanned openings in the causeway that allow lake traffic pass from Lake Texcoco to the lagoon on the other side. The bridges were no more than wooden beams, which could easily be removed if the city was threatened. The sight of several thousand canoes moving up and down the causeway left little doubt in our minds of our vulnerability should we be forced to retreat.

A league up the causeway we came to a halt before a fortress that stands at the junction of the Coyoacán causeway. Twin towers looked down upon walls 12 feet high, with but two narrow gates through which all traffic must pass. Which, I wondered, of their enemies did the Mexicans fear so much that they had to build this citadel. It took us the better part of an hour to pass through the gates, since nearly a thousand nobles were there to greet us. Each was obliged to place his hand on the ground and kiss it in the Mexican tradition of welcome before we could move on.

Beyond the last bridge, a broad avenue, nearly a league in length, led into the city. I called a halt, because 200 nobles, wearing robes of the royal court were coming toward us in single file, keeping close to the houses on both sides of the avenue. Each carried a brightly colored gourd filled with flowers, and as they approached, they kept their eyes fixed upon the ground. All were barefoot.

Behind them were three nobles with golden scepters, leading a litter shaded from the sun by a canopy of green feathers. Gold and silver pendants swayed gently from the canopy with every step of the bearers, and Cacama and Cuitláhuac walked on either side, unshod like the others. The bearers set the litter down 30 paces in front of us, and Montezuma stepped out. Cacama and Cuitláhuac took him by the arms and led him toward me as servants laid mantles on the ground before him.

Montezuma was about 40 years old, in the prime of his life. He was tall for an Indian, and although he was slender, he was well proportioned. His skin was somewhat faired than most Indians, and his hair was short, no longer than necessary to cover his ears. A scanty beard, which he kept trimmed, accentuated his long face.[ii] He wore a light blue robe clasped about his shoulders with a seashell the color of a fine emerald, and his golden sandals were inlaid with jewels. His turquoise diadem was worth a king's ransom.

I dismounted and walked toward him, but when I reached out to embrace him, Cuitláhuac stepped in front of me. I stepped back and bowed to Montezuma, and he in turn bowed to me. Then he placed his hand upon the ground and brought it to his lips in a gesture of welcome. He spoke to Cuitláhuac, and his brother came forward and took me by the arm. He led me up the avenue, staying a few steps behind Montezuma and Cacama. None of the Spaniards were permitted to follow us.

We halted in an open area, and one by one, the lords on either side of the avenue came forward to greet me. After each paid his respects, he turned and walked back to the city, keeping to the houses along the way.

When we stood alone, I took a necklace of pearls and glass diamonds from my corselet and held it before Montezuma. He hesitated for a moment, then bowed slightly, indicating that I might approach and place it about his neck. At his signal, a majordomo handed him a small packet, and he took out a pair of collars made of translucent shells with eight golden shrimps as large as a man's hand hanging from each. He placed both collars around my neck, then made a sign that I was to follow him into the city.

With the army close behind, he led me to a large palace with many rooms. As we crossed the threshold, he took me by the hand and led me into the courtyard, where he spoke to me for the first time.

"Now you are in your house," he said, "eat, drink, and rest from your journey, and when you are ready, I shall return."

The sun had nearly set when Montezuma, accompanied by a few nobles and majordomos, returned. I met him at the palace gates with my commanders, and we followed him to the reception chamber, where he motioned us to be seated. The majordomos laid out an assortment of gold and silver artifacts, some beautiful feather work, and many richly decorated mantles before us. When they had presented the last gift and we had offered our proper thanks, he dismissed the majordomos and motioned us to gather around him.

"Valiant captain, noble gentlemen," he said, "I am pleased to welcome you to my kingdom and my home, where you will be accorded the respect that is rightfully yours. If I troubled you in the past with my demands that you turn back from your journey to Tenochtitlán, rest assured that it was only because my people are afraid of you. We have been told that a single Christian is more than a match for a thousand of our warriors; we have heard that you can shake the earth by bringing down thunder and lightning from the heavens; and we have seen you kill men without their knowing how they met with death. It is also said that you can cut a man in half with a single blow from your swords, and that you kill men for no other reason that they displease you. But as much as we feared you, we feared even more the great beasts that carry you on their backs.

"We have also heard that you are overfond of another's realm, and that you are determined to rule all who live in our land. We have been told that you have an unquenchable thirst for gold and silver, and that there is no limit to the violence you would commit to obtain it. We have also heard that you eat as much and more than ten of our people, and we wondered how the land could provide for your needs as well as ours. These tales frightened us, and we were determined to do everything in our power to keep you away from Tenochtitlán.

"My nobles, who have been your constant companions since you made war on the Tlaxcalans, however, have had many opportunities to observe your behavior, and they report that although you have great powers, you are mortals, no different from us. They tell me that you are men of good character, that you are loyal to your friends, and that you do no harm without good reason. They say that you make war only when you must to defend yourselves, and that you are ever willing to protect those who approach you in a civil manner, as good servants should. Just as the Tlaxcalans once misjudged you, I too was convinced that you were wicked and heartless. But now I know better: now I know your true nature, and knowing this, I offer you not only my friendship, but also the same affection that I hold for my closest relatives.

"My father, who heard it from his father, told me that our ancestors were not natives of this land but immigrants who were brought here by a great lord. It was a time when the Otomies ruled the land, and they were very powerful. The Otomies allowed our people to settle here, but they drove the lord away, and he returned to his native land. Many years later he returned to take his people home, but by now they had married and begotten children, and a lord of their choosing ruled in his place. Once again the lord was forced to leave, but as he departed, he warned the people that one day his sons would return, and they would enforce the laws and the religion of their forbears. If they should refuse to accept his sons, however, they would find themselves ruled by force of arms. This prophecy has been passed down from one generation to the next, and we, like our ancestors, have awaited the day when his sons would return from a land to the east and rule over us in peace.

"Now you have come to us from beyond the great sea, from the direction of the rising sun, and you tell us that you have been sent by a lord from a faraway land who knows of me and my people. You may well be those the prophecy has spoken of, but if this is not so, if what has been foretold has not yet come to pass, you will still be honored guests in my court. Therefore, honored captain, if there is no deceit on your part; if there is no artfulness in your dealings; your wishes will be our command, and we will share all that we possess with you.

"There are many who say that I am a god. Others say that I can turn myself into a lion, a jaguar, or a serpent, but this is not true. I am a mortal, just like all men. I hold myself, however, to be above ordinary men, to be more than any man in my realm, but only because the gods have granted me a high station in this life. Here, touch my arms! Touch my body! See for yourself that I am no more than flesh and bone." He held out his hand and offered it to me.

"The Cempoalans, the Tlaxcalans, and the Huexotzinca say that the roofs and walls of my houses and all my utensils are made of gold. As you can see, my houses are made of timber and adobe, and my palaces are made of cut stone. It is true, however, that I possess great wealth. I inherited silver, gold, precious jewels, and priceless artifacts that have been passed down from one generation to the next, for that is the custom of kings and princes. I have protected them and kept them safe in anticipation of your coming, and they are yours for you and your companions to enjoy."

Montezuma paused, and suddenly his eyes were moist. "You must rest now," he said, "for I know that you are very tired."[iii]

I sensed that Montezuma's reception was more politic than sincere. He had chosen a somewhat permissive attitude, possibly based upon fear and uncertainty about the future than his fondness for our company, but his belief in the prophecy of his ancestors offered us an opportunity not to be overlooked.

"Great prince," I replied, "I came here for no purpose other than to greet you in the name of the Emperor of the Christians, and to bring you his message. Although his kingdom is far removed from here, he would have you know that he looks upon you as his friend, and he will place everything within his power at your disposal.

Conversation between Cortés and Moctezuma

Behind Cortés is La Malinche, his Indian interpreter

"He has ordered me to tell you of the sciences that were left to us by our ancestors and to bring you the knowledge that will guide you in the administration of your kingdom. These teachings contain the laws by which man must live by if he is to lead a life of virtue and godliness, and the fundamental truths that have been ordained for his immortal soul. The soul of man, as you will learn, leaves his body when he dies, and at that time he must give God a true and exact account of the good and evil he has done on earth. Our God is the true judge of mankind, he who gives everlasting life to those who have lived the good life and condemns those who have followed the evil ways of the devil to endless torment.

" My lord's greatest concern is about the false gods you worship, and he realizes that this is not your fault but that of the devil, who has led you into the path of unspeakable sin. He wishes you to know that his greatest desire is to lead you along the path of truth, to bring you the faith that will permit you to renounce this demon and save your immortal soul from eternal damnation.

"Be assured that the great lord for whom you have waited these many generations is indeed the Emperor of the Christians, the lord of the world and the rightful heir to your house, and he has decreed that you must not die in the shadow of the devil's deadly sins. Therefore receive us as one of your own; love us, care for us, for we come only to serve you, only to point out the way of righteousness and to bring you peace and contentment in God's light.

"As for the treasure that you have offered my lord, I kiss your hands for your generosity and good will. In time, you will understand that our serving you and your people is far more important than all the worldly goods of Mexico."

I could not be sure just how much Montezuma understood when the interpreters finished, but he smiled and shook my hand. He asked me if all the Christians were my vassals, or if some were only slaves. I told him that each man was my brother and my companion, although some held a higher station in life than the others.

He departed, but he left a majordomo behind to speak with the interpreters. The following day, palace servants arrived with gifts for the common soldiers and gifts worthy of a prince for the commanders.

---

[i] Ixtaccihuatl, "The Sleeping Woman." The altitude of the volcano is 17,343 feet. The top of the mountain was blown off in some prehistoric eruption, and the dimensions of the crater indicates that it was higher than Popcatepetl at one time.

[ii] The physical description of Moctezuma is given by Bernal Díaz

[iii] Moctezuma's welcoming speech to Cortes is highly controversial. Some historians contend that the conversation was an invention of Cortés to establish a legal basis for establishing Spanish sovereignty over Mexico. Others. based upon the writings of eyewitnesses, hold that there is no reason to doubt Cortés, though he may have taken considerable latitude in expanding and dramatizing the meeting.

It is important to note, however, that by now Cortes was well aware of Moctezuma's fear of Quetzalcoatl, and he used it to his advantage.

The conversation, however, contains elements that are consistent with Moctezuma's beliefs. As Octavio Paz points out, the Mexicans, due to their historiacal isolation, held the world view of a universe ruled by gods, but not of another civilization and its inhabitants. Moctezuma is thus left with only two possibilities for the origin of the Spaniards: they must either be gods or descendants of some legendary hero of the past.

It is interesting to note that 16th century faced the same dilemma to account for the origin of the Indians. Christian dogma ordained that all humanity was descended from Adam and Eve, and that only Noah and his family survived the flood. Thus if it could not be established that the Indians were Noah's descendants, they were not human. In the Papal Bull of Paul III in 1537, however, the church declared them to be human, and another explanation had to be found for their existence.

Theologians argued that they were most probably descended from the Ten Lost Tribes of Israel, while secular intellectuals postulated that they came from the lost world of Atlantis, or that they migrated across the ocean from Scandinavia, Central Asia, China, Korea, or India. The only writer of the 16th century to suggest an overland migration was Fray Jose de Acosta.

Cortes's response to Moctezuma, on the other hand, is entirely in character, since he gave the same sermon time and time again during the course of the conquest. Although Moctezuma never mentions Quetzalcoatl to Cortes, the name may have been lost in translation. Variations of the Quetzalcoatl saga could be used to support Moctezuma's story, but it is far beyond the scope of this work to pursue the complexities of the myths and legends of the Feathered Serpent. Suffice to say, the name Quetzalcoatl may have been used by one or more individuals at different times, by priests fostering the cult, or it may have been a title of office for the priesthood.

16. Bernal Díaz del Castillo:

Six Days in November

Four days had passed since our triumphant march into Tenochtitlán, but neither the captain nor any other member of the company left our quarters save to relieve themselves in the outbuildings or walk about the palace grounds. Cortés, knowing that we needed release from the monotony of our confinement, decided that a trip to the temple of Huichilobos,[i] the god of Mexico, would do wonders for our spirits without inviting any undue risk. He sent Jeronimo de Aguilar, Doña Marina, and his young page Ortegulla, who had learned something of the language, to seek Montezuma's permission. The emperor readily agreed to the outing, but fearing that we might affront his idols, insisted that we delay our departure until he could receive us in the great plaza of Tlatelolco.

We did not have to wait long for an escort, and the company, fully armed and accompanied by horsemen, followed them up the broad avenue leading to Tlatelolco. They led us through the plaza and into the marketplace, where Indians from every corner of the land had come to sell their goods. As we walked about, we saw that the crowd was kept in good order by magistrates, constables, and supervisors, who regulated all commerce.

We marveled at the number and variety of wares sold here, for they far surpassed those offered at the weekly fairs in Medino del

Campo, my home in Castile, and their goods were displayed in the same systematic manner used by the Spaniards.

Along one avenue we saw dealers who sold feathers, mantles, precious stones, and artifacts made of gold and silver. Others sold gold nuggets from mines and streams in the sierra, which they packed inside of transparent goose feather quills. These quills were the master currency of the realm, against which the value of every commodity was weighed. Accounts were calculated by the length and thickness of each quill; what it was worth in terms of mantles, slaves, cacao beans, and whatever else they barter and sell in Mexico.

In another quarter of the market, merchants sold ropes, sandals, robes, and other items woven from henequen, a material more coarse than cotton. Here hunters sold pelts of tigers, mountain cats, and jackals, furs of the beaver and the otter, and deer hides, some tanned and others raw.

In the food markets we saw heaps of beans, sage, herbs, fresh vegetables, fruit, and cacao. Butchers sold chickens, turkey, rabbit, deer, and small dogs, some alive and others dressed and ready for the table. In another section women sold jars of honey, molasses, and prepared foods, such as corn paste soaked in honey and sugar. They also sold cooked tripe, and a delicacy made from a flour paste that tasted like honey nut. Fisherwomen sold cakes they make from an ooze that they skim from the surface of the great lake, which, when curdled, tastes like cheese.

In another quarter they sold earthenware of every size and variety; from large jars to small jugs, cups made from gourds, and pitchers carved from wood. Everything was painted with bright colors.

Beneath the gates of the marketplace, merchants sold flint knives, copper hatchets, cradles, benches, lumber, and pitch pine for their torches. Here we also found paper, which they call *amal*, and reeds scented with the sap of the sweet gum tree, which they filled with tobacco, salt, and grain. They also have a slave market, where men and women with wooden yokes about their necks are sold, and this market is as large as the markets where the Portuguese sell slaves from Guinea.

I am well aware that many Spaniards will laugh at me for this, but they also sell human excrement from canoes tied in the marshes, for they claim they cannot make salt nor cure hides as well without it.

Moreover, they build latrines screened with cane and straw along the streets, where those who have a mind to evacuate their bowels cannot be seen, and in this way the filth is not lost for the trade.

One could not see all the merchandise sold in that marketplace in two days. Soldiers who had been to Constantinople, Rome, and other parts of the world swore that they had never seen a marketplace as big as this, nor one so well administered.

From the marketplace, Montezuma's nobles led us through the gates leading to the great *cue*,[ii] and the courtyards about it were as great as those in the plaza of Salamanca. The inner courtyard, where the great *cue* towered above the city, was paved with white flagstones, and in places where the courtyard was not paved, the bedrock was plastered and highly polished. Nor could a single bit of straw or a speck of dust be seen anywhere.

We moved to the foot of the *cue*, but before we reached the first step, six priests were waiting to assist us up the 114 steps leading to the summit. When the priests reached out to take Cortés's arm, however, he stepped back and motioned them away.

The summit contained a sacrificial altar made of large stones, a massive stone serpent, and several evil-looking idols. Fresh blood covered everything in sight.

Montezuma emerged from the *adoratorio* of his accursed idols and asked Cortés if the climb had tired him. Cortés replied that nothing ever tired him or his men. Montezuma took Cortés by the hand and led him to the edge of the *cue*, where they could look out over his city and all the other cities that lay along the shore of the lake. He pointed below, and he told Cortés that if he had not seen as much of the marketplace as he would have liked, he could see it all from up here.

That great and evil temple was so high that it dominated the city and its surroundings as far as the eye could see. To the south, we could see the Ixtapalapa causeway by which we had entered the city. To the west, we saw the causeway that leads to Tacuba [iii] and the aqueduct that brings fresh water to the city from Chapultepec, and to the north, we could see the causeway that crosses the lake to Tepeyacac. At intervals along the causeways we could make out bridges where the lake waters passed from one side to the other. To the west was the great lake of Texcoco, where hundreds of canoes were converging upon the city, bringing provisions, merchandise, and other goods.

Directly below us a network of canals gave canoes access to every part of the city, and where the canals intersected the streets, wooden bridges allowed traffic to cross from one side to the other. The city itself, with every house freshly whitewashed and every *cue* and palace faced with gypsum, was a wonderland in white.[iv]

The captain, as I remember him doing so often, turned to Fray Bartolome de Olmedo and said, "Senor Padre, this might be an opportune time to ask Montezuma for permission to set up our church here on the *cue*. The padre replied that the idea was certainly worthwhile, but he believed that it was not Montezuma's nature to yield to another god, and in any event, this was not the time to press the issue.

Cortés ignored him and turned to Montezuma. "Your Majesty," he said," you have favored us by showing us your city, but since we are here on your temple, may I ask you to show us your gods?"

Montezuma summoned the priests to his side, and after a brief consultation, he led us into a large chamber with an ornately carved wooden ceiling.

Inside the shrine were two altars, and upon each sat a massive figure. Both were monstrous giants with grotesquely fat bodies. The idol on the right side of the shrine was Huichilobos, the god of war. The face was broad and the eyes fiendish. The body was inlaid with jewels and gold, and seed pearls were cemented into the idol from head to foot with a paste they make from roots. Huge serpents coiled about its waist, and precious stones imbedded into the coils reflected the dim light of the chamber. About its neck hung necklaces of blue stone, with figurines of human faces fashioned in gold and hearts of silver set among the stones. In one hand the idol held a bow, and in the other an arrow. By the side of Huichilobos, a small idol held a lance and a shield decorated with gold and jewels. This, they said, was the god's page.

The blackened hearts of three Indians sacrificed that day lay smoldering in braziers before the altar. The floor was bathed in blood and encrusted layers of blood, one on top of the other, blackened the walls of the shrine. The stench was overwhelming.

The idol on the opposite side of the shrine was as large as Huichilobos, and its body, like that of Huichilobos, was inlaid with precious stones. This idol had the face of a bear, and its mirrored eyes seemed to glow with a light from some inner source. The waist was girdled with figures that resembled tiny devils with tails like serpents. This was Tezcatepuca,[v] the god of the infernal regions, who was charged with the souls of Mexicans, and he was said to be the brother of Huichilobos. That day they had offered the idol the hearts of five Indians, and the stench that rose from the floor, still slippery with fresh blood, was more sickening than that of any slaughterhouse in Castile.

Another idol, half man and half alligator, stared out of a recess in the uppermost part of the *cue*. The recess was inlaid with ornately carved woodwork, and the body of the creature was inlaid with jewels. The human half was covered with a mantle. They say that the body of the idol is filled with every variety of seed in the world, and that it is the god of the fields and orchards, but I do not remember its name.

Leaving the shrine, we examined a large drum mounted on a platform near the edge of the *cue*. The drumhead was made of snakeskin, and when they beat this instrument of hell, its hollow throbbing could be heard for a distance of more than two leagues.

We saw other things on top of that great *cue*; diabolical things like conch horns, trumpets, large knives, and the burnt remains of numerous hearts they used to cense their idols. I cursed them for the dried blood that covered everything in sight, and I could not wait to leave the stink of this slaughterhouse and the abominable sight before us.

The captain, half in jest, turned to Montezuma and said, "Lord, how a man as enlightened as Your Majesty cannot see that your idols are not gods but evil monsters truly confounds me. Allow me to place a cross on the top of this temple, and give us a separate area in the shrine of Huichilobos and Tezcatepuca where we can place an image of Our Lady. When She is here, you and your priests will soon see how these idols will come to fear Her."

The priests glared at Cortés, and Montezuma said, "Lord Malinche,[vi] had I known that you would insult my gods, I would never have shown them to you. We hold them in great esteem,

197

because they grant us health, they nourish the land, they bring the rains and the seasons, and they bestow victory in battle upon us. For these gifts, we worship them and sacrifice that which they demand of us. Please say no more to dishonor them."

Cortés did not pursue the subject any further. Instead, he smiled and said, "I think it is time we left, so that you may return to your rituals."

Montezuma replied that it was well we leave: he must return to the gods and offer sacrifices for allowing this profanity to occur.

We descended the 114 steps slowly, since those soldiers who were afflicted with abscesses and humors on their legs were sorely pained from the steep descent.

Let me now speak of the temple and its surroundings. Any who has seen these *cues* on the coat of arms of a conquistador, such as mine, can picture the shape of it far better than I. The base of the temple covers an area of six large city lots, as they are measured in this land. From this broad base to the summit, where the cue narrows to the small platform that contains the idols, there are five hollows, one spaced directly above the other on the centerline of the temple. These hollows resemble barbicans,[vii] save that they are open and have no screens.

According to the Indians, when the foundations of the *cue* were laid, the blood of countless prisoners was poured into them. Then, before the mortar set, the residents of the city cast all their jewels, gold, and silver into them, and the priests sowed the seeds of every plant in the land into them. This was done, they said, so that the gods would grant them victory in warfare, riches, and bountiful harvests.

The inquisitive reader will, of course, want to know if we found any basis to this native folklore, now nearly a thousand years old. After the fall of Mexico, we resolved to build the church of our patron and guide, Santiago, and the site chosen encroached upon that of the *cue*. Before the foundations of the church could be laid, we had to dig out the old foundations of the *cue*, and among the debris we found a considerable amount of gold, silver, turquoise jewelry, and many pearls. An inquiry was conducted among the chieftains and nobles, including Guatemuz,[viii] who was alive at that time, and all confirmed that the ancient Mexicans had thrown their valuables into the foundations of the temple. Upon further investigation, our priests found this custom recorded in their books and paintings.

Some time later, a Spaniard who was granted a building site in the same area discovered a number of valuable artifacts. His Majesty's treasury officials ordered him to surrender them to the royal treasury, since by law, they rightfully belonged to the King, and a lawsuit took place. I do not recall the outcome, but in the end, the treasure paid for the construction of the Holy Church of Santiago.

Returning to our tour of the city, we stopped to examine a small temple not far from the *cue*. This was a house of idols, and it was a veritable hell. The entry passes through a gaping mouth, such as those the native painters portray in pictures of hell, where frightful mouths with vicious fangs devour the souls of the condemned. Images of devils and serpents stood by the entry, and nearby was a sacrificial platform, bloodstained and blackened with encrusted blood. Like the slaughter houses of Spain, chopping blocks and knives were conveniently arranged alongside it. Firewood was piled in heaps some distance behind the temple, and beyond the stacks of firewood stood a large reservoir filled with water. Inside the temple there were vats and jugs and pitchers of water for the priests to cook the flesh of the poor Indians they sacrificed. I have always called that charnel house the *Inferno*.

We passed beyond the courtyard to a *cue* where they bury the great lords of Mexico, and like the others, it had its idols and its faces from hell, and it was blackened with dried blood and smoke. Nearby was another *cue* filled with skulls and bones, all stacked in perfect order-skulls in one pile and bones in another. In every temple we entered, priests watched our every move. They wore long black robes and hoods that resemble those worn by the Dominicans, and their hair was so long and matted with dried blood that it could neither be combed nor untangled. All had scarified ear lobes. They lived in low-lying buildings adjacent to the temples with the Indians who attended the idols

We visited cues where marriage brokers sought proper wives for men and made their sacrifices to idols that were distinctly female, and we saw others where upper class women lived like nuns.

Every province and every city in the land had its own gods, and in Tenochtitlán, every barrio had its own temple and worshipped its own idols. Temples larger than the cue of Tenochtitlán stood in Cholula and in Texcoco, where a temple rose to the height of 117 steps above the courtyard. The idols were countless, and each demanded its share of blood. The wholesale slaughter of human beings practiced in Mexico was enough to sicken the very soul.

By now we were tired of walking about the city, and the sight of blood and idols nauseated us. We returned to our quarters and set up an altar between two tables, as we had done ever since we arrived in Mexico, and mass was said.

Later, when the altar was dismantled, the captain and the padre Olmedo decided that they had enough of this makeshift form of worship. Since Montezuma would not permit us to set up a cross and build a chapel on the temple of Huichilobos, Cortés and the padre sent a request to Montezuma for his permission to build a chapel here in our quarters. Montezuma gave his permission without hesitation, and he ordered his majordomos to provide us with whatever materials we needed.

In two days the chapel was finished, and a cross was erected before the gates of the palace. There was little enough wine for mass, since Cortés, the padre, and some of the captains drank most of it when they had been taken ill during the war in Tlaxcala. When the wine was gone, we still held services and prayed on our knees before the altar, since we were obliged to confess our sins before God. We hoped that our praying and chanting the Ave Maria would set a good example for Montezuma and his chieftains, and make them favorably disposed to accepting our religion.

While we were trying to decide upon the best place to set up the altar, a carpenter called Alonso Yanes noticed an area in the wall of one of the palace rooms that had been freshly plastered. It seemed to us that there was once a doorway there that had recently been sealed up and concealed with mortar. Yanes reported his discovery to his captains, Juan Velázquez de Leon and Francisco de Lugo, who were my kinsmen.

We had all heard the rumor that the treasure of Axayaca,[ix] Montezuma's father, was hidden somewhere in the palace, and we suspected that it might be in a chamber behind the doorway, because the mortar was relatively fresh. We broke open the door and Cortés was speechless when he saw the wealth of gold plates, jewelry, precious stones, and other riches heaped inside the chamber. I was a young man at the time, and never in my life had I seen such wealth. I was certain that there could be no treasure as great as that before me in the whole world.

The captains agreed that we would not touch the treasure, and we sealed the doorway just as we found it. It was further agreed that our discovery would not be discussed lest word of it reach Montezuma's ears.

On the fifth day of our residence in Tenochtitlán, two Tlaxcalans arrived with letters from Vera Cruz. The consequences of the battle between our men and the Mexican garrison at Nautla were far worse than we had been led to believe at Cholula. Three days after our men returned to Vera Cruz, Juan de Escalante, the chief constable, and six other Spaniards succumbed to their wounds. Worse, our Indian allies, sensing that the colony was in trouble, withdrew from the garrison and refused to bring food to the men. Now Cempoala and every Totonac town in the sierra threatened the colony. God alone knew the despair we felt when we heard this news.

Four captains and 12 soldiers, including myself, met with Cortés in the chapel to consider a course of action. The threat to the colony had left us inside a fortress surrounded on all sides by water, and our host could become our warden simply by opening the drawbridges on the causeways. We reminded Cortés that the people in every town we passed through on our way to Tenochtitlán warned us that Huichilobos had instructed Montezuma to allow us to enter the city, and once there, he could offer us to the god whenever he pleased. We reminded Cortés that the hearts of men were fickle-more so those of Indians-and that he would be a fool to place his trust in the continuing good will of Montezuma. If he turned against us and opened the drawbridges, then cut off our food and water, we would be at the mercy of thousands of Mexican warriors. Our Tlaxcalan allies could not come to our aid, since they could easily be cut off at the canals that lay between them and our quarters. If Montezuma so decided, then Axacaya's treasure and every bite of food he had given us would turn to arsenic inside our bodies. If any in our company told him otherwise, he was either a fool or a mindless ass, unable to see the face of death before his very eyes in his blind lust for gold. These were the fears, we said, that kept us awake night and day. For our safety, and for the safety of the colony, we believed that we had no other course than to take Montezuma hostage.

Cortés was silent for a few moments, lost in thought before he replied.

"Gentlemen," he said, "do not think for a moment that I do not share your fears-I am not asleep to the danger facing us. But do we dare seize this great lord in his own palace? Dare we defy the army of guards and warriors that surround him day and night? Do any of you have a plan in mind to prevent him from summoning his warriors? "

The captains-Juan Velázquez de Leon, Diego Ordaz, Gonzalo de Sandoval, and Pedro Alvarado, had a plan in mind. Cortés, they said, should invite Montezuma to our quarters on one pretext or another, and once we had him here, we could lay hold of him and threaten to kill him if he tried to shout for help. If Cortés had no better plan, then he should give them permission to act upon theirs. Better to take the initiative and seize him rather than wait for him to attack us, they argued, since we could expect no assistance from any quarter.

We deliberated well into the night whether or not we could seize Montezuma without undo risk, and a consensus was finally reached that we had no choice but to take him prisoner. Cortés agreed, and in one way or another, Montezuma would be our prisoner tomorrow.

That night we prayed to God that in His Holy Service, he would guide us and protect us in this perilous business.

At first light, Cortés ordered the entire company on full alert, and the horses bridled and saddled, then he sent word to Montezuma that he would like to meet him in the royal palace. When word came back that the emperor would receive him, he set out with his captains, the interpreters, Doña Marina and Jeronimo de Aguilar, and a party of foot, of which I was a member. We felt secure in the knowledge that Montezuma would not be duly alarmed when Cortés arrived with an armed escort, since this had been our practice ever since we arrived in Mexico.

Cortés took the offensive as soon as we entered the palace. "Lord Montezuma," he said, "it is truly difficult for me to believe that you, a valiant prince who has so often declared his friendship for me, would order your chieftain at Nautla to take up arms against my Spaniards. I can scarcely believe that you would send him to raid towns that are under my protection for men and women to be sacrificed. Now your warriors have killed one of my brothers and a horse, and I will tolerate no more."

Cortés was careful not to mention the men who had died of their wounds at Vera Cruz, since we were certain that Montezuma was not yet aware of the extent of our losses.

"Because I held you as my friend, I ordered my captains to serve you as they would our emperor, yet you opposed us every step of the way to Tenochtitlán. When we were in Cholula, you invited us to your city, but you ordered your squadrons to set an ambush beyond the city. I chose to overlook your duplicity on that occasion only because of my great esteem for you, but now your vassals and your chieftains once again meet in secret to decide how they will kill us.

"I do not propose, however, to start a war or destroy your city. Instead, I shall forget your scheming against us if, silently and without outcry, you accompany us to our quarters. We will serve you and honor you there as if you were in your own palace, but if you raise your voice or refuse to go with us, my captains stand ready to kill you."

Montezuma was pale and his eyes open wide. When he was able to speak, he stammered that he had never ordered his chieftains to take up arms against us. He took the seal of Huichilobos from his arm, a device he used only for orders of greatest consequence, and gave it to a messenger. This, he said, would bring the chieftain of Nautla to Tenochtitlán at once, and when the truth was known, he would be punished. As for Cortés's demand that he leave the palace, however, he was not a person to whom such an order could be given.

A lively discussion followed. Cortés offered any number of good reasons why he must come with us, and Montezuma countered with even better ones why he must remain in his palace. They argued for nearly an hour, until Juan Velázquez interrupted and demanded to know what Cortés expected to accomplish by arguing with Montezuma. Seize him or kill him, he said. Tell him we are ready to die fighting if we have to.

Juan Velázquez's manner of speaking was loud and intimidating, and by the tone of his voice, Montezuma knew that the captains were angry and impatient. He turned to Doña Marina and asked her what they were saying.

"Lord Montezuma," she replied, I believe it best that you go quietly to their quarters before they kill you. I know that when you are there they will still honor you as befitting the great lord you are until the truth of this matter is known."

Montezuma turned to Cortés and said, "Lord Malinche, since you are determined to pursue this course, let me instead offer you my son and my two daughters as your hostages. Take them-do not dishonor me thus. What will my chieftains say if they see me taken away as a common prisoner?"

Cortés replied that he had no alternative but to take him hostage. More arguments were raised, but in the end, Montezuma agreed to leave voluntarily.

Cortés and the captains then paid court to him, and begged him not to be angry with them. They asked him to tell his chieftains that he was going with us of his own free will, because Huichilobos told him he must go with us or die. A majordomo called for his litter, and accompanied by an honor guard, we took him to our quarters and placed him under heavy guard.

In the days that followed, Cortés and the company did everything in their power to please Montezuma. He was free to hold court with his chieftains and his nobles, to hear lawsuits brought to him from distant lands, and to receive his tribute from the provinces. He kept 20 nobles of the royal court as his personal retainers, and he was free to enjoy his women and his daily baths. Cortés even allowed him to be escorted to the temple to offer his prayers to Huichilobos, provided he sacrificed no men. Once there, however, even with the Padre Olmedo present, he broke his promise, and we could do no more than pretend not to notice.

Although Montezuma never showed resentment toward Cortés or any other member of the company, the captain took care to watch for any sign of depression. Each day after prayers-we still had no wine for mass-he went to Montezuma's quarters, usually accompanied by Pedro de Alvarado, Juan Velázquez, or Diego de Ordaz. They did everything they could to keep his spirits up, and they assured him that his orders were being carried out just as if he were in his own palace.

Montezuma never failed to reassure them that he was not upset with them. He was here, he said, because either Huichilobos had willed it or because our gods had granted us the power to seize him.

In time, they attempted to explain our Holy Faith to him, and to describe the grandeur of the court of our emperor.

On several occasions his nephews and other ranking nobles visited him, and each time, they told him that they were ready to attack us whenever he gave the order. But Montezuma ordered them not to arouse the people, because he was here only to share some leisure time with us. They must not grieve for him, because the priests who served Huichilobos told him that it was the god's will that he remain with us.

Montezuma and Cortés often passed the time playing *totoloque*[x]. Each took a turn tossing gold balls and gold discs across the floor, and after five tosses, one would win or lose whatever jewels and other articles he had wagered with the other, depending upon the distance and accuracy of his throws. Pedro de Alvarado marked Cortés's counters, and a nephew marked Montezuma's. Alvarado always gave Cortés one more toss than he was entitled, but Montezuma only turned to us with a little smile and said that he did not like Tonatio[xi] to keep Cortés's score, because he used too much *yxoxol*, meaning he cheated. Cortés and the soldiers on watch always laughed at this, for although Alvarado was handsome and had gracious manners, he was a vicious man and talked too much.

Juan Velázquez, the captain of the guard, seldom found it necessary to remind us to show this great chieftain every courtesy, and he in turn was most generous to us with jewels, clothing, and pretty women.

I was a young man at the time, and whenever I was assigned to guard Montezuma, I never failed to remove my helmet when he passed by. He knew my name and my rank, and he learned from the page Orteguilla that I had come to Mexico twice before. When I asked Orteguilla to ask Montezuma for a pretty woman, he summoned me to his quarters and said, "Bernal Díaz, they tell me that you have very little gold and clothing. Today I have ordered my majordomos to give you gold and mantles, and a pretty girl. Treat her well, for she is the daughter of an important noble."

"I kiss your hands for this great favor," I replied. "May the Lord our God grant you all prosperity."

He asked the page what I had said, and when it was translated for him, he said, "I think Bernal Diaz is a gentleman."

That day I received three gold plates, two cargos of mantles, and a noblewoman, whom we baptized Doña Francisca.

Thus Montezuma passed the days of his confinement, at times cheerful and laughing, but more often lost deep in thought.

---

[i] Huitzilopochtli

[ii] temple

[iii] Spanish name for Tlacopan

[iv] Diaz's text has been edited here to reflect his intent to describe the city as a network of canals and streets.

[v] Tezcatlipoca

[vi] Malinche was the name given to the interpreter Marina. As she was always with Cortés in his dealings with the Mexicans, he was given the same name.

[vii] An outwork of a fortified structure.

[viii] Cuautémoc. Guatemuz is derived from Cuahtémoctzin. The honorific tzin has been omitted here, since it applies to all Mexican nobles.

[ix] Axayácatl

[x] No better description of the game has been found.

[xi] Tonatio, or Tonatiuh, "the sun," was the name given to Pedro de Alvarado because of his reddish-brown hair.

17. Ecatl:

The Rape of Anahuac

"The gods have ever warned us not to welcome a lord into our house who would cast us out and take away our kingdom, for when we seek to remedy our mistake, we will have neither the time nor the means to do so."

How often had Cuitláhuac spoken his mind about the Christians, how often had he proposed bribes, an ambush, or any other means within our power to keep them away from our city? In a single day, Cortés had rendered the Triple Alliance of Tenochtitlán, Texcoco, and Tlacopan powerless.

Had the lords of Mexico heeded Cuitláhuac when there was still time, neither he nor they would be keeping Moctezuma company in his gilded prison. The day he was seized, Moctezuma ordered Cuitláhuac, his brother Cuauhpopocatl, Cacama, and Tetlepanquetzal, the lord of Tlacopan, to join him in his confinement. The following day Cortés seized Chimalpopoca, his eldest son, and Itzcuauhtl, the military governor of Tlatelolco. Only Atlixcatl, the lord of warriors, and Tepeutl, the lord of the javelin house, escaped Cortés. When they heard that Moctezuma was a prisoner of the Christians, they fled the city and nothing more was heard of them.

Those nobles who were still free cried out for war, but there was neither a commander in high places to heed them nor a priest to rally the chieftains, since the high priest of Huitzilopochtli was also in the custody of the Christians.

On the twentieth day of Moctezuma's captivity, Quauhpopoca, the chieftain of Nautla, arrived in Tenochtitlán with his son and fifteen nobles. Before entering the palace, he removed his sandals and his mantle and wrapped the coarse maguey cape of a commoner about his shoulders. After a long wait, a majordomo ushered him before the emperor. With his head bowed and eyes fixed upon the ground, he paid obeisance to Moctezuma. When he was granted permission to speak, he rose and said, "My lord, most powerful emperor, you have ordered me seized, and now your slave Quauhpopoca kneels here at your feet, as you commanded."

Moctezuma's response was cold and unfeeling. "You have done me great harm by making war on the Christians in my name," he said, "and you are no longer welcome in my palace. For your lies, you will be punished as a traitor to your emperor." Quauhpopoca protested, but Moctezuma refused to listen, and a majordomo led him away and delivered him into the hands of the Christians.

We knew little about what was going on behind the palace walls, but it was rumored that Cortés was pressing Quauhpopoca and his nobles to admit that Moctezuma had ordered him to attack the Christians. The nobles, however, insisted that the Christians had first made war upon them, and that they had fought only to defend themselves. They admitted that they had killed some Christians, but they had done so honorably, in battle, according to the rules of warfare. Cortés, however, persisted, threatening them with torture until they told the truth.[i]

The truth may never be known, but it was said that the nobles confessed that they had waged war against the Totonacs and the Christians at Moctezuma's order.

Quauhpopoca himself said very little. Only when Cortés asked him if he was a vassal of Moctezuma did he speak. "Could there be any other lord in the world whose vassal I would be?" he replied.

"The emperor of the men you killed is far more powerful than Moctezuma," Cortés replied, "and for your crime, the time of your death is near at hand. There is no power on earth that can save you now."

Cortés sentenced Quauhpopoca to be burned at the stake alongside his son and his nobles. It was reported that when Quauhpopoca learned of his fate, he said that he regretted having to die for killing the Christians, but Moctezuma had ordered him to do so, and he had no choice. As the Christians bound Quauhpopoca and led him to the plaza with his nobles, Cortés and his commanders went to Moctezuma's quarters.

"Lord Moctezuma," he said, "you denied that Quauhpopoca acted under your orders when he killed my Spaniards, but now we know the truth. Today a great lord of Mexico will die with his son and his nobles, even though the blame lies upon your shoulders. Your actions have not been those of a great lord, but of a contemptible villain. You refuse to accept the fact that truth is far more powerful than all the princes in the world, and the laws of God and man would condemn you to death with the others had you not shown consideration for us in other matters.

"But you will not go unpunished. You will be chained in irons and you will remain there until you and your people understand the value of truth and the value we place upon the lives of our men."

Moctezuma was stunned. He tried to stammer his innocence, but he could scarcely find the words. He begged Cortés not to be angry with him, and pleaded with him not to take away his last shred of pride, but Cortés walked away without looking back.

The gods must have wept with Moctezuma when he saw himself, the mightiest prince Anahuac had ever known, chained like a common slave. His kinsmen gathered about him, weeping as they held the heavy chains away from his arms and legs while stuffing their mantles inside the manacles to prevent them from cutting into his flesh. None dared cry out to the people to take up arms, knowing that the sentries would kill their lord if they did.

In the plaza, Quauhpopoca and his nobles were tied to stakes while the Spaniards gathered bows and arrows from our armories and broke them into firewood. The lords were permitted to say a brief prayer to their gods before the fires were lit. In an instant, flames swept up around them, and when the fires dwindled and died, their bodies had been reduced to nothing but cinders and ash. Not a single outcry was heard from the Mexicans who stood by and watched one of the greatest lords of the realm consumed by fire.

That afternoon Cortés returned to Moctezuma's quarters, and with a reassuring smile, he removed his chains. He told the emperor that he deserved a far greater punishment for his crime, but he had spared him only because of his love for him. Tears rolled down Moctezuma's face as he embraced Cortés, and later that day, a grateful emperor celebrated his freedom with gifts for his captors.

As Quauhpopoca's ashes were scattered into the wind, messengers carried the great seal of Huitzilopochtli to every vassal lord in the land with a summons to Tenochtitlán. In three days they arrived with all the pomp and pageantry due the royal house, and Moctezuma, seated on the jaguar throne received each in turn. This time, however, he was not alone. Cortés sat beside him in a chair no less elegant than his. When the last lord paid his obeisance to Moctezuma, he raised his hand and began to speak.

"Beloved servants, cherished friends and relatives," he said. "I have been your lord and emperor for these 18 years now, and above all else, I have endeavored to seek peace, tranquillity, and prosperity for all. Just as you have loved me, so have I loved you. Were this not so, I would not stand before you and urge each of you to accept what I am about to propose, for I truly believe that it lies in your best interest.

"Our ancestors, our learned soothsayers and priests, those who speak each day with the gods, have, from one generation to the next, told us that we are not natives of this land, and that our sovereignty over these dominions will not endure forever. They have told us how a great lord led our forebears from a far-away country, and how the Otomies forced him to return to his native land. As he left, however, he promised our ancestors that if he could not return, he would one day send his sons to rule over them.

"From the time of our great-great-grandfathers, we have awaited his sons, and now, as many of you have heard, they have arrived. The great Emperor of the Christians, who knows of us even though he lives in a land far from here, has sent Hernando Cortés and his companions to us, and from what they have told us, we know them to be our relatives. Let us offer our thanks to the gods for having seen fit to send the sons of our ancestral lord in our time.

"Now, however, we must do that which we must do, that which gods demand of us, even though it may not be to our liking. I have rendered myself to the King of Spain as his royal servant, and as such, it is my duty and the duty of all my vassals to pay homage to his captain. Henceforth, even though this Emperor of the Christians is far away, you must pay him his tribute and obey him just as you would obey me. By doing as I ask, I will know that you love me and that my love for you has not been in vain."

Moctezuma halted, unable to continue. Many of the nobles wept quietly, and even the Christians brushed a tear or two away as this great lord stood before them in silence. Cortés rose and took him by the hand, and he led him back to his throne.

There was a brief conference among the nobles, then a leader among them stepped forward and knelt before the emperor. When he was given permission to rise, he gave Moctezuma their answer.

"Great lord," he said, "we, your friends and relatives, your servants and your vassals, have listened carefully to what you have said this day, and we shall do our duty as the gods demand of us. We shall offer ourselves as vassals to the Emperor of the Christians, and we shall obey his servant, Hernando Cortés, as we would obey you. We are, however, deeply troubled to see our emperor suffering such pain and sorrow. Nevertheless, we shall do as duty commands, even though we know not how we can endure this change that will overturn our laws and banish our religion."

Cortés rose to his feet to speak to the assembly.

"Princes and beloved friends," he began, "my lord the emperor will be most pleased that you, of your own free will, have followed the example of your lord Moctezuma and offered him your vassalage. For these many years he has longed for your enlightenment, for your sharing with him the knowledge that can come only from the True God, our Lord, which will bring you peace and tranquillity. Although you many mourn this new order that seems so unfriendly, one day you will realize benefits that lie far beyond your understanding at this time.

"My lord offers you his promise that Moctezuma will be the same great lord that he has always been, and that you will enjoy all the privileges befitting your noble rank. The Emperor of the Christians solicits only your friendship; his intent is no more than to free you from the heresy that rules your lives, and to defend you from all your enemies. As his representative, I will serve you in any way that I can."[ii]

Cortés summoned his scribes and his translators, and when the words of Moctezuma and his vassals were written down and sworn to, the council was adjourned.

With the leadership of our nation firmly in hand, Cortés turned his attention to our religion. He began his attack on the gods with Moctezuma, hoping that he would set an example for his people by embracing Christianity.

"Great lord," he said, "in time you will learn that your dominions have been granted to you by Almighty God. He could have granted your throne to any of your vassals, but for reasons hidden from us, God has chosen you to sit upon this throne. God alone-not one of your countless idols, for they have not the power-has chosen you to rule this land. In time you will come to know that there cannot be many gods, for if many gods did indeed exist, they would have no unity of purpose, and without unity of purpose, they cannot guide the affairs of man.

"For the time we have known each other, our laws and our way of life have seemed good to you, and I am led to believe that you have shown an inclination toward becoming a Christian. Let you be the first, then, to renounce these evil delusions that rule your life; let me destroy your false gods, who are so cruel that you must worship them with the blood of innocents. Let me replace them with the image of Christ, the True God, and the image of his Blessed Mother, so that your people will know the god who created them, the god who will redeem them and receive them into eternal bliss. Let you be the first to become a Christian so that others may follow, because you are their lord, loved and obeyed by all. Have no fear of any who would rise against you, for I shall stand beside you, and with the help of God, we will impose your will upon them and they will abide by it."

By now Moctezuma realized that although he was a hostage, he need not fear for his life, The improbable turn of events that had reduced him to a chained captive and the execution of Quauhpopoca had left him demoralized and bewildered, expecting the worse at any moment. Now, however, supported by his relatives who shared his prison, he knew that without him, the Christians had no bargaining power with the people, and without him, they could not leave the city alive.

Moctezuma remained silent after Cortés had finished his sermon, searching out the conflicting emotions in his heart. Finally he spoke. What Cortés suggested did not appear to be sinful, he said, but this was not the time for it. Even if he were inclined to accept the religion of the Christians, his people would not necessarily follow his example. They had been reared from childhood to worship their gods, and they held them to be greater than their emperor, which was proper. Nor could he accept Cortés's assumption that his gods were false gods. Rarely had they failed to bestow health, abundant harvests, and victory in warfare upon them; only when the gods were offended did they become angry and sent bad years to the earth,

But Cortés was adamant: the idols Moctezuma worshipped were demons, not gods but willful creatures condemned to eternal punishment in hell. Good came only from the hand of God, even though his demons had convinced him otherwise. Moctezuma's refusal to accept Christianity was based upon the lies whispered to him by the devil, who had kept him in darkness all his life.

Moctezuma refused to carry the discussion any further. If Cortés insisted upon overthrowing the gods, his people would rise up in arms, he said, and if the Christians prevailed, he would achieve nothing-they would abandon the city and move on to another kingdom.

If the people revolted, Cortés replied, he would crush them into submission, and if they dared leave the city, he would bring them back by force.

Moctezuma raised his hands in resignation. "Since you are determined to pursue this course," he said, "do as you wish. But I warn you; your men will be killed-if not in battle, then from hunger, because my people will refuse to feed them. Should you come to grief, do not appeal to me, for I shall not be a party to appeasing them."

"They may do as they please," Cortés replied, "but they will soon see that they are powerless against us. God, for whose honor and glory we came here, will be at our side. I have promised Him that I will cast down your idols, and when I do, you will be the one to suffer for your empty fears and your refusal to accept our faith."

Three days later, more that 400 porters, nobles, and warriors assembled in the great plaza. The porters carried heavy straw mats to the top of the great temple, where they wove them together to form cradles big enough to hold the images of Huitzilopochtli and Tlaloc. They lowered the gods from the altars and tied them into the cradles, and when they were secure, they passed ropes as thick as a man's arm through heavy metal rings attached to the cradles. They lashed the cradles to heavy wooden beams greased on the underside, and began to ease them down the temple steps. Even the skill of the porters and the loving care with which they lowered them, however, was not enough to prevent small pieces from being broken from the images, and priests followed behind, gathering each precious fragment and shard in their mantles. All worked silently as they lowered the gods from the temple, and the Christians watching could not help but shudder at the deathlike silence that filled the plaza.

When the gods were safe on the plaza floor, hundreds of nobles, warriors, and porters lifted them to their shoulders and carried them across the causeway, and they were never seen again. Moctezuma had ordered them hidden to spare his people from witnessing their desecration.

The following day the Christians filed from their quarters and marched to the temple, chanting one of their mournful dirges as they climbed the steps. Their priests led the way, carrying a cross and an image of the woman they worshipped. When they reached the summit, they placed their idols in the shrine of our gods and knelt before them, singing and weeping tears of joy.

That same night Moctezuma ordered 400 brothels in Tlatelolco burned to the ground and the public women who lived in them put to death. He chose to blame their sins for angering the gods and bringing the Christians down upon us.[iii]

Although Moctezuma was firm in his resolve to adhere to the religion of his ancestors, he readily yielded to Cortés upon matters that affected the security and future of the empire. When Cortés asked him about our sources of gold and silver, he was only too willing to provide him with guides to lead the Spaniards to our gold-bearing rivers in the sierra.

Armed with no more than a safe-conduct from Moctezuma, the guides led them to Zozollan, in the land of the Cloud People,[iv] where the natives panned high-grade gold nuggets from three rivers. Another party journeyed to Malinaltepec, where the natives gave them nuggets found in the great river that flows to the eastern sea. At Tochtepec, the southernmost province on the coast of the Eastern Sea, third party found not only gold, but a land so fertile that Cortés persuaded Moctezuma to grant him holdings for another colony.[v]

The fourth party worked its way upstream from Malinaltepec to Chinantla, the mountain home of Coatlicamatl, a powerful chieftain hostile to Moctezuma. Although Coatlicamatl's province was small and his warriors few, his enemies were never able to penetrate the rugged terrain. His warriors carried lances a full 30 palms in length, and were among the fiercest in Anahuac.[vi]

Coatlicamatl granted the Spaniards permission to enter his territory, but insisted that the Mexicans remain outside the borders. Once inside, the Spaniards found a new ally for Cortés. Coatlicamatl led them to several streams where gold was washed down from the high sierra, and after gathering enough samples, the chieftain sent them back to Tenochtitlán with gifts and a pledge of allegiance to the Emperor of the Christians.

By granting his captors access to the sierra, where sovereignty depended solely upon the man who sat on the jaguar and eagle throne, Moctezuma had damaged Mexican authority over the Cloud People beyond repair.

If this disastrous blunder was not enough, Moctezuma ordered a map of the entire eastern seaboard drawn up for Cortés. Now he could seek out an anchorage for more ships, ships that would soon bring more Spaniards to our country.

Although Moctezuma's map showed no large bays or inlets between Potonchán and the Panuca River, the Spaniards found an inlet at Coatzacoalcos, which was fed by a river where ships could sail more than a league upstream.

The province was populous, with many large cities along the riverbanks, and the people were Nahuatl speakers. Tuchintl, their chieftain, had successfully resisted Moctezuma's efforts to expand his empire eastward into his territory. Tuchintl was well aware of Cortés's victory over the Chontal Maya, and caught between the Mexicans to the west and the Chontal Maya to the east, he deemed it prudent to form and alliance with the Spaniards. When the chieftain offered to pay tribute to the Emperor of the Christians, Cortés sent 150 Spaniards to Coatzacoalcos to establish a second colony on the eastern seaboard.

With garrisons at Quiahuitzlan and Coatzacoalcos on the coast, and allies at Cempoala, Tlaxcala, Cholula, and Huexotzingo, Cortés's foothold in Mexico and his line of communications to the sea was seemingly secure. His only obstacle was the strong Mexican garrison at Tepeaca, which controlled the approaches to the pass across the sierra. But with Moctezuma held hostage, the Mexican commander was powerless.

Moctezuma's generosity to his captors did not end with his granting the wealth of Anahuac to them. When Cortés complained that the Emperor of the Christians, who waged one war after another, was hard pressed to support his armies, Moctezuma pledged his wealth and that of his vassals to him. Yet this was not enough; Moctezuma gave the priceless treasures of the royal aviary to the Spaniards.

In the house of the hunting birds, where birds of prey and wild animals were kept, majordomos led the Spaniards past the cages of panthers, jaguars, and wolves to a small chapel. Gold and silver tiles, inlaid with turquoise and pearls, lined the four walls of the chapel. As the Spaniards began measuring the tiles and estimating their worth, Moctezuma's dwarfs, albinos, hunchbacks, and other deformed creatures, who lived in the loft, gathered about to watch.

The majordomos led them through the gardens to the House of Feathers, where waterfowl flocked in a dozen ponds; some filled with fresh water, others with water from the sea. Inside they saw vast quantities of plumes, elegant clothing, rich tapestries, shields, and other articles decorated with feathers of the most exotic birds in the land. In another room, the Spaniards saw the blowguns that Moctezuma used for the hunt. Each was fashioned of wood and gold foil; some were inlaid with figures of tiny birds whose wings and feathers were made of miniature pearls, others were painted with flowers and trees so natural and detailed that they appeared to be real. A mesh pouch, woven from gold and silver thread, which contained pellets and pellet molds, lay beside each weapon,

When the Spaniards had pried out the gold and silver tiles from the chapel, and set all the jewels aside, the goldsmiths of

Atzcapotzalco melted the gold and cast it into ingots. Each ingot was stamped with the seal of the Emperor of the Christians and stored under a heavy guard in one of the palace rooms. The Spaniards divided the finest turquoise among themselves, and the Tlaxcalans stole the rest. Moctezuma, knowing that the featherwork had little worth for the Spaniards, asked them to set it aside, but it was thrown in a heap and burned with the clothing and the tapestries.

Cacama, at the insistence of Moctezuma, agreed to surrender the treasures of Acolhuacán to the Spaniards, provided they not touch the turquoise and precious feathers used in their religious ceremonies. Reluctantly, he sent his brothers, Nezahualquentl and Tetlahuehuequitl, to take the Spaniards to the treasure chambers of his ancestors.

As they prepared to depart for Texcoco, a messenger arrived, warning them that Moctezuma would be the one to suffer if the Spaniards were not satisfied with the gold and silver they found. As the messenger spoke to Nezahualquentl however, the Spanish commander became suspicious, and he struck the Texcocan, knocking him to the ground. He took him to Cortés and accused him of plotting against the Spaniards, and without a word spoken in his defense, the captain ordered Nezahualquentl hanged.

Cacama was furious when he heard of the mindless execution of his brother, but he could do no more than send another to replace him.

In Texcoco, the Spaniards filled a chest as long as a man is tall and half again as wide with the vast treasure of Nezahualcóyotl, but the sight of such wealth only increased their appetite for more. They sent the young princes into the city to order every noble to bring all the gold he possessed to the palace, and they returned with enough gold to fill another chest as big as the first.

With the coming of the Spaniards and Cacama's subsequent imprisonment, Ixtlilxochitl, the rebel prince who ruled the northern regions of Acolhuacán at Otumba, and Coanacoch, who now ruled Texcoco, formed a truce of convenience, and together they governed a loosely united nation. With the execution of Quauhpopoca, however, resentment against the Spaniards was so strong in the northern cities that the people were arming themselves and preparing for war. Ixtlilxochitl, now an ally of Cortés, was forced to return to Otumba to restore order. Meanwhile, in Texcoco, the execution of

Nezahualquentl and the looting of their homes had aroused the nobles, and Coanacoch, fearing for the lives of Moctezuma and Cacama, was hard-pressed to keep them under control.

Cacama's unexpected escape from Tenochtitlán, however, brought Ixtlilxochitl back in a hurry, and the nobles of Texcoco pronounced for their legitimate lord. In the name of the Triple Alliance, Cacama called for a council of war, and every chieftain in the Valley of Mexico responded to his call of arms. They gathered in secret, in the great hall of Nezahualpilli's palace, and when the last chieftain had sworn his allegiance, Cacama spoke.

"Lords and vassals," he said, "I have summoned you here today to speak of these foreigners who have made slaves of our people. You have seen how they seized my uncle, the great Moctezuma, a lord in whose veins flows the blood of our noble ancestors. You have seen them defile our temples, deprive us of our sacred rites and ceremonies, which we have observed from time immemorial, and, above all else, make way for their god by taking away ours.

"Must we, who are many, continue to grovel at the feet of so few? Have we no pride, have we no manhood? Can we let them continue to use our wives and our daughters as they please? Can we allow our relatives and friends to serve them as if they were their slaves?

"I say no, my lords! We must cast them out of our homes, we must reclaim our religion, our liberty, our honor, and our country. And we must return the great lord Moctezuma to his rightful throne. Let us not wait until others come to swell the ranks of the foreigners. Think! If these few have done so much, what will they be capable of when others come to join them? Let us attack them now, let us force them to release Moctezuma if they would save themselves.

"If they kill Moctezuma, then I will be your emperor, and I will avenge his death. If that should come to pass, I vow to you that I will never tolerate the shame of serving them as he has.

"Take up your arms, my loyal vassals. Ready your bows and arrows, polish your *maquahuitls*, and provision your homes for what is to come. And you, valiant captains, you who are charged with the affairs of war, ready your warriors, for the time has come to free our friends and relatives from their chains.

"Let me warn you, however, if we undertake this affair, there can be no turning back. If we are defeated, we will lose our homes, our honor, and all that we hold dear, for the wrath of our enemy will leave us nothing to live for. If there are some among you who fear this war, now is the time to counsel me: tell me what course I must take, tell me what I must do."

The young chieftains, confident of victory, did not hesitate to commit their warriors and all their resources to Cacama, and they urged him to attack at once, since delay would not work to their advantage. The elders, however, those who were nearing the end of their lives, advised Cacama to reflect carefully before committing his nation to war

"Do not allow pride and the courage of youth to deceive you about these foreigners," they said. "Their captain is a great warrior, and he has gained victories over forces greater than Texcoco can bring against you. Nor can you count upon the Mexicans for support, since Moctezuma, fearful for his life, is now a friend and ally of the captain. And most important, do not use religion and liberty to further your ambition for the throne of Mexico. Others have a rightful claim to it, and affairs motivated by greed often turn out badly for all."

Theirs was but a small voice, however, and none would listen. All but one of the chieftains raised their voices in support of Cacama. The lord of Matalzingo demanded the throne of Mexico for his support, and when Cacama ridiculed him, he informed Moctezuma of the plot.

Cortés wanted to launch an attack against Cacama before he had time to organize his forces, but Moctezuma, fearing an uprising in Tenochtitlán would result, prevailed upon him to reason with Cacama first. He warned Cortés that the Acolhuacáns would defend Texcoco with every warrior they had, and notwithstanding Cacama's lack of experience in warfare, he commanded many battle-hardened chieftains. He advised Cortés to send a conciliatory message to Cacama. Remind him, he said, of the friendship they shared when he had first come to Mexico, and warn him that a young lord might find it exciting to take up arms, but he would soon find that using them would prove difficult and bloody. Better he face his responsibilities as the lord of many vassals, he said, and join his uncle in accepting the King of Spain as his emperor rather than risk the lives of his people in a war he could not win.

Cacama responded that he would not lay aside his arms for the friendship of one who would strip him of his country and his honor.

219

He would not serve a captain who would enslave his people and deprive them of their religion. Furthermore, he knew nothing of the Emperor of the Christians, and he would never acknowledge him as his lord. Until the day he had avenged his uncle and his gods, and brought freedom to his nation, there could be no other course than war.

Cacama's reply, however, did not discourage Moctezuma. He invited him to come to Tenochtitlán and meet with Cortés, hoping that war might be averted if they met face to face.

Cacama's reply to his uncle was as defiant as his message to Cortés. If Moctezuma were a man, Cacama replied, if he truly believed in the gods, the foreigners would never dare keep him in chains. They had trampled the gods beneath their feet as if they were dirt; they had profaned the fame and glory of his ancestors; they had levied harsh laws and strange customs upon the people; and with each passing day, they claimed more and more of his kingdom. But since Moctezuma was too cowardly to defend himself and his country, he would do it for him, and he would die before he turned away from his duty.

Yes, he said, I shall come to Tenochtitlán, and I shall come soon. But I will come with a *maquahuitl* in my hand, not with my hands between my buttocks.

What Moctezuma could not obtain by diplomacy, he could, like all the lords of Tenochtitlán before him, gain by guile. Neither Ixtlilxochitl nor Coanacoch held any affection for him, but he knew that either one would sell his birthright for the throne of Texcoco.

It was Ixtlilxochitl who proposed that Cacama meet with him to discuss his support for the coming war. They could meet on neutral ground in the palaces of Tepetzingo, a forested island less than a league from the shores of Tenochtitlán. From there, with the eastern shore of Tenochtitlán in clear sight, they could lay out a workable plan to blockade the city and agree upon a date to launch a ground attack. Cacama agreed, and when the day appointed arrived, he and his commanders set out for the island on the royal barge, but it was the Christians, not Ixtlilxochitl, who awaited him.[vii]

Betrayed by his brothers, chained to the other lords who shared Moctezuma's prison, Cacama's plan collapsed and all resistance to Cortés ceased. As a guarantee against another uprising, the

Acolhuaque were forced to send four princes of the royal family to Tenochtitlán as hostages. Neither Ixtlilxochitl nor Coanacoch, however, realized his ambition to rule Texcoco. Cortés, not Moctezuma, chose the young lord Cuicuizcatl to succeed Cacama to the throne.

The people, however, had heard Cacama's voice. His words were and inspiration to all of Mexico, and they were heard time and time again in the streets of Tenochtitlán. Lord and commoner alike hailed his defiance of Moctezuma and Cortés. Too long had they waited for Moctezuma to send the word that would set him free. Too long had they watched him allow the Spaniard to strip Mexico of its wealth, and too long had they been forced to stand by as one province after another fell away from the empire.

Bur Moctezuma was still their lord. If it were his will to leave his captors, they would free him and serve him as they had done before, and Cortés would never dare seize him again. If, however, he chose to remain with his wardens, they would elect a new lord in his place. Sooner or later, they said, he would suffer the same fate as Quauhpopoca.

No matter what course he chose, Moctezuma knew that Mexico would tolerate the Spaniards no longer. Unless they left the country of their own free will, there would be a war that would cost many lives and leave Tenochtitlán in ruins. Cortés too must be concerned about the mounting tension in the city, and sooner than later he would call upon him to control the people. This, he knew, he could not do while a single Spaniard remained on Mexican soil. He summoned Cortés to his quarters, then sent an order to his generals to mobilize an army, but well out of sight of the Tlaxcalans.

When Cortés entered his quarters, Moctezuma took him by the hand and led him to a room where they could not be overheard.

"Captain Cortés," he began, "the gods are angry with me because I took them from their temple and allowed you to erect a cross in their rightful place. Now the priests tell me that our gods will hold back the rains, destroy our crops, send pestilence upon the land, and do that which I fear most-place my country in the hands of my enemies. I must therefore ask you to leave the city and the country before my people rise up and kill you, for they will tolerate you no longer. Ask what you will of me, and I shall give it to you, for, as you well know, my love for you has not withered. If this were not so, I would not warn you to leave, for I still hold the power and the ability to do you great harm. I say this to you with all sincerity, and I shall not warn you again. Take what you want of my treasures and leave satisfied with your gains, because you can no longer live among my people against their will and against the will of the gods that nourish them. Therefore go, for the sake of your honor as well as mine."

When the interpreters finished translating Moctezuma's words, Cortés spoke.

"I shall always be grateful for your love, my lord, and I too know that we cannot continue to live within a society that will never accept us and our ways. Since it is the will of your vassals and your gods, we shall leave as you command us, for our god would not have us remain at the cost of your life."

Moctezuma was pleased, and he said, "I shall not order you to leave until you are prepared to do so. Take such time as you need, and when you are ready, I will give you four measures of gold, your captains two measures each, and a measure to every common soldier."

Cortés thanked Moctezuma for his generosity, but he reminded him that he had destroyed his ships when he first arrived in Mexico. To build others, he would need some time and his shipmaster would need many carpenters to cut and shape timber. Moctezuma could assure his gods and his vassals that he would leave as soon as the ships were ready.

This seemed reasonable to Moctezuma, and he sent his carpenters to the forested lands of the eastern seaboard with orders to work with all possible haste.

Pine trees were felled and timber was dressed, but as the days passed into weeks, little was accomplished as the shipmaster found one reason after another for delay. By now Moctezuma had reached his patience with the lack of progress, but before he had the opportunity to protest, news arrived from Cuetlaxtlan that cast all other concerns aside.

A large fleet lay offshore, and even now an army was landing on the beach with cannon and horses. Before news of the fleet reached Cortés, it was imperative that Moctezuma learn the intent and identity of the new arrivals. Keeping Cortés at arms length, he sent ambassadors to meet with them.

When his ambassadors returned, they told Moctezuma that the new men were kinsmen of the Spaniards, but they had come to seize Cortés and his companions. Their captain informed them that he, not Cortés, was the lawful ambassador of the Emperor of the Christians and captain-general of all Spanish forces in Anahuac. Cortés and his men, he said, were nothing but greedy adventurers who had come to Mexico against the will of the emperor, and he had sent him here with 800 men to arrest them and make restitution to Moctezuma and his people for the crimes they had committed. Every one of them would be taken into custody and punished according to the severity of his crime. Some would be hanged, and others would be given long prison sentences. As for the lord Moctezuma, he sent him assurances that he would set him free as soon as he reached Tenochtitlán, and after he delivered his emperor's message, he and all his men would return to their own country. The ambassadors had no doubt that the new captain spoke the truth, since three of Cortés's own men stood by his side and translated every word to them.

Moctezuma now faced a dilemma. Should he accept the new captain's word that he and not Cortés spoke for the Emperor of the Christians? And if he did, could he depend upon his promise to release him and leave the country after he arrested Cortés? Should he cast his support behind him and his superior forces now, or should he await further developments and perhaps lose his best opportunity for regaining his throne? Although the new captain's forces far outnumbered the battle-weary troops of Cortés, his men were firmly entrenched in an impregnable city, and they were veteran soldiers who had proved themselves more than once against overwhelming odds. If Cortés chose to defend the city, he could very well prevail against the new captain if the Mexicans remained neutral. At the very least, a war was brewing that could cripple both sides and leave Mexico with the balance of power.

Three more days passed, and word of the arrival of the Spanish fleet had not yet reached Cortés, but Moctezuma dared not keep the news from him any longer. He called upon Cortés to meet him at once in the palace gardens.

"Great captain," he said, "ships from your country have arrived upon our shores. Now that we have no need wait for your ships to be built, and you must prepare to leave Mexico a soon as possible."

Cortés stared at Moctezuma as if he did not quite understand what he was saying. "Lord," he replied, "you do me a kindness by warning me to leave, and though I am not pleased to go, it is my duty to obey you. But how am I to leave? My ships are not ready."

Moctezuma nodded to a majordomo, who spread a cloth before Cortés. On it was a painting of ships lying off the coast and a large army with horses and cannon encamped upon the beach. Cortés was silent for a moment, then he raised his arms to the sky and tears streamed down his cheeks.[viii]

"O true and omnipotent God," he cried, "Thou has sustained us in our hour of greatest need!"

Moctezuma embraced him, then took him by the hand and said, "Come, let us dine together.

In the days that followed, the captains sent messages back and forth between Tenochtitlán and the coast, and it soon became obvious that relations between the two were strained. From the activity about the palace, we knew that Cortés was preparing for war. Soldiers were cleaning their weapons and horsemen were exercising their mounts daily, and the foot was practicing with long lances equipped with twin copper blades for use against cavalry. The lances were gifts from Coatlicamatl, Cortés's ally in Chinatla. When his army was ready to march, Cortés met with Moctezuma.

"Lord," he said, "when we agreed that the time had come for me to leave your country, you allowed me to stay on until I could build my ships. Now, however, my brother Pánfilo de Nárvaez has arrived with 11 ships, and I am leaving for the seacoast to inspect them, because they will need repairs after sailing so far. When I am finished, we will come to Tenochtitlán together.

"Be advised, however, that there is no conflict between me and my brother, no matter what your vassals have told you. If Pánfilo de Nárvaez led them to believe that he came here to do me harm, I feel obliged to warn you that he did so deliberately to test your intentions and those of your people toward us. Had you risen against me, he would have come here with his army, and together we would have destroyed you and laid waste your city.

"We are both vassals of Don Carlos, the Emperor of the Christians, who sent me here to offer you his friendship. When I failed to return to Spain at the appointed time, however, he feared that I was either dead or lost and unable to reach your city. Consequently, he sent another caballero with an army much larger than mine to find me or to avenge my companions and me had we been killed.

"This new captain, however, now knows how you have favored me and of your desire to be a vassal of the emperor, and he has sent me a letter that states his intentions. Since you have proved yourself to be my friend despite the hostility he has feigned toward me, he has asked that I escort him to Tenochtitlán so that he can kiss your hands and present his gifts to you. Then, when you have given him your reply to our emperor, we shall return to our country.

"While I am gone, I shall leave Pedro de Alvarado here in my place. He is a distinguished caballero and your good servant, and he will serve you as I would until Pánfilo de Nárvaez and I return with the emperor's message. After that, we will take our leave of you.

"In my absence, I appeal to you not to encourage an uprising among those of your vassals who stand in opposition to us. If there should be a revolt, you and your people will suffer, for now you know the power and strength that our god has bestowed upon us. Therefore, Your Highness, if we must make war upon your people, do not blame me: it is my intent to leave your country as soon as possible."

Moctezuma weighed his answer carefully. It was well known that there was a great deal of ill-will between Cortés and the new captain, and with each passing day there were more reports of their growing hostility toward each other. He also knew that his generals would not hesitate to use these reports to goad him into a war with the Spaniards. But instinct told him that at least for the present, it might be to his advantage to accept Cortés's story. Cortés was dividing his forces, and it would be prudent to wait until he was sure of his course of action.

"Valiant captain," he replied, "from the first day you landed upon our shores, you have had no reason to doubt my affection for you. Long before we met, I sent you gifts and ordered my governors to see to your every need. When you came to my city, I received you as if you were an emperor. I quartered you in the house of my father and ordered my vassals to attend you as if you were a king. I have entertained your men and given them many gifts, and they in turn have shown me every courtesy and served me as if I was their king.

"But my people resent you, and my gods, who you consider false and evil, have advised me to sacrifice you for the outrages that you have committed against them. I have, however, yielded neither to my people nor to my gods, for this is not in keeping with laws of hospitality we must observe toward ambassadors, laws that we must honor and obey above and beyond those of our religion.

"My regard for our laws as well as my love for you compels me to warn you that you must leave. I granted you sufficient time to construct your ships, but they were never finished. This angered my people, because they believed that you were purposely delaying your departure. Since you say that you came here only to visit me and teach me about your religion, there is no purpose in your remaining any longer. As one who loves you, I advise you to leave as soon as possible now that ships have come.

"You say that this new captain is your brother, and that he has spoken badly of you only to test the intent of my people. If this is so, go to him, receive him, and let us hope he will welcome you. But return soon, I cannot hold my people back much longer. Though your men may be more powerful than my warriors may, you are but few, living in a foreign land, and my people are many, and they are prepared to die for their homeland.

"Until you return, I will show Pedro de Alvarado and those who remain with him every consideration, and I give you my word that I will instigate no uprising. But warn them not to break our laws, because if they do, my people will seize any opportunity to attack them. If this should happen, I cannot help them-the people are weary of my pleading for peace with you.

Let me also advise you to make it known to all that there is no strife between you and the one you say is your brother, and that your departure from Mexico will be delayed no longer. Now may your god be with you and may he favor your meeting with him."

The following day Cortés and 70 Spaniards began the long march to the seacoast. Moctezuma, with an honor guard of Spaniards and an escort of nobles, accompanied them as far as the Ixtapalapa causeway, where Cortés called a halt and dismounted. Moctezuma stepped down from his litter, and the two embraced. The column moved down the causeway, and Moctezuma returned to the palace with Pedro de Alvarado riding close behind him.[ix]

---

[i] There is little evidence to support Cortes's claim that Moctezuma ordered the uprising at Nautla. More likely, Quauhpopoca was a convenient scapegoat to justify his seizing Moctezuma.

[ii] Cortes himself is the undoubtedly the source of this account of the transfer of power from Moctezuma. The account found in Gomara, his secretary who had never been to Mexico, and that of Cervantes, who had access to the conqueror, are nearly identical.

[iii] The evacuation of the gods from Tenochtitlán and the destruction of the brothels is an eyewitness account of Alonso de Ojeda, as told to Cervantes. Note that Tlaloc, the god of rain, not Tezcatlipoca, sits beside Huitzilopochtli in the temple of Tenochtitlán.

[iv] The Mixtecs and Zapotecs of Oaxaca

[v] Cortes sent four parties into Mixtec territory. The first party took the highland route (Now highway 190) leading to Zozollan, 180 miles south of Mexico City as the crow flies. Cortes gives the distance traveled as 210 statute miles, using the Spanish league of 2.6 miles. Two more parties took a more easterly route to Malinaltepec 160 miles from Mexico City. While one party explored the rivers for gold, the other party worked its way 32 miles to the Gulf Coast province of Tochtepec.

[vi] Chinantla was the principal city of the province, which was populated by Chinantec speaking Mixtecs. Neither Cortes nor any other source provides insight as to how the Spaniards, accompanied by Nahuatl speaking Mexicans, communicated with the Mixtecs.

[vii] The chronicler Fernando Alva Ixtlilxochitl is the only chronicler who names Coanacoch and his ancient namesake Ixtlilxochitl, as Cacama's betrayers. He does not, however, denounce them, instead he commends them for facilitating the conquest. Ixtlilxochitl was an ally of Cortés, but Coanacoch supported Cacama's revolt and was one of Cortés's most outspoken enemies.

[viii] Andres de Tapia states that Moctezuma received two paintings of of the arrival of Narváez's fleet. The first painting showed 18 ships some 270 miles southeast of Vera Cruz, probably along the coast of Tabasco between Laguna de Terminos and Potonchán. Five of the ships, however, were shipwrecked and lying on the beach. The second painting that Moctezuma showed Cortes was of the surviving ships lying at anchor off Vera Cruz.

[ix] Cortés varies on the number of Spaniards he left behind with Alvarado. In the Second Letter, MacNutt translation, he states that 500 men were left behind. In the Second Letter, Rasmusio version, he sets the number

at 150. The latter number is accepted here, since it is relatively consistent with the forces available to him in Tenochtitlán at this time.

Assuming that he left Vera Cruz with 484 men; allowing for 45 more men killed at Tlaxcala (Bernal Díaz); 150 taken by Juan Velasques de Leon to Coatzacoalcos; and the 70 men that Cortés took to fight Narváez, no more than 219 Spaniards remained in Tenochtitlán. Only if one includes some of the Tlaxcalan allies left behind can a force of 500 men be realized..

18. Juan Cano:

The Expedition against Cortés

Grijalva's commander, Pedro de Alvarado, brought the *Trinidad* safely back to Cuba on the 24th day of June, 1518, and when the governor saw the gold idols, medallions, and the jewelry, he sent the priest Benito Martín to Spain with the king's fifth of the treasure and a petition for a warrant to colonize the new land. Without waiting for Grijalva to return, he set about organizing another expedition and began looking for a new commander.

The governor's first choice to lead the expedition was Baltazar Bermúdez, but when he demanded 3,000 ducats for arms and equipment, Bermúdez refused, stating that the cost would be greater than the profit.

Others were considered, but his ultimate choice was Hernando Cortés. Cortés had some military experience, but more important, he had two thousand castellanos in gold, a lucrative partnership with Andrés de Duero, and a number of friends who were willing to invest in the enterprise.

With his appointment as captain-general, Cortés turned his full attention to the undertaking. He raised money by using his estate as security, borrowed money from his friends, and sold shares of the profits to the wealthy. According to Cortés's friends, he invested five thousand castellanos for the purchase of three ships, borrowed two thousand castellanos more from Diego Velásquez, and assumed a note to buy enough salt pork to feed the company for five months. With the aid of friends, he secured enough capital to buy four more ships and underwrite the expenses for every member of the company who was short of funds.

The contribution of Velásquez is not clear, but word had it that he provided three weatherworn ships and provisions, which he sold to the company at outrageous profits.

The objectives of Cortes's mission were threefold. The Crown required him to encourage the Indians to become vassals of the King of Spain, to search for six Spaniards that had been lost in the area, and to determine the resources of the country. The Church urged him to spread the Catholic faith among the natives, and to learn more about a cross that had been observed in native villages.[i] Diego Velásquez's demands were that he update the charts along the coast of New Spain, and send news of his progress as soon as possible with all the gold, jewels, and other products of the land that he obtained.

No instructions were given Cortés to establish a colony in New Spain, inasmuch as Diego Velásquez had not yet received a warrant from the Crown, and the *Audienca* in Santo Domingo had granted him only the right to trade with the natives.

By now, however, Velásquez began to have second thoughts about his choice for a commander. Relatives reminded him of his past difficulties with Cortés, and he was further troubled when a court jester called out, "Have a care, master Velásquez, or we shall have to go ahunting someday or other after this same captain of ours!"

The governor spoke of his concerns to Andrés de Duero and Amador de Lares, but Cortés was heavily indebted to them, and they had no intention of jeopardizing their investment in the expedition. They urged Cortés to leave as immediately if he was to retain his command.

Cortés had not yet a full complement of ships, men, and provisions, but he weighed anchor and sailed out of port that same day. Stopping only long enough to pick up rations and a crew along the coast, he rounded Cape San Antonio on the western end of Cuba on February 18, 1519, and set sail for New Spain.

More than six months passed before first word of the expedition reached Cuba. In August 1519, the governor received a letter from an encomendero who lived on the western shore of the island, and it sent him into a colossal rage.

A caravel from Cortés's fleet had anchored near the encomendero's hacienda, and two hidalgos, Francisco de Montejo and Alonso Hernandez de Puertocarrero, came ashore to bargain with him for bread, cassava, wild hogs, and sufficient fresh water for the crossing to Spain. The encomendero, who was a good friend of Montejo, was invited aboard, and after being sworn to the utmost secrecy, was taken below. There, according to his letter, he saw a cargo of gold, silver, and jewels worth no less than 300,000 castellanos. The ship carried so much gold that he swore the pilot was using it for ballast.

The following day, the caravel departed, taking a course around the northern coast of Cuba, where the waters are dangerous and poorly charted.

Diego Velásquez dispatched two ships to intercept the caravel, but the quarry was gone. All he could do now was document his claim for the treasure to the King and request that the ship be impounded as soon as it reached Spain.

Benito Martîn returned from Spain early the following year with a grant from the Council of the Indies appointing Diego Velásquez governor of all the lands he should discover and colonize. Armed with the warrant, Velásquez set about purchasing another fleet and recruiting and army larger than that of Cortés. He found no difficulty finding volunteers, since reports of the wealth in the land that Grijalva called New Spain had spread from one end of the island to the other.

Diego Velásquez planned to lead his army in person to New Spain, but when word of his intent reached Santo Domingo, the *Audiencia* sent a message insisting that as the King's governor, his duty demanded his continuing presence in Cuba, and he felt it prudent to obey the directive.

Reluctantly, he turned to his most trusted friends to choose a commander. He would have preferred his nephew, Baltazar Bermudez, but so many of the principals who had invested in the enterprise objected that he turned to the highly regarded Vasco Porcallo de Figueroa. The governor's faith in the loyalty of his friends, however, had always been short-lived, and, as was the case with Cortés, he began to vacillate in his support for Porcallo. The cooling of their relations was not lost on Porcallo, and there was an angry confrontation with the governor before the most prominent backers of the enterprise.

"Senor," Porcallo said, "you honored me when you chose me to lead this undertaking, but I have no intention of suffering your insulting behavior now that you favor another. As of this moment, I resign my commission, and even though the King himself should urge me to lead this mission, I would refuse. But when you choose one of my many rivals to succeed me, I caution you to choose him carefully, for he alone must face Hernando Cortés, who will not only defend himself stubbornly, but given the least opportunity, will take the offensive. May it please God that this affair does not follow the path you have chosen, for although many boast of their ability to compromise, there are few who can deal with Hernando Cortés without resorting to arms."

With this, Porcallo turned his back and left without giving Velásquez an opportunity to reply.

Porcallo's pride would prevent him from reconsidering his resignation, no matter what, and the governor turned to his friends again to choose a commander. After considerable debate, the post was offered to Pánfilo de Narváez, a well-respected hidalgo known for his courage, but considered by many to be inordinately arrogant.

In March of the year 1520, we assembled at Guaniguanico, on the western end of Cuba. We were more than 600 strong, with some 400 foot, 80 horse, 150 crossbowmen, and 90 musketeers. Our artillery consisted of 20 heavy guns and falconets. Nineteen ships, manned by 200 mariners, stood ready to take us to New Spain. As we prepared to board the ships, Diego Velásquez arrived to bid us farewell and give instructions to his captain-general.

"Senor Pánfilo de Narváez," he said. "I chose you from many able and respected caballeros as my captain-general, and I bestow upon you all of the powers that lie within my authority to carry out your mission,. Now the time has come for you to do your duty and seek redress for the wrongs done by Hernando Cortés. Now you must restore the honor and dignity of the office of Governor of Cuba, which he has shamed by his unpardonable conduct.

"When your task is done, you will receive your fair share of this enterprise, and I shall do everything in my power to further your career. Many of your friends go with you, and many who remain here wish you every success. Use prudence and discretion in all things, and see that Cortés does not deceive you with his lies. I have provided you with an army far superior to his, and good fortune will be yours if you are vigilant and judicious. Now may God go with you and favor you in all you do."

The governor embraced Narváez, and the captain replied, "Senor, even though my army were half as large, I would bring back Cortés as my prisoner. When I reach New Spain, he will honor me as his captain, and I will receive as I would a son. But this will not prevent me from doing my duty: I will send him to you in chains for the way he has repaid your many favors, and nevermore will he lift his head in pride. I shall colonize the land in your name and do whatever is needed to secure it, and when this is done, the King will know that it was your diligence and your initiative that brought success.

Before our ships could get underway, however, Lucas Vázquez de Ayllon, the Appellate Judge of the Indies, arrived with an order signed by the Jeronymite Friars[ii] and Rodrigo de Figueroa, the *juez de residencia,* prohibiting the fleet from leaving port. This expedition, he said, would drain badly needed manpower from Cuba and leave the Indians mismanaged and the island vulnerable. Furthermore, the Jeronymites were convinced that if the fleet sailed for New Spain, a civil war with Cortés's army was unavoidable. The war would risk the loss of the most promising territory found in the New World and the loss of many prominent Spaniards, and this would create more problems in Cuba. If Velásquez had a grievance against Cortés, he must petition the Crown to resolve it, not take the affair into his own hands.

There was, however, a condition upon which the Jeronymites would permit the fleet to leave Cuba. The Crown was seeking to colonize new lands, and Narváez could sail if Velásquez agreed to seek out lands other than New Spain to plant his colonies. If the governor accepted this condition, he could serve God and King and still realize a profit for his investment.

The governor, however, was aware that the Jeronymites no longer held administrative or judicial powers in the Indies. Its responsibility to the crown in Indian matters was finished, and it served only as an advisor to Rodrigo de Figueroa, who had arrived in the Indies less than seven months ago. One month after his arrival, the Crown established the Council of the Indies in Seville and appointed the Bishop of Burgos as president. With such a powerful friend in court and the authority of Santo Domingo so poorly defined, Velásquez did not hesitate to take issue with Ayllon's order.

"Senor," Velásquez replied, "I complied with the wishes of the Jeronymites when I yielded command of my ships and my army to one of my officers. Now, however, I am asked to submit to the unreasonable demand that I give up the enterprise as well, no matter what financial loss I may suffer. The land that Cortés has unrightfully occupied is prosperous, it falls within the territories granted me by the king, and it lies within my right to enforce my grant. I can assure you that there will be no civil war in New Spain-Cortés cannot have no more than 300 men, and some of them may be dead by now. No matter how able he is, he cannot stand against 900 good men under the command of Pánfilo de Narváez.

"If we seek other lands, as the *audiencia* insists we must, we are more likely to lose everything than realize a profit if we hesitate. Therefore, I am determined to pursue this venture. By doing so, I serve God and my Emperor, and I shall proceed no matter how many injunctions you serve against me."

"Senor *licenciado*," Narváez said," you have shown no cause to prevent our leaving. We are all vassals of the Emperor, and everything we do, we do in his name, even though some may perceive his service differently than others. We believe that we must conquer that fair land and colonize it for the King, and that we are duty-bound to prevent Hernando Cortés from appropriating that which rightfully belongs to a loyal servant of the King. I ask that your reflect upon your orders, sir, for even though I go to New Spain by the order of Diego Velásquez, I go in the service of the King, for he is his governor and he holds the King's authority to pursue this course of action.

"You need have no concern about war, for I know Hernando Cortés well, and he knows me. I cherish him as I would a son, and he respects me as he would a father. If he chooses to resist, the men in his company are not fools-they will not stand by him when they are faced with the governor's army. Furthermore, many of his men are our friends also, and some are even relatives of Diego Velásquez.

234

"Now, sir, I must go. In two hours the tide will be with us, and we are ready to depart."

Ayllon could do no more to prevent the fleet from sailing. Diego Velásquez obviously believed that the order from Santo Domingo was subordinate to his warrant from the Crown, and he was willing to risk the displeasure of Figueroa and the *Audiencia* to enforce it. All the licenciado could do was to exercise his right to accompany the expedition as an officer of the King to keep Narváez and Cortés from each other's throats.

We followed the same southwesterly course as Grijalva to reach the Island of Yucatán, then we followed the coast north until the land turned eastward. When we passed beyond the Laguna de Terminos we encountered a heavy norther, with winds so strong that one of the ships foundered, drowning the captain and all hands aboard save for five that managed to reach the shore. We salvaged what we could of the ship's gear, then resumed our journey along the coast until we reached San Juan de Ulua, where we anchored on the 23rd day of April, 1520.

We had no trouble learning the whereabouts of Hernando Cortés and his army. We had not yet put the cargo ashore when three Spaniards from his company arrived. They were seeking gold in the sierra when the Indians brought word of our fleet, and they lost no time in reaching the coast. From them, Narváez learned that Cortés and the greater part of his army were beyond the sierra in a city called Tenochtitlán. We also learned that he had established a colony some twelve leagues north of our position, where he had left a garrison of 70 men, and had sent 150 foot to establish another colony fifty leagues south of San Juan. All three were disenchanted with Cortés. Cervantes, the most outspoken of the three and a drunken fool, claimed that Cortés had amassed a fortune in gold and refused to share it with his soldiers. The others, Escalona and Alonso Hernandez, were relieved to be out of Cortes's grasp and away from Tenochtitlán, fearing that they would be killed by the Indians if they returned.

But it was their description of the vast Indian empire that lay beyond the sierra and the great city on the lake that gripped our imagination. The lord of the empire, Montezuma, was in Cortés's hands, and he exercised such control over the empire that no chieftain, no Indian lord, dared challenge him or his men as they traveled from one end of the country to the other, taking what they pleased.

Cortés, however, was in a precarious position. According to Cervantes, he was surrounded by more than 10,000 Indians, who were kept at bay only by the continuing submission of his royal hostage.

Narváez sent the priest Juan Ruiz de Guevara, his notary, and a hidalgo called Amaya to Gonzalo de Sandoval, the commander of the garrison at Vera Cruz. They bore a message that Diego Velásquez was now His Majesty's governor and chief justice of New Spain, and an order to surrender the colony to him at once. He also sent an invitation to Juan Velásquez de Leon, a kinsman of the governor and now commander of Cortés's troops at Coatzacoalcos, to come to San Juan where they could discuss how they might best serve the new governor of New Spain. His next move, based upon information from Cortes's deserters, was to send a ship to Cempoala, and after a few rounds were fired to frighten the Indians, he moved the company into the city and set up quarters in the temples.

We had not been in Cempoala more than a few days when a party of Indian nobles, wearing multicolored robes and graceful feathered plumes, arrived in camp. They brought greetings from the lord Montezuma and gifts for our captain, and they told him that the Emperor had ordered his vassals to provide him and his companions with food and whatever else they might need.

By now the three deserters had learned something of the Mexican language, and when the ambassadors asked Narváez if he were a brother of Cortés, he replied that all were servants of the Emperor of the Christians, but Cortés had come to Mexico against the wishes of his lord. When their lord heard of how Cortés had seized Montezuma and mistreated his people, he sent him here to arrest Cortés as a common criminal. When he took Cortés into custody, he would release Montezuma and return him to his rightful throne. He would also make restitution for all the wrongs done by Cortés, and after this was done, he would return to his own country.

A few days after the Mexicans departed, messengers arrived with a letter from Cortés. He asked that we identify ourselves and state our objectives in Mexico, and he wanted to know if we had been sent by the King of Spain with a warrant authorizing us to establish a colony. If not, and if it was our intent settle here, he warned us that we were now in the dominions of the King of Spain, and that he was His Majesty's chief justice and captain-general of all his forces. If we failed to reply to his inquiry, he would assume that we were adversaries who had come to take the land away from the king, and he would march against us with his army and 10,000 Indian allies.

Narváez seized the messengers and did not bother to answer.

Two weeks later, the priest Bartolome de Olmedo arrived with another letter for Narváez. By now Cortés knew who we were and that Diego Velásquez had sent us.

Cortés wrote that he was disappointed that his old friend had not sent him greetings when he arrived in Mexico, and that he was concerned about his messengers, who had not returned. He was also disturbed to hear that Narváez was encouraging his men to desert, and he warned him that all such efforts must cease at once. The state of affairs throughout the country were now at a critical stage, and there was great risk that all he had accomplished would be lost if the Indians suspected that there was any discord between them. Even united, he wrote, we are but few, and the Indians outnumber us more than a thousand to one. If we set our forces against each other, the king's goals in Mexico will never be realized.

He informed Narváez that Montezuma, the lord of Mexico, was his prisoner, and that he had accumulated a great sum of gold and other valuables belonging to the King and to his company. He could not, however, leave the city to meet with Narváez at this time without risking an uprising.

He had also been informed that Narváez had created a municipality, named civil officers, and that he had assumed the tiles of Lieutenant Governor of the country and captain-general of all forces. Only the king, he advised Narváez, could grant such authority, since Villa Rica de Vera Cruz was a crown colony with proper tribunals and municipal bodies. If, however, he possessed valid warrants and directions from the king, he should present them to him and he would see that they were honored.

Narváez's next move was to send a priest named Guevara, a notary, and four soldiers to the garrison at Vera Cruz, where they were met with a cold reception by Gonzalo de Sandoval. When Guevara demanded he tender his submission to Narváez and the notary began to read his proclamation, Sandoval threatened him with flogging unless he first produced a warrant from the Crown. When it was not forthcoming, he ordered the party bound and tied to the backs of Indians and carted off to Tenochtitlán.

They were expecting the worse when they were taken before Cortés, but to their surprise, he released them and apologized for Sandoval's regrettable behavior. They spent the next two days as his guests, and he went to great lengths to entertain them and show them the city. When they left, he was generous to a fault, giving each gold and jewelry from a storeroom filled with priceless artifacts.

When Guevara returned to Cempoala he urged Narváez not to break with Cortés, but instead to take the lead in negotiating a compromise that would benefit all. The cities he had seen in his journey into the interior, he said, were beyond compare, and Tenochtitlán was as great a city as Constantinople. He warned Narváez that the land was so heavily populated that dissension and strife between them would risk losing the entire country.

Lucas Vázquez de Ayllon had also received a letter from Cortés, and the licenciado warned Narváez that it would be a disservice to both God and King if he chose to risk the lives of his men and those in Cortés's company by rousing the Indians. Narváez's attitude toward Cortés, he said, gave every indication that he had come to New Spain to avenge Diego Velásquez, not to serve the Crown. If he marched to Tenochtitlán to seize Cortés, his actions would be judged punishable by death in Santo Domingo. Furthermore, he was so blinded by his desire for revenge that he refused to listen to his commanders, who were men of good sense.

Ayllon's threat, Narváez knew, was intended to intimidate him and his men, but he was not one to have his authority challenged, not even by an officer of the King. His arrogance and stubborn pride got the better of his good judgement, and without considering the consequences, he ordered Ayllon seized and sent back to Cuba, where Velásquez could keep an eye on him. But Narváez failed to judge the authority carried by an officer of the King: Ayllon had no difficulty convincing the pilot major of the ship to change course and sail for Santo Domingo.

While the captains bickered about jurisdiction, however, the rank and file was more concerned with gold and jewels. The gifts that the priest Olmedo passed among them during his stay had been calculated to impress them. Furthermore, Cortés's hospitality and generosity to Guevara and his men was designed to assure them that all would realize a fair share of the wealth of New Spain.

Narváez, on the other hand, seemed bent upon risking their lives to punish Cortés, and he showed little concern for their stake in the venture. When Cortés left Cempoala for Tenochtitlán, he left behind a considerable amount of gold and jewelry for safekeeping, and Narváez took it all for himself. Nor did he share with them the precious gifts that Montezuma sent to him, not even with his closest friends. Also, many were troubled by his abduction of Ayllon, which could be judged high treason in Santo Domingo, and some who had no desire to share the King's retribution with Narváez planned to defect to Cortés at the first opportunity.

Discipline in camp grew worse every day, and the men, left to their own devices, treated the Cempoalans like dogs. They worked them night and day, and took whatever they wanted from them-ducks, turkeys, hens, and whatever valuables they possessed. Worse, they used their wives and daughters mercilessly. Soon the town was all but deserted; every able-bodied Indian had fled into the hills. Furthermore, Cortés was well aware of our unrest: not a single night passed without one or another of us receiving a letter from one of his men, telling of the spoils to be gained by joining them.

Having failed to convince Sandoval to surrender the garrison at Vera Cruz, Narváez now sent Alonso de Mata to Cortés with an ultimatum to surrender his forces immediately.

De Mata and his party met Cortés and his army on the road to Cholula, and when Cortés saw the unfamiliar faces, he dismounted and approached them on foot. De Mata handed him Narváez's directive, and he read it slowly, without expression. When he finished, he asked de Mata if he brought warrants from the King. De Mata said he had, but when he failed to produce them, Cortés arrested him for impersonating an officer of the King. Later he relented, and sent de Mata back to Narváez with a request that he present him with the proper warrants when he arrived in Tapaniquita.

De Mata returned with the news that Cortés was already on the march with 270 Spaniards, not more than 40 leagues from Cempoala, and he warned Narváez to prepare for an attack. Furthermore, the loyalty of the company was suspect, since he had met a number of deserters on the road. He urged Narváez to move the army into the field, where our superior numbers could be used to advantage rather than waiting for Cortés in the confinement of the city. But Narváez was more accustomed to flattery from his subordinates, not advice upon exercising his command, and he dismissed de Mata as an overcautious subordinate.

Juan Velásquez de Leon was an imposing man. Proud and lordly, he rode into Cempoala in full armor, wearing a polished steel corselet and a heavy gold chain thrown carelessly about his shoulder. He dismounted in front of the fat chieftain's house, where Indians surrounded him as if he were a lost brother. The sentries ran to inform the captain, and Narváez lost no time in coming out to greet him, certain that he had come to join his uncle's cause. They embraced in the street, and Narváez ordered his servants to see to his horse and baggage, but Juan Velásquez stopped him. He had very little time, he said, because he had come only to greet his companions and to ask Narváez if he would meet Cortés on more friendly terms. Narváez began to object, but Juan Velásquez held up his hand.

"Senor captain, he said, "when Hernando Cortés heard of your arrival, he offered you and your men opportunity not only to share the wealth of this land, but to serve God and the King as well. He also warned you that failure to reach a reasonable compromise would result in conflict, because every man in our company will die before he gives up that for which he has risked his life and suffered every hardship. The choice is yours and yours alone, Cortés says, and if you chose war, whatever happens will not lie upon his conscience.

"I am a near kinsman of Diego Velásquez, and it would seem that I am obliged to support him rather than Hernando Cortés. Justice, however, is of far more consequence than kinship, and I am relieved of my obligation because justice in this affair is clearly on the side of Hernando Cortés.

"When Diego Velásquez undertook this venture, he appointed Hernando Cortés as his captain-general, and Cortés committed all of his resources and the resources of his friends to the enterprise. When we arrived in New Spain, we founded a colony and elected him our chief justice and captain-general, and from that time on, he has shown himself worthy of our trust. He has been courageous and judicious; he has conquered many peoples; and he has subjected kings and princes to the Crown of Castile. With no more than a handful of men, he forced his way into Tenochtitlán, the greatest and most powerful city in the world, and seized the emperor Montezuma. Now, even though Montezuma is his prisoner, he looks upon Cortés as if he were emperor of the world.

We who came to this land with Cortés have suffered many wounds from the arrows, the javelins, and the *maquahuitls* of the Indians. But we persevered, and now even the Tlaxcalans, the most formidable warriors in the land, are our friends. We learned to speak their language, we cast down their idols, we baptized them as Christians, and now we live among them as if we were in our own homes.

"Now you have come here with a great army, unwilling to offer us terms and bent upon forcing your will upon us. Although my allegiance lies with Cortés, my duty to Diego Velásquez compels me to ask you to seek peace. God stands with right and justice, and even though we are few in number, we shall prevail if it comes to war."

Narváez could hardly contain himself. "How dare you speak to me in this manner!" he said. "How dare you ask me to seek terms with a traitor who has betrayed his governor and benefactor? I am captain-general of New Spain, and I shall do my duty as I see fit!"

"Cortés is no traitor," Velásquez responded, "and I ask you not to use that word in my presence. He is a faithful servant of His Majesty, and it is not treason but his right as a loyal subject of the Crown to appeal our case before the King."

There was talk among the principals to seize Juan Velásquez, but cooler heads prevailed, and he was led to quarters that had been prepared for him.

Narváez had planned to offer the post of second in command to Juan Velásquez, hoping that he would persuade his friends and relatives to abandon Cortés, but there was little prospect of that now. Nevertheless, he invited him to dine with him and his captains, hoping to persuade him to act as a mediator whereby he could convince Cortés to surrender his army. Narváez also invited young Diego Velásquez, another nephew of the governor, to join them.

Little was said during dinner, and what conversation took place was civil and light. As dinner was about to end, and Narváez was preparing to broach the subject, Diego Velásquez turned to his cousin and said that Cortés and all who supported him were traitors for refusing to submit to Narváez. Juan Velásquez swept his chair to the floor and jumped to his feet. "Senor captain," he said to Narváez, "I have warned you that I will not tolerate such insults against my captain and my comrades. Only a thoughtless fool would call men who have served their king so faithfully traitors."

Diego Velásquez rose slowly, and replied that his words were well-spoken, and that Juan Velásquez was not worthy of their honored name.

Juan Velásquez's hand flew to his sword. He called his cousin a liar, and asked Narváez to give him leave to prove it. But others jumped to their feet and stood between them. They led Juan Velásquez outside and told him that it was best he leave before there was more trouble.

When he was mounted and ready to ride, he turned to his cousin and said, "before many days have passed, we will see if your courage is a match for your tongue."

Cortés was now no more than 15 leagues from Cempoala, and war seemed inevitable. As determined as Narváez was to see Cortés in chains, however, he was not so pig-headed that he failed to see the difficulties that a bloody civil war would create with the Crown. In a last minute attempt to avoid the conflict, he sent Andrés de Duero, one of Cortés's closest friends, with a proposal for peace.

He offered to provide Cortés with ships and provisions, and he could take whatever he wanted out of the country, provided he yielded New Spain to him and recognized him as captain-general. These terms, he wrote, were the best he was prepared to offer, and he offered them only because Diego Velásquez had authorized them.

Cortés replied that he had yet to see a warrant directing him to yield the country to Diego Velásquez. Grants to the Governor of Cuba that were signed by the Bishop of Burgos carried no legal force in a crown colony, and he was bound by law not to yield the country without authorization from the King. If Narváez possessed such warrants, he would honor them if he presented them to him and to the municipal council of Vera Cruz.

Through intermediaries, efforts were made to arrange a meeting, hoping that they could reconcile their differences before one attacked the other. An agreement was reached whereby the two would meet in a deserted Indian village halfway between the camps, and Cortés would be given the opportunity to examine Narváez's warrants. Each signed a safe-conduct for the other, and each agreed to an escort of no more than 20 soldiers. Cortés, however, backed down at the last minute, claiming that he had evidence that Narváez had set a trap and planned to kill him, and he sent an ultimatum to Narváez.

If Narváez failed to provide a proper warrant from the king, he wrote, he was forbidden, under penalties set forth by the municipality of Vera Cruz, to call himself chief justice or captain-general, and neither he nor any of his appointees were to assume duties invested in the lawfully elected officers of Vera Cruz. Furthermore, his men were forbidden to recognize him as captain-general, and they were directed not to obey any orders he might issue as such. Instead, they were to report to Cortés at a designated time to receive his instructions and be assigned proper duties for His Majesty's service. If Narváez persisted in his unlawful activities, and if his men refused to report to him as ordered, he would proceed against them and see that they were prosecuted according to law.

Narváez ordered the foot, the cavalry, and the artillery into the fields outside of Cempoala, and when they were assembled, he rode to the forefront. He raised his arm for silence, and in a voice that could be heard at the rear, he shouted, "Comrades! Caballeros! You who have been chosen from many for this great enterprise! You have come to bring Hernando Cortés to justice!

"From the day this traitor left port in Santiago, he not only betrayed his benefactor, Diego Velásquez, but disobeyed every order set forth by the governor. He has assumed powers in New Spain that he is not entitled to, and he has taken for himself riches that rightfully belong to others.

"Now he dares to bargain with me by offering to share the wealth of this land with me. But I have steadfastly refused all his overtures. I would be no better than him if I accepted any compromise whatsoever, and I would be stealing what is rightfully the property of my governor.

"I know that many of you feel that we should not take up arms against our countrymen. We know that this land is populated and bountiful, and that it has riches enough for all. We also know that if it comes to war, our forces may be so weakened that everything will be lost to the Indians. To this I cannot disagree. But if we reach an accord with Hernando Cortés, will we still avoid strife? Hernando Cortés and his men are now established in New Spain, and you are the outsiders. Envy and disharmony are sure to aggravate our differences with them, and sooner or later we are bound to clash with them.

"They are few in number and poorly armed, however. We have more men, more horses, more cannon, crossbows, and muskets, and we are no less brave in spirit than our enemy. This I promise you-if it comes to war, little of your blood will be shed! You will be the masters of New Spain, and they will have no more than what you give them.

"I need not inspire you with words, since the rewards of this undertaking are inspiration enough, and I know that there is not one among you so stupid as to want more for Hernando Cortés than for himself. Our advantage is obvious to all-victory lies before our very eyes, and if we have but resolve, none can overcome us!

"Let us return to our quarters now, and may God favor us and aid us in our endeavor."

It was nearly twilight, and as we withdrew, some of the principals suggested, as had Alonso de Mata, that it would be better to meet Cortés in the open field than wait for him in Cempoala, where our superior numbers would be less to our advantage. But it was raining, and Narváez dismissed their concerns. Cortés would not dare attack us whether we were in the field or in the city, and notwithstanding Cortés's threats, he had no choice other than to accept whatever terms he was offered.

Back in quarters we discussed the captain's confidence of victory well into the night. His followers praised his rousing speech and approved of his decision to defend the city instead of meeting Cortés in the open field. Here the musketeers and crossbowmen had the advantage of high ground on the temples, and our artillery was positioned to cover each of the four entrances into the plaza. Cortés, they insisted, would be a fool to attack us.

Others were less confident that victory would come as easily as the captain predicted.

"You know little about warfare," said a veteran campaigner. From what his friends among us have told me about Hernando Cortés, he will prove to be a formidable enemy. He and his men have endured

Aztec: The Death of a Nation

many hardships, and they have overcome what many judge to be insurmountable obstacles. Moreover, they know the land and the Indians. Cortés may be in a difficult position, but history has shown time and time again that men who believe in the justice of their cause have defeated great armies. His men will fight like lions unchained to defend this country, and if we win, it will be done only after a long and difficult struggle. As they say, if we won't give them a leg of the bird they have hunted, they may as well defend the whole bird.

"Hernando Cortés has done what no other captain in the Indies have ever done. He is brave, he has earned the respect of his men by being the first to expose himself to danger, and he is shrewd. Mark my words, he will attack us, and he will choose a time when we are least prepared to defend ourselves."

Early the next morning the army awakened to the rattle of drums and the tattoo of trumpets sounding the call to arms. Our Indian allies had sighted Cortés less than a league from Cempoala.

We left the city at quick-march, with the cavalry in the van. When we reached the fields, the cavalry deployed as skirmishers while the foot executed a wheeling maneuver about Cempoala. We heard several artillery salvos from the direction of the city, but this turned out to be no more than a show of force, since no sign of the enemy was found that day.

It seemed useless to proceed further, because the Rio de Canoas lay up ahead, and its waters were in flood stage from the heavy rains that had fallen the past week. Narváez was certain that Cortés would not attempt a crossing, since our scouts had searched up and down both banks without finding a ford. Believing that the Indians had encountered nothing more than a small patrol beyond the river, he ordered the army back to Cempoala.

Narváez posted a hundred sentries on the outskirts of the city and in the plaza, and more at half-league intervals along the road. He ordered 40 horse to patrol the routes that Cortés would most likely use to reach the city, and stationed two lookouts along the near bank of the river in the unlikely event that Cortés was able to find a ford. He deployed his artillery to establish a field of fire covering all four entrances of the plaza.

I was quartered with 50 other men in the main temple, which was Narváez's command post. Three companies were posted in the lesser

245

temples of the plaza, and the rest of the army was positioned at strategic points throughout the city.

As we prepared to bed down for the night, a steady rain began to fall. Our quarters were still dank and miserable from the weeklong rains, and we huddled together to seek what little warmth we could from the wretched dampness of the temple. It rained so hard that the gunners were unable to keep the charges in the cannon dry, and they were forced to seal the touchholes with wax and place tiles over them. There was no moon: the only sign of life was a solitary light burning in the captain's quarters, shining like a beacon above the pitch-black plaza.

The hour was approaching midnight when we were shaken out of a fitful sleep by shouts from below. "To arms! To arms!" someone was shouting. "Cortés is coming! The enemy is upon us!"

Lights came on from one end of the plaza to the other, but we saw nothing bellow save the sentries and the gunners huddled about their cannon.

The soldier who had given the alarm was brought before Narváez, and we recognized him as Hurtado, the servant of Gonzalo Carrasco, whom the captain had posted along the road a league from Cempoala. Hurtado told Narváez that he and his master were alerted by the sound of men moving quietly along the road. Carrasco ordered Hurtado to hide in a nearby ravine, and fearing that his white corselet could be seen in the dark, went behind a plum tree to remove it. Hurtado heard a shout, and without waiting to hear anything more, fled for Cempoala.

Narváez asked Hurtado how many men he had seen, but the lookout was not sure. It was very dark, he said, but from the noise, he judged that there must have been at least eight.

Narváez smiled, and he said, "Hurtado my son, go to bed. I believe that you let your imagination run away from you in the dark, or else that you had a bad dream. Cortés will not come tonight, not in this rain."

He dismissed Hurtado, and sent a page to fetch him a glass of wine.

When Hurtado reached our quarters, we gathered about him, asking what had happened.

"Cortés is coming," he said, "and my master, Gonzalo Carrasco, is his prisoner, even though the captain does not believe me. He says I must have been dreaming, but when I heard Cortes's men, I was as wide-awake as I am this moment. Unless there are phantoms in this country, those voices I heard were speaking Spanish."

Juan Bono laughed and told Hurtado to be quiet and let him get some sleep. "Cortés is not fool enough to attack in a downpour in the middle of the night," he said, "not when he can't see what he is doing.

"You make an ass of me," Hurtado said, "but I swear to God that I was not asleep nor did I let my imagination get the better of me in the dark. And I was not drunk: it has been far too many days since I tasted a drop of wine. But if Cortés does not fall upon us before daylight, I will be the ass you say I am, and I will bray like an ass on the body of God."

We settled down again, trying to get some sleep before sun up, and the sentries returned to their posts, seeking shelter wherever they could against the steady downpour. Midnight came and passed. The only light was the lamp that shone from the captain's quarters, and the only sound was the steady beat of rain on the temple roof.

Then, in the distance, a sentry's challenge echoed into the night. Then another, this time closer, and as we scrambled to our feet, soldiers in the plaza below began to shout. Narváez ordered the drums sounded, but before he could put on his armor, the sentries at the foot of the temple shouted, "To arms! To arms! Cortés is here!"

Their shouts were answered by a drumbeat across the plaza and cries of "Espirito Santo! At them!" Below us a Negro ran out of a temple with a lantern, and by its light, we could see more than 50 soldiers rushing toward the temple. A lance thrust tumbled him to the ground, and his lantern went out. Then we saw points of light flickering in the darkness beyond, and it seemed that hundreds of musketeers were priming their matchlocks.

Below us our gunners were busy clearing their touchholes, but they succeeded in discharging only four rounds before the enemy was upon them. Our cavalry tried to drive them away from their cannon, but Cortés's foot, armed with long pikes, struck at their flanks, unhorsing riders and scattering their mounts.

We rushed down the stairs of the temple to meet their charge, but they pressed upward, driving us back inside the shrine, where we held

247

fast. As they fought to enter, we could hear Gonzalo de Sandoval shouting for Narváez to surrender. Narváez only laughed, and Sandoval's words made us fight all the harder.

Suddenly smoke filled the shrine, and above us the thatch roof burst into flames. The smoke drove us out onto the platform, choking us and making it difficult to see the enemy. The captain Diego Rojas was the first to fall, and as he fell, we heard him cry out, "O Holy Lady, save me!" Narváez rallied us, and we drove them from the platform, but more pikemen arrived and forced us back. We still might have won the day, but a pikeman thrust his lance into Narváez's eye, and he shrieked, "Holy Mary, protect me! They have killed me!"

With the fall of the captain, our spirit failed us, and the enemy about us shouted, "Espirito Santo! Espirito Santo! Narváez has fallen! Victory for Cortés!"

For those of us who fought beside Narváez, the battle was over. Gonzalo de Sandoval arrested him and led him away, and his men took our weapons. Of our comrades, we saw nothing of them as we fought off our attackers. Whether the enemy drove them away with our own cannon, whether there were more of Cortés's sympathizers in the army than we accounted for, or whether they mistook the fireflies that filled the air for matchlocks frightened them off, I know not.

As the enemy herded us to the plaza below, the only resistance in evidence was on a nearby temple, where 300 men stood fast. In response to Cortés's demand for surrender, they shouted "Diego Velásquez and Pánfilo de Narváez! Our governor and our captain by order of His Majesty! Long live the king!" The temple, however, afforded them no protection from the artillery. When a warning shot fired over the temple failed to dislodge them, the gunner placed a round through the roof of the shrine, killing two and dismembering several others.

Dawn saw Narváez's proud army herded into the plaza, and one by one, we surrendered our arms. As we laid down our weapons, we looked upon our captors with shame, for they were no more than a ragged band of brigands, less than half our number. They had no horses, their swords were rusted, they had few crossbows, and their filthy cotton armor was a humiliating contrast to our shiny steel corselets.

From the other side of the plaza we could hear the shrill voices of Francisca de Ordaz and her sister Beatriz, who had come to New Spain with us. "Rogues!" they shouted, "Cowards!" A fine account you gave of yourselves this night. "Now you can watch while these swine who have beaten you use us like whores! Women who follow men like you will always come to ruin!"

Narváez's forces, more than twice as great as those of our attacker, had been defeated in a battle that was little more than a skirmish between two squads, a struggle that lasted half an hour. Of our 700 foot, crossbowmen, and muskets, fewer than 100 engaged the enemy. The cavalry played no part in the action. One squad searched fruitlessly along the road and another scarcely had time to saddle their mounts before Cortés's pikemen were upon them. The artillery, for reasons known only to him, Narváez had deployed about the main temple, were captured before the gunners could clear the touchholes.[iii]

Our only casualties were Diego de Rojas, Fuentes the standard bearer, two foot, and one of Cortés's renegades. Of the enemy, we had killed but four, and two others drowned when Cortés crossed the river by the ford that Narváez could not find.

Prodded by our captors, we gathered about the main temple, where Cortés was waiting to speak to us. He raised his hand for quiet, and in a voice that echoed across the plaza, he began to speak.

"I, Hernando Cortés," he said, "have been elected Chief Justice and Captain-General by the captains, caballeros, and soldiers who serve under my banner by the authority given to them by Charles the Fifth, Holy Roman Emperor and King of Spain. I now proclaim to all the captains, caballeros, and soldiers of the army of Pánfilo de Narváez, that by my order, your commander has been arrested for just cause.

"As His Majesty's interests demand that his generals do not stand in opposition to each other, however, I invite every member of Pánfilo de Narváez's army, in the name of His Majesty, to appear before men and swear and oath to serve me as your captain-general. Those who take this oath and later defect from my command, however, will be hanged and all of his property declared forfeit."

Nearly half the company and several captains joined Cortés, and he returned their weapons and horses over the objections of his men, who claimed them as spoils of war. Many remained loyal to Narváez and Diego Velásquez, but they had no plan other than return to Cuba as soon as they could. They had no ships, however, since Cortés had seized the fleet. Francisco de Lugo had taken the ships to the anchorage at Quiahuitztlán and placed them under the command of Pedro de Cavallero, who, although one of Narváez's pilots, was one of his most trusted friends. To prevent any of Diego Velásquez's supporters from seizing one of the ships and escaping, he disabled them by removing sails, rudders, and rigging, which he stored under heavy guard at Vera Cruz.

With so many men at his disposal, Cortés decided that the time was opportune to establish more settlements along the seacoast. Narváez's arrival had prevented him from colonizing Coatzacoalcos, but now that the threat was over, he was able to send 120 men under the command of Diego de Ordaz back to the province, and another 120 men under the command of Juan Velásquez north to the Panuco River. Each force consisted of 100 men from Narváez's army and 20 from Cortés's company. By sending so many of Narváez's men away, he made our forces in Cempoala more manageable.

Cortés established his headquarters in the house of a wealthy Indian noblewoman called Doña Catalina, whom the chieftain of Cempoala had given him when he first arrived in New Spain. He stored the weapons of Diego Velásquez's loyalists inside Dona Catalina's compound, positioned his artillery around the perimeter, and confined Narváez in the house under a 24-hour watch.

We had not been in Cempoala more than a few days when the Indians began to sicken, and almost overnight their bodies and faces were covered with rashes and erupting pustules. We knew the symptoms well-it was smallpox. Their burning fevers drove them to the river by hundreds, and try as we would, we could not keep them from the water. They began to die faster than we could bury them, and soon a putrid stench spread over the city as bodies rotted in the streets. The town became a morass of filth, vomit, and excrement, and we feared the malignant vapors would bring the pestilence down upon us. Mercifully, an offshore breeze rose and swept the foul air far out to the sea.[iv]

A Negro in our company brought the epidemic ashore, and from that day forward, from Cempoala to every corner of the land, the plague followed us, taking its terrible toll of the natives.

Fortunately, only a few of us were infected with the disease, but it was clear that we could no longer remain in Cempoala, because hunger followed upon the heels of pestilence. There were not enough Indians now to provision us and feed us, nor enough women to make tortillas from what maize was left in the granaries.

The Indians were still burying their dead when a message appealing for help arrived from Pedro de Alvarado. The Mexicans had risen against the garrison in Tenochtitlán, and the entire company was under siege. Montezuma could not, or would not control his people. Several Spaniards had been killed, many were badly wounded, and unless help arrived soon, they would be massacred.

Cortés countermanded his orders to Juan Velásquez and Diego de Ordaz, and directed them to march at once to Tlaxcala, where he would join them. Then he summoned every able-bodied Spaniard to meet with him in the plaza.

"This army," he said, "is an army divided by conflicting loyalties. There are those of you who came here with me and supported me faithfully as we fought the Indians and conquered the land. There are among you those who came with Narváez, but you abandoned his cause for mine when you recognized it as a just cause. You accepted me as your captain-general, and for your allegiance, I returned your arms and invited you to join me in the conquest of this land and to share its wealth with my companions and me.

But many of you still oppose me and cling stubbornly to Narváez's claim that Diego Velásquez should govern this country. Now you find yourselves alone in this land. You have no weapons, you have no ships to take you back to Cuba, and you have no captain to protect you from the Indians.

"When Narváez brought you here, he did everything in his power to undermine my authority over the Indians. He wrote not to me, but to Montezuma, telling the emperor of his powerful army and his intent to execute my men and me. He promised Montezuma that he would return him to his throne, and Montezuma bargained with him. But Montezuma is no fool. He believed that I would be killed at Cempoala, and he rose against Pedro de Alvarado and the men as

251

soon as I left. With them out of the way, he would once again command his armies, and he would have to deal with only those of us who survived the war in Cempoala.

"Now Pedro de Alvarado and our companions are under siege in Tenochtitlán; his defenses have been undermined, and some of his men are dead. If we do not reach him soon, before our countrymen are sacrificed on the altars of Mexico's gods, the power of this great empire will be turned against us. Then the richest, the greatest city in the world will be lost, and our opportunity for wealth, honor, and glory will be gone forever.

"As one army, however, an army united in purpose and seeking to serve God and king, no power on earth can stand against us. To you who oppose me, I ask you now to join me in our common cause. Follow me, and I promise that you will be the equal of any man who takes part in this enterprise. I promise that you will share equally with those who have supported me from the first day we came to New Spain and with those of your company who have sworn their loyalty to me. Know also that every man in my company has given me his word that he will honor my promise, as has each of you who is now with us.

"Now pick up your arms. I return them with no conditions. You may follow me or go your own way, as you chose, but whatever course you choose, you will find no fortune greater than that which awaits you in Mexico. If honor and glory, if wealth and the service of God do not spur you to follow me, then neither God nor I would compel you to do so. But you must decide now. We must act swiftly to help our flesh and blood in Tenochtitlán. We must not permit our Christian brothers to be sacrificed on the altars of the devil."

Alonso de Ojeda and Juan Marquez began passing out swords and bucklers, and as each man took up his arms, he swore his allegiance to Hernando Cortés. What else could he do? Without ships, without provisions, left to himself in a plague-ridden city, where could he go?

---

[i] During the Córdoba expedition, Bernal Díaz noted, "On the other side of the idols were symbols like crosses." To the Maya Indians, the cross signifies the tree of life, and wooden crosses were erected on the borders of each village to guard it from evil.

[ii] The Jeronymite Friars, Luis de Figueroa, Bernardino de Manzanedo, and Alonso de Santo Domingo, were sent to Santo Domingo in December, 1516, by the Regent Cardinal Ximenez de Cisernos. Their mission was to bring an end to the abuses suffered by the Indians at the hands of the Spanish colonists by reforming the encomienda system. Cisernos, however, endowed them with powers beyond those called for to accomplish their stated mission, so that they were, in effect, royal governors. Even Alonso Zuazo, the juez de residencia, was obliged to consult them in all matters.

After the death of Cisernos in 1517, the Jeronymites, failing to resolve the Indian problem to the satisfaction of the Crown, the colonists, or the Indians. Bartolome de las Casas, who instigated their mission, requested Charles V to relieve them of their duties. Their judicial authority was removed in August, 1518, and by December of that year, their powers were transferred to the new *juez de residencia,* Rodrigo de Figueroa. But Figueroa did not arrive in Santiago until August 1519, during which time the Jeronymites continued to exercise judicial authority. They remained in Santo Domingo until 1520, serving in an advisory capacity to Figueroa.

[iii] The sealed touchholes of the cannon may not have been the only reason that Cortes took Narváez's artillery so readily. Bernal Diaz reports that a member of Cortés's company, one Usagre, was the brother of Narváez's master gunner, and Usagre had accompanied Olmedo to Cempoala. Olmedo's mission was to bribe key members of the company, and it is more than likely that a gold ingot found its way into the gunners hands. Cervantes also reports that some of the pieces had been filled with sand instead of gunpowder.

[iv] Cervantes reports that the smallpox epidemic was of such proportions that the Indians revised their calendar to mark the date of its appearance.

19. Ecatl:

The Death of Innocence

The approach of Toxcatl, the most festive of our agrarian rituals, found the people of Tenochtitlán troubled and in low spirits. Nearly eight months had passed since the Spaniards seized our lords, and they forbade our celebrating any but the least of our public ceremonies, eight cheerless months that saw the rites of Huitzilpochtli, Tlaloc, and Xipe Totec, the god of spring, pass unobserved. Only the Nemontemi, the five unlucky days that marked the end of the year, the days of fasting, and penitence, when the people observed abstinence in the privacy of their homes. Needless to say, there had been few sacrifices, all of which were carried out in secret, but far from sufficient to placate the gods.

Toxcatl heralded the end of the dry season and the return of life-giving rains to the land, a celebration for all our people, commoner and noble alike, and Moctezuma was determined to see his people sing and dance again. He sought out Pedro de Alvarado to explain the significance of the ritual and its importance to his people, and to seek his permission to observe it.[i]

The principal ceremony, he told Alvarado, would take place in the great plaza, where the people would gather on the first day to sing songs of praise and offer their gifts and prayers to the gods. On the second day, young nobles from the finest families of Mexico would gather to perform the ritual dance asking the gods for a bountiful harvest. There would be no human sacrifices, he assured Alvarado, and he promised that there would be no uprising. He invited Alvarado and his men to observe the ceremony and attend the rituals so he could see for himself that their only purpose was to honor the gods.

Alvarado was suspicious, but grudgingly gave his permission after warning Moctezuma of the consequences should there be any trouble.

Eight days before the festival, every household in Tenochtitlán was busy popping kernels of maize over open fires and making garlands, tiaras, and necklaces from the snow-white buds. These would be worn until the eighth day after the festival, which marked the end of the dry season.

Women who had observed a yearlong fast ground wild amaranth seeds into a heavy paste, added black maguey syrup, and kneaded it into heavy dough. They molded the dough onto a framework of sticks and shaped it in the image of Huitzilopochtli. They clothed him with a sleeveless jacket, a breechcloth, and a skirt cut from paper, and painted the breechcloth white and hung miniature heads and bones on the skirt. They wrapped his body in a black cape woven from nettles, and placed a shield of reeds in one hand and four arrows in the other. Then they painted diagonal stripes across his face, fastened turquoise earflaps decorated with golden thorns on his earlobes, and covered his face with a hummingbird mask. On his head they set a paper cylinder decorated with feathers. As a symbol of the blood of those sacrificed upon his altar, they tied a paper banner to a long staff and fastened a paper knife to the tip, and painted red stripes on both.

The priests carefully set him on a litter and paraded him around the plaza as the people sang and placed garlands of toasted maize about his neck. When they reached the foot of the great temple, they lifted him from the litter and carried him to the summit. When the god was properly seated in his shrine, a priest emerged. Facing east, he raised a flute to his lips and began to play. After a few moments, he turned to the north, then to the west, and finally to the south. At the sound of the flute, people knelt upon the ground and placed a handful of soil in their mouths, signifying that the earth was the source of all life.

The eagle gate stands at the main entrance to the plaza, guarded on one side by the Tenochca and the other by the Tlatelolca. That was before the coming of the Spaniards. Now, because of the proximity of the Spanish quarters, warriors are forbidden in the plaza, and the armories near the gate have been stripped of all weapons.

As I stood beneath the gate, watching heavily armed soldiers examining the temples and the other ceremonial structures within the serpentine wall that surrounds the plaza, I felt uneasy and apprehensive. In a few days, more than 600 nobles, sons of the greatest families of Mexico, would assemble here to worship their god.

My concerns led me to seek an audience with the Emperor, and when I was granted permission to speak to him, I said, "Lord, each day I have watched the Spaniards inspect every corner and every recess in the plaza. They are wary and suspicious of our intentions, and I fear for the safety of our nobles. I beg you to recall what happened in Cholula when the people of that city assembled in the plaza. What happened there could well happen here unless we are prepared to deal with them. Allow us to hide weapons inside the plaza so we can defend ourselves if the need arises."[ii]

"Have we now come to the point of war with the Spaniards?" Moctezuma replied. "This is but a small affair. We need have no concern for the safety of our people."

I bowed and withdrew, knowing that my warning had fallen upon deaf ears.

Early the following morning, women who had fasted uncovered the face of Huitzilopochtli and offered him food and rolls of amaranth paste. The musicians laid their rush mats on the plaza floor, and set out their reed flutes, conch horns, bone whistles, and drums.

By midday the plaza was transformed into a sea of white plumage as 600 nobles gathered for their sacred dance. Their dress was no more than a ceremonial breechcloth and a panache of feathers from the snowy egret, but their bodies were adorned with gold necklaces that hung to the waist, gold and silver breastplates, and gold neckbands inlaid with pearls and jade. Around their wrists they wore gold bracelets trimmed with feathers, and on their faces turquoise earflaps, jeweled lip plugs, and jade nose ornaments.

Quatlazol, a young lord who had taken four captives in battle, raised his arm and the musicians began to play. The nobles took each other by the hand and began their tortuous dance, their bodies swaying with graceful, sinuous motions as they moved in circles, chanting the dissonant rhythm of the music.

As they danced, the Spaniards fully armed as always, drifted through the gates of the serpentine wall to watch the ritual. Some ventured closer to the dancers to get a better view, while others remained at the gates.

As the dance approached its climax and the tempo of the music increased, the dancers, caught up in a trance, moved with more and more abandon, their feathered headdresses undulating like a giant serpent.

Then a shout rang out. Then another and another as soldiers ran toward the dancers. A heavy lance struck Quatlazol in the chest, and the Spaniards fell upon the old priests who played the drums. They struck off their hands and slashed at their necks with blows so hard that their heads flew into the air. For a moment, the dancers stood transfixed, as if they couldn't understand what was happening. The Spaniards began to hack at their naked bodies, and as their entrails spilled on the ground, they ran to the gates, only to be cut down by soldiers guarding the gates. They ran back into the plaza seeking an avenue of escape, but only a few managed to reach safety on the other side of the wall.

The Spaniards moved methodically about the plaza, seeking those who had hidden in the temple and those who feigned death by lying among the dead, and they put all to the sword. They rushed up the steps of the temple, sword in hand. The priests rolled a heavy beam down the steps, but it came to rest above them. They killed the priests and cast them from the temple with the amaranth figure of Huitzilopochtli. Then they killed the temple guards and the servants who swept the courtyard.

The massacre continued for three hours, until the floor of the plaza was strewn with mutilated bodies and severed legs, arms, and heads. Blood flowed along the pavement as if from a heavy rain and a foul odor rose from excrement oozing from the entrails that littered the courtyard. Then, as the screams of the dying diminished, an unworldly wailing rose in the city as wives and mothers realized what had happened inside the walls.

The Spaniards were oblivious to their screams as they stripped every item of jewelry from the lifeless bodies of our nobles, the flower of Mexico.

When Moctezuma heard the wailing, he knew in his heart what had happened, and his guards could not prevent him from rushing out of the palace. When he saw the carnage, he cried out, "O lords, enough! What have you done to my people? Why have you killed them? Why! They have no *maquahuitls*, they have no shields!"

Alvarado signaled his soldiers to fall back, and they withdrew in order, taking the Emperor with them, their weapons at the ready.

Panic, driven by the cries from the plaza and the sight of the dancers leaping over the walls with blood streaming from their wounds swept through the city. People rushed for the safety of their homes or hid wherever they could find shelter, expecting the carnage in the plaza to burst out upon them at any moment.

With the coming of dawn, however, word spread through the city that the Spaniards had withdrawn to their quarters. Few by few, they ventured back into the streets, searching for their loved ones. Shrieks and cries marked the discovery of a son or a brother, and all through the day, their anguish poured out of the heart of the city.[iii]

On the heels of grief came rage, and a demand for revenge. The chieftains sent runners into the streets, shouting "Mexicans! The Spaniards have murdered our lords and nobles! All have perished! All are dead! Bring your weapons and your shields! Now they must be avenged!" By midday the Spaniards were surrounded by a leaderless mob of warriors, shouting defiance and showering the palace with arrows and javelins, but they did little damage.

Now came the sorrowful task of removing the bodies of our friends and relatives from the courtyard. Now was the time for mourning as people carried their sons and brothers and husbands home. There they stripped them, bathed them, and dressed them for the last rites. They scrubbed their blood from the flagstones of the plaza, and brought their bodies there to lie in state, where the priests committed their souls to the gods. They took the bodies of the principal lords and cremated them in the Quauhxicalco, the eagle vessel, and they cremated those who had not yet taken a captive in battle to the *calmecac*, where they first learned the ways of nobility.

When the fires of the last funeral pyre was spent, we sent our warriors against the Spaniards, and neither cannon nor muskets nor even the deadly bolts of their crossbows could stay us. Our losses were frightening, but the attack went on, one wave after another, against the walls of the palace. Only when Itzcuauhtl, the lord of Tlatelolco, appeared on the roof of the palace with Moctezuma, did we pause.

"O Mexicans! O Tlatelolcans!" he shouted. "Take heed! The lord Moctezuma demands that you lay down your arms! If you make war on the Spaniards, the entire city will suffer, for they are too powerful for us to resist. If you do not yield, they will put your emperor in chains!"

"Sodomite of Moctezuma!" they shouted. "How can you ask us to lay down your arms? What does that wretch who stands behind you have to say to us? We will never give up our fight against these murderers!"

With this they let fly a swarm of arrows, stones, and javelins, and if the Spaniards had not shielded them, both would have been killed.

The Spaniards led Moctezuma and Itzcauahtl from the roof, but we had no heart to continue this attack that had cost us so dearly. It was time to consider a rational plan of action.

The plan we agreed upon called for keeping the Spaniards occupied by day with constant attacks while we and dug tunnels under the walls of the courtyard by night. When the tunnels were ready, we would mount an attack against the front gate while warriors in the tunnel attacked from inside the compound.

The plan worked well. As soon as the gate was breached, warriors rushed out of the tunnel and attacked the Spaniards from the rear. The defenders were hard-pressed from both sides, but others came to their rescue and drove our warriors back into the tunnel. As they worked to seal the tunnel, a second squadron breached the rear wall while we mounted another attack on the gate. The Spaniards were now engaged on all sides, and although we suffered heavy losses, our warriors refused to withdraw. But as night fell, the Spaniards still held the gate, and we were forced to withdraw. Five Spaniards were dead, and two others were in our hands, waiting to be sacrificed.[iv]

We now decided that it was best if we laid siege to the palace and starved the Spaniards out. We burned the small ships that Cortés had built when he reached Tenochtitlán to prevent them from escaping across the lake, and dug a wide ditch around the palace compound. We erected barricades across the avenues leading to the palace, and dug the canals on all sides of the palace deeper and wider. We closed the marketplace and posted sentries around the palace to prevent Moctezuma's sympathizers from bringing food to the Spaniards and fodder to their horses.

In spite of the heavy guard about the palace, however, enemies from abroad made attempts to smuggle food and weapons to their Spanish allies. The sentries halted a party of merchants bringing rabbit furs from the provinces, and as they examined their cargoes, the merchants warned us that among them were warriors from Chinantla. They were bringing weapons for the Spaniards, but the sentries found them and clubbed the merchants to death.

There was also distrust of our own people. Moctezuma's servants lived in constant fear of being accused of smuggling food and messages into the palace, and many were put to death with no more justification than an unfounded accusation. Before long, all of Moctezuma's pages and servants fled the city lest they be stoned to death in the streets. The nobles of the royal house, who were readily identified by their livery, kept clear of the barricades for fear that they would be suspected of carrying messages to Cortés.

On the twenty-third day of the siege, Cortés arrived in Texcoco with more than 1,000 foot, 90 horse, and 2,000 Tlaxcalan warriors. He entered the city with caution, watching for any sign of an ambush, but he found no resistance. The Texcocan warriors were now in Tenochtitlán, fighting alongside the Tenochca and the Tlatelolca.

The Spaniards remained in Texcoco for four days while their patrols scouted the lakeshore. On the fifth day, Cortés led his army around the upper lakes to the causeway at Tepeyacac.[v] The Spaniards started across, but one of the lead horses caught a foreleg between two beams at the first bridge, spilling the rider into the water. The army halted, suspecting a trap, but a careful search of the streets and houses found the town nearly deserted. The search party was fortunate enough to find provisions and good deal of maize, and the army settled down for the night.

The following morning a party went from house to house seeking porters, but every able-bodied man had fled the town. Much to their misgiving, however, they found a servant of the royal house hanged by the neck from a roof beam.

The army moved on, and as the Spaniards neared the causeway, they came upon a heap of tortillas and some 500 roast fowl, which, to all appearances, had been set out for them. Cortés called a halt while they searched the surroundings. When he was satisfied that no ambush awaited him, he ordered his fife and drum corps to the van and the army crossed the causeway.[vi]

Once inside the city, Cortés proceeded with caution as the Spaniards drew near the canals. The only Mexicans he encountered, however, were householders seated in their doorways, paying the Spaniards little attention as they passed. The Spaniards shouted curses at them, but the Mexicans only smiled and nodded.

The army reached the palace without incident, and their comrades, relieved at their deliverance, swung the gates wide. It was a lively homecoming for the Spaniards. Those who had gone with Cortés were flushed with their victory at Cempoala, and those who stayed in Mexico were glad to be alive to welcome their return. Moctezuma left his quarters to join the celebration, but when he tried to congratulate Cortés, the captain turned his back and walked away.

The following morning Cortés made an attempt to restore order in the city. He sent a messenger to some of the leading nobles with a request that they meet him at the palace gates. When they arrived, Cortés appeared the roof.

"My lords," he said, "no matter where the fault lies, I regret with all my heart the affair that brought us to this sorry state. If it was your doing, it grieves me deeply that you broke your word and rose against my men. If it was your doing, you have misjudged my love for you, and you have refused to acknowledge all my efforts on your behalf. If this is so, I have failed to deliver you from the bondage of the devil.

"Yet I forgive you-even if you are at fault, I forgive you, but only if you grant me the same measure of friendship that I hold for you and you keep the peace. If you rise again, your old enemies, who, by my good offices are now your friends, will once more be your enemies, and trouble will rain upon your shoulders. If I was able to overcome you with so few men, what do you think me capable of now, with so many more men, more horses, and more cannon? You have witnessed the courage and valor of my men, and you know full well how many

261

lives you have lost for those few you managed to kill. Even though we are lions in war, we are merciful and forbearing in victory, and we do not wreak havoc upon those we conquer.

"If, however, the blame lies with Alvarado, then my regret is only deeper, for it is our duty, nay, our very nature, to do only good and to prevent others from doing evil. If there is anything I can do to offer you peace of mind, speak up, and I promise that I will serve you better than ever before."

If he expected any response from his audience, he was disappointed. The nobles stood before him in silence, then one by one, they turned and walked away, leaving him standing alone on the roof.

Moctezuma was deeply disturbed by the way Cortés had slighted him. The first Spaniard to visit him since the Toxcatl massacre was the priest Olmedo. When Moctezuma asked him if Cortés held him responsible for the uprising, the priest said that Cortés was fatigued from the Cempoala campaign, and he assured the Emperor that he would pay his respects after he rested. Since presents never failed to prompt a warm response from Cortés, he told Olmedo that his goldsmiths would make a golden statue of him seated upon his horse. The day passed, but there was neither response nor acknowledgement of his offer from Cortés.

Only when Cortés, now burdened with the responsibility of feeding his new army, did he visit Moctezuma. He asked the Emperor to reopen the marketplace, but Moctezuma was hurt and angry, and word had reached him that Cortés had called him an Indian dog for failing to feed the Spaniards.

He refused to order the market opened, saying that he was no more than a prisoner. If Cortés wanted the market opened, any of the lords he held hostage had the authority to do so, and he was free to send whomever he chose. Cortés, however, insisted, and Moctezuma sent Cuitláhuac, who had opposed his allowing the Spaniards to enter the city.

The following morning a horseman rode out of the palace and took the avenue leading to the Tepeyacac causeway. As he entered Tlatelolco, he met a squad of warriors, and, secure in the belief that the Mexicans would gave way for him, he pressed forward. But with the release of Cuitláhuac, a new day had dawned for Mexico. They showered him with stones and arrows, and as he turned to flee, another squad armed with maquahuitls blocked his way. The Spaniard spurred his horse and charged through their ranks, but before he reached the safety of the Spanish quarters, the flanks of his horse were soaked with blood.

He had no sooner passed through the gates than Cuitláhuac attacked in strength, his warriors whistling and shouting as they fought to reach the defenders on the walls. The Spanish horse sallied forth, but our numbers were too great, and we drove them back inside. Only when 400 foot, led by the horsemen, charged out of the gate did we withdraw. They drove us back to the first canal, but fresh squadrons were there to attack their flanks while warriors on the rooftops pelted them with stones. In their abandon to close with the Spaniards, our warriors thrust themselves upon their swords, and the sheer pressure of our numbers forced them to give ground. But before they reached the gate, Cuitláhuac launched an attack against the palace, pinning them outside the compound while we fired the gates and opened breaches in the walls.

The battle lasted all day and well into the night, and they could not drive us off. We withdrew only when we succeeded in firing the palace. But the day was ours-fourteen Spaniards caught outside the compound were dead, and many of their comrades inside shared their fate. Well into the night we saw them fighting fires and repairing breaches in the walls.

Cortés now divided his forces, deploying one company to defend the compound while another attempted to seize the avenue leading to the western causeway. The causeway was the shortest route between Tenochtitlán and Tlacoapan, on the lakeshore. It was wider than the others and less than a league in length. The causeway was an earthen embankment, unbroken along its entire length, but between it and the palace were eight canals, and Cuitláhuac had dug them wider and deeper, and removed every other beam from the bridges.[vii]

Each day the Spaniards sallied forth in strength. Their crossbowmen and musketeers swept the rooftops to keep us back while the foot soldiers, each holding his shield above the head of his companion, worked their way along the avenue. They fired the houses as they moved forward, and when they reached a canal, they filled the gap with stones and timber.

By night, however, we cleared the canals of debris, built barricades across the streets, and piled stones on the rooftops leading to the crossing. Each day, the Spaniards were forced to fight hard to recover the gains of the previous day, and when they wearied from the day's battle, warriors hidden along the embankment rose and showered them with arrows and javelins as they withdrew.

The Spaniards now built armored vehicles from heavy timbers to shield them from our stones and arrows, and manned them with crossbowmen to provide cover for the foot. With these vehicles, which were much like turtles, the foot broke down our barriers and set up ladders to attack the defenders on the rooftops. They destroyed many of the smaller buildings, but we held the rooftops of the tallest, and in time we disabled the vehicles.

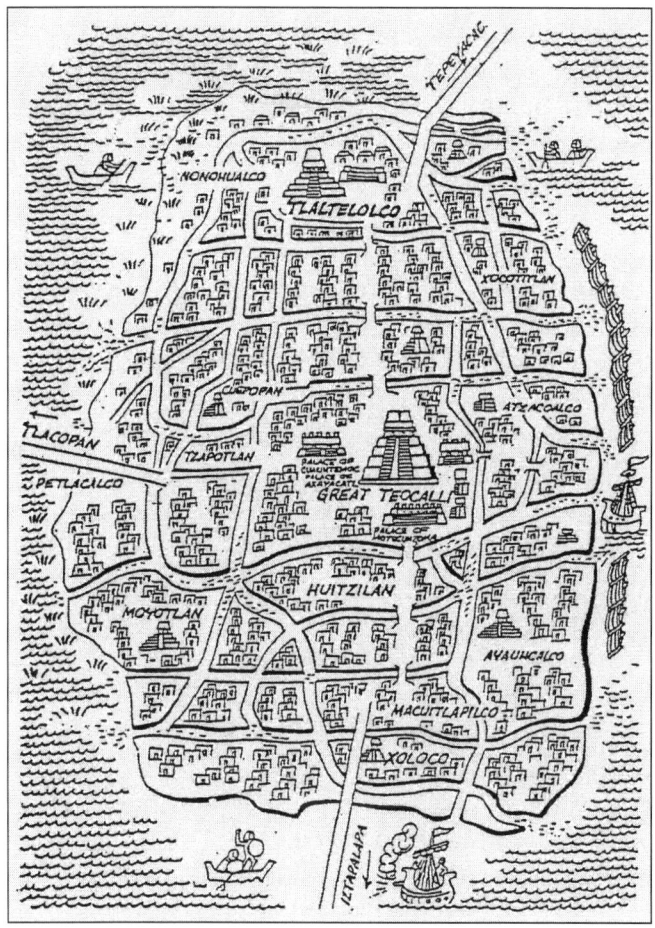

Early Map of Tenochtitlán

There came a day when there was no fighting, and the Spaniards called for a meeting with our chieftains. We gathered at the walls of the palace compound, and Moctezuma, guarded by soldiers on either side, came out to speak with us.

"My lords," he said, "you have fought valiantly for me, and you have suffered death and injury to set me free, and I am most grateful for your loyalty and your allegiance. While your intent is praiseworthy, however, your efforts are misguided because I am not a prisoner. I came to my father's palace of my own free will, and I live

265

here as I would in my own house. These men are my guests-they have come to visit me on behalf of their emperor, and I am here to attend to them as would for any ambassador of a great lord.

"Now I beg of you, put down your arms, do not persist in this foolish war. The Spaniards are too powerful for us: for each who falls in battle, they will kill two thousand of our people. You cannot win! Although they are few, they have won every battle that they fought in this land.

"These men are not barbarians-they have neither seized your property nor ravished your wives and daughters, and time after time, they have asked for peace. If it is your wish that they leave our country, they will go, for they have no desire to remain here against your will. If you want me to return to my palace, I shall do so, because I am not held here against my will.

"I have been told that you have elected another lord because of my goodwill toward the Spaniards, but this I cannot believe. You would never invite the wrath of the gods by forsaking your lawful lord.

"Therefore, for the love that binds us, stop this senseless struggle. Do not let hate and passion blind you, because this will accomplish nothing."

The chieftains prostrated themselves on the ground before him, but he bade them rise. With tears running down their cheeks, they told him that they prayed every day to Huitzilopochtli and Tezcatlipoca to spare him, but the gods responded that this could be until they killed them all. Then they told him that they had elected his brother Cuitláhuac lord of Mexico, and they begged his forgiveness.

Moctezuma stepped forward, away from the shields of his escort, as if to respond, but before he could speak, a noble in the crowd shouted, "Silence, effeminate one! You were born to spin and weave, not to lead us in warfare. These Spanish dogs you love so much hold you prisoner as they would a commoner. You are a coward, and they lie with you and use you as they would a woman!"

The noble let fly with a stone, and within moments, the air was filled with stones. Before Moctezuma's escort could raise their shields, a stone struck him in the temple and he fell. The sight of their emperor lying motionless on the palace roof halted the shower of stones and silenced the crowd. The Spaniards rushed to his side and stood guard while others carried him below.

The stones of our nobles had spoken-Moctezuma's fate was sealed. No lord of Mexico, not Tizoc, not Chimalpopoca, had suffered such abuse. May the gods forbid that the Spaniards prevail and return him to the throne: the time had come to cast them out or die fighting.

The temple of Huitzilopochtli was an ideal place for our command post, since it overlooked Axcayacatl's palace and the surrounding courtyard. From this vantagepoint, Cuitláhuac could direct his forces against the most vulnerable sectors of the compound. Late that night, he sent his chieftains and 300 warriors to the summit of the temple with enough provisions to last a week or more, and staged his veteran squadrons about the base to defend them.

Dawn broke with a pandemonium of whistles, horns, and drumbeats as Cuitláhuac's squadrons swept down upon the palace. Our attack was so swift and unexpected that the defenders had difficulty directing their crossbows and cannon where the threat was greatest. If they concentrated their fire upon one sector, a chieftain on the temple signaled for the point of attack to be shifted to another sector. When the Spaniards regrouped to counter that attack, the chieftain signaled again, and the Spaniards found themselves firing into empty space.

Never before had the Spaniards been forced to spread their defenses so thin. If they were to survive the day, the command post must be taken without delay. Cortés sent his horse into the plaza to clear our warriors from the base of the temple, but the flagstones were still wet and slippery from the morning dew, and they were forced to withdraw. Then the foot fought their way to the foot of the temple, but as they started up the steps of the temple, wooden beams and burning logs tumbled down upon them from above. Three times they started up the steps, and each time they were driven back.

Cortés led the fourth assault. He arrived with a party of musketeers and crossbowmen, and while they kept the defenders back from the rim of the platform, the Spaniards began another assault on the temple, protecting themselves with their shields. Logs and stones continued to tumble down upon them, but when the supply of missiles was spent, the Spaniards reached the summit.

Cortés was the first to reach the top, and as soon as he stepped onto the platform, two warriors seized him and dragged him to the edge, but before they could jump over the side with him, he managed to pull free. Our weapons were no match for Spanish steel, and the few who were not cut down hurled themselves from the temple.

The loss of the temple ended our assault on the palace, and, to our misfortune, the fowl and tamales that the warriors had taken to the summit provided a windfall for the hungry Spaniards. The defeat also provided a feast for the Tlaxcalans, who had nothing to eat but their daily ration of a single tortilla. That night they dined upon the bodies of our fallen warriors.

Our losses that day caused Cuitláhuac to call a halt to our assaults on the palace. Instead, we settled down to a siege we hoped would either starve them out or wear them down to the point that they could no longer defend themselves. To prevent them from making a run for the causeways, we dug the canals along the route to the Tlacopan causeway deeper and wider, and removed the bridges from the Ixtapalapa causeway. There was no way for them to leave the city.

Cortés, however, knew that escape was his only hope for saving the Spaniards. He took the offensive with a sortie along the avenue leading to the Tlacopan causeway. He fired 300 houses and reached the fourth canal, which he filled with earth, stones, and timber. After posting a guard of horse and foot at the crossing, he retired for the night.

The following morning he broke through the squadrons defending the remaining canals, and while his soldiers filled them in, his cavalry pursued our warriors across the causeway as far as the lakeshore. That day he commanded the entire route to the mainland, and had the Spaniards been prepared to leave the city, nothing could have prevented their escaping.

Late that afternoon our chieftains went to the palace with a peace offering. They promised to rebuild the bridges over the canals and repair the streets if Cortés gave his word that there would be no reprisals for the uprising. They asked to speak with Huitznahuacatl, the priest held captive with Moctezuma, and after meeting with them, he told Cortés that if he agreed, they would send word to all the chieftains that the war was over. Cortés seemed satisfied, and he returned to his quarters to dine.

But as darkness fell upon the city, we attacked the Spaniards guarding the crossings, and Cortés charged from the palace with his cavalry and drove us as far as the mainland. The foot, however, exhausted from the previous day's fighting, failed to follow him onto the causeway, leaving the crossing at the westernmost canal in our hands. Cortés was with the rear guard when the cavalry returned to the city, and by the time he reached the crossing, he found two horsemen dead and five horses swimming down the canal. We closed in about him, but he fought his way clear, and with a great leap, his horse cleared the gap and reached safety.

Four days after Moctezuma had been stoned, Cortés made signs that he wanted to speak to us. We gathered at the foot of the palace walls, and he came out upon the roof.

"A poor reward you gave the lord Moctezuma when you stoned him," he said. "The emperor you once worshiped and revered as a god now lies dead, but it was not your stones that killed him-it was his anguish and despair brought about by your disloyalty. Ever since the day you cursed him and stoned him, he has refused to take food and water, and when we tried to treat his wound, he turned us away. With each passing day, he has wasted away, and we could do nothing to save his life.

"Now I send his priests out to you with his body so that you can bury him according to your custom, and they will tell the new lord the truth of what I say."

"Why should we care whether Moctezuma lives or dies?" a noble shouted. Cuitláhuac is now lord, and what was done was well done-Moctezuma dealt with this affair like a woman. Keep him-he was your mistress! This war will not end until we kill every Spaniard in the country or every Mexican lies dead on the battlefield. We may die by the thousands for every Spaniard we kill, but thousands more stand ready to take our place. If you try to flee, you will die, because every bridge across the canals and every bridge across the causeways are open, and if you stay here, hunger and thirst will finish you. We will have our revenge one way or another!"

Cortés turned his back and left the roof.

A few moments later, the gates of the palace compound opened, and priests brought out the body of the Emperor wrapped in a mantle. As they made their way through the crowd, a chieftain who had just arrived asked them whose body they carried. When they told him that it was the body of Moctezuma, he motioned toward the palace and told them to take him back.

Some of the nobles wept at the sight of Moctezuma's body, and others cried out when they heard that the Emperor was dead, but none stepped forward to remove the body or make arrangements for his funeral. The body lay on the ground until one of Moctezuma's servants, out of pity for his master, picked it up and carried it into the city to seek a resting-place. He carried the body to one barrio after another, but none would relieve him of his burden. Only when he reached Acatliyacapan did he find people who would receive the body of the Emperor and cremate his remains. When nothing but ashes remained of this great prince, the servant put them in an urn and buried them under a rubbish heap.[viii]

---

[i] The feast of Toxcatl was celebrated from 19 May to 28 May.

[ii] Our narrator, the Tlatelolcan general Ecatl, appears for the first time in the native literature. (Codex Aubin, 55)

[iii] The native accounts of the massacre are found to be consistent in every detail, and none give any indication that the Mexicans planned anything other than the customary celebration of the end of the dry season. Ixtlilxochitl lays the blame for the massacre on the Tlaxcalans, who were seeking revenge for past sacrifices of their people at Toxcatl. The Texcocan claims that the Tlaxcalans convinced Alvarado that an uprising was planned.

The testimony of Bernardino Vazquez de Tapia, an eyewitness, given before the *Audiencia* at Santo Domingo, sheds more light upon the event. See Appendix 1

After the conquest, the Toxcatl massacre was portrayed on a wall mural in the hall of the native court of justice, which was intended to serve as a warning for the descendants of the Aztecs.

[iv] Bernal Díaz states that seven Spaniards were killed and two were captured and sacrificed before Cortés reached Tenochtitlán.

[v] Cortés chose the long march around the northern lakes to the Tepeyacac causeway rather than try to fight his way up the Ixtapalapa causeway.

[vi] Cervante's description of Cortés's entry into Tenochtitlán has all the characteristics of an eyewitness report. (Alonso de Ojeda's *Memoriales?*)

[vii] The number of causeways, their length and location, and the number of openings along each has never been adequately resolved. Cortés shows six causeways on the Nuremburg map of 1524, and two or more openings

along the Tacuba causeway. C. Harvey Gardiner, *Naval Power in the Conquest of Mexico*, suggests that only three may have been usable, since Cortés was able to contain the Mexicans by blockading them.

Gardiner sets the length of the Ixtapalapa causeway at seven miles, that of the Tepeyacac causeway at three miles, and the Tacuba causeway, the widest of the three (40 feet), at two miles with four breaches.

Cortés, however, in his account of his sorties to break out of the city, denies that there were any breaches along the causeway.

...fighting for our lives and honor...that street led to the only unbroken causeway crossing to the mainland

[viii] The question of whether Moctezuma was killed by the stone or by Cortés is still hotly contested by historians. See Appendix 2

20. Francisco de Aguilar:

La Noche Triste. The Night of Sorrows

The wound on Montezuma's head did not seem mortal, but from the moment we carried him from the roof and laid him on his bed, he refused every attempt to wash away the blood and dress his injury. He kept to his bed day and night, and he would neither take food or water from his servants, but we were too occupied with the unrelenting attacks on the palace compound to be concerned about him. When it became evident that his strength and vitality were diminishing, however, a majordomo advised Cortés of the emperor's condition.

Cortés went to Montezuma's quarters immediately, and as he knelt at his bedside, the emperor raised up and embraced him. He took Cortés's hands in his own and began to weep.

" I cannot begin to tell you of the despair that fills my heart," he said. "Am I truly he who the world once feared and venerated no less than the immortal gods? Am I that same lord who came forth to greet you, the one who received you with such pomp and majesty the day you arrived in my city? What change of fortune, what calamity has brought me to this pitiful state?

"I did not appropriate another's realm. I inherited this unhappy, this unfortunate kingdom, from my father and his fathers before him, and I have ruled it with fairness and justice. I have been victorious in battle, I have conquered many kingdoms, and I have brought about many benefits for my people. How dare those who once came barefoot before me with their eyes lowered, those who carried me upon their shoulders with their mantles beneath their arms, defy their lord and king? How dare they curse me with words that even the lowest of slaves would not stoop to use? How dare they cast stones at their emperor!

"Ah Cortés, Cortés! My heart is broken. My shame is more than any man can bear. A great rage burns in my soul as I lay here dying, vilified and despised as the most cowardly man on earth. Who among us would not seek revenge and witness their punishment? But for me there will be no retribution, no satisfaction. I shall soon die; not from their stones but from bitterness and rage.

"There is but one thing left for me now. As I die in your defense, I ask you to watch over my children, protect them and care for them in the kingdom of their father. I ask also that you punish those who have defiled my name, and that you redeem my kingdom from the one who rose against me. Remember, gallant captain, he who asks this is a king who has always been your friend. As a man of honor, I ask you to carry out my dying wish. Discharge it faithfully, and put my soul to rest."

For a moment, Cortés was silent. "Great lord," he said, "you must take comfort, you have done nothing or said anything unbecoming of a great king, The people have risen against you through no fault of your own, Do not blame yourself for what has happened, blame those who are at fault. And rest assured that I will carry out your wishes as I would those of the Emperor of the Christians. I will watch over your children as I would my own, and I swear upon my honor that I will avenge your death, even though I lose many men in doing so."

For a moment, Montezuma's face was calm and untroubled. "Great captain," he said, "as friends who know each other so well, as one whom I have always loved, your words bring great comfort to my troubled heart. The day will come when you will rule this land and lead my people, but before I die, I must counsel you what experience has taught me so that you may administer this great empire wisely.

"The natives of this land do nothing save from fear, and they are fond of pleasure and given to every vice known to man. They are lustful, they lie constantly, and they are greedy. They have little love in their hearts, and they are quick to forget any favor. Princes who

273

offer them kindness and generosity only spoil them. If I did not exact harsh levies upon every man and woman in the realm, even to the point of demanding that the poor pay a tribute of no more than body lice, they would not respect me. They must be punished for minor transgressions as well as despicable crimes; otherwise they become insolent and more difficult to control. I have punished them with slavery and even hanged them for stealing as little as a single ear of corn.

"Always deal cautiously with them; never tell them secrets of any importance, and subject them to endless humiliation. Show anger for the least offence, and never give them opportunity to commit greater ones. When you grant them favors, do so without familiarity or congeniality, for if you do, they will lose all respect for you and hold you in low esteem. And lastly, never forgive them for anything they do poorly-they must know that they will be held accountable for tasks not well done."

Cortés thanked Montezuma for his counsel, embraced him, and rose to his feet. He apologized for having to leave so soon, but the war was pressing, and he had to attend to his army. He promised the Emperor that he would look in on him often, and urged him to summon him whenever he needed him.[i]

The following day Montezuma's condition worsened, and Cortés hurried to his bedside. When he entered the room, Montezuma turned to him with empty eyes and said, "Death is the greatest sorrow of all sorrows."

"My lord," Cortés answered, "now more than ever, courage and a steadfast spirit are needed. This last debt is inescapable, for he who is born must necessarily die. Your death, however, need not be eternal, nor need you suffer the torments of hell. In the name of the True God, in whom alone you must believe, allow me to bring the Fray Olmedo here to baptize you."

Montezuma replied that he had no wish to adopt another religion in the little time left to him. He preferred to die in the bosom of the faith of his ancestors, because there could be no real meaning if he were to be baptized into a faith in which he had never been instructed. Our people are by nature fickle, he said, and he would only be the worse for it if he turned back to his gods before he died. Far better not to know the truth than abandon it once having known it.

Our powder was all but gone, and the gunners were forced to use turquoise stones and whatever rocks they could find for shot. Food was so scarce that our daily ration was no more than a handful of grain, and that of the Tlaxcalans but a single tortilla. For the past 14 days, we had nothing to drink save a trickle of brackish water that seeped from a tiny well in the courtyard. The walls of the compound were weak and crumbling from the breaches the Mexicans had opened, and it was evident to all that we could not withstand many more assaults. All but a handful of soldiers had suffered one or more serious wounds during the fighting. Had it not been for two Italians who were skilled in the art of curing, with nothing more than olive oil, a woolen pad, and a magic spell or two, many of the wounded would have died. I count myself among the fortunate ones who were healed by their miracles. At night, after the screaming savages withdrew, some of those fit to stand watch swore that they saw dead men and disembodied heads, including their own, dancing in the streets and along the canals.

One day after heavy fighting, Alonso de Ávila, the captain of the guard, returned wearily to his quarters, hoping to steal a few moments of sleep. When he entered the room he shared with Botello Puerto de Plata, he found him weeping sorely.

"Senor," Ávila said, "is this the time for tears?"

"Have I no cause for sorrow?" Botello replied, "Not one of us will live to see the sun rise tomorrow unless the captain orders us to withdraw this very night."

Ávila was not one to mistake Botello's fears for those of a frightened soldier. Every captain and soldier in the company believed that a guardian spirit watched over him and let him see into the future. At Cempoala, while we still celebrated our victory over Narváez, Botello approached Cortés and said, "Senor, we must leave Cempoala as soon as possible: the Mexicans have killed a Spaniard and laid siege to Alvarado's company. Even now they are trying to scale the walls of the compound. His words were hardly spoken when an appeal for help arrived from Alvarado.

Ávila summoned Alvarado and the other captains, and together they went to Cortés's quarters, demanding to know whether he planned to withdraw or hold fast in the palace.

"Senors," Cortés said, "we face great danger whether we choose to stay here or attempt to break out of the city. It is my opinion, however, that it is far more dangerous to stay than try to withdraw. But to succeed, we must leave at night when the Mexicans are off-guard, and we must maintain complete silence to prevent our alerting them.

The captain's words gave rise to objections from several of his commanders. Many of the bridges are open, they argued, and the beams had been removed from others, rendering them unsafe for transporting cannon and other heavy equipment. Furthermore, a light rain usually fell upon the city at night, rendering poor footing for the cavalry and poor visibility for the foot.

Cortés heard them out, and when those who supported a withdrawal had their say, he said, "Let us hear what Botello has to say."

"Senors," Botello said, "I see a man lying dead on the causeway and that man is either me or my brother, and I see many of our comrades lying dead in the streets and the canals at night. Yet we must leave this city this very night if any are to survive.

"For those who hold no faith in clairvoyance, consider that our cannon, the weapons in which lies our greatest advantage, lack both powder and shot, and they are of little use by day or by night. By night, we will be spared our greatest danger: the attacks from the rooftops. If we withdraw in complete silence, a good number may reach the shore before the enemy is fully alert. Even so many will die. The bridges are open, and it will be difficult to fill them and pass onto the causeway without suffering heavy losses. If we attempt to leave by day, every man in the company will die before reaching the opposite shore. It has also been revealed to me that our captain and many of our leaders will survive the night, and that a day will come when they will return and take the city by force of arms.

"This is my counsel, but you must be the ones to decide. Do not wait too long-if we are to leave tonight, you must decide within the hour."

Botello's words decided the issue, and the company made preparations for the withdrawal. Cortés directed the carpenters to construct a portable bridge and established the order of retreat. The van, led by Gonzalo de Sandoval and Antonio de Quinones, was to be

200 foot and 20 horse. Cortés was to follow with the main body of the army, and Pedro de Alvarado and Juan Velásquez would command the rear guard. Between the main body of the army and the rear guard, a force of 40 foot and 400 Tlaxcalan warriors were to protect the royal hostages. Among them were Motezuma's two sons and two daughters, four daughters of the ruling house of Texococo, one of who was heavy with Cortes's child, and the daughters of the lords of Tlaxcala who had been given to our captains. Forty foot and 400 Tlaxcalans commanded by a Spaniard named Margarino were charged with the formidable task of laying the portable bridge across the canals. To be sure that no man who was asleep or too ill to travel was left behind, Alonso de Ojedo was to search every quarter of the compound before the order to withdraw was given.[ii]

The vast treasure we had accumulated during our stay in Mexico, valued at some 7.000 ducats, was taken from the repository and heaped in the great hall of the palace. Cortés summoned Gonzalo de Mejia, the king's treasurer, and Alonso de Ávila, the king's accountant, and before witnesses, ordered them to count the royal fifth and ready it for transport. He assigned seven wounded horses, a mare, and 80 Tlaxcalan porters to carry it out of the city. This being done, he informed the King's officers that he bore no further responsibility for the King's share of the treasure, even though, as was most likely, it should be lost during the retreat.

When the royal fifth, consisting mostly of gold ingots, was set aside, a considerable amount of gold was left. Cortés declared all the property of the army, and any soldier was free to take whatever he wanted of it. Much of the treasure, however, was in the form of unwieldy artifacts and items of jewelry, which, unfortunately, was prized more by the Mexicans than the Spaniards.

At the hour of vespers, Montezuma gave up his soul to his creator. Now Cortés faced the problem of what was to be done with the lords and nobles who had been imprisoned with the emperor. Their offices had long since been assumed by others, they could neither be set free nor left behind to alert the Mexicans that a withdrawal was underway, and taking them with us would compromise the safety of the company.

Cortés met with his captains, and all agreed that they had no choice but to kill them. One by one they garroted them, and when this

277

terrible task was done, they cast their bodies outside the gates, hoping that grief and their funeral rites would draw the warriors away from the palace long enough for us to escape.[iii]

That night I stood watch on the palace roof, and at ten o'clock, more than a score of women emerged from the darkness, seeking the bodies of husbands, brothers, and sons by torchlight. My blood ran cold as I heard their screams upon finding a loved one, and when I could no longer bear to look upon the tragedy unfolding beneath the walls, I turned to my companion and said, "If you have never seen hell, my friend, look upon it now in the misery and despair below us."

Never, during the entire course of the war in Mexico, through every danger and hardship we suffered, did fear strike at my soul the way it did the night I witnessed the anguish of those women.

Cortés gave the order to withdraw, but to our dismay, the moon was bright and the city streets were flooded with the light of fires that blazed from every rooftop. Toward midnight, however, a light rain began to fall, obscuring the moon, then a thunderstorm passed over the city, followed by a hailstorm that drove the Mexicans indoors. To my dying day, I will always believe that the storm that descended upon the city that fateful night was no phenomenon of nature, but a miracle wrought by the hand of God to spare us from the Mexicans. Without His divine intervention, all would surely have perished.

The army left shortly after midnight, moving as silently as possible down the avenue that led to the causeway. Magarino and his crew set the portable bridge across the first canal, which lay a thousand paces from our quarters, but it soon collapsed beneath the procession of men, horses, and baggage. Now we had no means of crossing the remaining canals save for what God had provided for us- our baggage and the Indian porters who carried it. The press of the army thrust them into the canals, and as they drowned, their bodies formed a bridge for those who followed. We fled down the avenue in disarray, throwing baggage into the breaches over the bodies of those who had drowned.

By now the city was alert and the Mexicans were converging upon our flanks, and when we reached the sixth canal, they fell upon us in force. Canoes closed in about us from both sides, and as warriors swarmed upon us from the canals and the streets behind us, we panicked and pushed Indians, Spaniards, and anything else in our path into the breaches. Not a man had the courage to lift a hand to save his companion, not even if he were his own brother. In the darkness, above the howls and shrieks of the Mexicans, we could hear the cries of our countrymen.

"Over here!"

"Save me-I am drowning!"

"O my God! Have mercy on me!"

"Blessed Virgin! Spare me!"

"Oh my God!"

We were heartsick as the screams of our dying comrades followed us down the avenue, but we could do nothing to save them.

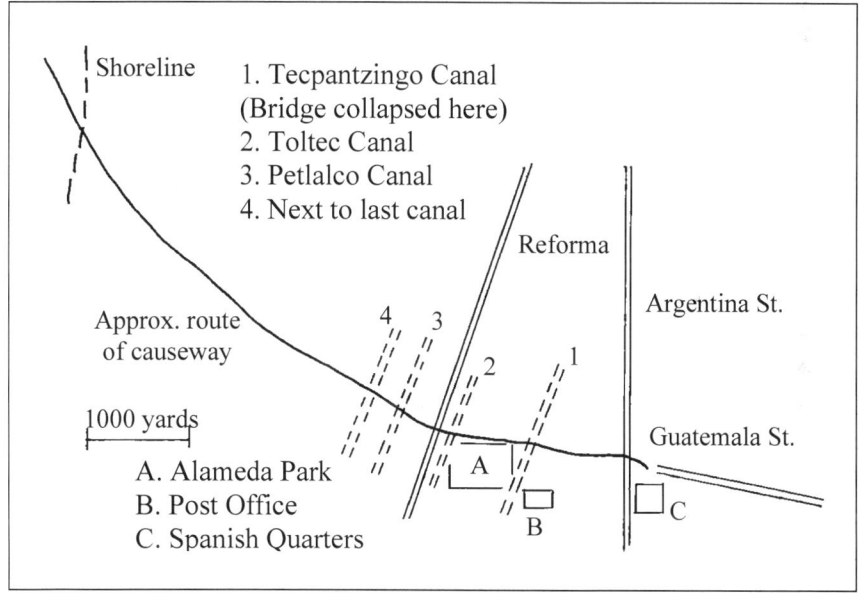

Spanish Retreat from Tenochtitlán, July 1, 1520

It was at the sixth canal that 40 Spaniards charged with transporting our heavy equipment were forced to turn back. They retreated to the palace compound with a horde of Mexicans at their heels screaming for their blood.[iv]

Those of us who were fortunate enough to cross the sixth canal found our progress easier as the enemy attacks slackened. The Spaniards who had turned back had drawn off many Mexicans, and others broke off their attack to ransack the baggage lost in the canals, cutting off each others hands in their frenzy to lay hold of the treasure we had abandoned.

We passed over the causeway and across the swamps of the lakeshore, then onto the road to Tacuba as the Mexicans continued to pursue us. Horsemen raced past us and back again onto the causeway, trying to reach the rear guard, which was still at the sixth canal. We kept to the road as best we could, but fields of ripening maize on either side provided cover for the Mexicans, and time after time they leaped out to seize a weary comrade. He was gone before we could react, and we could hear him screaming for help as he vanished into the maize.[v]

The Battle for the Causeway

In Tacuba, Cortés tried to establish order among the troops milling about in the plaza, but when he realized that there was no hope of finding more survivors, he ordered a withdrawal to the west. A large Mexican force was now close behind us, but by the grace of God, we encountered no Tepanec warriors in Tacuba, who, for whatever reason, chose not to attack us.

It was nine o'clock in the morning before we reached a clearing beyond the maize fields, and we made for a small temple on high ground. The rear guard and what remained of our cavalry held the enemy back until we could set up defenses about the temple.

That day we treated our wounded and Cortés took muster. Of the Spaniards, less than half the foot answered roll call: more than 700 of our comrades had perished at the canals and along the causeway. Of 80 horse, only 23, most of which were wounded or crippled, survived. The cannon, the muskets, and our remaining powder had been lost in the canals. The valiant Juan de Velásquez, who had forsaken his uncle for our cause, had fallen with the rear guard, as had Francisco de Saucedo and Francisco de Morla. The losses suffered by our Tlaxcalan allies, burdened with the baggage, the artillery, and the King's gold, numbered well over a thousand. All the royal hostages, save for two sons of the house of Texcoco, had been killed by their countrymen. Cortés's pregnant concubine was dead, and all the Tlaxcalan noblewomen, save for Doña Luisa, Alvarado's woman, had been captured or killed.

Once again we found ourselves without food or water, but early the following morning, another of God's miracles appeared. A party of Indians approached the temple, and we knew by their dress that they were not Mexicans. They brought us eggs, fowl, tortillas, and tunas, and they told us that they were Otomies, close relatives of the Otomies who lived in the province of Tlaxcala. Their ancestors founded the towns of Teocalhueyacán and Tliliuhquitepec many years ago on the western shore of the lake. They had lived in peace with the Mexicans for many generations, but when Montezuma gained the throne, his demands for tribute all but impoverished them. Their chieftain, Otoncoatl, was eager to offer Cortés his friendship, and if we chose to remain in Teocalhueyacán, he would house us and feed us and see to all our needs.

That day we set forth our plan to reached Tlaxcala, more than 30 leagues from or present position, where, we prayed, the Indians would not turn against us to avenge their relatives who died in the canals of Tenochtitlán. Cortés was determined to begin the march as soon as possible, since we could not afford the Mexicans an opportunity to regroup and attack in force.

Our route would necessarily take us north. If we attempted to move south to leave the valley the way we entered, we would be marching into the heart of Mexican territory, and we would have to fight our way across the heavily populated southern lakeshore to reach safety in Chalco. To the north, the country was less populated, and if we left without delay, before the Mexicans crossed the Tepeyacac causeway and intercepted us, we hoped to keep a safe lead over our pursuers.

Our journey would first take us to Teocalhueyacán. Where the Otomies would provision us and give us an opportunity to rest before we began the long march to Tlaxcala. From Teocalhueyacán, the army would march northward and circle the shores of Lake Zumpango and Lake Xaltocan, then take a southeasterly course toward Tlaxcala, across the territory of the Acolhuaque.

At midnight we let campfires about the temple as if we planned to spend the night, then assembled in the darkness below and prepared to march. Cortés organized the foot into companies of 40 men and appointed a captain for each. The men still able to fight were placed in the van, the rear guard, and along the flanks of the column to protect the wounded. No soldier, under penalty of death, was to stray from the column.

We left the temple as quietly as possible, guided only by the stars and the Otomies, who led us along a path that skirted the main trails. A half-league from the temple, our scouts met a squadron of Mexican warriors, but they routed them after a brief skirmish. The remaining two leagues to Teocalhueyacán were uneventful, but we were aware that the enemy was close behind, following as closely as they dared.

The Otomies provided us with fodder for the horses and gave us all the fowl, tortillas, and gourds we could carry, and at first light we departed for Tepozotlan, four leagues to the north. We encountered enemy squadrons along the way, but the terrain was so rough that neither the enemy nor our cavalry could fight effectively. The Mexicans fell back, but they continued to follow us.

As word of our approach reached Tepozotlan, the people fled into the hills, and we remained in the deserted city for two days while we tended our wounded, rested the horses, and satisfied our hunger with the provisions we found in their homes. We especially enjoyed the ducks the townspeople breed for their fine plumage and sell at a handsome profit in the markets of Mexico. We found them quite succulent when served with the proper condiments.

The next two days saw us complete the circuit of the lakes, halting first at Citlaltepec, then at Xoloc, the northernmost towns on the shores of Lake Zumpango. We found both towns deserted, but we encountered opposition on the outskirts of Xoloc. A party of Mexicans appeared on the crest of a hill, close to the road, and Cortés, suspecting that a larger force lay on the other side, set out with five horse and 12 foot. As he circled the hill, a squadron of warriors fell upon him, and before he could fight his way clear, a stone struck him on the head. The blow left him in a daze for the rest of the day.

Beyond Xoloc provisions were difficult to come by, and soon our scant supplies were exhausted. We found the region heavily populated, and we kept well away from the towns along our route. We had nothing to eat but herbs, Indian sorrel, and stalks of maize that grew alongside the road. Anything more that a step or two from the road was done without, since the enemy was all about us and the captains kept us in close ranks as we marched.

One Spaniard, half-crazed with hunger, cut open a fallen comrade and dined on his liver. Cortés would have hanged him on the spot if it were not for the pleas of his companions, who understood his temptation all too well.

When we came upon a grove of cherry trees not more than eight paces from the trail, Hernando Alonso broke ranks to gather a few cherries. As he reached into the tree, Alonso de Ávila hurled his lance at him. The lance passed through his right arm, and although he eventually recovered, he lost the arm.

Later that day the Mexicans attacked us, and Martin de Gamboa's horse was cut from under him. That night we roasted the horse, and knife fights broke out as men fought each other for a share. The captains stopped the fight before anybody was killed, but they had to post a guard while the food was rationed. When the meal was finished, not a single scrap of the horse remained, not even the entrails and the hoofs.

The following day the Mexicans attacked in strength, and Cortés, fearing that the worst was yet to come, readied the cavalry for action. He ordered the wounded riders to dismount, and we improvised crutches for them. This would soon to prove a wise decision.

We reached the crest of a small hill a day's march beyond Otumba, and before us we saw a great plain, which at first sight seemed to be covered with snow. But the snow that reflected the noonday sun quickly transformed itself into a host of warriors wearing white tunics, an army so great that it covered the plain and the slopes of the hills on either side. They appeared out of nowhere-no drums, no whistles, and no horns announced their arrival. It was as if they materialized across our path, silent and motionless, waiting for us to come to them.

Cortés dismounted and stared at the plain for a long time, then he turned to us and ordered each man to sit down and eat whatever food he had. When we were finished, he stood before us, and we could see tears in his eyes.

"Comrades," he said, "if we have want of courage now, it will avail us nothing but to die all the sooner. If we must die, let us die like men; let us sell our lives as dearly as we can rather be conquered by fear. We have yet to face danger with anything other than courage, and what we face today is nothing new.

"You have seen for yourselves how one miracle after another has sustained us in this enterprise, and you have witnessed the divine protection of God at every step of our journey. Today He will confound these dogs that stand before us, and before the day is over, we will have realized the greatest victory that Spain has ever won over the Infidel. We will emerge victorious and we will enter Tlaxcala in triumph, and one day we will return and take our revenge upon the Mexicans.

"Let us now ask God once more for His support, because it is in His cause that we fight. Let us pray that He will intimidate our enemy and strike terror into his heart, and let us commend us to the Virgin Mary and pray that She will be our mediator. Now let each man make his confession to God, since there is little time left to us."

We had no cannon, no powder for what few muskets remained, and few enough bolts for our crossbows: only our swords and a few lame horses stood between our Maker and us. As we prayed, many wept openly.

Cortés deployed the cavalry in rows of five horses abreast, one behind the other. The mounted men lowered their lances, and we advanced upon the enemy. When we reached the plain, the blare of conch horns echoed from the hills, and with an ear-splitting shriek, the Mexicans rushed toward us.

Our horsemen charged and met the lead squadron headlong, scattering warriors and crushing them underfoot as they opened a gap in their ranks. The foot rushed through the gap and the column moved forward. The Mexicans closed in about us, but before they could close the gap, the cavalry returned at full gallop, driving them back again. The cavalry charged through the Mexicans four times, but the crush of warriors about us was too great: the gap closed and we found ourselves in close combat with the enemy. The Mexicans were now inside our ranks and the line of battle ill defined. Cortés abandoned the offensive and used the cavalry to protect the foot, and for the next five hours we fought for our very lives, making little or no headway through the enemy ranks. Cortés was unseated twice, and several captains were wounded. The men, attacked by one fresh squadron after another, were exhausted.

To the east we could see an ornate litter that was unmistakably that of the Mexican general. The man seated in the litter carried a gold and silver shield, and a golden banner flew high above his head. The litter was surrounded by more than a hundred nobles ready to give their lives for him. Cortés, with Cristóbal de Olid and Gonzalo de Sandoval beside him, charged into their midst. Close behind were Alonso de Ávila and Juan de Salamanca, and together they fought their way through the escort to the litter. Juan de Salamanca crashed into the litter, and before the bearers could steady it, Salamanca tumbled the general to the ground with a thrust of his lance. Dismounting quickly, Salamanca cut off the Mexican's head and held it high for all to see. He raised the chieftain's banner, and we took up the cry, "Victory! Victory!"

What had been a sea of white tunics faded and vanished into the hills as the Mexicans, now leaderless, gave up the fight. The day was ours, and when we had seen the last of the enemy, we tended our wounded and buried our dead. We resumed our march to Tlaxcala, carrying the golden shields and jeweled weapons of the Mexican leaders and wearing their feathered panaches.

On the eighth day after we fled from Mexico, we entered the province of Tlaxcala. Only 440 men, including 12 crossbowmen, seven musketeers, and twenty horses had survived the flight from Tenochtitlán, and there were none who had not suffered one or more serious wounds.[vi]

We stopped to rest our weary troops in Hueyotlipan, a town of some 4000 inhabitants, located about ten leagues from Tlaxcala. The people were willing to give us food and lodging, but we had to pay for everything with gold and silver-they would accept nothing else. Their disposition offered us no assurance of the welcome we hoped for in Tlaxcala, and a message carved in a tree gave us even more concern. It read, 'The luckless Juan Juste passed this way with his woebegone companions, who were so hungry that they had to give the people a bar of gold worth 800 ducats for a few tortillas.' We knew nothing of the fate of his party, but we feared the worst.

We rested in Hueyotlipan for three days, not knowing if we would be received as friends or foes in Tlaxcala. On the morning of the fourth day, however, hundreds of women and children from hamlets more than a league away descended upon us. They gave us food and decked us with flowers, and they wept when they saw our weak and injured bodies and saw how few of us were still alive. They embraced us as they would their husbands and brothers, and they scolded us like lost children for not heeding their warnings about the Mexicans.

Later that afternoon Maxixca, Xicotencatl the Elder, and the lords of Huexotzingo arrived and received us like lost brothers. Although they grieved for their lost countrymen, they placed no blame upon us, instead, they praised our courage and our skill for fighting our way clear of the canals and causeways of Tenochtitlán and marching across a hostile land to reach them. We could do nothing but shed tears of joy as we praised God for our having found such compassion and generosity among these heathen people.

---

[i] The deathbed dialogue between Moctezuma and Cortés was written by Cervantes. Cortés, in his Second Letter to Charles V, makes no mention of such a conversation. He does, however, in a petition dated June, 1526, claim he made a deathbed promise to the Emperor to care for his surviving daughters.

[ii] Juan Cano claims that Cortes failed to notify all the men of the hour of departure, and that 270 men were left behind. This is contradicted by Cervantes, who states that Alonso de Ojeda returned to carry a wounded man who had been forgotten out of the deserted palace.

[iii] Aguilar's eye witness account confirms Sahagún's assertion in his Enmendada that the Spaniards killed the hostages. See Appendix 2

[iv] There are considerable differences among the chroniclers as to the number of Spaniards who were forced to retreat to the palace. Aguilar sets the number as 40, Cervantes at 100, but states that many conquistadors insist that 300 were driven back.

[v] Despite his heavy losses, Cortes managed to take a considerable quantity of gold out of the city, notwithstanding his claim that much of the gold was lost." Bernal Diaz claims that more than 80 Tlaxcalan porters bearing gold bars were the first to cross the causeway.

In March, 1981, a gold bar stamped with Charles V, weighing more than four pounds, was found at the site of the sixth canal. The gold bar is now on display in the National Museum of Anthropology.

[vi] See Appendix 3 for various estimates of fatalities during the retreat.

21. Ecatl:

Tlaxcala's Choice

It seemed improbable that we would ever see the Spaniards again. More than half their army lay dead or dying in the canals, and those who had escaped would learn soon enough that Tlaxcala was their prison. In weeks, perhaps days, the blind allegiance of their hosts would sink under the burden of feeding and caring for them, and when that time came, they would remember the brothers and husbands that the Spaniards had left dying on the causeways of Tenochtitlán. If they tried to reach the sea, they would find the passes across the sierra closed, leaving them easy prey for marauding warriors from every town along the way.

The days that followed their flight from the city were days of rejoicing and prayers for the Mexican people as they set about restoring order and repairing the damage done by the war. They removed the bodies of the dead Spaniards from the canals and laid them in neat rows along the causeway. They stripped them of their stolen plunder, their weapons, and their armor, and cast them into the marshes with the bodies of their horses. Then they stripped their concubines, and after they ravished them and painted their bodies yellow, they left them to the mercy of the streets. They impaled the bodies of the Tlaxcalans and the Cempoalans upon stakes, and set them out in the marshes for the vultures to tear at their flesh.

Then it was time to turn their attention to 40 Spaniards who waited in the palace for the inevitable. It was more sport than war as they offered them terms for surrender, terms that both knew would never be honored, but they stood fast, choosing to die honorably in combat. In three days it was over, and those still alive were led to the sacrificial altar. Inside the palace they found the body of Cacama, his hands and feet in chains, and his abdomen ripped open by more than 20 knife thrusts.

There was, however, no joy among the military and the nobility; the escape of the Spaniards and our defeat at Otumba brought down the wrath of Cuitláhuac upon chieftain and warrior alike. Who, he asked, had allowed the sentries to leave their posts the night the Spaniards escaped? How, he stormed, had the Spaniards reached the fourth canal before they were discovered? Where, he asked, were our Tepanec allies when the Spaniards, milling about their city disorganized and vulnerable, reached Tlacopan. And why, he asked, had his warriors given up the pursuit of the fleeing Spaniards when they could have destroyed their weak and crippled army?

Cuitláhuac's rage, however, fell more upon those unfortunate lords who smuggled food and other necessities to the Spaniards while his warriors were dying on the ramparts of the palace walls. Had Cuitláhuac been victorious at Otumba, he might have been more understanding of their plight, since their only crime was blind obedience to their emperor-they had no choice under the law but to do everything in their power to save his life. The ignominy of the defeat at Otumba and the rumor that Chimalpopoca, the eldest son of Moctezuma, had aided the Spaniards in their retreat, left no room in his heart for clemency.[i] None were spared a cruel and painful death, not the Cihuacoatl, not his kinsmen.

Cuitláhuac sent messengers throughout the provinces with the heads of the Spaniards and the horses killed in the retreat, and he offered a year's exemption from tribute for any lord who refused them sanctuary. He sealed the principal trade route to the sea by reinforcing the garrison at Tepeaca, and dispatched warriors to Zautla, Ixtacamaxtitlan, and Jalacingo to close the northern route to the sea. If Cortés chose to flee to Oaxaca, he would find Mexican garrisons at Izucar and Huaquechula blocking his line of retreat.

Cuitláhuac's efforts were not long in bearing fruit. Without the protection of Imperial Mexico, Spaniards journeying from the seacoast, unaware of the fate of their comrades, found themselves at the mercy of every warrior in the land. Spaniards travelling along the trade route through Tepeaca were ambushed and killed; a company of sixty was intercepted while travelling along the northern route; and the Acolhuaque captured 45 foot and five horse at Zoltepec, a town seven leagues east of Texcoco.[ii]

Perhaps the most gratifying incident for Cuitláhuac was the destruction of the Spanish settlement at Coatzacoalcos. Tuchintl, the lord of the province, fearing the wrath of Mexico, turned on his allies and attacked the colony, killing 80 men and five women. The emperor's message had been heard beyond the farthest reaches of Anahuac. Now only Tlaxcala, Cempoala, and Chinantla sheltered the Spaniards..

Cuitláhuac next sent a diplomatic mission to Tlaxcala. It was not an unreasonable undertaking, since support for the Spaniards lay primarily in the city. Many towns in the province were resentful of having to share their scarce resources with foreigners while receiving nothing in return, and forced to ration food among their own people to satisfy their demands. Also, there was dissension and divisiveness among the nobles. The majority stood by Maxixca in his steadfast support for the Spaniards, but a significant minority shared Xicotencatl's hatred of them.

Above all else, however, Mexico and Tlaxcala shared a common language and a common heritage: like our ancestors, their ancestors had migrated to this land from the seven caves. Even though a constant state of hostility existed between Mexicans and Tlaxcalans, many of our battles were little more than tournaments, fought solely for honor, glory, and captives to sacrifice to the gods.

Six Mexican nobles, bearing salt, feathers, cotton mantles, and gold, appeared before the gates of Tlaxcala, asking for an audience with the lords of the Republic. They were permitted to enter the city, and when the lords and chieftains of the Republic gathered in the assembly hall, the spokesman of the Mexicans stepped forward.

"Valiant lords," he said, "the princes, the great nobles, and all the people of Imperial Mexico send you their greetings. They have sent us here to speak for them and to submit their most sincere proposal to you, which, they assure you, is the will of all our people. They in turn ask for no more than a reply in good faith, which they pledge to honor in all confidentiality."

The ambassador stopped, waiting for a response.

"Continue, lord ambassador," Maxixca said. "The Republic recognizes you and we will hear you out as if you were the princes of Imperial Mexico"

"My lords," the ambassador began, "since time immemorial, our people and your people have waged cruel wars against each other. Both nations have suffered the loss of many good warriors, and vast resources now lay in the waste and ruin they have brought down upon us. Even though we share a common language, a common religion, and are subject to the same laws, we have waged these wars from one generation to the next.

"Although these wars have been manly wars, they have been so devastating to our people that that the lords of Mexico would like to bring them to an end for all time to come. They therefore propose that we put behind us the injuries of the past, that we forgive each other for the death and destruction that we have brought down upon our heads, and that we now embark upon a course of everlasting peace between our people.

"United, every nation of Anahuac will bow down before Tlaxcala and Imperial Mexico, and together we will share as equals the tribute realized by our confederation. From this time forward, your people will enjoy salt, precious feathers, silver, gold, jewels, and cotton clothing, and all else that you have lacked for these many years.

"For this alliance to be realized, Mexico insists upon one stipulation-that our enemies be your enemies, and that these Spaniards seeking refuge with you be punished for their crimes. They have cast down our gods and replaced them with their own, they have caused great suffering among our people by subjecting them to unjust laws, they have seized our property, and they have ravished our wives and daughters. Now they have killed the lord Moctezuma, who died for our common cause. They have strived to destroy our way of life, and for this, they must be punished-they must be sacrificed to the gods!

"Profit from our experience and heed our warning. If you choose to nurture them and protect them, you will heap wood on a fire that will one day consume us all. If you choose to help them, and by your

291

help they overcome us, you will give them the very power they need to enslave your people and your republic, and our empire will be lost forever. Never again will our gods grant us prosperity, health, and victory.

"You owe them no debt because they say they have come here to help you, and you are not beholden to them if they do not honor your laws. If their coming has brought nothing of value to your people, if you live each day in fear of what is to come tomorrow, and if you fear being eaten by the serpent lodged in your house, then beware of them.

"This is what the princes of Mexico say to you, and this is what they offer you. They seek only peace, and they appeal to you to protect the freedom of your people and your republic above all else. If you fail to do so, then the blame for the destruction and devastation that will come to pass will be yours and yours alone, and we, with you and your gods, will be cast aside forever."

The ambassador lowered his eyes, and Maxixca rose.

"My lords," he said, "an undertaking as important as this must be considered carefully. While we reflect upon our answer, rest from your journey in the quarters we have prepared for you."

After the ambassadors left, Maxixca turned to the assembly and said, "My lords, do not be deceived by the honeyed words of the Mexicans. Need I remind you that they have been our capital enemies from time immemorial? Need I point out that this offer of friendship is for their benefit alone? Need I warn you that if we accept their proposal, we will live to regret it?

"They ask that we no longer abide by the laws we have observed for generations, laws that govern friendship, which we hold above all others. We need not observe these laws, they tell us, for they are not of our religion, and that there are no moral grounds for offering friendship and protection to those born of another faith. Furthermore, they ask us to kill our friends, friends we trust and respect, friends we have taken into our homes. But what honor, what glory, lies in murdering those we have sheltered, those who are ill and weary and suffering?

"They speak as if our Republic were the greatest nation in all of Anahuac, as if their armies were the most powerful in the land, and that we have never once realized victory in the years we fought each other. If, however, we agree to this beastly, this inhuman deed, and if we do that which the gods have ever forbidden and kill our friends, rest assured that the Mexicans will rediscover the power of their great armies and recall their many victories against the forces of Tlaxcala. Then, without the protection of our Christian allies, they will wage war against us more ruthlessly, more savagely, than ever before. But you know them just as well as I; I need not belabor their motives.

"Even now the Spaniards are recovering from their wounds, and soon they will be strong and healthy. Once they are sound, they are not so few that, with our support, they cannot overcome the Mexicans. Therefore, I counsel you to turn away the Mexicans. Refuse their offer! Only a fool or an enemy of the gods, a traitor to his country, would accept it."

Xicotencatl could contain himself no longer. He jumped to his feet and demanded that the council accept the Mexican offer. The Spaniards, he argued, were an evil lot who not only consumed the precious resources of the county, but also gave nothing in return. Furthermore, they brought disgrace and dishonor upon our people by desecrating their gods. If Tlaxcala was to safeguard its religion, if the Republic was to preserve its honor, there was no other course but to kill the Spaniards.

Tempers flared in the council hall, and disorder threatened to disrupt the assembly as Maxixa and his supporters tried to shout down Xicotencatl and the chieftains. The dissension could easily have led to arms, but Maxixca lost his patience and struck Xicotencatl, knocking him down the steps of the platform. An abrupt silence fell over the assembly, and the council adjourned without a vote.

Our ambassadors, aware that the emotions of the council were running counter to their proposal, left without waiting for a reply.

For Cuitláhuac, the failure of his ambassadors was disappointing, but for Cortés it was a call to arms. The captain was well aware that he could not depend upon the continuing good will of his hosts if he lingered overlong in their city. Although the Spaniards had not been in Tlaxcala for more than 20 days, and many of his men were not yet recovered from their wounds, he gathered the company, now only 17 horse, 400 foot, and a squadron of Tlaxcalan warriors, and marched against Acatzingo, the Mexican garrison at Tepeaca.

The approach to Acatzingo passed through fields of maize as far as the eye could see, and the ripening stalks stood well above a man's head. The Mexicans had plowed soft furrows between the rows of maize to hamper the horses, and dug deep ditches where they could lay in ambush. Knowing that the Spaniards had no cannon or muskets, the Mexicans knew the advantage was theirs.

The battle lasted for three days as Spaniards and Tlaxcalans milled about in the maize, confused and disoriented by attacks that seemed to come from all directions. The soft footing of the furrows slowed the charges of the Spanish horse, and by the third day, the endurance and the spirit of the Spaniards were crumbling. Cortés was having difficulty mobilizing his forces, and the company could not find a way out of the fields. But once again his gods smiled upon him: a captain leading a squadron of Tlaxcalans stumbled upon Acatzingo, and after killing the defenders, he raised the standard of Tlaxcala on the summit of the highest temple. When Cortés saw the banner above the sea of maize, he led his army toward it, driving back the Mexicans before him. Unaware that the town had fallen, they rushed inside and closed the gates behind them, only to find the Tlaxcalans inside, waiting for them.

Once again the pass across the sierra was open, and to secure his line of communication with the seacoast, Cortés fortified Tepeaca and established his headquarters there.

He sent punitive expeditions against the towns where Indians had ambushed Spaniards travelling from the coast, and secured the northern route by attacking Ixtamacatitlan and Jalapa, where warriors had killed a party of 55 Spaniards and sent their dismembered limbs to towns throughout the area.

The fall of Tepeaca created panic in the provinces. The first to abandon Cuitláhuac was the lord of Huaquechula, the ruler of a large, well-fortified city ten leagues west of Tepeaca. The city, situated on a fertile plain, was protected on one side by rugged mountains and on the other by deep ravines carved out by rivers flowing down the sides of Popocatepetl. A high wall surrounded the city, and four narrow openings provided the only means of entry, and a strong Mexican garrison was nearby,

Cortés sent 13 horse, 200 foot, and a squadron of Tlaxcalans to attack the garrison, and with the help of the people, who seized the lookouts and sentries, took the city and drove the Mexicans into a blind canyon in the foothills.

With Huaquechula secured, Cortés turned his attention to Izucar, a town four leagues from Huaquechula that lies on the strategic route to Oaxaca

Walls, battlements, and a deep ravine surrounded Izucar, and a Mexican garrison lay close by, but the Spaniards entered the city without undue difficulty and drove the defenders into the ravine.

The lord of Izucar, who was married to a niece of Moctezuma, fled for Tenochtitlán, and with his defection, his people turned to the Spaniards for protection. Mexico was now isolated from its distant provinces in Oaxaca and the Isthmus of Tehuantepec.

In the days that followed, ships arrived, bringing more men, horses, and weapons to Cortés, and by the time six months had passed, he was once again ready to march.[iii]

But Cuitláhuac would not defend Tenochtitlán. Two months after we drove the Spaniards from our city, a foe more formidable than the Spaniards came down upon us, and for 60 days, death reigned over our people. Before the plague that the Spaniards brought to our land was spent, Cuitláhuac lay dead, and Cuauhtémoc, a youth barely past his twentieth year, son of the mighty Ahuitzotl, sat upon the jaguar and eagle throne.[iv]

---

[i] Chimalpopoca was killed on the night of the retreat.

[ii] Cortés estimates that he lost between 150 and 200 men and 5 horses in the sierra.

[iii] While the Spaniards were in Tepeaca, two ships arrived from Cuba: one from the first Garibay expedition, another from the second expedition, and two from Cuba. Neither Cortés nor Díaz give an accurate count of the increase of manpower brought by the ships.

[iv] Cuitláhuac reigned for approximately four months before he died of smallpox.

22. Hernando Cortés:

The Noose is Drawn

By the grace of God, Martín López had survived our retreat from Tenochtitlán. Now that the passes across the sierra were secure, I sent the shipwright into the mountains to cut timber for gunships, without which no army in Christendom could lay siege to that proud citadel.

When we first arrived in Tenochtitlán, López built four brigantines that we used to reconnoiter the lakes, take soundings of the depth, and record wind patterns during our cruises with Montezuma. These were relatively small craft that the Mexicans burned after Alvarado's foolish massacre on one of their feast days.[i]

The new ships would be larger, 40 or 42 feet long, with a beam slightly more than eight feet, which was narrow enough to pass through the canals of Tenochtitlán. Each of the brigantines would have a freeboard of four feet at the waist and six or more feet at the forecastle and the poop deck, and collision bulkheads would reinforce the prow for ramming. The ships would be rigged to carry sail, and in the event of light winds, there would be six oars on each side of the vessel. The flagship would be larger, 48 feet in length, and more heavily armed than the others. Thirteen brigantines, designed with sufficient speed and maneuverability to outrun the Mexican war canoes, would be built.[ii]

While the shipwright and his crew were cutting and shaping timber for planks and beams, I sent to Vera Cruz for sails, masts, anchors, rigging, bolts, and everything else we would need, including iron cauldrons for melting pitch to caulk the seams.

When the hulls were tested and proven in a nearby river we had dammed up, Lopez would disassemble them and ready the sections for transport across the sierra.

Some of the captains favored Ayotzingo, a port on the south side of Lake Chalco, as the assembly site. Ayotzingo's canals were deep and wide, but we would have to breach the Mexicalzingo causeway to reach the great lake, and I deemed the risk unacceptable. I chose Texcoco, on the western shore of the lake instead as the assembly site. We would have to widen the canals and dig them deeper to accommodate the brigantines, and we would have to extend them inland for security, but we would be well positioned to launch our attack on Tenochtitlán.

Leaving 60 men in garrison at Tepeaca, I moved the foot and the cavalry to Tlaxcala, where, to my sorrow, I learned that Maxixca, my greatest advocate, had died of the plague. His death, however, in no way diminished the support I received from the other lords of the Republic, and at their request, I chose Maxixca's son, a lad of 13 years, to rule the province in the name of His Majesty.

During the Tepeaca campaign, five ships reached Vera Cruz at various times; some from Cuba, seeking to reinforce Nárvaez, and others from Francisco de Garay's ill-fated expedition to the Panuco River. One ship's company was too thin and jaundiced from the hardships of the Panuco to be of any use, but the others added sufficient personnel to muster an army of 40 horse and 550 foot, and leave 60 men in garrison at Tepeaca.

Our arsenal now consisted of 80 crossbows and muskets, and nine field guns. Powder, however, was scarce, but this would soon be remedied: Alonso de Ávila was on his way to Santo Domingo with sufficient funds to buy enough provisions, weapons, and gunpowder for four ships. Good fortune, however, never failed us in our hour of need, and before Ávila returned, Juan de Burgo's timely arrival from Spain and the Canary Islands brought us more crossbows, muskets, and gunpowder, which I purchased at a fair price.

On the 28th day of December, 1520, the day of the Feast of the Innocents, we said mass and set forth for Texcoco. Our route would take us through the highest and most difficult pass in the sierra, where, I hoped, the Mexicans would least expect us to make our crossing. We reached the top of the pass on the second day of the march, and we found the cold so penetrating that we had to light roaring bonfires to keep us warm through the night. Morning, however, brought forth a warm and sunny day, and we began our descent into the valley.

We had not gone far when the scouts reported that the road ahead was blocked for more than half a league with pine and cypress trees. Beyond the barrier the road was no more than a narrow path that led through a dense forest, where they had to dismount and lead the horses. The Tlaxcalans moved forward to clear the road, and we resumed our march, with crossbowmen and musketeers on point. When we reached open ground, we could make out Tenochtitlán in the distance, but columns of smoke were rising from the floor of the valley, announcing our approach.

We met no resistance until we came upon a deep gorge spanned by a dilapidated wooden bridge, which was defended by several squadrons of warriors. The cavalry drove them back from the road, and we crossed the unsound structure cautiously, taking care not to make any sudden moves. Once on the other side, we continued our descent into the valley until we reached Coatepec, a village three leagues south of Texcoco, where we quartered for the night.

The following morning we had marched no more than a quarter league when we met four nobles, one of whom I knew, bearing a gold standard. They bowed before me and offered me the standard, which must have weighed at least four gold marks, and gave me to understand that Coanacoch, the lord of Texcoco, offered his hand in peace and was pleased to welcome me to his city. Their lord, they assured me, had taken no part in the war the Mexicans waged against us, and he asked that I do no harm to his people and his city.

I accepted the standard and extended my gratitude to their lord for his offer, even though I knew that they lied. At Zoltepec, not more than six leagues from where we stood, Texcocan warriors had killed five horses, 45 Spaniards, and more than 300 Tlaxcalan porters bringing gold, clothing, and other valuables to me. Yet, if at all possible, I hoped to avoid a war with Texcoco: there would be enemies enough when we attacked the Mexicans. Through my interpreters, I made it known to the nobles that I held them responsible for the massacre at Zoltepec, and for this, they deserved to die. But if they truly wanted peace, I would forgive them, providing they returned what they had stolen from my dead companions.

The attack on the Spaniards, they protested, was instigated by Cuitláhuac, and after the Mexicans killed or captured them, they took my valuables to Tenochtitlán and sacrificed my companions. They promised, however, to search for whatever treasure had been left behind in Texcoco.

They proposed that we spend the night in Coatlichan, a village on the outskirts of Texcoco, to give Coanacoch and his majordomo's time to prepare suitable quarters for us, but I had no intention of prolonging our march one-hour longer than necessary.

We reached Texcoco at midday, and the nobles led us to the palace of Nezahualpilli, a magnificent structure large enough to accommodate an army twice as large as ours. I posted the watch and issued orders that no man, under penalty of death, was to leave the palace without my express authorization. I had seen neither women nor children on the streets of the city, and I feared an ambush.

Pedro de Alvarado and Cristóbal de Olid took a party to the summit of the great temple, and from there, they saw why our escorts tried to prevent our reaching the city that day. The lake was swarming with canoes crossing the lake to Tenochtitlán, and the road leading north was congested with people fleeing the city. Had we arrived a few hours sooner, we would have trapped Coanacoch and his army in Texcoco.

We had not been in Texcoco more than three days when the Acolhuaque began to defect to us. The first to arrive and offer me allegiance were the lords of three cities south of Texcoco, claiming that they fought against me only because they feared the wrath of the Mexicans. Later, Otumba, the largest city north of Texcoco, would submit to me.

Acolhuacán was a province sorely divided. Not a single town in the entire province chose to resist us, since no lord had emerged to unite the Acolhuaque since the death of Cacama. Coanacoch's desertion had left his people leaderless, but if I were to unify the province behind me, I would have to find a native ruler who could command its loyalty and obedience.

I had hoped that the people would accept Cuicuitzcatl, the lord whom I appointed as Cacama's successor, as their ruler. He had survived the retreat from Tenochtitlán and the battle at Otumba, but for reasons known only to him, he chose to return to Texcoco, where Coanacoch executed him.

Fortunately, another lord of royal blood, a natural son of Nezahualpilli, had survived the retreat and was now in Tlaxcala, in my custody. Tecocoltl was little more than a boy, whom the priests had converted to Christianity and baptized as Don Fernando, my namesake. He proved to be a wise choice: he remained steadfastly loyal to our cause, and despite his youth, he could be exceedingly persuasive when dealing with his chieftains-even Ixtlilxochitl, who coveted the throne of Nezahualpilli, accepted him as lord.

With Texcoco secure and work underway to excavate the canals where the brigantines were to be assembled, I set out to test the defenses along the southern shore of Lake Texcoco. Leaving a force of 200 foot to defend Texcoco, I led 18 horse, 200 foot, and several squadrons of Tlaxcalans into the peninsula that separates Lake Texcoco from Lake Chalco and Lake Xochimilco. The peninsula is more than three leagues in length, and ends at the Strait of Mexicalzingo, where a levee holds back the higher waters of Lake Xochimilco from Lake Texcoco. Our goal was to reach Ixtapalapa, situated at the end of the great causeway leading to Tenochtitlán, but I had no illusions of an easy victory, since the Mexicans or their allies controlled every town on the peninsula.

We had not advanced a league before we came under attack on both flanks, and as we penetrated deeper into the peninsula, a flotilla of canoes converged upon us. Up ahead, in the vicinity of Ixtapalapa, columns of smoke warned of our coming. Our cavalry was fresh, however, the Tlaxcalans were well rested, and the musketeers and crossbowmen were well supplied with shot, powder, and bolts. We pressed forward, and on the outskirts of Ixtapalapa, a large force of Mexicans, armed with makeshift lances fashioned from the swords of our fallen comrades, engaged the cavalry. They held their ground for three hours, then broke suddenly and fled into the city. We charged after them, but half the houses were built over water, and a fleet of canoes stood by to rescue them. A few Mexicans failed to reach the canoes, but they were skilled in the art of swimming, and they swam to safety among the reeds. The town was ours, but it came within an hour of becoming our grave.

While the Tlaxcalans looted the town, we prepared to take up quarters on the houses built on dry land. Shortly after seven o'clock, the Tlaxcalans began shouting and running through the streets. In moments, a powerful current of water surged across the floor of my quarters, and as I ran outside, I could see water rising among the houses situated on land. The Mexicans had broken open the Mexicalzingo levee, and the waters of Lake Xochimilco were pouring through the gap. Ixtapalapa lay directly in the path of the torrent, and by the time I gathered the men and led them out of the city, we had to make our way through water above our shoulders and still rising. The Tlaxcalans, a mountain people, could not swim, and many were swept away in the current and drowned. We were a soggy, hungry lot that night, because the men had been too busy looting to stop and eat their rations.

Daylight saw the Mexicans waiting for us once again. A fleet of canoes lay offshore, and a host of warriors were gathered on the peninsula, barring our retreat. We dared not take the offensive, since the enemy was all about us, and as we had done at Otumba, we used our cavalry to open a path for the foot as we retreated. By the time we were clear of the peninsula, two Spaniards and a horse were dead, and the Tlaxcalans had suffered heavy casualties. The defeat left a bitter taste among the men, but there was no thought of reprisal-events on other fronts demanded attention.

When we first came to the Valley of Mexico, the lords of Chalco, a province bordering Acolhuacán, had indicated their willingness to become vassals of His Majesty, but there had been little contact with them since that time. With our return to the valley, however, word reached me that the Chalca still favored an alliance, but feared to approach us because of the strong Mexican garrisons along the western border of the province. It seemed that generations of Mexican dominance had taken its toll on their spirit.

At this time Gonzalo de Sandoval was due to escort a company of Tlaxcalans, eager to return home with their spoils, out of the valley. This seemed to me to be an excellent opportunity to rally the Chalca with a show of force. Following a route that would take him through the heart of Chalco, Sandoval left Texcoco with 20 horse and 200 foot.

Skirmishes along the eastern shore of Lake Chalco cost the lives of two Spaniards, but Sandoval delivered the Tlaxcalans safely beyond the reach of the Mexicans. Upon his return, he stopped at Tlamanalco, one of the principal towns of Chalco. After a brief stay, he returned to Texcoco with two Chalca nobles, sons of the lord of the confederation, who had recently died. His deathbed instructions to them were to visit me and look upon me as their father should I ever return to Chalco. They brought me a small quantity of gold and an offer of friendship that I knew to be sincere. During the days when Alvarado was under siege in Tenochtitlán and I was occupied with Narváez in Cempoala, when no Spaniard in the land was safe, the Chalca sheltered two of my men from the Mexicans.

Their mission accomplished, the nobles left Texcoco. Within days, however, they were back: the Mexicans were mobilizing their forces to attack Chalco, and they appealed to me for help.

The news was disturbing, since Chalca was rich in maize, timber, cotton, and other resources of importance to us, but at this time, I could ill-afford to offer the Chalca assistance. The brigantines were finished, and ready for transport to Texcoco, and I needed every man available to transport them across the sierra. The best I could do was to persuade our allies from Huexotzingo and Huaquechula to put aside their differences with Chalco and join them in their struggle against a common enemy. I promised them that I would attend to the Mexican garrisons in the area as soon as I could, since I had no intention of leaving them in a position to attack me from the rear when I laid siege to Tenochtitlán.

Gonzalo de Sandoval left for Tlaxcala with 15 horse and 200 foot to protect the porters who would transport the brigantines to Texcoco. His route took him through Zoltepec, a town near the Tlaxcalan border, where Coanacoch had killed 45 Spaniards the previous year. When he entered the town, he found it deserted, and mindful of an ambush, he climbed a temple to survey the surrounding territory for signs of the enemy. When he entered the shrine on the summit, he saw the faces of two Spaniards, flayed and tanned and their beards still as full as when they were alive, hanging above the altar. Beside them were the hides of five horses, their hoofs still shod with iron, mounted upon the walls. In one of the houses below, Sandoval saw the inscription 'here the unfortunate hidalgo Juan Juste awaits his fate' scrawled in charcoal upon a wall.

Since I was anxious that there be no delay, I sent Alonso de Ojeda, who was more familiar with the Tlaxcalans than any other man in the company, on ahead to see that the brigantines were ready for transport when Sandoval reached Tlaxcala.

Within five days of his arrival, Ojedo had mustered 8,000 porters and organized them into the crews that were to transport the hull timbers, the deck planks, and the rigging. On the sixth day he transported the parts to Hueyotlipan, a village four leagues from Tlaxclala, where every able-bodied warrior in the province was waiting to escort them to Texcoco.

Eight days passed without a sign of Sandoval and his men, and with each passing day the Tlaxcalans grew more and more impatient with the delay. They needed no help from the Spaniards, they insisted: as long as a single Tlaxcalan lived, no Mexicans would reach the porters, and when they arrived in Texcoco, the captain would find that not a single timber or plank had been lost along the way. But Ojeda held fast, warning them that the captain had given orders that the brigantines were not to leave the area without Spanish troops to protect them.

By now Ojeda was also concerned with the delay, and early the following morning, he left Hueyotlipan with a few Spaniards to look for Sandoval. Knowing that Sandoval had orders to take a route north of the great volcanoes, he made camp at Calpulalpan, a small town on the northwest border of the province, to wait for him.

Sometime after midnight, a Tlaxcalan roused Ojeda and led him beyond the light of the campfires. As they listened, they could hear faint jingle in the distance, signaling the approach of Spanish horse. In a few moments, three Spaniards, drawn by the light of the fires, rode into camp. Sandoval and the main body of the army, they said, were just now breaking camp in Zoltepec, not more than a league away.

Two days later, Sandoval, with eight horse and 100 foot, led a procession of 8,000 porters, laden with hull timbers, deck planks, and rigging, out of Hueyotlipan. Two thousand relief porters bearing provisions followed close behind, and every warrior and chieftain in

Tlaxcala marched alongside the column. By the time the rear guard saddled up to ride, the van was more than two leagues distant.

Once the van passed through Calpulalpan and entered Acolhuacan, Sandoval called a halt. The enemy, he felt, would be more likely to attack the van of a column of this length than the rear. Since the van was more encumbered than the rear, he considered it prudent to bring the hull timbers forward and shift the unwieldy deck planks to the rear. The transfer was made with little trouble, but Chichimecatl, whose squadrons were assigned to protect the deck planks, refused to move to the rear. He and his lineage, he insisted, always took their position at the point of attack, and he refused to suffer the indignity of entering enemy territory at the rear of the column. Nearly an hour of negotiations took place between Sandoval and Chichimecatl, and the chieftain yielded only when Sandoval convinced him that the rear was more dangerous than the van, and he agreed that no Spaniards would be assigned to the rear. Once again the column moved forward, and on the fourth day, the vanguard marched into Texcoco. We welcomed them with every trumpet and drum available, and by the time the rearguard entered the city, six hours had passed.

As Martín López and his men began to assemble the brigantines, I considered the task ahead of us. The siege, I knew, would not succeed unless the brigantines eliminated the lake traffic that supplied the needs of the city. If we were to destroy more than a thousand canoes that operated in a system of lakes with a shoreline of 45 leagues, we must have the ability to sweep broad expanses under sail. Our measurements of the valley winds during our outings on the lake with Montezuma, however, gave us every confidence that our brigantines were up to the task. Once the ground attack on Tenochtitlán was underway, however, the brigantines must be free to support the army by sweeping the causeways clear of the enemy. For this task, the brigantines would rely upon the oarsmen.

First and foremost, however, our forces must be secure from attacks on the flanks and from the rear. To do this, it was vital that we secure the lakeshore. After we had accomplished this, we could begin the siege, which, lest our allies lose heart and desert us, must be of short duration.

Leaving Gonzalo de Sandoval in command at Texcoco, I led a force of 25 horse, 300 foot, and several squadrons of Tlaxcalan warriors to scout the shores of the northern lakes, following, to some extent, the route we had taken in our withdrawal to Tlaxcala. The region is less populated than the southern shore, and I planned to use this route to provision our forces on the western shore of Lake Texcoco, where I planned to establish a base. Our task was to provide safe passage for our porters around Lake Xaltocan and Lake Zumpango by destroying enemy garrisons in the area. Our journey would take us as far as Tacuba, where I could assess the condition of the causeway to Tenochtitlán and the enemy strength at that junction.

The second day out of Texcoco, we came abreast of Xaltocan, a town situated on an island just offshore of the lake of the same name. The Indians opened fire with arrows, javelins, and stones as soon as we came within range, and a fleet of war canoes, reinforced against our crossbows and muskets with heavy bulwarks, attacked us along the shore. We could do no more than move out of range, since the Indians had opened a breach on the causeway and the road leading into the town was flooded.

One of our guides, who came from a town hostile to Xaltocan, informed us that the causeway was not as impassable as it seemed. A few days earlier, he saw the enemy open the breach and flood the roadway, and he assured us that the water was not very deep. I ordered the crossbowmen and musketeers forward, and while they maintained a steady fire against the defenders, the foot waded across the breach and up the roadway, although at times the water rose nearly to their shoulders. With the Tlaxcalans close behind, they came upon solid ground, and after heavy skirmishing, they drove the Indians into their canoes and out onto the lake.

The following day we reached Cuauhtitlán and found the town deserted. On the summit of a temple we came upon the bodies of three women impaled upright upon stakes. The heavy stakes had been thrust into the vagina and through the body until the tips protruded from the mouth. Their only sin was having consorted with our men.

We resumed our march and found Tenayuca and Atzcapotzalco deserted, but as we approached Tacuba, the enemy was waiting for us in strength. Trenches dug along the approaches to the city afforded them protection from the horse, and it was all we could do to force them onto the causeway.

We spent the next six days testing the defenses of Tenochtitlán, and on one occasion we forced our way along the causeway as far as the sixth canal. I managed to silence the Mexicans on the opposite side long enough to ask to speak with a noble, but they shouted back that they were all lords; whatever I had to say, I could say to them. I warned them that their people would die of hunger if they refused to yield, but they threw tortillas across the canal and offered to feed us.

The Mexicans were as clever as they were courageous, and in a careless moment, we met with disaster. In the heat of the chase, I pursued them across a bridge that was still open, but once on the other side, they fell upon us from the rooftops and the canals. In moments, the Alferez carrying the banner of Our Lady was in the water, and had Pedro de Ircio not gone to his rescue, he would have been carried off and sacrificed. We fell back, keeping our face to the enemy until we reached the safety of the lakeshore, but five Spaniards failed to answer muster that day.

On the sixth day, I decided to return to Texcoco. I had learned all I needed to know about the western defenses of Tenochtitlán, and the desertion of nearly a third of our Tlaxcalan allies had weakened our position.

When the Tlaxcalans were not fighting alongside us, they were busy looting Tacuba, and before long, we observed them wearing fine cotton clothing, elegant plumes, and jaguar pelts, which are worn only by royalty. What caught our attention, however, were the gold armbands and other pieces of fine jewelry they were wearing.

I allowed the Indians to keep the clothing and the feathered plumes, but each night I ordered them searched for gold and jewelry. The returns of the first night yielded gold worth some 3,000 pesos, but in the morning we found that many had deserted. The second night our search yielded 1,777 pesos, but the next day saw so many desertions that we estimated as much as 20,000 pesos had found their way to Tlaxcala. Among the treasures we took from them were two winged idols made of gold, a heavy gold chain inlaid with turquoise stones, and a large turquoise stone with the carving of a face engraved on one side. The stone alone would fetch at least 15 slaves in

Tlaxcala. On the third day, we halted the searches, fearing that the Mexicans would note our losses.

Two days after our return to Texcoco, the Chalco lords were back again, complaining of more Mexican attacks. I knew that several squadrons of warriors from Huexotzingo and Huaquechula were in the province, but it was evident that they had made no attempt to attack the Mexicans.

Nearly every man in the company was spent from the endless fighting, and many were too weak to take into combat. The physicians were also concerned about the men who were throwing up blood mixed with mud and dirt, but I could no longer avoid sending troops into Chalco. Casting about for able-bodied men and the walking wounded, I mustered a force of 20 horse and 300 foot, and on the twelfth day of March, Sandoval led them to Chalco.

Sandoval's mission proved to be a success. Leading his native allies, he launched attacks against the Mexican garrisons at Oaxtepec and Yecapixtla. He encountered no difficulty with the garrison at Oaxtepec, but Yecapixtla was a fortified town perched upon a bluff, and his Indian allies lost heart when they saw the heights. They did no more than watch as the Spaniards scaled the face of the bluff under heavy fire from above, but when the town fell, the river below the bluff ran red with blood of their captives. The courage of the Spaniards, however, had its effect upon the Chalca. Within a few days the Chalca sent me 40 Mexican chieftains they had taken in battle.

The last days of March and the first days of April were harbingers of good things to come. Four ships arrived in Vera Cruz, bringing us nearly 200 men, 80 horses, and a considerable store of arms and powder, and a few days later, a ship out of Jamaica brought two heavy cannon.

Among the new arrivals was the first representative of His Majesty to set foot in New Spain. Juan de Alderete, our newly appointed treasurer, had accompanied the Admiral Diego Columbus to Santo Domingo the previous year, and after purchasing a ship and supplies, he sailed to Vera Cruz to assume his new duties.

The strength of the company was now sufficient to begin the siege. We had enough weapons and horses, the logistics of supplying the army were ready to implement, and our Indian allies were overeager to begin the war. It was time to carry out our final preparations for the task ahead.

On Friday, the fifth day of April, I set out with 30 horse and 300 foot to clear the region south of the fresh-water lakes of Mexican garrisons. Our route would first take us along the western border of Chalco, through Tlamanalco and Chimalhuacan, then in a southwesterly direction, following a great circle through towns peopled by the Xochimilca but governed by Mexico. At Xochimilco we would test the strength of Mexico's most formidable allies, then, depending upon the outcome, we would either return to Texcoco across the Ixtapalapa causeway, or continue our journey around the lakes.

We reached Chimalhuacan the second day out of Texcoco, where the largest force of Indian allies yet to join us awaited. At the quarter hour before dawn, we mustered our army and entered Mexican territory. The plain before us was rough and uneven; its surface was split by vast lava fields and deep gorges formed centuries ago by streams and rivers that flowed from long-dormant volcanoes. Isolated mesas, carved from rock and lava by the erosion of wind and water, rose steeply above the plain, and nowhere did we see any evidence of water.

At two o'clock in the afternoon we came abreast of a mesa where the Indians had placed their families out of harm's way. Women and children watched us from the heights as warriors gathered around the edge, shouting insults and daring us to attack. I had no inclination to attack, since the mesa lay off our line of march and there appeared to be no path leading up its sheer walls. I was aware, however, that failure to attack would result in a loss of confidence among our allies.

I rode around the foot of the mesa, nearly a league in circumference, and at no point did is see any sign of a path to the summit. But I was committed, and I ordered an assault on the sides of the mesa that seemed less formidable.

At my signal, the men began their ascent, protecting themselves as best they could from the avalanche of boulders from above.

Soon they reached a point where they could climb no further: not a single foothold could be seen on the walls above. They halted, seeking what little shelter they could find against the hail missiles from above. Inasmuch I hated to suffer another defeat at the hands of the Indians, I sounded the retreat before they were swept from the walls of the mesa. When they reached safety, I counted eight good men dead and many others injured and unable to finish the campaign.

A second mesa nearby proved less of a problem. Although it seemed steeper than the other, a nearby hill stood above it. A squadron of warriors defended the hill, and when we moved forward, they evidently thought that we were preparing to attack their families on the mesa. They raced to defend their families, and abandoned the hill to us. We found the mesa well within reach of our crossbows and muskets, and it took no more than an hour before the women began waving their shawls, signaling that they were willing to make tortillas for us.

We spent the next two days in a small town at the foot of the mesa, and before we departed for Oaxtepec, the people on the first mesa came down to our camp and offered me their allegiance. They had little choice-there is no water on the mesas.

The land became increasingly fair as we approached Oaxtepec, and the natives, having been pacified by Sandoval, were friendly and hospitable. The lord of the city came out to greet us, and he led us into a city so lovely that few, if any, in Spain could be called its equal. A tree-lined stream, bounded by broad expanses of greenery and flower gardens, flows through the center of town, and beyond the gardens lie orchards, where every variety of fruit in the land grows. Oaxtepec was the favorite playground of Montezuma, and for his hunting pleasure, the natives stocked the entire region with fowl, rabbit, deer, and other game. We spent the night in summerhouses and oratorios set among boulders overlooking the town.

We left Oaxtepec at first light for Yautepec, a town protected by a large Mexican garrison. When we arrived, we saw that a large force of warriors had taken up a position in a field outside of the town, but as we approached them, they made what seemed to us signs of peace. As we drew nearer, they turned and fled to the west. We pursued them to the outskirts of Jiutepec, four leagues distant, where they turned and made a stand, but we had little difficulty driving them into the hills. I expected the lords of the city to come out and offer me their allegiance, but after waiting two days, I fired the town and moved on to Cuernavaca, a league and a half northwest.[iii]

Our first sight of Cuernavaca was discouraging. The city lies at the foot of a range of rugged mountains, and ravines more than 60 feet deep surround the city on all sides. The bridges spanning the ravines were raised, and as we approached, the Indians launched a broadside of javelins, arrows, and stones.

I led the horse around the perimeter while the foot surveyed the ravines. The defenders stayed abreast of us as we circled, keeping safely out of range of the crossbows.

The foot, meanwhile, were about to give up on their search for a crossing until a Tlaxcalan descended into a ravine to examine the trees on either side of a narrow stream. Descending carefully, he managed to reach the branches of a tree on the other side, and without a moment's hesitation, others followed him across. When they reached the rim and entered the town, they caught the Indians from the rear just as Cristóbal de Olid and Ándres de Tapia made a perilous crossing over a shaking and swaying bridge. At the sight of the horse and the foot closing in on them from behind, the Indians panicked and fled for the mountains.

We fired a good part of the town, then settled down for the day in the comfortable quarters of the lord of the city. Late that afternoon, some of the chieftains and leading nobles returned to surrender and offer their allegiance to me.

The following morning we set out across the mountains for Xochimilco. The day was hot and the path was steep and difficult as we climbed to a pass that rises nearly 5,000 feet above Cuernavaca. It took us most of the day to advance three leagues, and not a drop of water was to be found anywhere. An elderly Spaniard collapsed and died from heat and dehydration, and when the Tlaxcalans began to fall by the wayside, I called a halt. Our guides insisted that a pool of water lay up ahead, and I sent six horse up the trail to find it. We waited for their return in a grove of pine trees, where the shade offered us some protection from the sweltering sun.

The sun sank low on the horizon as one hour passed into the next, I feared that our men had met with misfortune, and I was preparing to resume the march when Bernal Díaz, one of the foot, approached me. Despite my orders to the contrary, he had slipped away with the horse in search of water and found a well in a small farm not far ahead, and he gave me a pitcher of water he had drawn from it.

We reached the farm just before sunset, but the well was small and had little water. We had been there only a short time when our six horse returned and reported that the pool lay some distance ahead, but they advised me to make camp for the night, since the countryside was swarming with warriors.

The men slept little that night. Their thirst was such that they spent the night sucking what moisture they could from the cactus that grows nearby, and by morning, their lips and tongues were raw and bleeding.

We began our descent of the sierra at first light, and by eight o'clock we reached the outskirts of Xochimilco. The city lay a short distance offshore, and a single causeway joined it to the land. The bridge on the causeway was open, and the Indians had raised defensive earthworks on the far side of the breach.

Leaving a squad of horse to guard the approaches to the city, I dismounted and led the foot along the causeway as far as the breach. On the other side warriors, armed with steel-tipped pikes, fashioned from our swords, waited for us behind the earthworks, where our crossbows and muskets could not reach them. We attacked, but one charge after another was driven back with a barrage of stones and arrows. Our position on the causeway soon became untenable as Indian canoes began to threaten our flanks, and we had no choice other than to charge across the breach in the face of enemy fire. The water was deep, and many of the men were half-drowned before we reached the opposite side, but we captured the earthworks and pushed our way into the city.

By late afternoon we gained control of that part of the city built on land, although many of the defenders escaped in canoes. The Indians made signs that they wanted peace several times, but when we lowered our weapons, they resumed their attack with stones, arrows, and javelins. Their actions, we soon learned, were delaying tactics to give reinforcements from Tenochtitlán time to reach Xochimilco.

The Mexicans attacked in the early part of the evening. Only six horses were saddled, but I led them across the shore while the others readied their mounts. As we approached the Mexicans, they closed ranks and braced for our charge by planting heavy steel-tipped lances in the ground. Without waiting for the others, we charged into their midst, and in the struggle, four horses were wounded and my horse fell, spilling me to the ground. In a moment the Mexicans were upon me, grabbing at my arms and trying to drag me off, but a Tlaxcalan came to my rescue, and with a Spaniard at his side, they held off the Mexicans long enough for me to remount. By the time I was back in the saddle, the rest of the horse arrived and scattered the Mexicans.

Four Spaniards, recent arrivals to New Spain, failed to report at muster that night. The Mexicans captured them while they were looting houses along the lakeshore and carried them off in canoes. After Cuauhtémoc sacrificed them, he sent their body parts to all the towns that had deserted him.

As darkness closed in about us, the watch sighted a large fleet of war canoes approaching from the direction of Tenochtitlán. I posted a watch around the perimeter of the city and assigned a squad of Spaniards at every dock and canal where the Mexicans might attempt a landing. I gave the Tlaxcalans the task of filling the breach in the causeway with stone and adobe, for I had no intention of allowing the Mexicans to bottle up my horse inside the city.

I spent the greater part of the night making my rounds of the watch. Some sentries reported hearing the sound of muffled paddles close offshore, but other than an occasional shower of arrows from the lake, the night passed without incident.

At daybreak I climbed to the summit of the highest temple, and to the north, less than a league from Xochimilco, the lake was swarming with canoes. How many I could not count. A thousand? Two thousand? How many carried two warriors? How many carried six? By sunrise the Mexicans were ashore and joined the warriors arriving by land.

We broke through the enemy with our first charge and scattered them along the shore. Before they could regroup, we attacked another Mexican force gathering about a nearby hill. When the horse drove them away, I ordered the foot up the hill as if it were our intent to occupy it, and took the horse around the other side. The Mexicans fell into the trap. They turned away from the hill, thinking we had taken it, and headed for Xochimilco. We continued around the hill and fell upon them from the rear, killing many and putting the rest to flight. By ten o'clock we were back in Xochimilco, arriving in time to repel an attack along the causeway.

We won the day, but after another day of heavy fighting against an enemy that greatly outnumbered us, I knew that it was time to withdraw. We could not hope to prevent the Mexicans from surrounding the city by land and by water much longer. We had no more powder for our muskets, and although we had bolts for the crossbows, we had to tip them with copper points, which were far less effective than steel points.

We assembled in the market place early the next morning. I assigned ten horse to the van and another ten to the rear, and placed the baggage and the wounded in the middle. We fired the city and moved out. The Mexicans fell upon us as soon as we were clear of Xochimilco, and they harassed us until we reached Coyoacán, a city two leagues to the north.

We found Coyocán deserted, which gave us an opportunity to survey the surroundings. At first light I took six horse and 200 foot to examine the Coyoacán spur, a causeway that joins the Ixtapalapa causeway at the Xoloc fortress. A barrier, defended by a large Indian force, blocked the causeway, but after heavy fighting and hand-to-hand combat, we drove them back to Xoloc.

From the top of the barricade, we had a clear view of the network of causeways that joins Tenochtitlán to the western and southern shores of the lake. To the north was a large lagoon between the Ixtapalapa and Tacuba causeways, and as we looked, we could see a large fleet of canoes bearing down upon us. I had no thought to wait for them, since I had seen all I needed to see: if the siege of Tenochtitlán were to succeed, I would have to secure a foothold here at Coyoacán as well as Ixtapalapa and Tacuba.

The following morning we departed for Tacuba, two leagues to the north, but our progress was slow due to repeated attacks from the marshes bordering the lagoon. Growing impatient with the delays, I took ten horse and dropped back, hoping to ambush the Mexicans, but I fell into one myself. Before I could withdraw, several horses were wounded and two pages who had followed me on foot were captured. They had served me well, and I grieved at the thought of the fate that awaited them at the hands of these savages.

A steady downpour began as we approached Tacuba, and we halted for an hour to seek shelter. The rainstorms continued as we moved northward to Atzcapotzalco and Tenayuca, and by the time we

313

reached Cuauhtitlán, which was deserted and knee-deep in mud, we were soaked and weary. All through the night, the Mexicans whistled and howled about us, but they kept their distance.

We reached Citlaltepec late the following day, and we spent another miserable night in a deserted sea of mud, but morning saw the sun rise and the rains stop. On the 23rd day of April, we straggled into Acolman, where Sandoval and a company of Spaniards were waiting for us.

Upon my return to Texcoco, I found the brigantines within a few days of being ready for launch. Eight thousand Indians had labored for more than 50 days to excavate a canal wide enough and deep enough to assemble them, and extend it far enough from the lakeshore to keep them safe from the Mexicans. Martín López had dammed the canal and constructed a series of locks at intervals along its length, and now he was ready to open them to float our ships.

My satisfaction with the progress made on the brigantines, however, was overshadowed when I learned that a plot against my life was underway. A common soldier, one Fulano de Rojas, approached me in secret and informed me that the leader was Antonio de Villafaña, and that he had a list of 300 men who were ready to support him.

I ordered Sandoval to seize Villafaña, but when the constables burst into his quarters, he thrust a paper into his mouth. Sandoval seized him by the throat to prevent him from swallowing it, but he came away with only a fragment bearing 30 names.

Villafaña confessed, but he was a man of honor, swearing that he and he alone had conceived the plot, and that the paper held only the names of those who he hoped would join him. I could torture him all I pleased, he said, but I would learn nothing more.

Although I knew better, I did not pursue the matter further. The conspirators had approached one of my trusted officers, and from him I learned that the real instigator of the plot was none other than Julian de Alderete, who, as the King's treasurer, was beyond my reach. I was not surprised: Alderete owed his appointment to Juan Rodriguez de Fonseca, the Bishop of Burgos, who was Diego Velasquez's strongest advocate in the Court of Spain.

I was to be assassinated during mass the following day. With the raising of the host, the conspirators would throw a hood over my head and stab me to death. When I was out of the way, Alderete would announce that Francisco de Verdugo, the brother-in-law of Diego Velásquez, was now captain-general and Antonio de Villafaña chief constable.

I hanged Villafaña from the window of his quarters and left his body there for all to see.

The next morning my most trusted companions armed themselves and accompanied me to mass. Alderete and his circle were seated in the chapel when we entered, and as we took our seats, I never took my eyes from his face. After the priest said mass, he rose and left without a backward glance. There was no more talk of mutiny-the conspirators had no way of knowing whose names were on Villafaña's paper.[iv]

On the 28th day of April, Martín López opened the locks and flooded the canal, and one by one, the brigantines rose to the level of the lake. When all were afloat, I ordered the entire company into the plaza for inspection. We mustered 86 horse, 118 musketeers and crossbows, and 700 foot, and our heavy weapons were three heavy cannon and 15 falconets. After my review, a scribe mounted the steps of a temple and read the articles of war.

> No man, he proclaimed, was to blaspheme our lord
> Jesus Christ, nor Our Lady, His Blessed Mother, nor
> the Sainted Apostles or any other saint.

> Each soldier must, at all times, wear armor, a neck
> guard, a helmet, and leggings, and maintain his
> weapons in good condition.

> No soldier, unless disabled by wounds or weakened by
> illness, was to sleep other than fully armed or shod.

> No soldier was to gamble for a horse, for armor, or for
> any weapon.

> No soldier, under penalty of death, was to leave his
> camp without permission from his captain, and any
> soldier found asleep on watch or convicted of desertion
> would be summarily hanged.

> No soldier, under the heaviest of penalties, was to
> mistreat our Indian allies, nor was he to take their food,
> their spoils of war, their women, or anything else from
> them.

The men were dismissed, and I sent runners to alert our Indian allies that the brigantines were ready and to inform them that they had no more than 10 days to arm themselves and report for duty. The Tlaxcalans were to report to Texcoco, and the Huexotzinga and the Cholulans to Chalco, on the eastern shore of the freshwater lakes.

On the day after Whitsunday, I organized the army into four commands and gave each their assignments. Pedro de Alvarado was to take 30 horse, 18 crossbowmen and musketeers, 150 foot, two field pieces, and half of our Tlaxcalan allies to Tacuba.

Cristóbal de Olid, with 33 horse, 18 crossbowmen and musketeers, 160 foot, and two field pieces, and the other half of the Tlaxcalans, would accompany Alvarado as far as Tacuba, and when that city was secured, he would march south and establish his camp at Coyoacán.

Gonzalo de Sandoval was given command of 24 horse, 13 crossbowmen, four musketeers, and 150 foot, 50 of whom were from my own company, and stand by in Texcoco until Alvarado and Olid were in place on the western shore of the lake.

The brigantines, with a complement of 150 soldiers and 150 mariners to man the oars, were under my command.

The Tlaxcalans were sent on ahead of Alavarado and Olid to clear the route around the northern lakes of Indians, but before Alvarado and Olid set out, Chichimecatl sent word that Xicotencatl had deserted his command.

Xicotencatl had been a thorn in my side from the day I crossed the sierra, a belligerent antagonist who made no effort to hide his hostility toward me. But Xicotencatl was like no other Indian I had ever encountered. For insight and strength of will, he was far superior to his peers, and unlike them, he held no delusions that I was of divine origin. Twice he brought shame and disgrace and the wrath of his father upon his head for defying the will of the Republic, yet he persisted to gain sovereignty for his people. Rather than yield it to a foreign invader, he was willing to fight alongside Mexico, an ancient enemy so powerful that he risked servitude for generations to come for his country.

But when I undertook the Tepeaca campaign, when I could not have established a foothold on this side of the sierra without the support of Tlaxcala, Xicotencatl was the first of offer his services, and he fought alongside us until the pass across the sierra was secured. For his support, willing or unwilling, I could not treat him as a common deserter without making an effort to return him to his command.

I chose two of his closest friends to urge him, for the sake of his honor, the honor of his country, and that of his father, to return of his own volition. If he failed to appear, I would declare him a deserter and order him executed.

His friends found him on the road to Tlaxcala in the company of Piltechtl, an injured chieftain, who, Xicotencatl claimed, had been beaten senseless by the Spaniards. They found him in no mood to listen to them. If it was honor that concerned them, he said, better they look to his father and the other lords who had delivered their proud nation into the hands of a foreigner. He resumed his journey without looking back.

Alonso de Ojedo and his constables brought him back to Texcoco, chained like a common criminal, and after reading the sentence as prescribed by law, I sent him to the gallows and hanged him before his countrymen.

I could not help but wonder what course history might have taken had Xicotencatl rather than Montezuma been seated on the throne of Mexico. I could not imagine him allowing a handful of foreigners to take him prisoner without an outcry, nor could I believe that he would prohibit his army from attacking us to save his own life.

On the 22nd day of May, Alvarado and Olid set out for the western shores of Lake Texcoco. The captains had a falling-out over a trifling matter of quarters along the way, but through the offices of Fray Pedro Melgarejo and Luis Martín, they grudgingly reconciled their differences and resumed their march. They reached Tacuba on the 26th day of May.

Olid remained with Alvarado until the city was secure and the Chapultepec aqueduct was destroyed, cutting the supply of fresh water to Tenochtitlán, then he moved south to Coyoacán.

317

On the morning of the 31st day of May, Sandoval left at first light for Chalco, where he mustered his Indian allies and set out for Ixtapalapa. He reached the city shortly after midday, and when the first column of smoke rose high into the air, I ordered the brigantines out onto the lake. The siege of Tenochtitlán was underway.

---

[i] Brigantines, sometimes called bergantines, drew little water, ideal for the shallow waters of the lakes and penetrating into the canals of Tenochtitlán. The vessels were capable of sailing into the wind and against the currents. The four built during the first occupation of Tenochtitlán were ostensibly built for pleasure cruises with Moctezuma, but they were fitted with cannon and carried out gunnery exercises, presumably to impress the Mexicans with Spanish power.

[ii] Çervantes states that the brigantines were maintained and preserved as a memorial to the conquest at the public docks of Mexico City for 40 years.

[iii] The Nahuatl name for Cuernavaca is Quauhnahuac.

[iv] Cortes does not mention the plot to Charles V until the close of his Third Letter, but he makes no mention of Alderete's participation in it.

23. Ecatl:

Ahuitzotl and the Quetzal Owl

Not since the days of Itzcoatl, when Atzcapotzalco and the Tepanecs made war upon our emerging nation, had the Mexican people been so threatened. As it was in Itzcoatl's time, a great crisis was once again upon us, a turning point that would decide the fate and future of the Mexican nation for generations to come. And, like Itzcoatl, Cuauhtémoc inherited a royal house sorely divided.

With the return of the Spaniards to the Valley of Mexico, Moctezuma's surviving sons, Axayácatl and Xoxopeualoc, supported by the Cihuacoatl and their loyalists, demanded that Cuauhtémoc sue for peace. Let us appease Cortés, they said, give him his tribute and whatever else he wants so that we may be rid of him.

By now, however, too much Mexican blood had been shed for us to compromise with Cortés. Too many promises had been broken to place our future at his discretion, and the memory of our innocent youth, the flower of Mexican nobility, lying dead on the plaza floor while the Spaniards stripped them of their possessions, still burned in the minds of our elders, our priests, and our chieftains. Talk of appeasement, they told the young emperor, must be stopped before it passed beyond the palace walls and created unrest among the people.

Cuauhtémoc did not hesitate. He ordered Moctezuma's sons and the Cihuacoatl seized and put to death, and others accused of supporting them sought out and executed without so much as a hearing.[i]

The leaders of the opposition were gone, but the loyalties of the royal household were still suspect, and for the sake of unity, a marriage was arranged between Cuauhtémoc and Tecuichpo, the only surviving child of Moctezuma and Tezalco, his legitimate wife.

Tecuichpo, who was only eleven years old, had been spared the fate of her brothers and sisters in the canals of Tenochtitlán when the Spaniards fled. Cortés, for reasons unknown, sent the child to her relatives in Tlacopan when he left to make war upon Nárvaez, but when he returned and sent for her, fate stepped in. While on her way to Tenochtitlán, a squad of warriors attacked her escort and took her to Cuitláhuac.[ii]

As internal strife abated and Mexico turned to the business of war, Cuauhtémoc began taking reprisals against towns that had defected to Cortés and attacking Tlaxcalan porters bringing supplies to the Spaniards. On the southern front, he reinforced his garrisons west of Chalco and launched a series of attacks on Chalca towns.

Meanwhile, we prepared for the coming siege. We stockpiled weapons, filled our granaries and water reservoirs to capacity, and built barricades along the causeways.

We were confident that we could control the causeways, where the Spanish horse would be of little use and their soldiers exposed to fire from Tlatelolco shield boats. Control of the lake, however, would be difficult in view of the craft the Spaniards were assembling in Texcoco. Cuauhtémoc made several attempts to destroy them before they could be launched, but the assembly site was far back from the shore and heavily defended. Fortunately, the lakes were vast, and it was unlikely that the Spanish craft could intercept every canoe bringing supplies to the city.

Our southern shores were, we felt, secure. Culhuacán, Ixtapalapa, Mexicalzingo, Huitzilopochco, and Xochimilco were our allies, and with 10,000 canoes at their disposal, they could provision us and supply us with fresh water from the streams south of the lagoon.

One hundred and forty days after he occupied Texcoco, Cortés set the siege of Mexico in motion. The first attack came from Alvarado. He marched out onto the Tlacopan causeway in force, where he met Temilotl, the captain-general of Tlatelolco. Temilotl attacked his flanks with his shield boats, and his warriors, protected from the Spanish crossbows by heavy bulwarks, were able to maintain a steady fire of darts and javelins on the column. But the Spanish soldiers, beneath the protective cover of their shields, continued to advance.

As the column moved forward, the warriors on the causeway drew back and slid into the water without a fight. The Spanish van crossed the first breach and drove the defenders back toward the city. Sensing a rout, their companions poured across the breach and joined the chase.

This was the moment that Temilotl awaited. His warriors, armed with lances tipped with Spanish steel, attacked the oncoming Spaniards. The onslaught drove the Spanish van back toward the breach, where they tumbled down upon those pushing their way across. As the Spaniards floundered in the water, clawing at each other to reach safety, the shield boats closed in from both sides and began to carry them off.

Fighting desperately to pull their men out of the water, the Spaniards pulled back, only to find their Tlaxcalan allies blocking their path of retreat. Step by step, the Spaniards forced their way back along the causeway, gathering their wounded as best they could beneath a merciless barrage of arrows and javelins from the shield boats.

Alvarado learned his lesson well that day: eight men were dead, and scores were wounded. He made no more forays until Cortés was prepared to support him.

The major thrust came nine days later. Sandoval, after driving the defenders of Ixtalpalapa into the lake, marched onto the causeway. At the same time, smoke signals rising from the summit of Uixachlan informed us that the Spanish gunboats were now on the lake and headed toward Ixtapalapa. Cuauhtémoc ordered 500 shield boats onto the lake to intercept the gunboats, and sent his warriors to take up positions on Tepepolco, a steep eminence that rises from the lake near Ixtapalapa.

Cortés chose to pass by Tepepolco, but after having second thoughts about leaving a fortified position to his rear, turned back and sent a landing party to secure the heights.

By the time the Spanish fleet was ready to resume its course, our shield boats were closing upon them. The fleet changed course to intercept, but as they bore down upon them, their sails sagged and fell as the afternoon winds died. The ships lost headway, and in moments, they lay dead in the water. The advantage was ours, but the shield boats hesitated, just beyond range of the Spanish crossbows and muskets.

We paid dearly for that lost opportunity, that brief moment when the ships, heavier and slower without sail, were vulnerable to our lighter and faster craft. From the northeast, a strong breeze rose and swept across the lake, and one by one, their sails billowed out and the ships were underway again, headed directly for the densely packed boats in their path.

Our fragile craft shattered and disappeared beneath the heavy prows of the Spanish ships, and in their wake, broad trails of debris and mangled bodies rose to the surface. The shield boats fled in every direction to escape the path of destruction; some managed to cross under the bridges on the causeway and reach safety in the lagoon; others, less fortunate, fled into the open lake, where the Spaniards overtook them and sent them to the bottom.

The next attack came from Cristóbal de Olid at Coyoacán. He marched out on the causeway with a large company of horse and foot and fought his way as far as the Xoloc fortress, where he hoped to join forces with Sandoval, but our warriors held their ground. Our hold on the fortress, however, lasted only until Cortés arrived with his gunships, and with the support of his cannon, he was able to capture the fortress. The Spaniards brought three heavy cannon ashore, but when the first cannon was fired, a powerful explosion rocked Xoloc as all the gunpowder exploded.

By midnight we had mustered enough forces to mount a counterattack on the fortress, but once again the Spanish gunships decided the issue. They cruised up and down the causeway, sweeping it clear of attackers.

The following morning Cuauhtémoc launched another attack against Xoloc, but Cortés, with gunships and support from Sandoval and Olid, mounted a counterattack that drove his warriors back into the city. The Spaniards, however, paid dearly for their success that day. Our shield boats raked their flanks with a withering fire of darts and javelins from the lagoon, where the gunships could not reach them.

Cortés withdrew to the fortress and opened a breach wide enough to pass four gunships into the lagoon. Now he could attack our warriors on both sides of the causeway and drive our shield boats back into the canals. The gunships sought to pursue them, but heavy stakes set just below the level of the water blocked the entrances. Two gunships, however, managed to reach the outskirts of the city, but after firing a few houses, they turned back.

Six days of heavy fighting on the causeways followed. While the gunships prowled about the city, foraging along the canals and firing houses, our allies at Mexicalzingo and Huitzilopochtlo cut communications between Sandoval at Ixtapalpapa and Olid at Coyoacán by opening the dike between Lake Xochimilco and the lagoon. The Spaniards, however, placed a gunship in the breach and used it as a footbridge.

By the end of the sixth day, Cortés had cut off all approaches to the city by land and by water. Sandoval and his company were now in Tepeyacac, sealing the causeway and cutting our route to the north, and closing the old spur leading to Atzcapotzalco. By opening breaches in the Tlacopan causeway wide enough to pass his ships into the swampy lagoon to the north, Cortés could now provide gunship support for Sandoval as well as Alvarado.[iii]

On the seventh day, Cortés launched his offensive against the heart of Tenochtitlán. With gunship support on either side of the Ixtapalapa causeway, he moved north with 200 Spaniards. At the same time, Alvarado, with gunship support on either side of the Tlacopan causeway, moved in from the west, and Sandoval attacked from the north.

When Cortés reached the first the first breach, he found it wider and deeper than before, and on the opposite side there was a barricade of stone and adobe. Several salvos from his cannon were sufficient to knock down the barrier and drive off the defenders, and the Spaniards crossed the breach.

Cortés brought the Tlaxcalans forward and set them to work filling the breach, and resumed his march on the city. When he reached the outskirts, he was halted by another breach with a barricade on the opposite side. He ordered the gunships forward, and a few rounds demolished the barrier. The Spaniards moved forward, leaving their allies to fill the gap.

Meanwhile, two gunships discovered a canal wide enough to allow them to penetrate into the city. They moved into the nearest barrio, firing houses on either side of the canal. The shield boats gave battle, but darts and javelins were no match for the cannons that swept away everything in their path. The boats that were not torn apart fled into shallow canals beyond the reach of the gunships.

Cortés's company was now facing a wide canal defended by heavy earthworks and a host of warriors on the rooftops of houses on either side. The column halted until crossbowmen cleared the rooftops and the cannon demolished the earthworks.

Two hours passed before the Spaniards secured the crossing, since Cortés would not move forward until the Tlaxcalans had packed the breach with enough adobe and logs to allow him to bring up his horse.

The bridge across the fourth and last canal was still in place, and they crossed it without resistance. The cavalry reached the great plaza, and after a brief fight, drove the defenders behind the serpentine walls and onto the roof of the Coacalli, the Serpent House. The Spaniards positioned a heavy gun at the Eagle Gate, and when its thunder echoed from the walls and clouds of black smoke filled the air, the defenders fled and scattered into the streets.

The Spaniards moved the cannon forward and set it on the stone of the gladiators, where it could cover the entire enclosure. They searched the temples and the shrines, but the only sign of life was two priests playing drums and chanting on the summit of the Temple of Huitzliopochtli. Two men climbed to the top and threw them into the plaza.

Cortés divided his horse into foraging parties and sent them into the streets to search out our warriors, and we were quick to take advantage of his change of tactics. When the Spanish horse was dispersed throughout the city, we mounted a counterattack on the plaza and sought out horsemen who had strayed too far from his companions.

One horseman pursued a warrior into the courtyard of Moctezuma's palace and ran him through with his lance. The warrior was mortally wounded, but he held the lance long enough for his companions to topple the Spaniard from his horse and kill him.

The Spaniards in the plaza, finding themselves without the support of the horse, broke and fled down the avenue, abandoning their cannon. Only the return of the horse, allowing Cortés to form an orderly withdrawal, prevented a complete rout of the army.

Repeated charges by horsemen in the rear guard kept our warriors at bay, but before the retreating army reached the causeway and the protection of the gunships, stones and boulders rained down upon the soldiers from every rooftop on the avenue. Had Cortés not been so prudent as to fill every breach along the path of his retreat with stones and adobe, we would have filled them with the bodies of his comrades.

The battle had proved to be more costly for Mexico than we anticipated. Help from the cities south of the fresh-water lakes never materialized, since detachments of Spanish horse kept their warriors away from the causeways, and their war canoes, fearing the Spanish gunboats, never ventured onto the lake. Our only spoils of the day were the cannon abandoned by the Spaniards. At nightfall, we set it on a barge and dropped it into the depths, of the lake at Tepetzingo, where Mexico's royalty once bathed among green forests.

Cortés's second attack followed the first by three days. The Spaniards found the going more difficult, since the breaches were wider and deeper, the barricades stronger and better defended, and every rooftop stockpiled with weapons and teeming with warriors.

But we fared no better than before: once again the Spaniards gained the plaza, and while the cavalry skirmished in the streets, the gunships penetrated deeper into the city, destroying everything that stood in their path.

As daylight faded and the sky grew dim, the Spaniards began their withdrawal from the plaza. As they marched down the causeway, the Tlaxcalans waved the limbs of our comrades that they would soon dine upon.

Before they had gone far, a great fire rose in the center of the city. One by one, flames that rose as high as the temple of Huitzilopochtli consumed the palaces of Moctezuma Ilhuicamina, Axayácatl, and Moctezuma Xocoyotl. When the fire reached the bamboo cages in the royal aviary, our souls cringed as the piercing screams of egrets, hawks, and songbirds filled the evening air.

The Spaniards were up and on the march again at first light, but despite hunger, fatigue, and a night without sleep, we had once again opened the breaches at the canal crossings. Cuauahtémoc himself directed the effort, forcing us to work from dusk to dawn, unmindful of those who died of exhaustion. At first light we put down our tools and fought with the enemy until late afternoon, and when the Spaniards withdrew, we took up our tools and filled the breaches again with adobe and timber.

Our efforts, however, had not been in vain. The Spaniards advanced no further than they had the day previous, and they too were beginning to weary. The strain and fatigue of continuous fighting had taken its toll, mentally as well as physically, upon them. Their powder and shot were nearly spent, many carried broken pikes and shields battered to the point of uselessness, their swords were nicked and scored and beginning to rust, and not a man wore a helmet that had not been scored by a stone or *maquahuitl*.

While Cuauhtémoc and the Tenochca fought against Cortés, Temilotl and the Tlatelolca waged an aggressive campaign against Alvarado and Sandoval. Like Cuauhtémoc, Temilotl opened the breaches by night, but when the Spaniards returned the following morning, there was always an unpleasant surprise waiting for them.

On one occasion the Spaniards found the opposite side of the breach lightly manned, and in their rush to cross, they plunged into pits where stakes sharpened and fire hardened to penetrate the heaviest boot were planted on the bottom. Nor could the Spanish gunboats offer them much protection: heavy stakes along the shore of the lagoon kept them away from his warriors.

Nevertheless, we found Alvarado a formidable opponent. He did not, like Cortés, withdraw from the causeway after the day's fighting was over. Instead, he posted a company of Spaniards at every breach he took to prevent us from reopening it. Once the causeway was secure, he set up camp inside the city and tore down every building in the vicinity to deny us the rooftops.[iv]

Temilotl now launched his attacks at any hour of the day or night that suited him: midnight, daybreak, or eventide, when the Spaniards were settling down for supper. At times he announced his attacks with whistles, shrieks, conch horns, and drums, and at other times he struck from the darkness without warning. He also used hit and run attacks against the watch for no purpose other than to deny the enemy a good night's sleep.

Alvarado was forced to keep a third of his company on watch at all times. He used three shifts from nightfall to daybreak: while one watch stood guard, the other two slept nearby, and at dawn, when an attack was most likely, the entire company was alerted for action. Some nights Temilotl kept the entire company up all night with forays, and when Alvarado took the offensive, he rotated fresh squadrons into battle as often as possible.

With the Spaniards in control of the causeways and the lake, the burden of provisioning the city also fell upon Temilotl. Taking every precaution to avoid the Spanish fleet, his supply craft crossed to the cities along the western and northern shores of the lagoon by night and returned to Tlatelolco before daybreak. The quantity of food and water needed, however, was so great that many supply boats could not reach Tlatelolco before dawn, and not a day passed without the Spaniards capturing a piragua or two and hanging the unfortunate oarsmen from the yardarm of a gunship.

Temilotl responded by hiding 30 piraguas with heavily armed warriors in the reeds of the lagoon. When two gunships approached, the piraguas broke cover and showered them with arrows and javelins. The gunships turned to attack, but before they could close, they struck heavy stakes below the surface. Before the crews could break out their oars and pull their craft into deep water, Temilotl's warriors were on board. That day we killed the crews and a captain before another gunship arrived and drove us off.[v]

Without aid from the cities and towns along the shores of the lake, however, we could not hope to supply enough food and water to meet our needs with canoes. We had lost all hope of receiving help from the eastern shore, since Coanacoch had failed to rally support from the Acolhuaque. Furthermore, his brother Ixtlilxochitl had mustered every warrior in the province and joined the Spaniards.[vi]

Yet we were steadfast in our belief that we could withstand the siege. The cities along the southern shore, Mexicalzingo, Culhuacán, and Huitzilopochco, and the cities that controlled the fresh water lakes, Xochimilco and Cuitláhuac, had reaffirmed their promise to fulfill their obligations to Mexico.

The lords of Xochimilco and Cuitláhuac sent us their warriors and their shield boats, and we welcomed them into our homes and set gourds of hot chocolate before them. We gave them shields, weapons, and devices, and we assigned them a place in battle where they would find honor and glory alongside us.

But when the Spaniards came again, they were nowhere to be seen. In the heat of battle they deserted us; they abandoned us to loot our homes and our temples, and to rob our defenseless women and children. They seized our maidens and our young men, and they were preparing to carry them off when a party of Mexican warriors happened by.

Our warriors hastened to inform their captain, and by land and by water our squadrons fell upon them. We drove their shield boats into the canals and pursued their warriors into the streets, and by day's end, all were dead or captive, and our children were once again with their parents.

We took them the sacrificial stone, where Cuauhtémoc and his brother Mayeuatl, the lord of Cuitláhuac, awaited them. Mayeuatl's shame for the his chieftains knew no bounds, and when they stood before him, Cuauhtémoc passed the knife to him and said, "My brother, do your duty."

With the defection of the powerful Xopchimilca, the lords of Mexicalzingo, Culhuacán, and Huitzilopcochco denounced Cuauhtémoc. They ordered their people to build shelters along the causeway to protect the Spaniards from the unending rains, and they sent their canoes each day, laden with fish and fresh food, with provisions we so desperately needed, to them.

Mexico now stood alone. Without help from outside, we could not defend our perimeter. Reluctantly, Cuauhtémoc ordered Tenochtitlán abandoned. He sent his warriors in the streets to gather the women and the children, allowing them no more time than needed to pack a few belongings. Once again Huitzilopochtli was lowered from his temple, and the priests carried him to Amaxacac and placed him in his new shrine in the Telpochcalli, the House of Youth.

Cuauhtémoc gathered his court and abandoned the palace of his father, the great Ahuitzotl. He took up residence at Yacacolco, not far from the sprawling marketplace of Tlatelolco, and his nobles came to live with the elite of Tlatelolco. They came to us with jewels, precious feathers, and gold bracelets. "Lords," they said, "here are all our worldly possessions; take them, they are yours."

The chieftains and warriors gave us their insignias and their devices. The quauchic, the proud military order whose duty is to take the position of greatest danger in battle, cut off the braid of hair that hangs from their shaven heads, and for the rest of the war they fought with their heads covered. Their women felt shame for their husbands and lovers, and when they went to war, they ridiculed them and vowed that no woman would ever again adorn herself or make herself attractive for them.

Now only the Tlatelolca wore the lock braided with a red ribbon; only the Tlateloca painted one side of his head red and the other side blue; only the Tlatelolca guarded the roads leading to the city.

An uprising among the Tenocha followed upon the heels of Cuauhtémoc's surrendering the city to the Spaniards. The disastrous defeats in the plaza created dissension among the nobility about his leadership and his conduct of the war, and the revolt that followed left the priests of Tlaloc, Huitzilopochtli, and Tezcatlipoca dead before it had run its course.

To Tecocoltl, the puppet lord of Texcoco, these events were a clear signal that an opportunity was at hand to drive a wedge between the Tenochca and the Tlatelolca. His messengers came to us in secret, and after we acknowledged them, the eldest lifted his hand to his mouth and began to speak.

"Lords of the Tlatelolca," he said, "Tecocoltl and the lords of the Chichimeca grieve that your people suffer the misfortunes of this war. Like you, he is also a victim, for he has lost the royal robes and devices of his illustrious ancestors. If this war continues, he fears that our nation will perish from the face of the earth.

"Cuauhtémoc is lost-not many days will pass before his people abandon him. Many have fled to Atzcapotzalco, to Cuauhtitlán, to Tenayuca, and to Coyoacán. Each day Tecocoltl sees fewer and fewer Tenochca among the defenders, and soon the brave Tlatelolca will find themselves fighting the Spaniards alone, for the cowardly Tenochca will leave them orphaned.

"Tecocoltl hopes that this war can be ended before this comes to pass. The captain Cortés proposes peace, and he will wait 20 days for your decision. As one who has proven to be a friend of the innocent and the trustworthy, our lord Tecocoltl prays to the gods that you will heed his words."

The ambassador stepped back and waited for our response.

"Our younger brother has ever been our trusted friend," we replied, for have not the lords of the Acolhuaque and Chichimeca been like mothers and fathers to our people?"

The Acolhuaque departed, and although we could not dispute the logic of his words, we could do nothing. We had committed treason for listening to them, and we never spoke of it again, not even among ourselves.

The southern barrios of Tenochtitlán had been abandoned to the Spaniards, the canal crossings were filled and leveled, and Cortés was now in a position to launch a major offensive.

The attack came by land and by water. His gunships, supported by a fleet of canoes from Xochimilco, struck at us from the lake while his horse and foot moved west to join forces with Alvarado. They captured the first three canal crossings, but by the time the Tlaxcalans filled them, darkness forced them to withdraw.

Alvarado, meanwhile, had grown careless. As his forces moved east to join Cortés, Temilotl attacked his rear from the causeway, his flanks from the north and the south, and his van from the city streets. The Spaniards had some difficulty with the attacks on the van, but they soon drove our warriors back to a canal. The warriors, caught between the Spaniards and the canal, turned and broke for the opposite bank. The Spaniards, seeing that the water was not deep, dashed across in pursuit. Some 50 foot and a horseman were well beyond the breach when an army of warriors hidden behind the houses closed in on them, and others from the rooftops pelted them with stones.

They turned and fled for the canal, but it was more than 70 paces across, and Temilotl's shield boats were there, blocking their escape. They raced along the bank to the nearest crossing and plunged into the canal, only to find themselves floundering in pits dug below the surface of the water. As they struggled to reach the opposite bank, Temilotl's shield boats closed in upon them and began to carry them off. The gunships came to their rescue, but they ran aground on heavy stakes planted along the bottom, leaving the crews exposed to volleys of arrows and javelins from the banks. Only the cannon, which the Spaniards hurriedly brought into play, prevented us from overrunning Alvarado's camp that day.

That day our boatmen brought five Spaniards to the sacrificial stone, a horseman and his mount were dead, and many others were killed or wounded.

The next four days saw Alvarado's company was busy filling the canal crossing in pouring rain, from which they had no shelter. We had not neglected to destroy their ramshackle huts.

Two days after the Spaniards made their repairs, Sandoval left Tepeyacac and joined forces with Alvarado, and we knew that another offensive was imminent.

The battle that could well decide the fate of Mexico began when three columns of horse and foot left the plaza and marched up the avenues that led to Tlatelolco. The lead company took the main thoroughfare, and the others the lesser streets on both sides. Cortés assumed command of the company assigned to the narrower street.

My squadrons were directly in the line of march of the lead company. This company, unhindered by canal crossings, was some distance ahead of the others, and having met no resistance, they grew less cautious as they neared Tlatelolco. Accompanied by fife and drum and their proud banner leading the way, they halted at the first canal only long enough for the Tlaxcalans to fill the crossing. The canal was wide and deep, but instead of allowing them time to gather enough wood and adobe to fill it properly, the Tlaxcalans used branches, reed grass, and whatever else was handy and threw it into the canal.

The Spaniards crossed safely and moved on to the barricade. When they reached it, our moment arrived. The heads of three Spaniards tumbled down the side of the barricade and rolled along the flagstones, coming to rest at the feet of the standard bearer. We stormed across the top and warriors hidden behind the houses converged upon the column.

I was the first to reach the standard bearer, frozen where his stood before the heads of his comrades. With a single blow I struck him down and seized his banner, and we charged headlong into the Spaniards. They turned to flee, but the flimsy bridge collapsed under the weight of the first men to cross, and those following were driven into the canal by the press of those behind.[vii]

We jumped into the canal, and in moments, it was filled with struggling bodies. Many who were weighted down with heavy armor

331

drowned, and others, trying to swim, were carried off in our shield boats.

At the height of the fray, I heard a voice shouting, "Hold fast! Hold fast! Turn back and face the enemy!" I looked up and saw Cortés standing on the opposite bank. He was on foot, in the company of 12 Spaniards. Others saw him at the same time, and they broke off the fight to lay hands on him. Outnumbered, his escort could not hold us off, and we seized him by the arms. We were dragging him off when two Spaniards, one no more than a youth, rallied their companions and pulled him away. Before we could reach him again, a page brought his mount, and he vanished into the crowd fleeing down the avenue.

The avenue was barely above the level of the canals on either side, and soon the surface was covered with mud and water as we drove the Spaniards back toward Tenochitlán. The footing became so treacherous that the Spanish horse could not mount an effective rear guard action, and after two men and a mount were killed, they retreated with the foot. Only when the army reached the broad avenue leading to the Tlacopan causeway was Cortés able to regroup, and we had to break off our attack.[viii]

Clouds of smoke and the fragrance of copal filled the air as the priests proclaimed our victory over the Spaniards, but we had no time relish the victory, since our warriors were still fighting Alvarado and Sandoval in the streets. We sent every warrior available into the western barrios, and they announced their presence by throwing the heads of five Spaniards at Alvarado's company.

"Here are the heads of Cortés and Sandoval," we shouted. Then we threw six more at Sandoval, claiming that the heads of Alvarado and Cortés were among them. We closed in, and neither their muskets, their crossbows, or their swords could hold us back. Step by step they withdrew, making a stand only when they reached the protection of the cannon posted before their camp.

That day the gunships fared no better than the Spanish foot and their horse. Two gunships, one following another down a narrow canal, came to a halt when the first ran aground. As the oarsmen struggled to break it free, the great drum on the temple began to beat, announcing that a sacrifice was taking place. As the crews watched, 15 Spaniards were stripped naked and led up the steps of the temple at

Yacacolco, and one by one, their hearts were torn from their chests and cast into a smoldering brazier.

When the last Spaniard had gone to meet the gods, we took their breeches and doublets and threw them to the men aboard the stranded ship. In desperation, the oarsmen tried to pull the ship into deeper water, but only succeeded in wedging it farther into the reeds. We scrambled up the sides and fell upon the crew, tearing the sails into shreds and breaking the oars, but in the heat of battle, we failed to see the other ship coming alongside. With a great leap, the captain led his crew across the gap and drove us back into the streets. The attack gave the Spaniards enough time to pull the stranded craft into the channel, and before we could attack again, they moved into safer waters.[ix]

As daylight faded, we came upon another gunship stranded across a breach between two canals. The Spaniards had opened the breach that morning to pass the gunship from once canal to another, and it became lodged fast. The Tlaxcalans were still struggling to break it free when Sandoval began his withdrawal, and at the sight of our warriors, they fled.

This was the prize of the day. We fastened ropes to the hull and began to tow it toward the city when Sandoval arrived with a party of horse and foot. The horse drove us off and the foot leaped into the canal to free the ship. It seemed that the Spaniards would never get the ship across the breach under the shower of stones and arrows that fell upon them, but prodded by Sandoval, they gave a mighty lunge and lifted the prow high enough to slide it through.

In another barrio our warriors attacked a gunship and killed the captain, and another barely escaped our shield boats after running onto hidden stakes. We captured no gunships that day, but we had met their challenge.

When the last Spaniard was beyond our reach, we presented them with a sight they would not soon forget. More than 50 Spaniards, some weeping, others praying, and a few singing, stood in line for Cuauhtémoc's inspection. The Emperor chose six or seven men, and we stripped them naked and led them up the steps of the great temple, where they could be seen from Alvarado's camp. We put plumes on their heads, painted them blue, and forced them to perform a little dance for the benefit of their companions. Then the conch horns sounded and the drum began its beat, and we dragged them to the sacrificial stone.[x]

Our spirits buoyed by victory, we moved our squadrons to the threshold of the enemy camps and dug the canals deeper and wider. Then, each day at sunset, to remind the Spaniards what awaited them in Tlatelolco, the temple drum announced the hour of sacrifice, and we led another group of naked Spaniards up the temple steps to dance the dance of death.

When all but five were left, we took them to Alvarado's camp and forced them to fire on their comrades with crossbows we had taken in battle. When the last bolt was spent, we took them to the temple and sacrificed them.

When the last Spaniard was dead, Cuauhtémoc flayed their faces and sent them to the provinces with the heads of their horses. With them went incentives and rewards for those who would join us, and warnings to those who refused.

The first to hear the call to arms was the Malinalca, who promptly attacked the Spanish garrison at Cuernavaca. Next the Matlatzinga, natives of the Valley of Toluca, promised Cuauhtémoc their support and attacked Cortés's Otomie allies. Cortés and his battle-weary troops were still nursing their wounds, but they were left no choice but to go to war again before every province in Anahuac rose against them.

The consequences of the Spanish defeat had not been lost on the Tlaxcalans and the natives of the cities that had betrayed us. More than 1200 Indian allies had met their end in the streets of Tenochtitlán and Tlatelolco, and now only 80 Tlaxcalans, 40 Alcohuaque, and 50 Huexotzinga remained in the city.

Cortés made a daily show of force, but with so many men in the provinces, he made no attempt to go beyond the plaza in Tenochtitlán. Alvarado continued to maintain his camp inside the city, trusting to his cannon to keep us away. The gunships stayed away from the canals, doing little more than chasing canoes and attacking boatmen skimming algae from the lagoon, which our women use to make cakes.

Fifteen days later, however, we knew that a new offensive was imminent. The wounds of the Spaniards were on the mend, the victorious Spaniards were back from the provinces, their native allies were making their way back to Tenochtitlán, and Alvarado was preparing to march.

But this time the Spaniards would find the city well defended. Open spaces where the cavalry could operate were strewn with heavy boulders, sturdy barricades had been erected along the avenues, and fortified platforms rose along the canals to keep the gunships away.[xi]

Our principle concern was providing enough food and water to last out the siege. We could not feed our people adequately with our canoes, and the only water inside the city came from a few brackish wells and what we gathered from the daily rains.

The new offensive found Cortés more cautious. Before he moved, an army of laborers from the provinces, armed with digging sticks and copper axes, tore down every building along the line of march and filled the canal crossings with the rubble of our houses and our temples. When he withdrew, he had no fear of attacks from the rooftops, and when he returned the following day, he could begin his advance where he had halted the day before.

As our defense perimeter tightened, every man and woman was drawn into the conflict. Women wore the insignia and devices of fallen warriors and fought alongside their brothers and husbands; mothers with children manned the rooftops; women to old or too lame to fight ground stones for our slings; and our maidens raised their skirts while their grandmothers swept dirt in the eyes of the Spaniards.

Soon only Yacacolco stood between Cortés and the marketplace, and on the 50th day of the siege, he attacked Cuauhtémoc's stronghold. The Spaniards moved up the avenue while the gunships, supported by a fleet of canoes from Xochimilco, entered the canals.

The canoes were no match for our shield boats. We closed about them from all sides, and the arrows and javelins that descended upon them were so dense that they hid the sun behind a yellow cloud. The canoes fled, and we turned to meet the gunships. One moved under a platform set above the canal, and a heavy stone crushed the skull of the captain. Another ran aground on stakes, and as our shield boats closed in, the commander leaped over the side and fled.

Twice that day we drove the Spanish gunships down the canals, but as the sun began to set, they came back and attacked in pairs, and we could no longer hold Yacacolco.

The chieftains and the warriors gathered their women and children and led them to Amaxacac, a barrio on the northeast corner of Tlatelolco.[xii] There they built shelters on the rooftops of the houses, and when the rooftop of the last house on land was occupied, they built more shelters on the rooftops of the houses that stood in the lake.

Now hunger began to test the strength and vitality of the people. Sandoval had cut off the last supply route across the lagoon, leaving us little more to look forward to other than our near-empty granaries and whatever food the lake could provide.

On his early morning forays, Cortés had to first clear the streets of women, children, and the elderly foraging for herbs, bark, and whatever else might ease the pangs of hunger. The gunships found only fishermen trying to reach shore before daybreak. Inside the barrio, people were eating lizards, dry stalks of maize and saltgrass, and when they could find nothing else, they gnawed sedum leaves and bark.

One night the watch heard a voice call out, asking them to come to the barricade. The captain of the guard was wary, but he took two warriors and rowed down the canal. As the canoe approached the barricade, he could make out a Tlaxcalan chieftain accompanied by several warriors. When he pulled alongside, however, he saw that the chieftain was not a Tlaxcalan, but a Spaniard we called Xicotencatl Casteñada, who resembled the great captain-general of Tlaxcala.[xiii]

We knew him well. He was a crossbowman of exceptional skill who always wore the feathered panache of a Tlaxcalan chieftain, and his appearance in the streets immediately raised the shout "Xicotencatl! Xicotencatl!" with a stream of insults. He never failed to respond with a smile and good-natured banter, but the last thing any warrior who exposed himself saw was the upward sweep of his crossbow before a bolt caught him between the eyes.

The Tlatelolcans asked Xicotencatl Casteñada what he wanted, and he replied, "Are you Tenochca or Tlatelolca?"

"Tlatelolca, the chieftain replied.

"Good," he replied," you are the ones we seek. Come, the captain Cortés wishes to speak with you."

Watchful and suspicious, they followed the Tlaxcalans to Ayaucalco, where they found Cortés in council with the chieftains of his native allies.

Xicotencatl Casteñada led them to the woman interpreter.

"Here before you are the lords of Tlaxcala, Huexotzingo, Chalca, Cholula, Acolhuacan, Cuernavaca, Xochimilco, Mixquic, Cuitláhuac, and Culhuacán, and all have abandoned Cuauhtémoc," she said. "Yet he has learned nothing; he continues to oppress the spirit and the will of those he still rules. Now the Tenochca will be destroyed. Do not the hearts of the Tlatelolca grieve that they too may perish with him? My captain asks, is Cuauhtémoc a child who has no compassion for the suffering of his women and his children? Is he so immature that he has no concern for the elderly, who will surely die a slow and cruel death if he prolongs this war?"

She turned to the chieftains and said, "Is this not true, my lords?"

"Would that the gods hear our prayers and bid the Tlatelolca to abandon Cuauhtémoc to his fate. May the gods will that they choose not to die with him," they replied.

Then Cortés spoke for the first time. "If the lords of Tlatelolco are to survive this war, they must abandon Cuauhtémoc now. If they decide to do so, they may send a message to me in Teucalhuiacán. I must leave now, for the brigantine that is to take me to Coyoacán has arrived."

Cortés dismissed them, and when they were alone, the chieftain said, "We must leave at once. We are in great danger. Even if what Cortés says is true, we would be put to death for listening to him."

As the gunship departed into the darkness, they turned and shouted after it that they would never desert the Tenochca, and word of their meeting never reached the ears of the lords of Tlatelolco.

Two days of heavy fighting followed the fall of Yacacolco. On the third day Alvarado fought his way to the temple of Huitzilopochtli and fired it, then pushed his way into the marketplace. At the sight of smoke pouring from the temple, however, our warriors rallied and fell upon the Spaniards with a fury that left three horses lame and bleeding before they could withdraw.

From the south, Cortés reached a temple due east of the marketplace, where he found the heads of several Spaniards mounted on stakes. When the fighting was over and he withdrew for the day, there remained but one canal between him and the marketplace.

This day marked the last stand we were to make against the Spaniards. Our warriors were spent. During the 27 days that followed our victory over Cortés, hard fighting, meager rations, and sleepless nights spent filling canals and building barricades had taken its toll upon us.

When Cortés returned the next morning, he found the last canal crossing so poorly defended that three Spaniards entered the marketplace with little trouble. By the time the Tlaxcalans filled it with rubble, Alvarado had taken the marketplace.

Cortés and Alvarado entered the marketplace cautiously, aware of the warriors gathered above the gateway arches looking down upon them in silence. With Alvarado and his men standing guard, Cortés crossed the plaza and dismounted at the foot of the great temple. He climbed to the summit and took off his helmet, then he knelt in prayer before the heads of his comrades mounted upon the skull rack. He raised his banner above them, and descended from the temple.[xiv]

Now only Amaxacac, a barrio with an area no more than one-eighth of Tenochtitlán, was left to us. The outcome of the war was no longer in doubt. But Cortés did not attack. Instead, he sent Mexican nobles to Cuauhtémoc with an offer of amnesty.

While waiting for an answer, the Spaniards occupied themselves with the construction of a catapult in the center of the marketplace. As this odd combination of beams and ropes took form, the Tlaxcalans never ceased taunting us. When it was finished, they claimed, the Spaniards would destroy our homes with a single stroke. As if to bear out their allies, the Spaniards laughed and pointed to the center of Amaxacac.

The day the device was finished, the Spaniards set a huge boulder in a cradle attached to a beam and began to twist ropes that secured it to the framework. Suddenly they jumped aside and the beam came upright with a resounding crash. The boulder soared high into the air, climbing higher and higher above the marketplace. It paused for a moment, and then it fell back to earth, gathering speed as it descended. It struck the catapult and sent the beams flying in all directions, and we heard no more from the Spaniards and the Tlaxcalans.

That day Cuauhtémoc sent his answer to Cortés. There could be no hope of peace between his people and the Spaniards, he said, for they were determined to fight until the last Mexican warrior fell in battle. Mexico had lost its tributaries, its vassals, and most of its great city. There was little left to be lost. For the Mexican people, life would be hollow without the company of their friends and relatives who had been lost in battle, and the sooner the war was over, the sooner they could stand before them with pride and honor for having fought and died as their ancestors had done. As for the treasure that Cortés so coveted, it was now at the bottom of the lake in water so deep that he would never find it.

The following day the Spaniards entered Amaxacac in force, only to find women and children, now no more than skin and bones, searching for scraps of food, and unarmed men watching in silence from the rooftops. Cortés asked the men of any could speak for Cuauhtémoc, and when none stepped forward, he asked if any would appeal to Cuauhtémoc for peace before more of his people were killed in a hopeless cause. Several hours passed in fruitless discussions. The men on the rooftops insisted that they wanted only peace, and Cortés repeatedly asked for a ranking noble who could speak for the Emperor.

Cortés finally lost patience with them. Convinced that their intent was to delay him until Cuauhtémoc gathered his forces, he ordered the army into Amaxacac. We fought as best we could, but in a few hours the barrio was overrun.

We lost many good warriors that day, and when the Spaniards withdrew, the wrath of the Tlaxcalans fell upon our people. The Spaniards could not control them, and like wild animals they ran through the streets, butchering women and children. Their aim was loot, but more important, their objective was to purge the next generation and generations yet to be born of Mexicans.

That evening we gathered our dead from streets filled with broken bones and severed limbs, from homes splattered with blood, brains, and matted hair, and from canals that ran red with blood. We took their bodies and hid them in our homes and on the rooftops, out of sight from the Spaniards lest they learn how few of us remained. In the heat and humid summer air, the stench of rotting bodies grew by the hour.

With the coming of night we gathered about fires, preparing our only meal of the day from lizards, mice, worms, clay, and anything else that might sustain us for another day. The less fortunate, the children, widows, and the elderly, ate dry stalks of maize and salt grass, and when there was nothing else, they chewed on bark and the wood of the skull rack.

Rich and poor, we suffered alike, for wealth would bring no more than what a starving people could offer. Gold, turquoise, precious feathers, cotton mantles-anything of value-would fetch at most 20 parcels of salt grass. Slaves were sold for two handfuls of maize, and ten winged insects from the lake might be worth a single tortilla. Only a child, a young girl, or a strong lad would yield enough for our daily fare.

Water could not be bought at any price. Warriors stood watch around our only well as families came for their daily ration of a single bowl of water, now foul and brackish and stained red with blood. With each passing day, more and more people died from the bloody flux it brought down upon them.

Nobles and commoners alike prayed for death to release them from their wretched lives. Some sought death at the hands of the Spaniards, and they waited at the barricade in the early morning light for the attack that was sure to come. But Cortés was unwilling to grant them the release they sought.

"Lord," they said to him, "during the golden years that we ruled Anahuac, we, like all men, feared the eternal sleep of death. But now we are the living dead. With each passing day, life becomes more and more intolerable, and only death can deliver us from our suffering. If you are truly the son of the Sun, if you are devoted to your god, and if there is mercy in your heart, kill us now; put and end to the unbearable misery you have brought down upon us. We beg you, send us to heaven so that Huitzilopochtli may reward us with peace and eternal rest, for we die in his cause."

Christian law, Cortés replied, did not permit him to kill a defeated enemy. Instead, he was obliged to see that they lived out their lives in peace and freedom. They would sooner realize the peace they hey desired, he said, by yielding to his Christians than seeking it in an afterlife with Huitzilopochtli.

He was, however, clearly moved by their pleas, and instead of ordering his troops into Amaxacac, he withdrew and sent for Xochitl, a wounded chieftain from a nearby barrio that the Texcocans had captured 20 days earlier.

The following morning two Spaniards led Xochitl into the marketplace and set him down gently at a place where, in better days, our merchants sold incense.

Warriors took him to the temple of Tezcatlipoca, and hearing that he carried a message from Cortés, a priest took him to Temilotl. The general heard him out, then sent word to the chieftains that there was to be no more fighting that day.

They took Xochitl to the royal barge, where Cuauhtémoc held court, and when given permission to speak, he said, "My lord, the bearded captain asks why you continue to ignore his pleas to yield before all is lost. Why, he asks, if you and your generals have no concern for the destruction of your great city, if you set no value on white corn, turkeys, and tortillas, why must you sacrifice our women, our children, and the elderly, who will perish by the hundreds in this war that is hopelessly lost.

"What say you, Cuautémoc? Will you yield, or will you wait until all abandon you and leave you to die alone?"

Cuauhtémoc was silent for a few moments, then he turned to generals and asked for their counsel. Before they could speak, however, the priest of Tezcalipoca, a savant of the sacred books, stepped forward.

"Great lord," he said, "our god Huitzilopochtli has assured us that this war will come to an end in 80 days, and we lack but four days to see his prophecy fulfilled. We must wait for him to carry out his promise."

"We will wait," Cuauhtémoc replied, "but we must seek an omen that will bear out his prophecy. Bring me the most valiant of our warriors, one who is worthy of wearing the battle dress of my father, the mighty Ahuitzotl."

We sought out a celebrated chieftain from Coatlán, and when he stood before Cuauhtémoc, the majordomos wrapped the green-feathered robes of Ahuizotl about his shoulders and set his panache of 600 feathers, embroidered with silver threads, upon his head. Cuauhtémoc then gave him an ancient bow and the arrows that once belonged to Huitzilopochtli, he gave one of Ahuitzotl's weapons to each of the four warriors who would accompany him.

"Now you are the Quetzal Owl," he said, "you bear the magic war devices of Ahuitzotl, and you carry into battle the weapons of our

341

god, which will render you invincible. Take these warriors with you and seek out and seek out our enemies. Do battle with them, for they will know fear at the very sight of you."

Then the Cihuacoatl Tlacotl spoke to them. "Tenochcas! Tlatelolcas!" he said. "Huitzilopochtli, who is the source from which the very strength of our nation flows, once fought with this same dart, this same arrow we call the skewer, the turquoise serpent. Do not waste it. If you raise it against our enemy and it finds its mark, this will be the omen we seek: this will be the proof that our god still stands by us, this will bear out his word that our end is not yet near."

As the priests led Xochitl to the sacrificial altar, the Quetzal Owl and his chieftains led the remnants of our army into the streets.

The sight of this magnificent warrior and the fury of his attack caught the Spaniards by surprise. They fell back, and the Quetzal Owl leaped from one roof to another in pursuit, urging his warriors on. It was if the spirit of Ahuitzotl himself buoyed them as they carried the battle to the enemy.

From the top of the granary, the Quetzal Owl shouted, "Christian dogs! Is there one among you who dares to battle with me? Look-my only weapon is a sword I took from one of your cowardly companions. Come-do battle with me! I will stay here until all who challenge me lie dead or you kill me!"

The swordsman Osama, who never refused a challenge, crossed the rooftops and approached the Quetzal Owl, his shield in one hand, his sword in the other, and his arms spread wide apart. The Quetzal Owl leaped forward, bringing his sword down with a force that split the Spaniard's shield in two. He raised his sword above his head, ready to deliver the killing blow, but the Spaniard, with the counterthrust that no Mexican had ever mastered, drove his sword into his body until a palm's length of the blade came out of his back. The Quetzal Owl looked down in surprise at the hilt of the sword thrust into his bowels, then dropped his sword and collapsed into a heap of green feathers. Osama took his headdress and held it high to the cheers of his comrades.[xv]

The death of the Quetzal Owl marked the end of our resistance that day, but Cuauhtémoc had his omen-a horse lay dead in the streets and three prisoners stood before him.

The Spaniards met with no resistance when they marched into Amaxacac the following morning. Only a handful of nobles, waiting for death to claim them, waited at the barricade. Cortés rode forward and spoke to them. He gave his word that he would stay out of Amaxacac if one of them could convince Cuauhtémoc to meet with him. None spoke up, but he persisted, insisting that needless bloodshed could be avoided only if Cuauhtémoc met with him. They were not convinced, but several left to speak with Cuauhtémoc. The greater part of the day passed before they returned, but they brought Cortés the answer that pleased him. Cuauhtémoc would meet with him in the marketplace the following day.

The next day saw an elegant table set for the Emperor in the shade of Cortés's pavilion, but midday came and passed without his appearing. Instead, five nobles arrived with gifts and apologies, and a message that Cuauhtémoc was ill.

Cortés nevertheless received them and invited them to dine with him. When they finished their meal, he called upon them to return to Cuauhtémoc and tell him how important it was for them to meet. If it was fear that kept him away, he would guarantee his safety no matter what he decided. He gave them food and they left, only to return in a few hours to inform Cortés that there would be no meeting: Cuauhtémoc was determined to continue the war.

But Cortés was not a man to be put off. He persuaded them to speak again with Cuauhtémoc, and the following day they returned to inform Cortés that the Emperor had changed his mind, and he would meet with him later that day.

Preparations were made again for the meeting, and Cortés sent the Tlaxcalans from the city to ease the fears of the Mexicans. Cortés sat and waited, but after three hours, he had waited long enough-he ordered the Tlaxcalans to return and he sent his army into Amaxacac.

We had no javelins, no arrows, and few enough stones to cast down upon the enemy, and we had no leader to marshal our forces. There was little resistance, and when the Tlaxcalans arrived, they raged through the streets, killing and looting as they pleased. Even the Spaniards were sickened by the atrocities they inflicted upon us that day, but outnumbered ten to one by their allies, the could no longer control them. By nightfall, when the Tlaxcalans had enough of the stench of rotting bodies, they left us to our misery and despair.

The last hope of ending the conflict without more killing ended when Cortés brought up his cannons and demanded that Cuauhtémoc surrender. It was the sad duty of Tlacotl, the Cihuacoatl, to meet with Cortés and inform him that Cuauhtémoc preferred to die with his people rather than surrender. They spoke for a few moments, then embraced, and Tlacotl returned to the royal barge.

The people panicked when they saw the Spaniards preparing to attack, and they rushed out into streets that were choked with the enemy. In the crush, nearly all were pushed into the canals, and they drowned beneath the bodies floating on the surface. The artillery opened fire, and their screams were lost in the thunder of the cannon.

When the first salvo failed to dislodge our warriors, Cortés sent in his foot, and those still able to fight were either butchered or driven into the lake to drown.

But Cuauhtémoc was not among them. He ordered his barge into the lake and fled for the opposite shore, only to find Sandoval and his gunships waiting for him. The war had ended.

Late that night, as a light rain fell upon the city, a pillar of flame rose in the northern sky. Like a whirlwind, it descended upon Tlatelolco, crackling and showering sparks as it made a circle about Amaxacac. Then it turned eastward and disappeared into the night.[xvi]

---

[i] The Anales de Tlatelolco set the uprising and the executions in 1521 (3 Calli), shortly after Cortes established his base in Texcoco.

Torquemada, citing a document written by an eyewitness, states that the nobles were executed for smuggling provisions to the Spaniards in Axayácatl's palace.

Tezozomoc, *Cronica mexicocóyotl,* insists that Moctezuma's sons, seven in all, were killed by the Spaniards at the Canal of the Toltecs during the retreat.

[ii] "Cortés, prior to leaving Tenochitlán to attack Narváez at Cempoala, sent a daughter of Moctezuma to Tacuba for safekeeping. Upon his return, Mexican warriors intercepted the escort returning here to Mexico." -Bernal Diaz. If we presume the daughter to be Tecuichpo, it would explain the survival of Moctezuma's only heir, since the others were killed during the retreat or executed by Cuauhtémoc.

[iii] Cortes discloses a fourth causeway not recorded by present day historians. This causeway was most likely the old one connecting Tlatelolco with Atzcapotzalco.

There is no mention in any of the sources what, if any, role Nezahualcóyotl's dike played in the siege of Tenochtitlán. As of November, 1519, Bernal Diaz noted lake traffic on both sides of the dike, indicating that the gates were open. Since the Mexicans had ample time to close them between July, 1520, when the Spaniards retreated, and June, 1521, one must wonder if the gates were damaged or too weather-worn to be closed 68 years after they were constructed. Cortés makes no mention of the dike.

[iv] Bernal Díaz, who served with Alvarado during the siege of Mexico, is the only chronicler to provide us with an account of the assault from the west.

[v] The ambush cost the life of a commander named de Potillo and nearly that of Pedro Barba, who commanded the other.

[vi] Tecolcotl, the puppet king of Texcoco, gave command of the Acolhuaque warriors to Ixtlilxochitl, a youth of some 23 or 24 years, who arrived to support the Spaniards during the first offensive.

[vii] Both Sahagun and the Anales de Tlateloloco identify Ecatl as the chieftain who led the attack against Alderetes column and captured the Spanish banner.

[viii] Cortés claims that he was hesitant to undertake the failed offensive of June 30 against Tlatelolco. Pressured by Juan de Alderete, however, who insisted that the army was anxious to end the war, he consulted with his senior commanders an ordered the attack.

[ix] Cristóbal Florez commanded the brigantine that ran aground, and Jeronimo Ruiz de la Mota, a Cervantes informant, came to his rescue.

[x] Cortes sets the Spanish casualties at 35 or 40 dead or captured, and the Tlaxcalan casualties at more than a thousand. Bernal Díaz claims that more than 60 foot and eight horse were dead or missing. Sahagun, Florentine Codex, claims that four horses were killed and 53 Spaniards taken captive.

[xi] Cervantes is the only chronicler who mentions the fortified plaforms the Mexicans erected in the canals.

[xii] Amaxacac lies approximately one mile east of the Plaza of Three Cultures in the northeast sector of Mexico City. It is bounded on the west by Argentina Avenue and on the north by Canal Street.

[xiii] Rodrigo de Casteñada, called Xicotencatl by the Mexicans, appears in both Spanish and Mexican chronicles. Fluent in Nahuatl, Cortés chose him to speak with the Tlatelolco sentries.

[xiv] The capture of the marketplace occurred on or about August 1, 1521.

[xv] The presumption that Hernando de Osama fought his duel with the Quetzal Owl and not some other Mexican chieftain is based solely upon

Cervante's statement that the Mexican's vestments were "the most beautiful that had been seen until that occasion."

[xvi] The pillar of flame that descended upon Tlatelolco is found in Sahagún, Tolosana. No other source reports observing the phenomenon.

Epilogue

Cortés received Cuauhtémoc with all the respect due royalty, and gave him every assurance that he had nothing to fear before sending him to Coyoacán, where appropriate quarters awaited him. But in spite of Cortés kind words and promises, Cuauhtémoc had hardly settled down before the Spaniards began to torture him.

Convinced that he had hidden the treasure they had abandoned the night they fled from Tenochtitán, they tormented him mercilessly to reveal its location. Each morning they took him from the royal suite and oiled his feet, then pressed them onto a glowing brazier. When they failed to make him talk, they carried him back to his quarters, where Isabel,[i] his young wife, dressed and bound his raw and bleeding feet.

Two hundred gold ingots were missing, they claimed, and when they threatened to torture Tlacotl, the *Cihuacoatl* told them to look to the Tlatelolca for the treasure. Theirs were the shield boats, he said, and only they had the means to recover it from the canals. The Tenochca, he added, had no boats.

Cuauhtémoc was furious. "Why do you accuse the Tlatelolca?" he demanded. "They were prisoners when they were sent out to search the canals, and everything they recovered they took to the Spaniards in Texopan. Turning to the Spaniards, he said, "There is nothing-all the treasure that exists lies here before you," and he pointed to a heap of gold and jewelry on the floor.[ii]

Among the natives, however, it was rumored that the Tlatelolca recovered the missing gold in the Canal of the Toltecs, and that they threw it in a deep subterranean pool known only to them. No such pool was ever found, however, and if Cuauhtémoc had hidden any gold, he took the secret to his grave.

Cortés abandoned his search for the gold, and for the next five years, he busied himself with the more important matters of governing his conquered nation and profiting from its resources.

Other than the central authority, his colonial government did not differ much from that which was in effect during Moctezuma's time. The *tlatoanis* and their descendants still maintained native rule over the cities in the Valley of Mexico; the barrios, save for the names, remained unchanged; and the *calpulli* still assigned the arable land within their communities to the people. By preserving native rule at the local level, Cortés left the tribute system of Moctezuma intact for the benefit of the Spanish Crown and its colonial administrators.

Labor, needless to say, was provided by the conquered. When Cortés granted lands and native villages to his conquerors, he assigned them an *encomienda* of Indians. The *encomendero,* for no more than the welfare and religious instruction of the natives, was entitled to their tribute and unrestricted personal services.

Cortés's first project was the restoration of Tenochtitlán. He tore down the temples and palaces of the city, cleared away the rubble of war, and filled the canals. As he made improvements, he began moving the native population into the barrios of Tlatelolco to make way for colonists arriving from Spain and Cuba.

In January, 1524, Cortés set out to find the elusive passage to the Southern Sea. He assembled a fleet at Vera Cruz, and sent a force of 400 Spaniards under the command of Cristóbal de Olid to survey the eastern shore of Yucatán and establish a permanent settlement in Honduras.

Olid, however, while provisioning his ships in Cuba, fell under the influence of Diego Velásquez, and he decided to establish an independent colony in Honduras. When Cortés learned of Olid's defection, he sent Francisco de las Casas to arrest him, but Las Casas was shipwrecked off the coast of Honduras and fell into Olid's hands.

Cortés decided it was time to take the matter in his own hands, and in October of 1524, he delegated his civic responsibilities to others and led a company of 90 horse, 30 foot, and 3,000 Mexican warriors out of the city, bound for Honduras. Rather than spend the time and money to outfit another fleet, he committed himself to a hazardous land journey of 300 leagues, one that would take him into the uncharted swamplands of the Maya and through the treacherous passes of the rugged mountains beyond.

To insure that there would be no native uprising in his absence, he took Cuauhtémoc, Tetlepanquetzal, the lord of Tacuba, and Coanacoch, the lord of Texcoco, with him. Other prominent nobles who accompanied him were Tlacotl, the *Cihuacoatl,* Motelchiuihtl, a Tenochca general, and the Tlatelolca generals Temilotl and Ecatl.

He halted at Coatzacoalcos long enough to gather intelligence from the natives of Tabasco of the best route to Honduras and a map of the territory that included the principal towns along the way. It was nearly Lent when Cortés reached Acalan, a province deep in the swamplands and wandering waterways of the Chontal Maya, where he allowed the company to break from the rigors of the trail.

The men were spent from the constant struggle against the swamps and the backbreaking labor of building one bridge after another across rivers that seemed to appear from the forest at every step. Many had fallen ill from swamp fevers; death and desertion had thinned their ranks; and lack of adequate provisions had taken its toll on the stamina of the men.

The Chontal Lords received Cuauhtémoc with the respect due a Mexican emperor. With Tetlepanquetzal and Coanacoch, they escorted him to a pavilion, and beneath a canopy of quetzal feathers, they gave them gold pendants and jade necklaces. Then they shod their sore and blistered feet with new sandals, and bade them rest while they drank pinole and atole.

Their kindness and generosity touched Cuauhtémoc. "My lords," he said, "you honor me with the goodwill you have shown me today, and when the captain takes me to Castile, I shall present your gifts and present them to the Emperor of the Christians. Although I must go to Spain-perhaps never to return-I pray with all my heart that you will never have to leave your country and be compelled to abandon your women, your children, and your elders. Let it be the will of the gods that your people will never be taken to a foreign lands, and let it be their will that you may love them and cherish them forever in your own homes."

It so happened that a dwarf called Cozoololtic, whom Cortés had appointed to a position of authority in Mexico, was quartered close by the pavilion. He made a painting of the meeting between Cuauhtémoc and the Maya lords and took it to Cortés, claiming that they were planning to attack the Spaniards.

Cortés was in a difficult position. His men were spent from the arduous journey, his Mexican warriors outnumbered his Spaniards more than six to one, and the Chontal might prove hostile. Before he reached Acalan, they burned villages and destroyed crops along his path to keep him away. Furthermore, if he was forced to make a stand, he could expect no relief from Mexico. Many of his veterans were in Honduras with Olid, Alvarado was in Guatemala, and a large expeditionary force was in Michoacan. Only a cadre of green troops, newly arrived from Spain, remained in Mexico.

Cortés seized the Chontal lords, and they readily confessed that Cuautémoc was planning an uprising, but denied that they were involved. The word of the dwarf, however, was sufficient for Cortés: neither Cuauhtémoc nor Tetlepanquetzal were given an opportunity to refute the charges against them. The Spaniards threw ropes around their necks and dragged them to a nearby ceibo tree, and after a brief confession before a priest, Cortés hanged them and left their bodies for all to see.

Others, however, told a different story. Cozoololtic, they said, was only a scapegoat; it was the *Cihuacoatl* Tlacotl and Motelchiuitl who accused Cuauhtémoc to gain favor with Cortés. This may have been so: before the Spaniards left Acalan, Cortés dressed Tlacotl in Spanish armor, gave him a sword and dagger, then placed him on a white horse and proclaimed him lord of Tenochtitán.[iii]

If Tlacotl had indeed betrayed his lord, he had little time to enjoy his high office; he died of pestilence in Honduras. Temilotl also died along the way, and he was succeeded by Ecatl. After his return to Mexico, Ecatl governed Tlatelolco for three years before he retired to his estate in Tziuhcoauac, and he spent his autumn years writing the history of his great city.

The company had to cope with another hundred miles of swampland, rivers, and tropical forest before they reached the savannas of Guatemala and Tayasal, the city of the Itza. Tayasal lay on Lake Peten, on an island no more than a hundred yards from the shore, and, according to Bernal Diaz, "...its houses and lofty teocallis, glistening in the sun, could be seen from a distance of two leagues."

Canek, the ruler of Tayasal, gave Cortés a cordial reception, and he remained in the city long enough to lay the groundwork for the conversion of its inhabitants by preaching a sermon against the evils of idolatry. Upon his departure, Cortés left a horse that had been crippled by a stake at Tayasal.

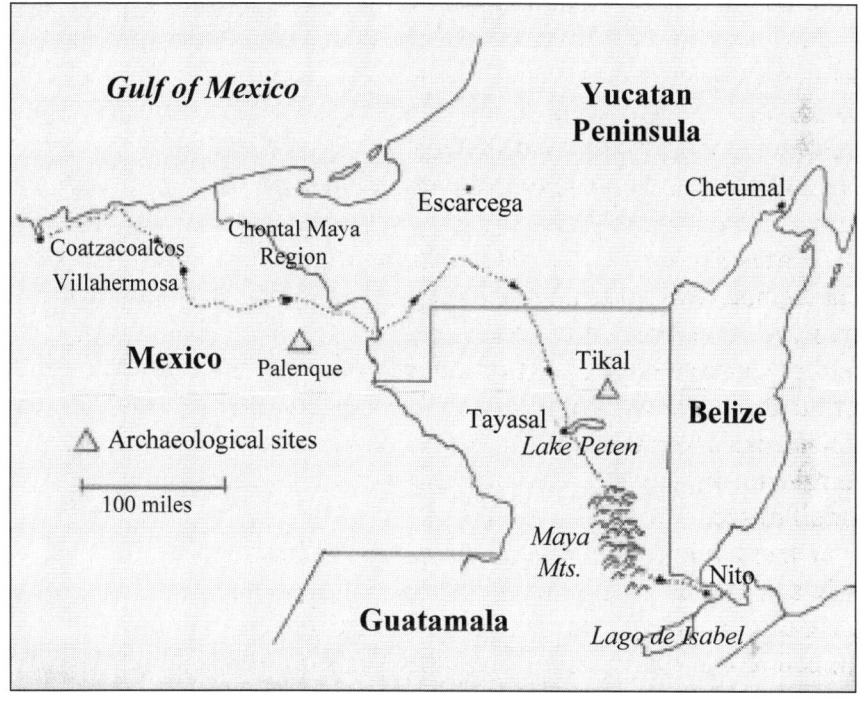

Cortés' March to Honduras

The Itza, having never seen a horse before, held the animal in great reverence, and they made offerings of flowers and poultry concoctions to the poor beast, and he soon died from the unusual diet. In commemoration, the Itza erected a stone statue of the animal and worshiped it as Tzimin Char, the god of thunder and lightening.

Seventy-five miles southeast of Tayasal, the company reached the Maya mountains, a low-lying range, but rugged out of all proportion to their size. Twelve days were required to cross these 'mountains of flint,' and in transit, Cortés lost 78 horses, most of which fell over precipices and into deep ravines.

On the other side of the mountains, they reached a large river swollen by weeklong rains. The current and turbulence prevented the men from building a bridge, but a scouting party found a slab of level rock with 20 fissures worn into it by the current. By felling trees and cutting beams, they were able to make a series of crude bridges spanning the fissures.

Cortés's goal was to reach San Gil de Buena Vista, a Spanish settlement where the Golfo Dulce flowed into the Bahía de Amatique. Before he reached the settlement, however, his scouts returned with the news that Olid was dead.

In 1526, nearly two years after he left for Honduras, Cortés arrived in Vera Cruz, ill and fatigued from the rigors of the campaign. His return marked an end to the anarchy that prevailed in his absence.

As he made his way from the coast, natives gathered along the route and spread flowers on the road before him, and when he reached Tenochtitlán, his companions hailed his arrival with all the pomp and circumstance due an emperor.

Cortés secluded himself in the monastery of Saint Francis for six days before resuming his civic duties. His first item of business upon leaving his retreat was to honor a deathbed promise he claimed he made to Moctezuma; that he would assume responsibility for his daughters.[iv]

Isabel was Moctezuma's only surviving child by Tezalco, his lawful wife, and according to Spanish law, she was entitled to inherit his entire estate. Consequently, Cortés drew up a grant conveying Tacuba and its subject villages, an estate of some 1240 houses to Isabel, and to work her land, he gave her a generous *encomienda* of natives.

With the execution of Cuauhtémoc, Isabel was now a seventeen-year-old widow in need of a husband to manage her estate, and Cortés arranged a marriage with a prominent hidalgo whom he had recently appointed Inspector General of New Spain.

Few, if any, understood why Cortés would award Alonso de Grado with the hand of the young princess and her prime estate. Although he was an able administrator and a member of a prominent family from the same province in Spain as Cortés, he had demonstrated nothing but disloyalty to his captain from the time the Spaniards set foot in New Spain. During the journey to Tenochtitlan, he constantly agitated among the men and officers, urging them to abandon Cortés and return to the seacoast, where he was certain that Diego Velásquez would soon arrive with more men and arms.

Cortés was well aware of de Grado's seditious activities and his lack of appetite for warfare, but he chose him without a moment's hesitation to command the garrison at Vera Cruz when the Totonacs killed Juan de Escalante.

Upon assuming his new office at Vera Cruz, de Grado set about enriching himself by appropriating gold and jewels from every town in the province, and arousing the wrath of the Totonacs by demanding their prettiest women for his bed. During this time, he again set about organizing another conspiracy against Cortés.

Word of unrest among the Totonacs was not long in reaching Cortés's ears, and he ordered de Grado transported to Tenochtitlán and shackled in the public stocks. A common soldier would have been sent to the gallows for a like offense, but de Grado, as articulate as he was artful, managed to work his way back into Cortés's good graces.

De Grado, however, had little time to enjoy his good fortune-he died of natural causes within a year, leaving no issue. The Crown now declared Isabel a ward of the state, and she joined the household of Hernando Cortés.

Cortés's taste for pretty women was common knowledge among the servants of his household. Doña Marina served him as interpreter and mistress until she bore him a son, whereupon he gave her to Juan Jamarillo. During the months he held Moctezuma prisoner, he flaunted his lechery throughout the royal palace. He bedded Doña Ana and Doña Elvira, Moctezuma's daughters, and when he tired of them, he spent his nights with Doña Francisca and Doña Juana, the daughters of Nezahualpilli. Doña Ana and Doña Juana were with child when the Spaniards fled Tenochtitlán, but neither survived the flight across the causeway. He bragged to one and all of his affairs with the daughters of the royal families before and after the fall of Mexico, but if he ever serviced Doña Catalina, the daughter of the fat chieftain of Cempoala, he kept it to himself.

Among his own people, Cortés had no regard for whose wife, whose sister, or whose daughter he took to his bed. On occasion he organized debaucheries well away from the city, and when his men were sufficiently drunk, he stole back to philander with their women. His rutting was so gross, according to the testimony of his majordomo at an inquiry into his conduct, that he forced himself on a woman who came to complain about his seducing her young daughter.

It came as no surprise, then, when his 17-year-old ward found that she was four months pregnant. In Doña Isabel's case, however, an illegitimate child could have embarrassing consequences for Cortés, since the Crown recognized her as a living symbol of the sovereign Mexican state. To forestall public gossip, he arranged a hasty marriage for Isabel with Juan Gallego de Andrade, who came to New Spain with Narváez. Five months later, Doña Leonor was born.[v]

Dona Isabel and Gallego had scarcely grown accustomed to their new life when Cortés set sail for Spain, and with his departure, a change of civil government brought them to the brink of ruin.

While Cortés was in Honduras, his enemies succeeded in arousing suspicion that he had misappropriated revenues due the Crown. Furthermore, they pointed to his appointment of friends to key government offices and his influence over the natives as indications that he was preparing to declare Mexico an independent sovereignty.

Within a month of Cortés return to Mexico, Juan Ponce de Leon arrived with the Crown's authority to assume control of the government while he investigated the charges against Cortés. Before Ponce de Leon could begin his investigation, however, he fell ill of fever and died within the month. The Crown then appointed Alonso de Estrado, the royal treasurer, as governor until a royal *Audiencia* could replace him to pursue the inquiry against Cortés. To avoid civil strife, Cortés was ordered to Spain, where the Crown could bestow appropriate honors upon him.

The man chosen to preside over the first *Audiencia* of New Spain was Beltran Nuño de Guzman, who, among all the Spaniards who ever set foot in Mexico, knew no peer for cruelty and greed. He and his deputies, Diego Delgadillo and Juan Ortiz de Matienzo, took up residence in Mexico in December, 1528, and their coming marked an era of brutality and corruption unsurpassed in the history of the country. From the day they arrived, they set about enriching themselves without regard for the law or the rights of the colonists or the natives, who suffered more than any from their greed.

Prior to his appointment to the *Audiencia,* Guzman served as the governor of Panuco, where, in a period of less than two years, his slaving raids nearly depopulated the province of Huasteca. To each man in his company, he sold licenses that allowed them to brand 20 or 30 natives as slaves and send them to work in the mines and fields of the islands. This profitable enterprise attracted other slave traders from offshore, and their raids eventually drove the natives into the safety of the wilderness. Before Guzman left Panuco, it was said that more than 10,000 Indians were shipped off to the islands, where they died before their time from exposure, overwork, and diseases foreign to their native land.

In Mexico, Guzman continued to profit from the misery and suffering of the Indians. Ignoring the king's laws prohibiting abuse of the Indians, he profited by conscripting free natives to carry supplies to slaves working in mines far from Mexico. Before the practice was stopped, the route to the mines in Tepeaca alone claimed more than 3,000 lives.

Nor were the Indians held in *encomienda* by the colonists safe from his administration. Upon them he levied an exorbitant tribute of labor, the most unconscionable of which fell upon the encomienda of Hernando Cortés in Huexotzingo. Each day Cortés's Indians carried burdens of chickens, eggs, quail, maize, wood, and charcoal 18 leagues across a snow-covered pass to the members of the *Audiencia* and their staffs. Before Guzman's tenure came to an end, more than 130 men, women, and children died from exhaustion along the way.

From the native lords and nobles, he demanded their fairest daughters and sisters for the personal pleasure of the *Audiencia,* and if they dared refuse, his interpreter Pilar threatened them with the gallows. He even violated the sanctity of the cloister when he sent Pilar to the convent school in Texcoco for two pretty girls to service him.

Among the colonists, he singled out Cortés and his conquerors for the harshest measures. The *Audiencia* gave ear to all who held a grievance against them, whether merited or not, and without hearing evidence to the contrary, they seized their properties and sold them at auction. Using the same procedure, they took away their *encomiendas* and awarded them to their friends.

355

For his mills, Guzman appropriated land in Tacubaya, and to operate them, he drained off the water needed to irrigate the surrounding fields. His deputies, Delgadillo and Matienzo, followed his example by seizing Tacuba and the lands belonging to Doña Isabel.

Without revenue from the land, life became trying for Isabel and her family. Juan Gallego appealed to the *Audiencia* for the return of Isabel's patrimony, but they made it known that there would be a price. Guzman received five bed linens worth more than 130 castellanos, Delgadillo received gold nuggets worth 30 pesos and a prime piece of land belonging to Doña Leonor, Isabel's half-sister, and Matienzo accepted 150 fanegas of wheat and land for his two mills.

Guzman refused the bribe, but he gave Gallego a bundle of clothing worth less than ten pesos in exchange for his "contribution" to the *Audiencia*. Consideration of his suit, however, was postponed for a more expedient time.

Only Don Fray Juan de Zumárraga, the Bishop Elect of Mexico and Protector of the Indians, dared raise his voice against Guzman. He demanded that the *Audiencia* obey all laws protecting the natives, and he insisted upon signature approval of all tribute schedules. Guzman retaliated by refusing to recognize his authority, citing that he had not yet been confirmed as Bishop of New Spain. Frustrated, Zumárraga initiated hearings for grievances of the colonists and natives alike, and threatened to expose Guzman to the Crown.

Guzman was not intimidated. He threatened any colonist who complained to Zumárraga with deportation, and he decreed that any native who met with the Bishop would be sent to the gallows. He threatened to bar Zumárraga from the pulpit if he continued to preach against the *Audiencia*, and he spread scandalous rumors against the clergy to turn people away from the church.

The conflict between church and state came to a head on Whitsunday of 1529, when Fray Antonio Ortiz, the Bishop of Tlaxcala, rose to the pulpit to defend the clergy against Guzman's lies. Guzman shouted at him to stop, but when Ortiz continued, Delgadillo ordered the constables to drag him from the pulpit. Guzman would have sent him to Vera Cruz strapped on a mule and deported to Spain, but Ortiz claimed sanctuary in the church.

Zumárraga then excommunicated Guzman and Delgadillo, but relented when Guzman agreed to withdraw his libelous statements against the church.

The damage, however, was done. The incident united the church against Guzman and the *Audiencia*. Only his agents, who controlled the ports and censored all dispatches from New Spain, prevented his crimes from being laid before the Council of the Indies.

Guzman's hold upon Mexico was broken in August, 1529, when Zumárraga persuaded a Basque sailor to smuggle a letter to Spain in a barrel of oil.

In April of the following year, the Crown appointed a new *Audiencia*, allowing Guzman, albeit with reduced powers, to remain in office until the *Audiencia* arrived in New Spain. Shortly afterward, Guzman received a royal directive regarding Gallego's suit.

> It has been brought to our attention that the President
> and judges of our Royal *Audiencia* did seize the town
> of Tacuba and the surrounding irrigated lands from
> Dona Isabel, the daughter of Montezuma and wife of
> Juan Gallego. It was our will that Tacuba and its
> immediate lands be entrusted to her and her husband
> Juan Gallego for their support, and the loss of these
> lands have caused them great hardship. As these lands
> belonged to her father, I therefore command the
> President of our *Audiencia* to return the town of
> Tacuba to her immediately, to restore her lands to their
> original condition, and that all tribute lost during this
> time be repaid to her.
>
> By command of Her Majesty, the Queen
>
> Juan de Semano, Secretary of the Council of the Indies
>
> Madrid, June 9, 1530

With the arrival of the new *Audiencia* in December, Matienzo and Delgadillo were arrested and sent to Spain to stand trial. They were found guilty of their trust and spent the rest of their days in prison. But Guzman was not one to wait for the inevitable. Knowing that his days in Mexico were numbered, he recruited 500 Spaniards, most of whom were loyalists of Diego Velásquez, and 15,000 native porters, and marched off to the western provinces of New Galicia, where he continued to pillage the land and enslave the people. The new *Audienca*, bowing to pressure from Spain, allowed Guzman to complete the subjugation of New Galica before sending him to Spain for trial.

The recovery of Isabel's patrimony was followed by the return of Cortés, now Marquis of the Valley of Oaxaca. With his new bride, Juana de Zuñiga, a Spanish noblewoman, he had returned to claim dominions more vast than any before granted by the Crown.

The heart of the Marquisado lay some 10 leagues south of the Valley of Mexico, in the fertile region between Cuernavaca and the Cuauhtla River. This was where Moctezuma once hunted deer and rabbit and rested from the cares of his empire among the gardens and orchards of Oaxtepec. In the Valley of Mexico, the Marquesado encompassed the region between Coyoacán and Tacubaya along the eastern shore of the lake, and west of the Valley of Mexico, it encompassed a substantial part of the Valley of Toluca. To the southeast, the Marquesado claimed tributaries at Tepeaca, at Cuetlaxtlan, and at Tuxtla, and in the province of Tochtepec. The most distant lands of the Marquis were in the Valley of Oaxaca, the land of the Zapotecs, and at Jalapa, on the Isthmus of Tehuantepec.

In these fruitful lands, Cortés would introduce sugar cane from Cuba and build mills to process it into raw sugar, pasture sheep and cattle in Tehuantepec, breed the silkworm in his mulberry trees, and mine gold along the Rio Tehuantepec. And from a thousand tributaries, maize, cotton, clothing, fabrics, and cacao exports would provide him a yearly income due a prince.

With her title to Tacuba once again secure, and an *Audiencia* of reputable men holding office, the future seemed bright for Isabel and Gallego. But with the coming of spring, Gallego fell ill, and by April, Isabel was a widow for the third time.

She was now 21 years old and the mother of two children, having given birth to Juan de Andrade Montezuma two years before Gallego's death. As the patrona of one of the most productive *encomiendas* in the Valley of Mexico, however, Isabel found no lack of suitors for her hand. Before the year was out, she marred Juan Cano, the *encomendero* of Macuisuchilo.

In the years that followed, Isabel gave birth to three sons; Gonzalo, Pedro, and Juan; and two daughters, Isabel and Catalina. As her family grew and prospered, so did Isabel's responsibilities to her household and her new faith. Each day, Isabel and her half sisters, Doña Leonor and Doña Francisca, met with more than a hundred wives, sister, and daughters of the native workers to instruct them in the Holy Faith and the Spanish language. Early every morning and again before bedtime, she supervised their prayers, and heaven help any who neglected to pay attention, for her back was sure to find Isabel's stout cane laid across it. And her generosity to the church, whose demands upon the resources of its parishioners were never-ending, became so excessive that the Order of Saint Augustine refused to accept any further gifts from her.

But these times were yet to come. By 1532, the rapid growth of Mexico began to outstrip the means of supplying the population, and the new *Audiencia*, though honest men all, turned envious eyes to the rich farmholds of Isabel and Cortés, which were less than two leagues from the heart of the city. The President of the *Audiencia*, Don Sebastian Ramírez de Fuenleal, decided that Mexico could not survive without annexing the lands along the western shore of the lake, and his deputy, Francisco de Ceynos, submitted a petition to the Crown to confiscate Coyoacán, Tacubaya, and Tacuba.

Ceynos, however, found that the Marquesado was inviolate-Cortés's prerogatives in New Spain were those of the Crown itself, and the Queen's support of Isabel against Guzman was still fresh in the minds of the Council of the Indies.

The Crown reaffirmed Isabel's title, but the rapid growth of the Marquesado at Tacubaya threatened to reduce the productivity of her land below the basic needs of the estate. Each day Isabel and Cano were faced with a struggle to protect their crops from Cortés's livestock and to prevent him from drawing off all the available water on the western shore. Finding the Marquis unapproachable, Cano once again petitioned the Crown, and in April of 1538, the Queen ordered the *Audiencia* to prohibit the Marquis from allowing his horses, oxen, hogs and chickens to range freely over Isabel's newly-seeded lands. Furthermore, the Marquis was directed to restore the river he had diverted from her field, and to operate his mills on its original course.

Ever since his triumphal return to Mexico in 1530, Cortés's restless spirit gave him no peace, driving him on one quest to another, seeking new horizons in the Southern Sea. From 1532 to 1539, he financed the construction of ten ships and sent four expeditions in search of fruitful lands along the western seacoast.

The first two expeditions foundered from mutinies and attacks by savages that cost the lives of many men. The third expedition took the Marquis into the lands across the Sea of Cortez, where one disaster after another kept him away from New Spain so long that it was feared he was lost. The fourth and last expedition reached the narrows at the upper end of the Sea of Cortez, but the land on either shore provided to be barren wastelands. His investment of 300,000 castellanos failed to yield a single ducat in return and before long, he was heavily in debt.

Nevertheless, he proposed to build five more ships to continue his explorations in the Southern Sea, but now a higher authority than the *Audiencia* stood in his way. In 1535, while he was struggling with storms in the Sea of Cortez, the Viceroy Antonio de Mendoza arrived in Mexico.

Mendoza, fascinated by tales of the Seven Cities of Cibola[vi] north of New Galicia, authorized Francisco Velásquez de Coronado to assemble a company of Spaniards and natives for the mission. Cortés objected, claiming his right as Captain-General of New Spain to explore and pacify all lands north of New Galicia. Mendoza, however, ruled that as the Crown's regent, his warrant took precedence over that of Cortés. The two quarreled, and when Cortés refused to yield, the Viceroy opened an investigation of the number of vassals he claimed above those assigned by the Crown. Cortés was left little choice but to seek support from the King.[vii]

In 1540, Cortés departed for Spain, never to return to the land where he built one empire upon the ruins of another. Leaving behind his wife and three daughters, he sailed from Vera Cruz with his son, Don Martín, now eight years old, to seek an audience with Charles V.

He found his position materially changed since his visit ten years previous. His reception by the King was civil but cold, and he retired to a village on the outskirts of Seville. In February, 1544, he sent a letter to the Emperor, soliciting consideration his suit, but it was the last one he would ever write.

Hernando Cortés died on the second day of December, 1547.

In his will he left ten thousand ducats in dowry to Doña Leonor and Doña Maria, bidding them to marry with the advice of Martín Cortés. If either should die before she married or desired to pursue a religious life or another virtuous following, she was to receive a yearly allowance of 70,000 maravedis for her expenses; the remainder would revert to his son and heir, Martín Cortés.

> Bequest of Hernando Cortés to Doña Leonor, his
> daughter by the princess Tecuichpo.

> Seville, October 11, 1547

On the eighteenth day of April, 1551, Doña Isabel de Moctezuma died in the forty-first year of her life. Her early years were not happy times. The loss of her father and her home in a devastating war and marriage at an age more suitable for playmates and games deprived her of childhood, and five years of confinement with Cuauhtémoc after the war robbed her of adolescence, innocence, and her ethnic heritage. But her passing was noted in far away Spain and Rome, for although she was a native of a subject land, she was honored as the crown princess of a once-great empire.

It was her wish to be buried in the church and monastery of Saint Augustine in Mexico City, and on the day of her funeral, the entire native population of Tacuba and its subject towns joined the procession as it made its way to the church.

In her will, she bequeathed Tacuba to Juan de Andrade, her son by Juan Gallego, and stipulated that he hold it in primogeniture for his descendants to enjoy for all time. To Gonzalo Cano, her eldest son by Juan Cano, she bequeathed to the towns of Cuiacaque, Cupuenaque, Quaupanoaya, and Tepenaxuca, all subject to Tacuba. These properties were also to be held in primogeniture. All other properties were given over to Juan, Isabel, and Catalina, her children by Juan Cano, less a third that was set aside exclusively for Isabel and Catalina to divide in equal shares. Isabel and Catalina were also to inherit all her household goods, linens, tapestry, carpets, pillows, and personal apparel.

She also petitioned the Crown for all the lands that once belonged to Moctezuma, and specified that if her request was granted, that Isabel and Catalina would also inherit them.

Six hundred pesos were set aside for funeral expenses and the mass that followed. The odds and ends of her possessions not specified in her will and left unclaimed were passed on to Doña Leonor.

Leonor was now a twenty-three year old spinster, rapidly approaching an age when a suitable marriage would be beyond reach, with no dowry save the monies left her by a father she never knew, but one who cared enough to acknowledge her. If she had few material assets, however, she did not lack suitors. There were few eligible colonials who were unaware of the prestige a union with a direct descendant of Moctezuma Xocoyotl and Hernando Cortés would bring him.

The wealthiest of her admirers was Juanes de Tolosa, a Basque who fought with Nuño de Guzman in the conquest of New Galicia, and again with the Viceroy Mendoza in the Mixton War, when the Caxcanes rose to stop the northward advance of the Spaniards. After the natives were pacified, Tolosa received a commission from Cristobal de Oñate, a wealthy speculator, to explore the region north of New Galicia.

In September of 1546, Tolosa and his company of Spaniards and Indians made camp at the foot of a high promontory 50 leagues northwest of Guadalajara. In exchange for a few trinkets, the natives gave Tolosa several specimens of silver ore. The ore was promising enough for Tolosa to find the deposits and send a few wagonloads south to be assayed. His strike produced more wealth that Spain ever realized from Cortés and his conquerors.

Zacatecas, the city founded by Tolosa, rose and prospered at the foot of the promontory. Within four years, 34 mining companies built foundries and stamping mills, and in time, homes for colonists seeking instant wealth, churches, missions, stores, a government house, and mansions for the rich followed.

Juanes de Tolosa was now in his forties, and quite possibly the richest man in New Spain when he brought Leonor to Zacatecas as his bride. But Tolosa, like Cortés, was too restless and enterprising to appreciate the joys and comforts of conjugal life. The lure of the mother lode was always just beyond the horizon.

In 1557, he and his partner, Luis Cortés, Leonor's half[viii] brother, discovered a rich source of silver ore at San Martín, 40 leagues northwest of Zacatecas, that would one day yield more silver than all the mines of Zacatecas. San Martín, however, was to be his last successful venture. In the years that followed, one fruitless expedition after another consumed his entire fortune.

Leonor's union with Tolosa produced three children; Juan Cortés Tolosa y Moctezuma, Leonor Cortés y Moctezuma, and Isabel Cortés y Moctezuma. They would pass down the names of Moctezuma and his conqueror, bound together for all time, to generations yet to be born.

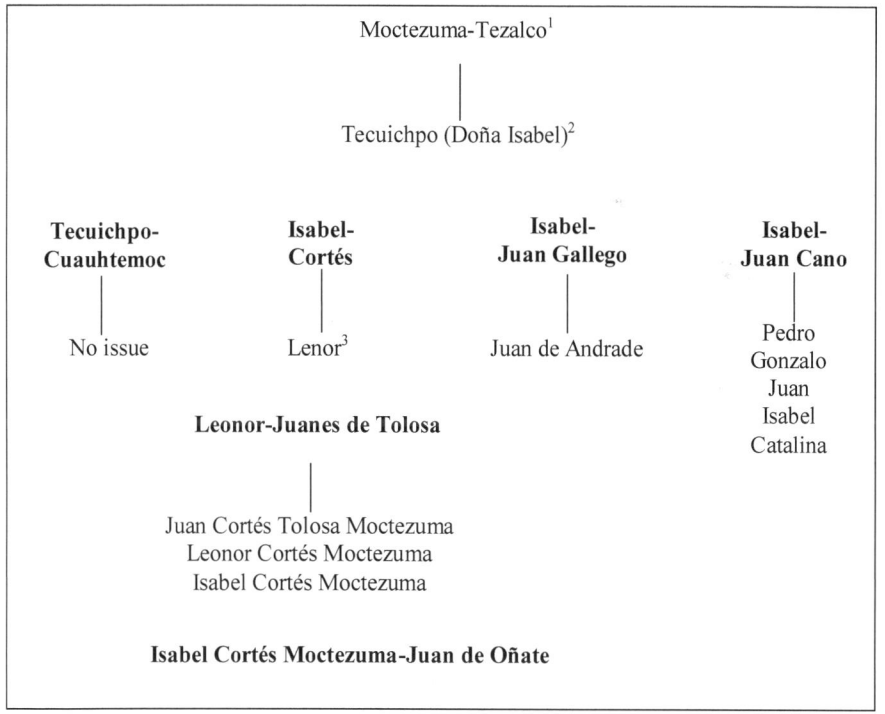

Moctezuma's Descendants

1. Moctezuma's legitimate wife.
2. Legitimate heir of Moctezuma and only child to survive the conquest.

3.   Illegitimate.
4.   Family moved to San Gabriel, Mexico in 1598.

In 1598, Juan de Oñate led a party of 129 colonists. 10 Franciscan friars, and 7,000 head of livestock to found a settlement at San Gabriel, New Mexico, 110 miles northwest of El Paso, Texas. With him came his bride Isabel, the namesake of her grandmother, who was once Tecuichpo, the little cotton snowflake, the royal princess of an empire in its golden age.

---

[i] The princess Tecuichpo

[ii] Cortés claims that Juan de Alderete instigated the torture of Cuauhtémoc.

[iii] Cortés and the Anales de Tlatelolco agree inasmuch as both state that Cozoololtic, a convert to Christianity, informed Cortés of a planned uprising, In Cortés's version, the dwarf described a plot to oust all the Spanish forces from Mexico, whereas the Anales de Tlatelolco infer that Cozoololtic, to gain favor with Cortes, told Marina that he overheard a plot to kill the Spaniards during the Chontal reception for Cuauhtémoc.

Bernal Díaz, however, accuses Tlacotl and Motelchiuhtl of fabricating the plot, and further states that the rank and file held the view that the execution of Cuauhtémoc was unwarranted.

Whatever the truth of the matter, Cortés was presented with an opportune time and place to rid himself of the Mexican monarch.

[iv] Cortes, in a document dated June 27, 1526, entitled *Grant of Cortes to Dona Isabel, daughter of the Emperor Montezuma,* justifies his award of Moctezuma's estates in Tacuba to Isabel, his only surviving daughter, to a pledge he made to the Emperor as he lay dying of his head wound.

"Fearing he might die from (his wound)…he prayed me and charged me very earnestly, that, remembering how much he loved me and desired to please me,I, should he die of the wound, would take charge of his three daughters, have them baptized and taught our religion, for he knew it was very good.…In his last moments, for he died of the wound, he called me again, and earnestly prayed me that I would care for these daughters, saying that they were the best jewels he had given me, that I should divide among them what he left, remembering especially the eldest, whom he loved very tenderly.…"

Other than Isabel, six surviving children of Moctezuma have been identified. Acalan, Moctezuma's second wife, bore him three daughters, and Dona Miagua Vhxuch, a royal princess of Tula, either a concubine or a third wife, bore him one or more sons. All were granted lands by the Crown.

---

[v] Vincente Rivas Palacio lists Isabel's second husband as Juan Gallegos de Andrade, a member of Narváez's company. Gallego is more often referred to as Pedro or Pero Gallego than Juan, but I have used Juan throughout the text to be consistent with Rivas Palacio and with the name of his son by Isabel, Juan de Andrade Moctezuma, whom I assume to be his namesake.

Juan Cano, Isabel's third husband, states that Isabel married "Pedro Gallego...who came to New Spain with the first group of conquerors." There was a Pedro Gallego in Cortés's first company, but he was captured and sacrificed by the Mexicans.

[vi] Acording to legend, seven fugitive bishops discovered these fabulous cities in the Sonora Desert. The legend was confirmed by Cabeza de Vaca, a Spaniard who had escaped from his Indian captors near Galveston, Texas, and walked barefoot to Onovas, in the Sonora Desert. Cabeza de Vaca's "confirmation" was all that Mendoza needed to launch the Coronada expedition, which cost the lives of so many men and resources that the Crown ordered strict limits on the funding of all future expeditions.

[vii] Cortes was particularly vulnerable to Mendoza's investigation into the claims of the Marquesado. The original grant from the Crown granted him no more than 23,000 vassals, but the number claimed by Cortes proved to be far greater. Inventories for the period 156-70 show more than 60,000 vassals for the Marquesado, and as late as 1597, the census count was more than 30,000.

Glossary

Adelantado	Title formerly given a provincial governor
Adoratorio	Name given by the Spaniards to a place of idol Worship
Aguada	Underground cisterns used to store water during the dry season
Alcaide	Warden of a castle or fortress
Alcalde	Justice or town council member
Alferez	Company standard bearer
Anahuac	Southeastern region of Mexico lying between 14 degrees and 21 degrees north lattitude
Arroba	A Spanish weight of 25 pounds or a measure of about four gallons.
Atlatl	Throwing stick for darts or javelins

Atole	Gruel made of boiling maize
Audiencia	Court of judicature in the West Indies
Aztlan	The ancestral home of the Aztecs, location Unknown
Barrio	A town subdivision
Calmecac	Pre-conquest school, primarily for upper class Boys
Calpixqui	A tax collector
Calpulli	Social group similar to a clan
Carga	Generally a load of two fanegas
Castellano	A monetary unit equivalent to one peso de oro
Cedula	A royal directive
Chalchihuite	A precious stone similar in color and quality to an emerald
Chontal	Seafaring Maya group occupying the delta region of the Usmacinta and Grijalva Rivers.
Cihuacoatl	Aztec vice-regent; literally "snake woman"
Citlaltepetl	Nahuatl name of the Orizaba volcano. The "Mountain of the Stars"
Cloud people	Natives of the Mixtec and Zapotec groups in Oaxaca
Coacalli	Guest house

Cochineal	A red dye made from the dried bodies of insects that feed upon cactuses in the warm regions of Mexico
Contador	An accountant
Copal	Incense made from the resin of any gum-yielding Tree
Corregidor	A Spanish magistrate
Council of the Indies	Jurisdictional headquarters of the New World in Spain
Cuauhnahuac	Nahuatl name for Cuernavaca
Encomendero	Possessor of an encomienda
Encomienda	Grant of land and Indians, mainly as tribute payers, to colonists
Fanega	A unit of dry measure, about one and a half Bushels
Fiscal	A government attorney, a prosecutor
Flota	A fleet of merchant ships
Guatemuz	Corrupted name for Cuauhtémoc used by the Spaniards
Hacendado	Hacienda owner
Hacienda	Large landed estate
Henequen	Fiber of the agave plant
Hueytlatoani	Great tlatolani, chieftain of chieftains. Literally "he who listens"

Huichilobos	Corrupted name of Huitzilopochtli
Itza	Maya group that migrated from Chichen Itza and settled at Tayasal, in Guatemala
Iztaccihuatl	"Sleeping woman," an extinct volcano south of Mexico City
Juez	A judge
Juez de Residencia	Presiding judge or presiding officer. See residencia
Jiquipile	A numerical unit of 16,000
Licenciado	A lawyer
Malinche	Name given to Cortés's interpreter, Marina. The natives used used the same name for Cortés, since he was rarely seen without her.
Maquahuitl	A war club with two rows of flint blades set along its cutting edges
Maravedi	Monetary unit: 34 maravedis equals one real
Mictlan	The land of the dead
Milpa	Plot assigned to native farmers for planting corn, generally about five acres.
Mitote	Ritual dance performed at weddings
Moctezuma Xocóyotl	Ninth heuytlatoani of Mexico. Literally, the "Angry Lord." Xocóyotl denotes the younger, or second of that name
Nemontemi	Five unlucky days at the end of the Mexican Year. The Mexican year has 18 months of

	20 days each. The nemontemi is needed to round out the year to 365 days.
Nahuatl	The language spoken by the Aztecs and other native groups throughout Anahuac
Nauhcampatepetl	A mountain 120 miles west of Mexico City 14,049 feet in altitude. Now called Cofre de Perote
Octli	A liquor made from the fermented juice of the maguey plant
Oidor	A judge of the *Audiencia* of Mexico or of the *Audiencia* of Santo Domingo
Otomies	A warlike race populating the region north of The Valley of Mexico and some settlements in The Rebublic of Tlaxcala
Patrona	Patroness of a hacienda or encomienda
Piragua	Spanish name for a native craft manned by as many as 60 warriors
Pochtecatl	An Aztec merchant
Popocatepetl	"Smoking Mountain." A volcano southeast of Mexico City
Pulque	Liquor obtained from maguey plant
Quauhchic	Military grade granted only to men of close kinship with royalty. They fought in the rearguard of the army to compel others to fight
Real	Monetary unit equal to one-eighth of a peso

Regidor	A councilman
Repartimiento	An assignemnt of native laborers to the encomiendas.
Residencia	Court or formal inquiry
Sapote	A fruit tree
Shield boat	Native war canoe manned by six or ten warriors
Tamale	Small meat or meal dumpling boiled in a corn Husk
Tameme	A native porter
Teotihuacán	Ancient city 26 miles northeast of Mexico City that flourished from 200 BC to AD 600
Tepepolco	A high outcropping in the southeastern part of Lake Texcoco
Tezcatlipoca	"Smoking Mirror." A god who assumed different forms; sometimes as god of the night sky, sometimes as the enemy of Quetzalcoatl. His powers were shared with other chief gods of the Toltec and Aztec pantheon
Tanquiz	A native market
Tierra Caliente	The hot lands of Mexico on the Gulf Coast
Tlacatecatl	A commander of warriors. One of the four highest ranking military posts, usually reserved for royalty

Tlacochcalcatl	Keeper of the Javelin House. Same rank as Tlacatecatl
Tlaloc	The God of Rain
Tlapallan	The destination of Quetzalcoatl-Topiltzin when he fled from Tula
Tlilancalqui	An Aztec priest, the "Keeper of the Dark House."
Toltec	Early post-Classic civilization of Mexico: AD 900-1200
Tortilla	A thin pancake of cornmeal
Toxcatl	A feast celebrating the end of the dry season
Tula	The site of Toltec civilization, 35 miles north of Mexico City
Tule	Marsh reeds
Tuna	A name given to the Nopalli cactus by the Spaniards
Tzompantli	A rack for mounting the skulls of sacrifices
Uixachalan	A promontory south of Mexico City where the rite of the binding of the years was performed. Now the Cerro Estrella National Park.
Vara	A rod or a unit of measure equal to 2.28 feet
Veedor	An inspector
Visitador	A visiting judge

Appendix 1

The testimony of Bernardino Vázquez de Tapia, an eyewitness, at an inquest into the massacre before the _Audiencia_ at Santo Domingo.

Cortes's departure for Cempoala left Alvarado in a bad mood. He began to treat Montezuma badly, and was overheard to curse him as a dog for not giving him as many gifts as previously. He also voiced his suspicions that the Indians were planning an uprising. When Montezuma approached Alvarado for his permission to hold the ceremony, however, [Montezuma] reminded him that Cortes had already given his approval.

Some Spaniards warned Alvarado that Montezuma proposed replacing the statue of The Virgin Mary in the temple with that of Huitzilopochtli, and Alvarado was so angry he threatened to cancel the ceremony. The Indians, however, assured him that since he was so upset, they would not take the god into the temple.

When Alvarado went to the plaza to inspect the preparations for the dance, he saw three idols set upon litters, waiting to be moved, and beside each litter sat an Indian with shorn hair, wearing new mantles.

Alvarado ordered the Indians taken to the palace, and he tortured them to reveal the plan for the uprising. The Spaniards took the first Indian and put live embers on his belly, demanding to know when the uprising was to begin, but he died without telling them anything. They cast his body from the rooftop, and put another Indian and two young relatives of Montezuma to torture.

The Indians confessed. Alvarado's interpreter was an Indian called Francisco, whom Grijalva brought back to Cuba from Guatasta.(Huaxteca?) The Spaniards kept asking Francisco if the Indians were planning to attack in ten days, and Francisco always responded. "Si, Senor."

Alvarado decided to kill everyone in the plaza, and although this witness advised him not to do this and that he would not take part in the attack, Alvarado ordered the entire company to take up arms.

He took half the company with him and left the other half in the palace with orders to kill all the Mexican hostages as soon as he attacked the dancers. When he entered the plaza, three or four hundred dancers were holding hands as they danced, and some three or four thousand spectators were watching them. Although the Indians saw him enter with armed soldiers, none made any effort to leave, and they remained silent as Alvarado moved around the plaza, stationing ten men at each of the gates. When the dancers were surrounded, he attacked....

Respuesta del Conquistador Bernardino Vázquez de Tapia al Interrogatoria formulado in la pesquiza contra Don Pedro de Alvarado. In Bernardino Vázquez de Tapia, Relacion de meritdos, etc.,   Appendix   II,   109-111.

Appendix 2

Historians have debated for nearly 500 years whether Moctezuma died from a head wound inflicted by his own people or whether Cortés, for one reason or another, killed him prior to the retreat from the city.

Some historians-Prescott for example-have accepted, without any definitive argument, that Moctezuma was killed by a stone thrown by the Mexicans. Orozco y Berra, on the other hand, after reviewing his sources, concludes that the Spaniards killed Moctezuma.

The Cronica X, as related by Duran, claims that after the Spaniards fled, the Mexicans found Moctezuma's body in the palace with chains about his feet and five stab wounds in his chest.

There is, however, reliable eyewitness testimony, which is supported by some native sources, that Moctezuma died before the Spaniards left Tenochtitlán. Duran cites native paintings to support his claim, and adds that the bodies of many noblemen and great lords lay next to him.

The native sources:

Chimalpahin, *Septima Relación*. The chronicler states that the Spaniards strangled Moctezuma, Itzcuauhtl, and Cacama.

Tezozomoc (*Cronica mexicóyotl*) States that the Spaniards killed Moctezuma, Itzcuauhtl, and Cacama.

Cronica X (Tovar, Codex Ramirez). After the Spaniards fled, the Mexicans found Moctezuma's body in the palace with five stab wounds. His head wound was either nearly healed or not visible.

Ixtlilxochitl *(Historia chichimeca)* The chronicler states that Moctezuma died of his head injury, and that the Spaniards stabbed Cacama before they fled.

The Spanish sources

Sahagún (Enmendada)

…in this manner the Spaniards resolved to defeat (the Mexicans) or die like men. Thus they advised all the allies (of their plan), and all were steadfast in their determination. The first thing they did was to garrote all the lords they held prisoner, and they threw their bodies outside the fort.

Torquemada had access to the Enmendada before it was taken to Spain, and repeats Sahagún's text, but with a crucial variation.

…all were steadfast in their determination. The first thing they did was to garrote Montezuma and Itzcuauhtzin, the lord of Tlatelolco, and the other lords they held prisoner.

Cortés

"…he received a blow on his head from a stone; and the injury was so serious that he died three days later. I told two of the Indians who were captive to carry him out on their shoulders to the people. What they did with him I do not know…"

Bernardino Vázquez de Tapia

The company alferez confirms Cortés's statement that Moctezuma's body was given to his people before the Spaniards withdrew. "…They put him in a bag and gave him to two Indians who had served Montezuma so they could carry him (out); whereupon when the warriors saw him, they believed that we had killed him, and that night all wept and burned the body in a funeral ceremony."

Juan Cano. Moctezuma's son-in-law, who had reason to dislike Cortes, unequivocally states that Moctezuma was killed by a stone.

Francisco de Aguilar, the soldier priest, maintains that Moctezuma died from died from his head wound, but his eyewitness account of women searching for their loved ones below his post confirms that most of the hostages were killed.

Bernal Díaz

"So as to convince them that Montezuma was dead, he ordered six Mexicans who were high chieftains, and the priests whom we held as captives, to carry him out on their shoulders, and to hand the body over to the Mexican captains, and to tell them what Montezuma had commanded at the time of his death; and they told Cuitláhuac the whole truth..."

We thus have five reasonably objective eyewitnesses to support Cortés's claim that Moctezuma was killed by the stone that struck him. Only one native source, Ixtlilxochitl, an ally of Cortes, supports his claim.

Thus it seems reasonable to assume that Moctezuma's body was carried outside the palace to be interred before the Spaniards left, and the body in the palace was not his, but possibly that of Cacama. The account of the eyewitnesses, de Tapia, Díaz, and Cano, however, only document the delivery of Moctezuma's body to the Aztecs. We have only Cortés's word that the emperor died of his head wound.

From a practical standpoint, Moctezuma may have had more value to Cortés alive than dead. Cacama, who despised Cortés, would be of no value to him alive, and would be a hindrance during the retreat.

Appendix 3

Fatalities on Noche Triste

Eyewitnesses	Spaniards	Tlaxcalans	Horses
Cortés	150	2000+	45
Aguilar	500+	——	——
Vázquez de Tapia	575-675	2-3000	57
Bernal Díaz	860	1000+	57
Juan Cano	1170	8000	—-

Spanish Chroniclers	Spaniards	Tlaxcalans	Horses
Cervantes	600-640	4000	46-57
Torquemada	290+	4000	46-47
Gomara	450	4000	46

Native Informants	Spaniards	Tlaxcalans	Horses
Duran	700	——	——
Tovar	340	——	——
Ixtlilxochitl	450	4000	46
Camargo	450+	4000	——
Sahagun	300+	4000	——

Abbreviations

AC	*Actas de cabildo de la ciudad de Mexico.* Title varies vols. Mexico, 1889-1916.
AGI	Archivo General de Indies, Seville.
BLMM	Mexican Manuscripts, Bancroft Library, University of California, Berkeley.
BAGN	*Boletin del Archivo general de la nación*, I (1930) et seq.
CDHM	*Colección de documentos para la historia de Mexico.* Joaquin Garcia Icazbalceta, ed. 2 vols. Mexico, 1858-66.
CDIAI	*Colección de documents ineditos, relativos al descubrimiento, conquista y organización de las antigas posesiones espaniolas de America y Oceana, sacados de los archivos del reina, y muy especialmente de las Indias.* Title varies, 42 vols. Madrid, 1842-95.
CDIHE	*Colección de documentos ineditos para la historia de Nueva Espania.* Martín

	Fernandez Navarrete and others, eds. 112 vols. Madrid, 1842-95.
CDIHIA	*Colección de documentos ineditos para la historia de Ibero-America.* Title varies, 14 vols. Madrid, 1927-32
CDIU	*Colección de documentos ineditos, relativos al descubrimiento, conquista y organización de las antiguas posesiones espanolas de ultramar,* 25 vols. Madrid, 1885-1932.
ENE	*Epistolario de Nueva Espana, 1505-1818.* Francisco de Paso Y Troncoso, ed. 16 vols. Mexico, 1939-42. Biblioteca Historica de obras ineditos, ser. 2
HMAI	Handbook of Middle American Indians
NCDHM	Nueva colección documentos para la historia de Mexico. Juan Garcia Icazbalceta, ed. 5 vols. Mexico, 1941
PNE	Papales de Nueva Espania, Francisco del Paso y Troncosco, 9 vols. Madrid and Mexico, 1905-48

Sources

Chapter 1

Codex Ramirez, tr. Paul Radin, "The Sources and Authenticity of the History of the Ancient Mexicans," University of California Publications in American Archaeology and Ethnology, XVII, (Berkeley, 1920) vol.17: 67-91 (Hereafter referred to as Codex Ramirez)

The Aztecs *The History of the Indies of New Spain by Fray Diego Duran,* tr. Doris Heyden and Fernando Horcasitas,) New York, 1964), 3-49,. (Hereafter referred to as Duran, HH ed.)

Chapter 2

Alvarado Tezozomoc, Hernando, *Cronica mexicana, escrita hacia el ano de 1598,* Manuel Orozco y Berra, ed., (Mexico, 1944), Chap. 13-70, 318. (hereafter referred to as Tezozomoc Mexicana)

Fray Diego Duran, *Historia de las Indias de Nueva Espania*

Y islas de tierra firme, Jose F.Ramirez, ed., 2 vols., (Mexico, 1951), Chap. 6-51, 356-57. (Hereafter referred to as Duran, Ramirez ed.)

Codex Ramirez, vol.17: 93-118

Duran, HH ed. 52-218.

Nigel Davis, *The Aztecs*, (Norman, 1980)

Robert H. Barlow, "The Extent of the Empire of the Culhua Mexica" in Ibero-Amercana, no. 28, (Berkeley and Los Angeles, 1949)

Bernardino de Sahagun, *General History of the Things of New Spain; the Florentine Codex*, ed. and trans. from Nahuatl to English by J.O. Anderson and Charles E. Dibble, 12 vols., Monographs of the School of American Research, (Santa Fe, 1950 et seq.), 8:41, 54-55, 62-65.7:3-9, 25-32, 12;1-3, (Hereafter cited as Sahagun, Florentine Codex)

Juan de Torquemada, *Los viente i un libros rituales i monarchia indiana* 3 vols.,(Madrid, 1723). Facsimile edition, (Mexico, 1944), 1:157-58, 1:186 (Herafter cited as Torquemada, facsimile ed.)

Jaques Soustelle, *Daily Life of the Aztecs*, trans. Patrick O'Brian, (Stanford, 1970), 106-107.

Anales de Cuauhtitlan and Leyenda de los soles, in Codex Chimalpopoca,59, 61) trans. Primo Feliciano Velásquez (Mexico, 1945). See Miguel Leon Portillo,

Aztec Thought and Culture, (Norman, 1963), 38-45.

Chapter 3

Bernal Díaz del Castillo, *The True Story of the Conquest of New Spain by Bernal Diaz,* A.P. Maudslay, trans. Vols. 23-25, 30, 40. Hakluyt Society, series 2. (London, 1908-16. Published in abridgement by Farrar, Strauss, and Giroux, (New York, 1956), 5-16 (Hereafter cited as Bernal Diaz)

Cervantes de Salazar, *Cronica de Nueva Espania,* (Madrid 1914), 63-63. (Hereafter cited as Cervantes)

Juan Díaz, Itinerario de la armada del Rey Catolico, a la isla de Yucatan, el ano 1518 CDHM, I: 57-75 (Hereafter cited as Juan Díaz)

Oviedo y Valdez, Gonzalo Fernandez, Historia general y natural de las Indias, (Madrid, 1851-1859), 2: 118-149. (Hereafter cited as Oviedo)

Juan de Torquemada, *Monarquia Indiana*, 6 vols; (Mexico, 1944), 19-21. (Herafter cited as Torquemada)

Gómara, Francisco López de, Cortes, The Life of the Conqueror by His ßecretary, trans.& ed. by Leseley Byrd Simpson, (Berkeley, 1966), 15-17 (Hereafter cited as Gomara)

CDIAI, 225.

Chapter 4

Tezozomoc, Mexicana, 483-88, 500-514.

Duran, HH ed. 255-58.

Duran, Ramirez ed. 490-524

Sahagun, Florentine Codex, 12:1-2

Miguel Leon Portillo, *The Broken Spears,* (Boston, 1966), 3

Nigel Davies, *The Toltecs,* (Norman, 1977), 392-97

Chapter 5

Tezozomoc, Mexicana, 528-536.

Duran, HH ed, 258-71

Fray Diego Duran, *Book of Rites and the Ancient Calendar*, tr. from *Historia de las Indias ce Nueva Espania y islas de tierra firme* by Fernando Horcasitas and Doris Heyden, (Norman, 1971), 210. (Hereafter referred to as Duran, Gods and Rites, HH ed.

Bernal Diaz, 47-64

Cervantes, 142-45, 47-48.

Sahagun, *Historia general de las cosas de Nueva Espania, Angel Maria Garibay K.*, ed. (Mexico, 1969) 4 vols,4:27-29. Hereafter referred to as Sahagun, Tolosana.

Elizabeth Carmichael, Turquoise Masks of Mexico, (London, BMP, 1970), 25

Hernan Cortés, *Letters from Mexico*, tr. and ed. A.R. Pagden, (New York, 1971), 40-46. (Hereafter referred to as Cortés, Pagden ed.)

William Hickling Prescott, History of the Conquest of Mexico, (Modern Library, New York, n.d.), 142-43.

Torquemada, 2:66

Chapter 6

Bernal Díaz, 79-113, 56, 58, 59, 80, 115-116.

Gomara, 61-93, 87-88, 93-94.

Cervantes, 148-85, 186.

CDIAI,v 12: 225-246, v22: 38-46.

ENE 1:44-50.

H.R. Wagner, The Discovery of Yucatan by Francisco Hernandez de Cordoba, (Berkeley, 1942), 23-24.

J.H. Elliot, in Hernan Cortés, Letters from Mexico, xviii-xx.

Cortés, Pagden ed., 3-46

Cortés, Letters of Cortez, F.A., Macnutt, tr. and ed., (London, 1908), 2 vols, 1:188, 1: 194. (Hereafter cited as Cortés, MacNutt ed.)

Torquemada, 2:101

Chapter 7

Torquemada, 1:223-25, 2:93, 124-25.

Duran, HH ed. 113-117

Bernal Díaz, 90-94, 95-96, 113-115n, 116-19

——————-, Historia Verdada de la conquista de la Nueva Espania, Garcia Genaro ed, (Madrid, 1928), 300-303.

Gomara, 76-79, 95-96, 177-78

Cervantes, 24, 164-67, 170-71, 189-90

Ándres de Tapia, *Relacion hecha por el Sr. Andres de Tapia sobre la Conquista de Mexico*, in CDHM, 2:562-63. (Hereafter referred to as Ándres de Tapia)

Cortés, Pagden ed., Nigel Davies*, The Aztecs,* 248.

Cortes, MacNutt ed., 1:236-37

Chapter 8

Diego Munoz Camargo, Historia de Tlaxcala, ed. Alfredo Chavero, (Mexico, 1948), 168, 172-73. (Hereafter cited as Camargo.

Cervantes, 192-98, 199.

Chapter 9

Cervantes, 201-20, 230-31, 241.

Bernal Díaz, 123-41

Francisco de Aguilar, Relacion Breve de la conquista de Nueva Espania, (Mexico, 1977), 70-73.(Hereafter cited as Aguilar)

Ándres de Tapia, CDHM 2:567-58

Cortez, MacNutt ed., 200, 201-205.

Torquemada, 2:111-21.

Gomara, 98-107.

Camargo, 186-87n.

Bernardino Vazquez de Tapia, Relación de meritos y servicios de conquistador Bernardino de Tapia, (Mexico, 1953), 31—32. (Hereafter cited as Bernadino de Tapia

Chapter 10

Cervantes, 220-35.

Cortés, MacNutt ed., 205-209

Gomara, 108-115

Torquemada, 2:121-24,125-28

Bernal Diaz, 137-39, 141-46, 233

Chapter 11

Bernal Díaz, 163.

Cervantes, 243-44.

Bernardino Vazquez de Tapia, 33-37

Chapter 12

Camargo, 190-211

Bernal Diaz, 148-49, 155

Cervantes, 238, 249-50.

Charles Gibson, *The Aztecs Under Spanish Rule,* (Stanford, 1964), 18-19, 472n.

Torquemada, 2:129, 2:132.

Gomara, 124.

Chapter 13

Cortés, MacNutt ed., 1:220-21, 1:216-23.

Cholula, *Guia Oficial,* Jorge Gurria LaCroix ed., (Mexico, 1970)

Diego Duran, Gods and Rites, HH ed, 130, 334.

Bernal Díaz, 169-84.

Camargo, 208-10, 211-13..

Cervantes. 251-58, 262-63.

Ándres de Tapia, CDHM, 2: 573-77.

Gomara, 123-30.

Torquemada, 2:134-41.

Chapter 14

Diego Duran, Ramirez ed., 2:202-205, 2:3-31

Diego Duran, HH ed., 253-60

Cervantes, 261

Cortés, MacNutt ed., 1:223-24, 223n

Sahagun, Tolosana, 39, 40-41

Torquemada, 2:144-46

Chapter 15

Cortés, MacNutt ed., 1:222-36.

Cortes, Pagden ed., 467 n42.

Cervantes, 264-79.

Bernal Díaz, 185-96, 208.

Aguilar, 79.

Hugh Thomas, Conquest, New York, 1994), 280-85.

Gordon Willey and Jeremy Sabloff, A History of American Archaeology, (San Francisco, n.d.) 24-26

Chapter 16

Bernal Díaz, 215-231

Bernal Díaz, *Historia verdadera de la conquista*, Garcia Genaro, ed., (Mexico, 1904), 286-301, 304-307, 314-18

Miguel Leon Portillo, *The Broken Spears*, (Boston 1962) xvi

Chapter 17

Torquemada, 2:144

Sahagun, Florentine Codex, 12:45, 66

Alvarado, Hernando Tezozomoc. *Cronica mexicoyotl,* tr. Adrian Leon, (Mexico, 1949), 149-50

Duran, HH ed., 293

Quauhlehuantzin Chimalpahin,(Domingo Francisco de San Anton Muñon), *Relaciones originales de Chalco Amequemecan,* tr.from Nahuatl to Spanish, Silvia Rencon, (Mexico, 1965), Septima relación, 235.

Cortes, MacNutt ed., 1:240-41, 269, 277.

Bernal Diaz, 134, 231-33, 240-44, 257-58

Gomara, 176-78, 182-85

Ixtlilxochitl, 2:382, 384-85, 387-88

Anales de Tlatelolco, unos anales historicos de la nacion mexicana y Codice de Tlatelolco, eds., Salvador Toscano, Heinrich Berlin, and Robert Barlow, (Mexico, 1948), 62. (Hereafter cited as Anales de Tlatelolco.

Cervantes, 341-343, 345-46, 354-56, 359-60, 366-71, 375-77, 382-85, 401, 412-15

Joseph W. Whitecotton, The Zapotecs, (Norman, 1977), 10-11.

Fragmento Numero 2, Codice Ramirez, Manuscrito de siglo XVI intitulado: Relacion del origen de los indios que habitan esta Nueva Espania, segun sus historias, eds. Manuel Orozco y Berra and others, (Mexico, 1944), 185

Torquemada, 2:142-43

Andres de Tapia, CDHM 2:570,2:586

Chapter 18

Cervantes, 388-403, 440, 448-49.

Cortés, MacNutt ed., 1:273-84

Bernal Díaz, 255-94, 279-80, 271-72.

Carta de Diego Velásquez, en la que relaciona la desobediencia de Hernan Cortés y ausencia que esto hizo con al armada que puso a su cargo, (12 Octubre de 1519) (1). CDIAI, vol.12, series 1, 246-52.

Leseley Byrd Simpson, T*he Encomienda in New Spain*, (Berkeley, 1982), 39-53.

Chapter 19

Sahagun, Florentine Codex, 12:51-59, 61

————- Tolosana, 4: 46-47

Duran, Gods and Rites, HH ed. 99-100, 107, 428-29,

———-. HH ed., 297-98

Anales de Tlatelolco, 63-64

Codex Aubin, tr. Charles E. Dibble, (Madrid, 1963), 55, 56-57, 58

Cervantes, 462, 465, 469-70, 477-78, 481-82

Juan de Tovar, Relación del origen de los yndios que havitan en este Nueva Espania segun sus historias, (Graz, 1972), 80-81

Ixtlilxochitl, 2:393-94

Torquemada, 2:204, 205

Cortés, MacNutt ed., 1:285

——————— Pagden ed., 130-37

Bernal Díaz, 294, 296, 298, 299-312

C. Harvey Gardiner, Naval Power in the Conquest of Mexico, (Austin, 1956), 42

Charles Gibson, *The Aztecs Under Spanish Rule*, (Stanford, 1976) 578, 88n

G.C. Vaillent, *Aztecs of Mexico*, (Baltimore, 1970), 201

Chapter 20

Aguilar, 87-93

Cervantes, 487-505

Cortes, Pagden ed., 137-43, 156, 161

Bernal Diaz, 313-23, 335, 396-97

Sahagun, Florentine Codex, 12:65-80

Fray Bernardino de Sahagún, *Relacion de la conquista de esta Nueva Espania,* ed., Carlos Maria Bustamente (Mexico, 1938), 70-71. (Hereafter referred to as Sahagun, Enmendada)

Torquemada, 2:214, 219-30

William Hickling Prescott, *History of the Conquest of Mexico,* John Foster Kirk, ed., (Philadelphia, 1873), 3 vols, 3: 446-50

Vetancurt, Augustin de, Teatro mexicano. Descripción breve de los svcesos exemplares, historicos, politicos, militares, y religiosos del nuevo mundo occidental de las Indias.(Mexico, 1698) 2 vols., 2:112

Oviedo, 4:462

Duran, HH ed., 304-305

Bernardino Vázquez de Tapia, 109-111

Ixtlilxochitl, 2:397

Alvarado Tezozomoc, Hernando, *Cronica mexicóyotl*, Adrian Leon, tr.and ed., (Mexico, 1949), 150

Camargo, 225, 227n

De Barrios, Virginia B. "How an Aztec Gold Bar was Found." R&D Mexico, vol.2, no.1, October, 1981, 4-6.

Chapter 21

Sahagún, Florentine Codex, 12:71, 81-84

Cortes, Pagden ed., 145-46

Bernal Diaz, 327-338

Cervantes, 518-546

Chapter 22

Cortés, Second Letter, Pagden ed., 156-57, 160-211; Bernal Díaz, 335-401; Cervantes, 567-654;

C. Harvey Gardiner, *Naval Power in the Conquest of Mexico*, (Austin, 1956), 68-70, 103-104, 130-32.

Chapter 23

Anales de Tlatelolco, unos anales historicos de a nacion mexicana y Codice de Tlatelolco, Salvador Toscano, Henrich Berlin, and Robert Barlow, eds., Mexico II, 1948), 10, 66, 70, 65-73;

Sahagun, Tolosana, 59-75; Sahagun, Florentine Codex, 12: 85-116; Bernal Diaz; 398-401, 415-24, 429-444; Cortes, 5th Letter, 210-264; Cervantes, 687-88, 699, 703-705,707, 726-729;

Epilogue

Gomara, 295-96; Sahagun, Florentine Codex, 12:125-26; Duran, HH ed., 320; Charles Gibson, *The Aztecs Under Spanish Rule,* (Stanford, 1964), 32-57, 58-97, 418-20, 423-26; William H. Prescott, *History of the Conquest of Mexico,* John Foster Kirk, ed., (Philadelphia, 1873), 3 vols, 3:446-50; CDIU, XVII, 33, 46, 52, 76, 98 XVIII, 43; CDIAI VI, 64 et seq.,XXVI, 422-23,XIII, 140-41; NCDHM (1941), III, 255, III, 256;

Amado Lopez de Menesis, "Tecuichpoctzin, hija de Moctezuma (1510?-1550)," Revista de Indias, IX (1948), 475-76, 478-79, 489-94;

Ixtlilxochitl, 396; Vincente Rivas Palacio, Mexico traves de los siglos, 5 vols., (Barcelona, 1888-89), 2: 858-63; Lesely Byrd Simpson, The Encomienda in New Spain, (Berkeley, 1982), 214-29; ENE, XV, 139 et seq.; Hernan Cortes, Estampas de su Vida, Instituto de Cultura Hispanica, (Madrid, 19470, 440-41; David Wayne Powell, *Soldiers, Indians, and Silver; The Northward Advance of New Spain, 155-1600,* (Berkeley, 1952), 4-25, Lewis Hanke, The Spanish Struggle for Justice in the Conquest of America, (Boston, 1965)

Biographies

Francisco de Aguilar, the Penitent Conqueror

A common soldier who arrived in the Mexico with Cortés, Aguilar soon distinguished himself for his valor. When Cortés seized Moctezuma, he assigned Aguilar to the watch that guarded the Emperor. After the conquest, he received lands and an encomienda of Indians, and established a hostelry on the Puebla-Veracruz highway. At the age of 50, he released his Indians and gave up all is possessions and wealth to enter the Dominican Order. He was assigned to the Dominican monastery at Oaxtepec, where he served for 42 years in a self-imposed menial capacity. When he was more than 80 years old, he wrote the story of his participation in the conquest at the request of his fellow monks.

Diego Durán resided for some time at the monastery in Oaxtepec, where he met Aguilar and spoke at length with the aged monk, who was now more than 90 years old and in poor health. Durán described him as "…a most honest priest, a man who was jealous of the glory of God and of His doctrines." Save for the Cronica X, Durán relies more upon Aguilar than any other source for material relevant to the conquest.

Diego Muñoz Camargo

Camargo was a noble Tlaxcala mustee, the son of a Spaniard who arrived in the New World in 1524 with Gonzalo de Salazar. Camargo's father married Maria Maxixcatzin, who, judging from her name and the date of Camargo's birth, circa 1525, was undoubtedly the daughter of Maxixca, one of the four lords of Tlaxcala at the time of the conquest.

Educated in the Christian faith, Camargo served at least four terms as governor of Tlaxcala, and he introduced sheep herding into the Republic. Some of the words and phrases that are found in his writing indicate that he visited Spain at one time.

Camargo produced four works, the most notable being the *Historia de Tlaxcala*. The original manuscript was sent to Philip II, and was eventually published in Spain in 1870. A copy of the manuscript was published in Mexico in 1871. Neither of these publications was edited or complete. In 1892, Alfredo Chavero republished the manuscript, and Chavero's edition was reprinted in 1948.

Prescott states that the original manuscript was evidently returned to Mexico and that it was preserved in the convent of San Felipe Neri, where Torquemada had access to it. The manuscript eventually found its way into the collection of Juan Bautista Muñoz, and was deposited in the Royal Academy of History in Madrid.

Camargo's work is one of the most important sources of the social and religious institutions of the Indians at the time of the conquest. For example, he provides an intimate glance into the cult of Quetzalcoatl, which was well known in Tlaxcala due to that city's long association with Cholula, the birthplace of the cult.

Camargo's biases toward the Tlaxcalans and their Spanish allies is reflected numerous times in his work. He all but ignores the war between Tlaxcala and the Spaniards, relating but a single skirmish with the Otomies during the siege of Teocacingo.

The Codices
Codex Aubin (Codice de 1576)

A text with poems and pictures of Mexican history from the time of the departure of the tribes from Aztlan through and beyond the conquest and into the post conquest era. Tlaxcala may have been its origin.

The Aubin offers a graphic description of the Toxcatl massacre, and it alleges that the Mexicans may have been expecting Alvarado's attack. The manuscript departs from some better known sources on several key points, such as the disposal of Moctezuma's body and the unusual selection of the five unlucky days for the coronation of Cuauhtémoc by the royal council.

Codex Chimalpopoca

The manuscript, so titled by the Abbe Brasseur de Bourbourg, contains three documents from three different sources: *the Anales de Cuauhtitlán* (anonimo de 1570), the *Breve relacion de los Dioses y ritos de la gentilidad, written by Pedro Ponce*, and the *Leyenda de los Soles*. Only the first and third of these documents are relative to the text.

Anales de Cuauhtitlán

Although the manuscript was compiled in Cuauhtitlán, it contains important information about other towns in and beyond the Valley of Mexico. It begins with the story of creation; continues with the legendary history of the Toltecs and the destruction of their civilization by the Otomies; and concludes with a chronological account of Tenochtitlán, Texcoco, and Chalco. There is an increasing emphasis upon Mexico-Tenochtitlán beyond the 14th century.

The document contains lists of the tributary towns of Tenochtitlán and Texcoco, and the names of the tlatoanis of the principal towns in the area when the Spaniards arrived. It also records plagues, eclipses, and the appearance of comets.

The document is one of the foremost sources of Mexican history if used critically in the period following the 11th century. The original manuscript belonged to Fernando Alva de Ixtlilxochitl.

Leyenda de los Soles

Written in Nahuatl, the manuscript provided the most complete account available of the legend of the five suns of Aztec mythology, and how each of the first four were destroyed before the time of Moctezuma II. The descriptions of the suns corresponds in number and order to those engraved upon the Monument of the Fifth Sun, now on display in the National Museum of Anthropology in Mexico City.

The monument was carved circa 1470 during the reign of Axayácatl, and excavated in the Zocalo in 1790. The manuscript is considered to be an explanation of the various suns depicted in the paintings of a lost native codex.

Codex Florentino:

See Fray Bernardino de Sahagún

Codex Magliabecchianus

The manuscript was prepared by a scribe for Cervantes de Salazar when he was mayor of Mexico City. The document contains accounts of the gods, religious ceremonies, and the Mexican calendar in pictures and text.

Codex Mendoza

The Viceroy Antonio de Mendoza sent the document to Charles V shortly after the conquest to describe the wealth of New Spain to the King. The ship transporting the document, however, was intercepted by a French privateer and taken to Paris, where it remained until a chaplain of the British Embassy purchased it from the government. After its publication in England in 1685, the document disappeared for more than a century. It came to light again in the Bodelian

Library, and a facsimile edition was published by J.Cooper Clark (London, 1938)

The document is divided into three parts: the civil history of Mexico; tribute and tributaries; and the manners and customs of the Mexican people. The manuscript lists 400 tributary towns of Imperial Mexico and more than 50 *calpixque* (tribute collectors) in the Valley of Mexico in the period 1516-1518. Some authorities consider it to be an incomplete listing of the tributary towns of the Mexican Empire, but Charles Gibson offers the premise that it is a complete record of tribute payers during the reign of Moctezuma II.

Hernando Cortés

Hernando Cortés was born in 1485, in Medellin, a town in the province of Estremadura,. He was the son of Martín Cortés de Montroy, a captain of infantry, and Doña Catalina Pizzaro Altimarino. Although of moderate means, the family was well respected in Castile.

When he was fourteen, Hernando was sent to Salamanca to study grammar in preparation for an eventual career in law, but the young Cortés showed little interest in formal schooling, and he returned to his parent's home within two years. His time in Salamanca was not entirely wasted, however, since he learned some Latin and developed remarkable writing skills.

At age seventeen, two prospects appealed to Cortés. One was to go to Naples with Gonzalo Fernandez de Córdoba, the Great Captain, and the other to sail to the New World with Nicolas de Ovando, whom the crown was sending to succeed Columbus. He chose the latter course, but a misadventure kept him from departing with the fleet. While climbing a garden wall to keep a rendezvous with an inamorata, the wall crumbled and gave way, tumbling him down onto the pavement and burying him under the stones. Cortés's injuries were severe enough to confine him to bed until well after Ovando sailed.

Cortés departed for the New World in 1504, the year Isabella died. In Santo Domingo, Cortés received a *repartimiento* of Indians and an appointment as notary of the town of Azua, where he engaged in trade for five years. During this period, his philandering continued, and upon several occasions, resulted in affairs of honor that cost him life-long scars. For diversion from the routine life of the farm, he often took part in the ever-recurrent wars that Diego Velásquez, Ovando's lieutenant, waged against the Indians. In 1509, Diego Columbus succeeded Ovando, and in 1511, the eldest son of the Great Admiral assigned Velásquez the task of pacifying Cuba. Cortés accompanied him as clerk to the royal treasurer to keep an account of royal revenues and the King's fifth.

He began to court Catalina de Xuárez, one of three sisters who had come to Santo Domingo from Granada with their parents. He may have proposed marriage to Catalina, but if so, time passed without any indication that he intended to keep his promise. The Xuárez family pressed him for a decision, as did Diego Velásquez, who was interested in one of Catalina's sisters, and his inaction cost him the favor of the governor.

Cortés had other difficulties with Velásquez at this time. Many of the hidalgos who joined Velásquez in the conquest of Cuba felt they had been denied their just rewards with land and Indians, and Cortés's sympathy with their cause landed him in jail. It was said that Cortés had in his possession documents complaining of the governor's abuse of authority, and that he was planning to take them to the *Audiencia* in Santo Domingo.

Cortés, however, either by bribery or by skill, managed to escape from prison and take sanctuary in the church. In time he got careless, and while standing outside the church door, a constable arrested him.

One has to doubt the loyalty of the governor's constables, however, since Cortés lost no time in escaping and again took sanctuary in the church, but not until he had spoken with Juan Xuárez and agreed to marry Catalina. There followed a reconciliation between Cortés and Velázquez, evidenced by the governor's presence at his wedding.

Although Cortés lost his appointment as secretary to the treasurer, Velásquez granted him a generous *repartimiento* of Indians and in time, he was appointed mayor of St. Jago. He now devoted himself to agriculture, and raised sheep, cattle, and mares on his estate. He enjoyed some success in gold mining, and eventually gained sufficient wealth to invest 2,000 castellanos into a partnership with Andrés de Duero, Velásquez's secretary.

This was the state of affairs in Cuba when Pedro de Alvarado returned with the news of Grijalva's discoveries.

Cortés's letters to Charles V, apart from his disposition to exaggerate his military successes over vastly superior forces. Are the foundation upon which the conquest of Mexico rests. The First Letter, written at Veracruz on or about July 6, 1519, has never been found, despite intensive searches throughout Europe, although Gómara saw a copy of it. The Second Letter was written at Segura de Frontera, and dated 30 October, 1520. The letter begins with the march of the army from the seacoast on 16 August, 1519; encompasses Cortés's victories at Tlaxcala; his meeting with Moctezuma; the retreat from Tenochtitlán; and ends with the regrouping of his army in Tlaxcala. The ship taking it to Spain was lost, however, and the letter did not reach Spain until sometime in 1521.

The letter was an overnight sensation in the Spanish Court. Cortés's description of a great native empire and his evidence of certain wealth seemed to fulfill the Crown's expectations of the New World and guarantee him an ear in Court.

The Third Letter, dated 15 May, 1522, from Coyoacán, Begins with Cortés mustering his army in Tlaxcala to return to the Valley of Mexico, and ends with the fall of Tenochtitlán. The Fourth Letter, dated 15 October, 1524, from Tenochtitlán, follows Cortés's continuing subjugation of the country and his expedition to the Panuco River. The Fifth Letter, undated, deals with Cortés's expedition to Honduras and his subsequent return to Mexico.

Two excellent translations of Cortes's letters are available: Letters of Cortez, tr. and ed., F.A. McNutt (New York and London, 1908), 2 vols. and Hernan Cortés, Letters from Mexico, tr. and ed. A.R. Pagden, (New York, 1971)

There are no major differences between the two, and both authors provide notes of considerable importance. Pagden's notes offer new information for tracing Cortés's route from Veracruz to Tenochtitlan.

Francisco Cervantes de Salazar

Cervantes came to Mexico in 1551, at the age of 37, and in 1553, he was appointed to a lectureship at the newly founded University of Mexico. He took holy orders in 1555, and in 1560, he was appointed Historian of the Imperial City of Mexico and began to write the *Cronica de Nueva Espania,* the first history of the conquest written in New Spain. In 1563, he obtained an additional appointment as canon in the Cathedral of Mexico.

Cervantes's manuscript was completed in 1567 and taken to Spain by the licenciado Valderrama, who was leaving his post in the *Audiencia* to take a position in the Council of the Indies. The manuscript that Valderrama took to Spain is apparently the only known copy of Cervantes's work, since no other copy has been found, either in Spain or in the archives of Mexico.

After Cervantes's death in 1575, the manuscript reverted to his nieces, Maria Peralta and Maria Espinoso. In 1597 it was re-titled *Libro de la Nueva Espania que escribe el Dr. Cervantes*, and sold to the Council of the Indies and subsequently transferred to Antonio de Herrera, who held the post of Historian of the Indies. In 1662 Herrera returned the manuscript to the Council of the Indies with other materials provided to him for his *Historia general de las Indias Occidentales.* The manuscript evidently remained with the Council of the Indies until Don Gaspar de Guzman, the Count of Olivares, who, as a favorite of Philip V, had access to papers of the state for his work, removed it. After Guzman's death in 1645, the manuscript was again returned to the Council of the Indies. In the 18th century, it was loaned to the biographer Gonzales Barcia, who catalogued it under the title *Cronica de maestro Cervantes.* In 1723, it was transferred from Barcia's library to the private library of the King, which eventually became the Biblioteca Nacional de Madrid. At this time, possibly due to the loss of the cover pages bearing Cervantes's name and the heavy-handed notations of Herrera, the manuscript was catalogued as '*anonymous.*'

Subsequent searches for the manuscript in the 19th century proved fruitless, including that of the eminent Mexican historian Joaquin Garcia Icazbalceta. In 1912, Zelia Nutall discovered it while she was researching an unrelated project in Madrid, and in 1914, it was published in its present form by the Hispanic Society of America.

Prior to his coming to Mexico, Cervantes became friendly with Cortés, and he had frequent discussions with the Marquis about the conquest. In Mexico, Cervantes had access to a number of valuable chronicles, among them Cortés's letters and dispatches to Charles V; dispatches from the settlement at Vera Cruz; the chronicles of Alonzo de Ojeda and Ándres de Tapia, two of Cortes's officers, and the *Cronica de Nueva Espania* of Francisco Lopez de Gómara, Cortés's secretary.

Cervantes copied much of Cortés's letters dealing with the march to Tenochtitlán and the subsequent conquest of the city, as well as several parts of Gómara's *Historia*. He does cite Gómara upon occasion, but only when he chooses to disagree with him. Cervantes work, however, cannot be judged by his using a practice that was deemed acceptable by 16th century chroniclers. His work ranges far beyond that of Cortés and Gómara in scope and detail, and adds a broader perspective to the conquest with his ready access to eyewitnesses and native informants.

Among his sources were the conquistadors Diego Ordaz, who made the first ascent of Popocatepetl; Alonso de Mata, from whom he obtained a first-hand account of Narváez's defeat at Cempoala; Jeronimo Ruiz de la Mota, who provided him with the only detailed description of canal warfare during the siege of Tenochtitlán; Rodrigo Rangel, Francisco de Montaño, and Diego Hernandez.

Cervantes also may have obtained some of his material from Jeronimo de Aguilar, Cortés's interpreter, as he is the only chronicler to write so extensively about Aguilar's captivity in Yucatán. Cervantes frequently cites Motolinia, but there is no record of Motolina ever having written a history of the conquest. O'Gorman believes that Cervantes had access to a now-lost manuscript presumably written by a Franciscan friar, an eyewitness to the conquest, who later became superior of the monastery in Tacuba, and Cervantes mistakenly attributed his manuscript to Motolina. Since the document appears to have been used by Gomara, it is obviously dated prior to 1552.

Of particular interest to historians and antiquarians are Cervantes frequent citations of Alonso de Ojeda's *Memoriales*, a document that has never been found. Ojeda, fluent in Nahuatl, was Cortés's point man with the Republic of Tlaxcala, and his observations provide considerable insight into the culture and customs of these principal allies of the Spaniards.

A native scribe prepared the Codex Magliabecciano for Cervantes, which contains accounts of the gods, ceremonies, and the Mexican calendar, and Fray Alonso de Veracruz,a fellow professor at the University of Mexico, served as his consultant for Indian rites and ceremonies.

One of the enigmas surrounding the work of Cervantes lies in the fact that none of the prominent chroniclers who wrote in 16th century Mexico, contemporaries of Cervantes, mention his work or seem to be aware that a historian appointed by Mexican officials was working in their midst.

In 1615, in Decada VI of his history, Herrera states "I also saw 32 parts of manuscripts and treatises of various authors...and the Memorials of Doctor Cervantes, Dean of the Holy Church of Mexico, a diligent and learned man; which it is certain that the author who produced the *Monarquia Indiana* (Juan de Torquemada) did not see..." It is obvious, however, that Torquemada made liberal use of Cervantes's material, including many of his dialogues, which Torquemada repeated almost verbatim. A comparison of Torquemada's work with Herrera's marginal notes on Cervantes's manuscript shows that Torquemada's access was via Herrera.

The Cronica X

Juan de Tovar, the Codex Ramirez, Diego Duran, and Alvarado, Tezozomoc, Hernando

Cronica X is the name given by Robert Barlow to a long-lost history of Mexico that was written by natives of Tlatelolco shortly after the conquest. The book was written in Nahuatl and illustrated with a series of native paintings.

Alfonso Caso, by correlating dates in Duran's *Historia de las Indias de Nueva Espania y islas de tierra firme* and the dates of the feast of Toxcatl given in the Codex Ramirez with the Julian Calendar, which was in effect when Duran's History was written, concludes that the Cronica X was written between AD 1536 and 1539.

The document traces the history of the Mexican people from the time of their migration from their legendary home in Aztlan to the siege of Tenochtitlán. It has served as a primary source for five 16th century historians-Duran, José de Acosta, Torquemada, Tovar, and Tezozomoc.

Juan de Tovar was the mestizo son of the conquistador Juan de Tovar, who participated in the campaigns of Mexico, Michoacán, Colima, and Oaxaca. He was born in Texcoco in 1541, ordained in the Jesuit Order and later appointed prebendary of the Cathedral in Mexico City. He was fluent in Nahuatl, Otomi, and Mazahua, and taught at the native colleges in Tepozotlan and San Gregorio de Mexico.

The Viceroy Don Martín Enríquez commissioned Tovar to write a history of the Mexicans based upon a collection of native documents and drawings he had assembled for that purpose. Tovar completed the manuscript about 1568, but it was lost when it was taken to Spain, and has never been recovered. Tovar then set about the task of rewriting his chronicle in a manner best described in his own words.

I made a very complete history, which, being finished, I took to the same Dr. Portillo, promising to make two copies of (the) very rich pictures, one for the King, and the other for us. Upon this occasion, he (Dr. Portillo) went to Spain, and he was never able to fulfill his promise, nor (could we) recover the *Historia*, but then as investigated and tried much later, there remained much in my memory, the rest of which I saw in a book that was written by a Dominican friar, my kinsman (Duran) which was most in accordance with the ancient libreria that I saw, which aided me in refreshing my memory to finish this *Historia*, which V.R.has now read.

Tovar's second work, *Relación del origen de los Yndios*, was completed about 1580, and a copy loaned to Jose de Acosta, which was his source for Lib. VII of his *Historia natural y moral de las Indias,* although he fails to credit Tovar.

Tovar's work was not published until the 19th century, when two distinct printings were made from manuscripts he found in different places. The first printing was made from a manuscript purchased by Sir Thomas Phillips in 1836, who published a portion of it in his private press, which is known as *Tovar de Phillips.*

In 1856, José Ramirez discovered a manuscript in the library of the friary of San Francisco in Mexico, which used the same source material as Duran in his *Historia,* but in considerable less detail. Ramirez concluded that the manuscript was a translation of the same document used by Duran and Acosta as their source. Manuel Orozco y Berra published the manuscript in 1878 as the Codex Ramirez.

In 1879 the Swiss anthropologist Adolf Bandalier compared the Codex Ramirez with Tovar's manuscript, and he came to the conclusion that both were the work of the same author. But when Robert Barlow compared the two, he came to the conclusion that they were not only written by the same author, but that they were the same work. The differences between the two were "no more than the sporadic differences that one may be accustomed to notice between two different copies of any manuscript." Barlow concluded that the copy of Tovar's manuscript published by Phillips and the Codex Ramirez can be considered short versions of Duran's Historia… "with an occasional fact, perhaps taken from another source."

The Tovar manuscript and the Codex Ramirez are, however, of limited use for the period of the conquest, and Tovar's account of the coming of the Spaniards is copied from Sahagún. Tovar's manuscript was later obtained by the John Carter Brown Library in Providence, Rhode Island.

The scope and content of the Cronica X, however, is best seen in Duran's *Historia* and Tezozomoc's *Cronica Mexicana.*

Information about the life of Diego Duran is sketchy at best. He was born in Seville about 1537, presumably of common parentage. He came to New Spain as a small child, and resided in Texcoco until he was about 12 years old, at which time he moved to Mexico City.

His formal schooling in Mexico is unknown. At the age of 19, he became a novice in the Monastery of Santo Domingo in Mexico City, and he was ordained in 1559. He resided for a number of years in a number of monasteries in what is now the State of Morelos. For a time, he resided in the Dominican Monastery at Oaxtepec, where he met Fray Francisco de Aguilar, the Penitent Conqueror, who was now more than 90 years old and in poor health. Aguilar provided Duran with a wealth of detail about the conquest.

A prodigious worker and a prolific writer, Duran produced three known works, *The Book of the Gods and Rites, The Ancient Calendar,* and the *History of the Indies of New Spain*, which relates the history of the Aztecs from the 9th century until the fall of Tenochtitlán. His sources were native informants, written and pictographic material, and the Cronica X. He finished his Historia in 1581, at which time he wrote that he planned another work, but whether it was written and lost in the archives of some monastery, or never written at all, is a matter of conjecture. Horcasitas and Heyden (43-44) postulate that it may have been a critical commentary, based upon material obviously censored in Duran's original manuscript, such as the invasion of Moctezuma's harem by the Spaniards, and the execution of Cuauhtémoc. Since Duran's activities from 1581 to 1585 are not known, he may well have been engaged in such a project. Duran died in 1588.

Don José Fernando Ramirez discovered Duran's manuscript of the *Historia* in the National Library of Madrid, and ordered an exact copy of it made in 1854. The first publication of the *Historia de las Indias de Nueva Espania y islas de tierra firme* appeared in 1867, which contained Duran's text up to chapter 68, which precedes the coming of the Spaniards. The remainder of Duran's manuscript was eventually found by Alfredo Chavero, rotting away in a moldy storehouse in the College of Mines, where it had been preserved with other valuables during the last years of Maximilian's rule. Chavero published the remainder of Duran's chronicle in 1880.

Fernando Alvarado Tezozomoc was born sometime between 1525 and 1530, the son of Diego Huantzin (Panitzin), a nephew of Moctezuma and Francisca Moctezuma, a daughter of Moctezuma. By virtue of his royal birth, he had access to documents rescued from the sack of Tenochtitlán. His two known works are the Cronica Mexicóyotl, which was written in Nahuatl, and the Cronica Mexicana, written in Spanish in 1598 and based upon the Cronica X.

The Cronica Mexicana is quite possibly the most faithful reproduction of the material contained in the Cronica X, and Tezozomoc's style is far more dramatic that either Duran's Historia or the Codex Ramirez.

The Cronica Mexicana ends with the entry of the Spaniards in Tlaxcala, and in the last sentence of the final chapter, Tezozomoc states.

"He, Moctezuma, convened the chieftains of his territories to reach and agreement, as will be told later, in another book."

Unfortunately, no other manuscript of Tezozomoc's work has ever been found, and most Mexicanists believe that it was never written.

Fray Francisco López de Gómara

Gómara was born in Old Castile, in the province of Soria, in 1511. After ten years of residence in Italy, Gómara joined the expedition fof Charles V to Algiers, where he met Cortés. Cortés joined the expedition in 1541 as a volunteer, and barely escaped when he was shipwrecked on the Mediterranean coast.

After the Algiers fiasco, Gómara entered Cortés's service as his secretary and chaplain, and remained with the Marquis until his death in 1547. Gómara retired to Valladolid, and spent the next five years completing his history of the conquest.

The first edition of the *Istoria de la conquista de Nueva Espana*, was published in Medina in 1552, and was promptly suppressed by Prince Philip; perhaps due to the contrast between Gómara's heroic treatment of Cortés and his irreverent treatment of Charles V; perhaps by Bartolome de Las Casas, a bitter enemy who had the Crown's ear. Censorship of Gómara's work, however, did not keep it from either Bernal Díaz or Cervantes de Salazar, who had access to his work before 1560.

Other than Cortés's Cartas and Motolinea's Memoriales, Gómara makes no mention of any other sources. He does mention a conversation with Ándres de Tapia, but it is not known if he met with other eyewitnesses returning to Spain.

Gómara's style was crisp and clear, a welcome departure from the rambling and confusing style of contemporary historians. His accounts of the events of the conquest were well organized, although overly brief in many cases. Cortés's letters to Charles V and the eyewitness accounts of Bernal Díaz, Ándres de Tapia, and Francisco de Aguilar confirms his exacting chronology.

No historian of the conquest has been deprecated and decried as much as Gómara, yet none has been more plagiarized and quoted by his contemporaries, including some of his severest critics, such as Antonio de Solis and Juan Bautista Muñoz.

Gómara's history was translated into English from the edition published by Joaquin Ramirez Cabañas by Lesley Byrd Simpson in 1966. Simpson edited Gómara's work by abbreviating the chapter headings and repeating the antecedents of relative pronouns that were often lost in his lengthy sentences. Simpson also eliminated chapters 200-248, in which Gómara interrupts the narrative of the conquest with Motolinia's account of Mexican religion and society.

Fernando de Alva Ixtlilxochitl

Ixtlilxochitl was a descendant of the principal wife of Nezahualpilli, and held the post of interpreter to the Viceroy due to his fluency in Spanish and Nahuatl and his knowledge of the ancient hieroglyphics. In the early 17th century, he was appointed governor of Tlalmanalco and Texcoco.

His noble heritage gave him access to persons of the highest station in Mexico, who made their large collections of Indian manuscripts and paintings available to him. He had his own extensive library, and used aged people who had known the conquerors and the conquered as informants. Although Ixtlilxochitl's works were primarily historical, they included songs and traditions of the Acolhuaque.

The authenticity of his historical works were certified in 1608 by officials of the Province of Otumba, who provided written testimonials that they were in agreement with their ancient records. His manuscripts were discovered by the Abbe Francisco Javier Clavijero in the Jesuit Library of Mexico City at the end of the 18th century.

Ixtlilxochitl's faults as a historian lie in his reaching conclusions that border on the improbable and his exaggeration of the contributions of Texcoco and Ixtlilxochitl, his namesake, to the conquest of Mexico.

Fray Bernardino de Sahagún

Sahagún's Historia *general de las cosas de Nueva Espania* consists of 12 books, the first 11 of which give an extensive picture of Mexican religion, philosophy, and social order prior to the Spanish conquest. The 12th book relates the conquest from the Mexican viewpoint. Sahagún's *Historia,* however, has a history of its own, a history of political and religious problems that plagued this exceptional scholar's work for the greater part of his life. A brief portion of Sahagún's works is given here to keep citations in the text in proper perspective.

Sahagún was born about 1499 in León, and after taking his vows in the Franciscan Order, came to the New World in 1529. After spending a number of years in convents, he was appointed to a lectureship at the College of Santa Cruz in Tlatelolco, a Franciscan institution devoted to teaching Latin, logic, philosophy, and theology to sons of the Mexican elite and ruling classes. His work was primarily linguistic, but in 1547, his *Historia* began to take shape, beginning with Book 6, *Rhetoric and Moral Philosophy.*

An exacting chronicler, Sahagún made a systematic use of native informants. His methodology consisted of submitting questions to natives who spoke only Nahuatl, and they in turn gave their answers in the form of hieroglyphic paintings. He then submitted their paintings to his students at the College of Santa Cruz. After consulting among themselves, they presented Sahagún with a written text of the paintings. Much of his source material was gathered from upper class Indians in an Acolhuacan town on the east side of the Valley of Mexico and from the pochteca (merchant) class in Tlatelolco. His access to the priestly class, however, was limited. After collecting substantial information from his sources, he took the material to Tepepulco, a non-merchant town, to verify and amend it.

Sahagún's liberal views eventually led to disciplinary action from the Franciscans-his stipend was withdrawn and his copyists dismissed.

Sahagún then took it upon himself to sent an abstract of his work in May of 1570 to Juan de Ovando the President of the Council of the Indies. The Franciscan Provincial, Alonso de Escalona, interpreted his action as insubordination and retaliated by distributing his manuscripts among various convents in the province.

Ovando received Sahagún's abstract in 1571, at a time when he was engaged in gathering historical and geographic data on the Indies, and he directed the Archbishop Pedro Moya de Contreras to provide a history of Mexico. The Archbishop, aware of Sahagún's work, believed that it would satisfy Ovando. He directed Fray Rodrigo de Sequera, the General Commissary of the Franciscan Order in New Spain, to commission Sahagún to produce his manuscript in Spanish and Nahuatl.

Sahagún finished the manuscript in 1576-77 and gave it to Sequera, who presented it to the Viceroy Don Mártin Enríquez for transmittal to Spain. Unfortunately, Ovando died in 1575, and by the time that Sahagún's manuscript was finished, the political and religious climate in Spain had changed. The Council of the Indies and the Holy Office of the Inquisition condemned all works by missionaries as being heretical and dangerous to the true conversion of the Indians, and a *cedula* was issued that all Sahagún's works were to be sent to Spain.

Sahagún wrote to the Council that it was his understanding that his manuscript had been sent to Spain on the 1578 *flota,* but foolishly added that if it did not arrive, to advise him, so that it could be copied again, revealing that he possessed copies. The Council was duly angered now, and issued another *cedula* ordering Enríquez "to take what was left so that no draft remains." The 1576-77 manuscript never arrived in Spain, and no trace of it was ever found. But for some unknown reason, the order of the Council was never carried out.

Sequera, meanwhile had been appointed censor for the Holy Office in Mexico, and he actively encouraged Sahagún to prepare a second copy of the *Historia general,* which was completed circa 1579, and taken to Spain by Sequera in 1580. The manuscript eventually found its way to the Biblioteca Medicea-Laurenziana in Florence, where it is now retained in the Palatina Collection as MS 218-20.

This manuscript was first described in the catalogue of Angelo Maria Bandini, published in 1793. It was Joaquin Garcia Icazbalceta who named the manuscript the *Florentine Codex* in his Bibliografia Mexicana de siglo XVI, published in 1886.

The Florentine Codex is the most extensive version of Sahagún's *Historia* general extant: the text is written in both Nahuatl and Spanish, and it contains approximately 1850 illustrations. It was translated from the Nahuatl language into English by Charles E Dibble and Arthur J.O. Anderson, and first published in 1950 with black and white illustrations. There is a microfilm copy of the *Florentine Codex* in the Library of Congress for reference use.

The *Tolosana*, which derives its name from the convent of Tolosa, where it was found, contains the Spanish text of the *Historia general.* The origin of the manuscript is not known, but Charles Dibble and Howard Cline consider it to be a contemporary or near-contemporary copy of the Spanish text of the *Florentine Codex.*[i]

The *Tolosana* has various presentations in style, and contains both additions and omissions with respect to the *Florentine Codex*. It does not bear Sahagún's signature. In 1783, Juan Bautista Muñoz transferred the manuscript to Madrid, where it is kept today in the Biblioteca de la Real Academia de la Historia, and is identified as A77, Colección de Muñoz, 50.9-4812. It contains 683 pages and one illustration.

In 1585, Sahagún was motivated to write another version of Book 12 of the *Historia general*, which deals with the conquest and is sometimes called the *Enmendada*. He gives his reasons for rewriting his account of the conquest in the prologue.

"When I wrote the 12 books of the history of New Spain in this town of Tlatilulco, (Which our lord King Philip sent for, which he has there), the ninth book[ii] was written about the conquest of this land. When this manuscript was written, (now more than 30 years ago), everything was written in the Mexican language, and afterwards everything was translated into Spanish. Those who helped me were old chieftains, and very knowledgeable in all things equally of idolatry as well as of the government, and the functions of it, and they were also present in the war when this city was conquered.

In the ninth book where this conquest was discussed, several errors were made, and it happened that some things were put in, and others were left out. For this reason, in this year 1585 I corrected this book, and for this reason it is written in three columns. The first is in the Indian language in this manner, unpolished as they pronounce it, and it is written so in the other books. The second column is a correction of the first as in terms as in sentences. The third column is in Spanish, obtained according to the corrections in the second column..."

The Enmendada was taken to Spain by Juan Francisco Montemayor y Cuenca, the president of the *Audencia,* where it eventually passed into the hands of Augustin de Vetancurt. During the French invasion of Madrid in 1808, a copy of the manuscript was stolen from the Biblioteca de la Academia Historia, which was later purchased by he Count of Cortina in 1828 and loaned to Bustamante, who published it for the only time in 1840.

The original manuscript, with its bilingual text, is lost. The copy used by Bustamente was returned to Spain, and as late as 1935 was in the hands of a Barcelona bookseller. In 1968,a copy was either lost or sold to an unknown person. A copy was made for Prescott while it was in Mexico, and is now in the Boston Public Library.

Bernardino Vázquez de Tapia

Vázquez was the son of a prominent Oropesa family, who, after the death of his parents, was raised by his uncles, Pedro Vázquez, a professor in the University of Salamanca, and the Inquisitor Francisco Alvarez, the Bishop of Toro.

Vázquez left Spain in 1514 with the Pedrarias Davila expedition to the Castillo del Oro, where he stayed for two and a half years before moving to Cuba. In Cuba, he entered the service of the governor Diego Velázquez, and was eventually granted land and an *encomienda* by the governor.

In 1518, he joined the Grijalva expedition to Mexico as the *Alferez General,* and in 1519, he sailed once more to Mexico with Cortés., who appointed him king's agent, charged with overseeing the financial interest of the Crown.

After the conquest, Vázquez held a number of important posts in Mexico City, and was awarded one of the largest encomiendas in the Valley Of Mexico. When the *Juez de Residencia* was convened in 1526 to investigate charges brought against Cortés, Vázquez was summoned to appear as a witness. In the course of the inquiry, whose proceedings were secret, Vázquez testified that Cortés precipitated the massacre at Cholula for insufficient reason, and criticized his former captain for allowing Alvarado to go unpunished for ordering the massacre at Toxcatl. Vázquez freely admitted that he had participated in the Toxcatl massacre, offering as his only excuse that he was forced to obey the orders of his superior. Some 18 years later, at a time when Cortés enjoyed the favor of the Crown, he revised his account of the Cholula massacre in a manner more favorable to Cortés.

Vázquez was assigned to carry the proceedings of the *Residencia* to Spain, and while passing through Seville, was unfortunate enough to encounter Cortés, who had him jailed, ostensibly as a debtor, for he owed the Marquis a large sum of money, but more likely for his participation in the *Residencia.*

Vázquez's *Relación de meritos y servicios de conquistador Bernardino Vázquez de Tapia* was written about 1544, and addressed to the Crown in response to the New Laws, issued by Charles V in 1542. Influenced heavily by Bartolome de las Casas, the Emperor disregarded the advice of his council and issued the New Laws, which limited or revoked the right of the encomenderos to the services of Indians, who were to be placed under the jurisdiction of the Crown and administered by royal appointees. The New Laws led to a rebellion in Peru, in which the Viceroy was killed, and a near-revolt in Mexico. The New Laws particularly enraged the conquistadors, since many held large encomiendas and large numbers of Indians without proper title, and felt that the Crown acted unjustly in view of their contributions to the pacification of the New World. As a result many of the conquistadors wrote letters to the Crown to justify their exclusion from the New Laws.

Fortunately for history, Vázquez did not limit his Relación to his own efforts, but provided an independent eyewitness account of the conquest.

Vázquez's *Relación* was first published in 1939 by D. Manuel Terreros.

Anales de Tlatelolco

Anales de Tlatelolco, unos anales historicos de la nación mexicana y Codice de Tlatelolco. (Manuscript 22, National Library, Paris.)

The document is the oldest historical narrative written by Mexicans in Nahuatl with Latin characters, in which the authors express themselves free of Hispanic influence. Written probably 1524-28, perhaps by Pablo Nazareo, a nephew of Moctezuma, it is a collection of five independent documents.

Document I. A register of the kings of Tlatelolco

> 1. The pre-Cortesian history of Tlatelolco from lost paintings.

> 2. Reminisces of Cortes's expedition to Honduras. The execution of Cuauhtémoc and the subsequent fate of Temilotl and Ecatl, the ranking generals of Tlatelolco.

Document II. A register of the kings of Tenochtitlán.

> Rulers from the time of the Tepanec governors to the rule of Moctezuma II.

Document III. A genealogy of the kings of Azcapotzalco.

Document IV. Supplement to the kings of Azcaptzalco.

Document V. The history of Tlatelolco from its earliest origins; from the migration of the original tribe from Aztlan to the conquest of Mexico.

The material of principal interest to this book are the sections of Document V that deal with the arrival of the Spaniards and the siege of Tenochtitlán, and part 2 of Document I, which deals with the execution of Cuauhtémoc.[iii]

The Spanish version used in the text is 'Unos Anales Historica de la nación Mexicana. Edited and commented by Heinrich Berlin', in

Fuentes para la Historia, no.2 (Antigua Libreria Robredo, Mexico, 1948)

Bernal Díaz de Castillo

Bernal Díaz was born of middle class parents in Medina del Campo, Castille, in 1492. In 1514, he accompanied Pedro Arias de Ávila, the governor of Tierra Firma, on his expedition to Panama. He remained in Nombre de Dios for three or four months, but when an epidemic broke out among the soldiers and a dispute arose between Ávila and Balboa, one that would cost Balboa his life, Díaz set sail for Cuba to join his kinsman, Diego Velásquez.

After three years of inactivity in Cuba, Díaz joined Fernando de Córdoba's ill-fated expedition to the islands off the coast of Honduras, now known as the Islas de Bahia. Córdoba's three ships were driven off course by a storm, and after 23 days at sea, they came upon the coast of Yucatán. Despite the disastrous experiences of the Córdoba expedition, the meager amount of gold and treasure brought back by the survivors provided the stimulus for the Grijalva expedition, and Díaz joined for a second voyage to Mexico.

In 1519, he sailed once more for Mexico with Cortés. During the course of the conquest, Diaz engaged in 119 skirmishes and battles, and he suffered numerous wounds, one quite serious. He narrowly avoided capture several times, and he shared all the hardships, hunger, and other privations of the army from the time it debarked until the final victory in Tenochtitlán. After the conquest, he took part in Cortes's ill-fated march to Honduras, where he witnessed the execution of Cuauhtémoc, the last Emperor of Mexico.

Díaz was granted an encomienda in Guatemala for his participation in the conquest, where he lived from 1541 until his death in 1584. He wrote the *Historia veradadera de la conquista de la Nueva Espania* during *the* 1560's and at some point in his effort, he came across Francisco López de Gomara's *Istoria de la conquista de Mexico*. Affronted by Gomara's lionization of Cortés and his neglect of others that played prominent roles in the conquest, he set about setting the record straight, so to speak.[iv]

Díaz's manuscript has remained in Guatemala in the archives of the Municipality of the Capital from the time he wrote it until the present day. In the 16th century, a copy was sent to Philip II, and the friar Alonso Remon published it in Madrid in 1632. In the 19th century, Francisco Antonio de Fuentes y Guzman, the great-grandson of Bernal Díaz, who had he manuscript in his possession, pointed out that Remon's differed from the original in several aspects. Remon made several alterations in his text to exaggerate the role of Father Olmedo, Cortés's confessor, and the other friars of the Order of Mercy, to which Remon belonged, who took part in the conquest.

It was not until 1895 that a photographic copy of the manuscript left Guatemala, when it was sent to Mexico as a gift. The gift was conditional upon a promise that it would not be reproduced or printed. In 1901, however, Garcia Genaro appealed to Manuel Estrada Cabrera, the President of Guatemala, for permission to print the original manuscript, which Cabrera readily granted. In 1908, the Haklyut Society published A.P. Maudslay's English translation of the *True History of the Conquest of New Spain* from Genaro's copy.

Antonio de Herrera and Juan de Torquemada had access to the manuscript in the 16th century.

Chimalpahin Quauhtlehuantzin (Domingo Francisco de San Anton Muñon, 1579 circa 1660)

Chimalpahin was a prominent noble of the province of Chalco, a direct descendant of the ruling family of Amecameca at the time of the conquest. While very young, Chimalpahin was enrolled in the convent of San Antonio Abad, in Mexico City, for his education.

He began his chronicle in 1620, at the age of 41, at the request of the governor of Amecameca, and his father, a court clerk, in response to an order from the Viceroy Mendoza to compile native histories of the provinces.

There are eight separate chronicles in his *Relaciones*, each of which appears to be independent-not because of the subject material, which is often repeated from one chronicle to the next, but because Chimalpahin used different sources for each. He developed his *Relaciones* from individuals who were intimate with the Chalco nobility and knowledgeable about the antiquities in the area. His work is more a history of an elite class of pre-Cortesian society than that of the conflicts between Chalco and Tenochtitlán.

Fray Diego Durán

Diego Durán came to the New World as a child circa 1542, and spent his childhood in Texcoco, the center of Aztec culture in pre-Conquest years. In 1556, at age 19, he entered the Dominican Order and served in the monastery of Santo Dominic in Mexico City until 1561, when he was transferred to Oaxaca.

Fluent in Nahuatl and well versed in Aztec culture from his early years in Texcoco, he began his massive work in Oaxaca about 1574 and finished *the Historia de Las Indias de Nueva España e Islas de la Tierra Firma* in 1581. After that date, the manuscript was not seen again until the 19th century.

The historian José Fernando Ramírez discovered the manuscript in the National Library of Madrid, and ordered an exact copy made in 1854. It was not until 1867, however, when the first part of Duran's *Historia* was published. The remainder of the manuscript and the plates were never published and considered lost.

Alfredo Chavero, who published the entire manuscript, which included the Rites and the Calendar, found them some years later in an old storehouse of the College of Mines.

The first part of the Historia is Duran's interpretation of the Cronica X. In the second part, Rites and the Calendar, Durán, portrays an incomparable picture of Aztec life and religion in pre-Conquest years. The text is illustrated by 127 color drawings.

Gonzalo Fernández de Oviedo y Valdez

Oviedo was born in the province of Asturias in 1478, and at an early age was introduced to the Spanish Court and appointed page to Prince Juan, the only son of Ferdinand and Isabella. Upon the prince's premature death, he accepted a post with King Frederick of Naples. After a brief period of service in Italy, he returned to Spain and accepted a commission as keeper of the royal jewels.

In 1513, Ferdinand appointed Oviedo as inspector of the gold foundries in the New World, and he journeyed to Panama, where he received an appointment as notary to Pedrarias (Pedro Arias de Ávila), the governor of Darien.

In 1526, Oviedo published his *Summario de la natural historia de las Indias,* a study of the climate, the geography, the people, and the flora of the New World.

In 1535, Charles V appointed him *alcaide* of the fortress of Santo Domingo in Hispaniola. In this strategic location, the crossroads of all traffic between the New World and Spain, Oviedo spent the next ten years interviewing every prominent Spaniard who passed through the port and any others who had a story to tell.

Oviedo completed the first volume of his *Historia general y natural de las Indias* in 1535, shortly after he took his post in Santo Domingo. In 1536, he returned to Spain to prepare his *Historia* for the press, and was honored by the Crown with an appointment of Chronicler of the Indies. He died in 1547, at the age of 79, before he could finish his work.

The *Historia general* is divided into three parts and contains 50 books. The first part, containing 19 books, expands upon the subject matter of the Summario and adds a narrative of the discoveries and conquests of the islands. The other two parts deal with the conquest of Mexico, Peru, and other countries of South America.

Upon Oviedo's death, his manuscript was sent to the Casa de Contratación in Seville, and sometime later, found its way to the Dominican monastery of Monserrat. It was discovered in 1775 by Francisco Cerda y Rico, an officer in the Indian Department, who supervised its preparation for publication.

Oviedo also wrote a six-volume work in which he devised dialogues between the most eminent Spaniards of his time.

Juan de Torquemada

Torquemada came to the New World as a small child about the middle of the 16th century, and grew up in Mexico City. He took his vows in the Franciscan Order sometime between 1579 and 1583, and served in the Convent of Santiago in Tlatelolco from 1604 to 1611. At one time he may have been a student of Sahagún, and like Sahagún, he was responsible for the instruction of upper class Indian youths in the Colegio de Santa Cruz. During his tenure at the institution, however, it was not the first class school that it had once been.

Torquemada spent 50 years gathering material for the Monarquia Indiana, which was first published in Seville in 1615. It includes in its scope Mexican religion, the calendar, geography, conversion of the Indians, the missionaries, the conquest, and a pre-Cortesian history of Mexico. Torquemada's sources were more extensive of any other chronicler of the 16th century, which included conquistadors, native documents and paintings, early missionaries, and Indian informants. He had access to the chronicles of Bernal Díaz, Camargo, Hererra, and Sahagún, whose work, at least upon one occasion, he was able to examine before it was sent to Spain, Among the native documents he had access to were the Cronica X, and the Anales de Tlatelolco.

Much of his account of the conquest originates in the work of other historians, such as Herrera, Sahagún, Díaz, and Camargo, but it is Cervantes, via Hererra's heavy-handed use of Cervante's manuscript, which he depends upon most often for the chronology of and major events of the conquest. Torquemada does, however, add a significant amount of original material from native sources that are found in not other account of the conquest, including dialogues such as those spoken by the ruling lords of the royal council as they attempt to deal with the Spanish invasion.

---

[i] Howard F. Cline, "Sahagún and His Works. HMAI, 4:199. Cline states that the *Tolosana* may have been prepared under Sahagun's supervision or copied from an intermediate original of the *Florentine* Codex.

[ii] The account of the conquest was originally Book 9 of the *Historia general*.

[iii] Jorge La Croix, 20-22, makes a strong case that the Mexican general Ecatl contributed to the Anales de Tlatelolco either as an author or an informant.

[iv] From the notes of William Hickling Prescott, *The Conquest of Mexico*:

The two pillars, on which the story of the conquest mainly rests, are the Chronicles of Gomara and Bernal Diaz, two individuals having as little resemblance to each other as the courtly and cultivated churchman has to the unlettered soldier.

...Even in his relation to Cortés, while he endeavors to adjust the true balance between his pretentions and those of his followers, and while he freely exposes his cunning or cupidity, and sometimes cruelty, he does ample justice to his great and heroic qualities.

Bibliography

Acosta, José de, S.J. *Historia natural y moral de las Indias,* Edmund O'Gorman, ed., Mexico City: Fondo de Cultura Economica, 1962.

Adams, Richard W.W. *Prehistoric America,* Boston: Little Brown & Co., 1977.

Aguilar, Francisco de. *Relación breve de la conquista de Nueva Espania.* Mexico City: Universidad Naciónal Autonoma de Mexico, 1977.

Alcocer, Igacio. "Apuntes sobre la antigua Mexico-Tenochtitlan." Tacubaya: Instituto panamericano de geografia e historia, (19350, 14.

Alvarado Tezozomoc, Hernando. *Cronica mexicana escrita hacia el ano de 1598.* Manuel Orozco y Berra, ed, Mexico City: Editorial Leyenda, 1944.

———————— *Cronica mexicóyotl.* Adrian León, trans. and ed. Mexico City, Imprenta Universitaria, 1949.

Anales de Cuauhtitlán, Published in the Codice Chimalpopoca, 3-118.

Anales de Tlatelolco, unos anales historicos de la nación mexicana y Codice de Tlatelolco. Salvador Toscano, Heinrich Berlin, and Robert H. Barlow, eds. Mexico City: Fuentes para la historia de Mexico, II, 1948.

Anonymous Conqueror, Narrative of Some Things of New Spain, trans. M.H. Saville, New York: 1917.

Aubin, J.M.A. Histoire de la nation mexicaine despues le depart d'Aztlan jusqu' a l' arrive de conquerants espanols. Paris: 1893.

Bakewell, Peter. Silver mining and Society in Colonial Mexico. Zacatecas, 1546-1700. Cambridge: 1971.

Ballentine, Douglass K. *Ally of Cortes, by Fernando de Alva Ixtlilxochitl.* El Paso: Texas Western Press, 1969

Bancroft, Hubert Howe, *History of Mexico.* 6 vols. San Francisco: 1886-88. Works IX-XIV.

Bandelier, Adolph. "On the Art of War and Mode of Warfare of the Ancient Mexicans," in Tenth Annual Report of the Peabody Museum of Archaeology and Ethnology, vol 2, 95-161. Cambridge:1887.

Bandelier, Fanny. A History of Ancient Mexico by Fray Bernardino de Sahagun. Nashville: Fisk University Press, 1932.

Barlow, Robert H. "Dos documentos de principios de siglo XVII, referentes a Tlatelolco," in Memorias de la Academia mexicana de la historia, IV, 101-110, 1945.

——————- "La Cronica 'X,' "Revista mexicana de estudios antropologicos," VII, 65-87, 1945.

——————- "Los caciques precortesianos de Tlatelolco en el Codice Garcia Granados (Techialoyen Q)," *Memorias de la Academia mexicana de la historia,* IV, 467-83, 1945.

——————- "Some remarks on the Term 'Aztec Empire, '*The Americas,* I, 345-49, 1944-49, 1944-45.

——————- *The Extent of the Empire of the Culhua Mexica.* Berkeley and Los Angeles: 1949. Ibero-Americana:28.

Beyer, Herman, Volume I of *Beyer's Complete* Works, tr. Carmen Cook de Leonard, in *El Mexico Antiguo,* vol. X, Mexico:1945.

Boturini Benaduci, Lorenzo. Catalogo del museo historica indiano del cavallero Lorenzo Boturini Benaduci. Madrid: Bound with Idea de una nueva historia general de la America septentrional.

Braden, C.S. Religious Aspects of the Conquest of Mexico. Durham: 1930.

Broda, Johanna, Carrasco, Davíd, and Moctezuma, Eduardo Matos, The Great Temple of Tenochtitlan, Berkeley, Los Angeles, London: 1987.

Brundage, B.C. *The Jade Steps: A Ritual Life of the Aztecs*. Salt Lake City: University of Utah Press, 1985.

Burland, Cotti A. *Montezuma*. New York: 1973.

Camargo, Diego Muñoz. *Historia de Tlaxcala,* ed. Alfredo Chavero. Mexico: 1948

Carmichael, Elizabeth. *Turquoise Mosaics of Mexico*. London: BMP 1970.

Caso, Alfonso. *El Pueblo de Sol*. Fondo de Cultura Economica. Mexico: 1954.

——————— *The Aztecs,People of the Sun*. Trans. Lowell Dunham. Norman: 1955.

Cervantes de Salazar, Francisco. *Cronica de la Nueva Espania.* Madrid: 1914.

Chavero, Alfredo. "Historia antigua y de la conquista." *Mexico a traves de los siglos,* vol.1. Vincente Riva Palacio, ed. Barcelona: Espasa y Compania, 1888.

——————— Pinturas jeroglificas. 2 vols. Mexico: 1901.

Chimalpahin, Quauhlehuantzin (Domingo Francisco de San Anton Muñon), *Relaciones originales de Chalco Amequemecan,* tr.from Nahuatl to Spanish, Silvia Rendon, Mexico, 1965.

Clavigero, Francisco Javier. *Historia de Mexico*, 4 vols. Mexico: Coleccion de escritores mexicanoa, 7-10, 1945.

Cline, Howard F. "Sahagún and His Works," HMAI, 4:199

———————- *Conquest of New Spain:1585 revision/by Bernardino de Sahagún*; reproductions of the Boston Library and Carlos Maria de Bustamante 1840 edition; translated by Howard F. Cline; edited with an introduction and notes by S.L Cline.

Coe, Michael. *Mexico*. Thames and Hudson, New York: 1999.

Codex Aubin. (Codice de 1576) Trans.from Nahuatl into Spanish by Charles E. Dibble. Madrid: Ediciones Jose Porrua Turazas, 1963.

Codex Boturini. See Tira de la Peregrinación.

Codex Florentino. See Sahagún, Bernardino de.

Codex.Magliabeccianus XIII.3. Florence Edition, the Duc de Loubat. Rome: 1904

Codex Magliabecchiano: The Lost Prototype of the Magliabecciano Group. Elizabeth Hill Boone. Berkeley, Los Angeles, London: 1983.

Codex Mendoza. 3 vols. Trans.and ed. James Cooper Clark, London: 1938. See also El Codice Mendecino y la economia de Tenochtitlán

Codex Telleriano-Remensis. Manuscrit mexicain de cabinet de Ch.-M. Le Tellier, archeveque de Reims a la Bibliotheque national (M.S.Mexicain No.385). Paris: E.-T. Hamy,ed., 1889.

Codice Azcatitlan, Journal de la Societe des americanistes, n.s., vol. 38. Paris: 1949.

Codice Chimalpopoca. Anales de Cuauhtitlán y Leyenda de los soles. Primo Felliciano Velazquez,.trans. Mexico: 1945

Codice Ramirez. Manuscrito del siglo XVI intitulado: Relación del origen de los Indios que habitan esta Nueva Espania, segun sus historias. Manuel Orozco y Berra and others, eds. Mexico: Editorial Leyenda, 1944.

Codice Xolotl. Charles E. Dibble, ed. Mexico: Publicaciones del Instituto de Historia, 1st series, no. 2. 1951.

Colección de documentos ineditos relativos al discubrimiento, conquista y organización le las antiguas posesiones espanoles de

America y Oceana, sacaso de los archivos del reino, especialmnte del de Indias. Title varies. 42 vols. Madrid: 1864-84.

Colección de documentos ineditos relativos al descubrimiento conquista y organizacion de las antiguas posesiones espanolas de ultramar, 1st and 2nd series, Madrid: 1885-1925.

Colección de documentos para la historia de Mexico. Joaquin Garcia Icazbalceta, ed., 2 vols. Mexico: 1858-66.

Colección de documentos para la historia mexicana. Antonio Penafiel, ed. Mexico: 1904

Conway, G.R.G., La Noche Triste. Documentos: Segura de la Frontera en Nueva Espana y de 1520. Mexico: Gante Press, 1943.

——————— The Last Will and Testament of Hernando Cortés, Marquis de Valle. Mexico: 1939.

Cook, Sherburne F. "Human Sacrifice and Warfare as Factors in the Demography of Pre-Colonial Mexico." Ancient Mesoamerica, John A. Graham, ed. Palo Alto: Peek Publications. 1966.

——————— and Lesley Byrd Simpson. The Population of Central America in the Sixteenth Century. Berkeley and Los Angeles: 1948. Ibero-Americana: 31.

Cortés, Hernando. Cartas de relación de la conquista de Mejico. 2 vols. Madrid: 1942.

——————— Cartas y otros documentos de Hernan Cortes novisimamente descubrietos en el Archivo general de Indias de la ciudad de Sevilla. ed. Mariano Cuevas. Sevilla: 1915.

———————*The Letters of Cortez*. trans. Francis A. MacNutt. 2 vols.New York and London: 1908.

——————— *Letters from Mexico*. trans. and ed. A.R.Pagden. New York: 1971.

Davies, Nigel. The Aztecs. Norman:1973.

———————The Aztec Empire. Norman: 1987.

Davila, Padilla Augustin. Historia de la fvdcacion y discurso de la provincia de Santiago de Mexico de la Orden the predicadores, por las vidas de sus varones insignes, y casos notables de Nueva Espana. Madrid: 1596.

Denhardt, Robert M. "The Equine Strategy of Cortez." Hispanic American Historical Review. 18: 550-55.

Díaz del Castillo, Bernal. *Historia verdadera de la conquista de la Nueva Espana.* Madrid:Espasa-Calpe, 1928.

—————-*The True Story of the Conquest of New Spain by Bernal Díaz del Castillo,* trans. A. P. Maudsley. Vols. 23-25, 30, 40. Hakluyt Society, series 2. London: 1908-16. Published in abridgement by Farrar, Strauss, and Giroux, New York: 1956.

Díaz Juan. Itinerario de la armada del Rey Catolico, a la isla de Yucatán, en la India, el ano 1518. Mexico: Juan Pablos, S.A., 1972.

Diccionario Porrua, Mexico: Editorial Porrua, 1964.

Dioses del Mexico Antiguo. Antiguo Colegio de San Idlefonso. Ciudad Mexico: 1995.

Duran, Fray Diego. *Historia de las Indias de Nueva Espania y islas de tierra firme.* 2 vols. Jose F. Ramirez, ed. Mexico: Editoria Nacional, 1951.

—————-*The Aztecs. The History of the Indies of New Spain, by Fray Diego Duran.* Doris Heyden and Francisco Horcasitas, trans. New York: 1994.

—————-*Book of the Gods and Rites and the Ancient Calendar, by Fray Diego* Duran. Fernando Horcasitas and Doris Heyden trans and eds. Norman: 1971.

Epistolario de Nueva Espania 1505-1818. Francisco del Paso y Troncoso, ed. 16 vols. Mexico: Biblioteca historica mexicana de obras ineditos, ser.2. 1939-42.

Fuentes, Patricia de. *The Conquistadors*. New York: 1963.

Garcia, Genaro, and Carlos Pereyra, eds. *Documentos ineditos o muy raros para la historia de Mexico*. 36 vols. Mexico: 1905-07.

Garcia Granados, Rafael. *Diccionario biografico de historia antigua de Mejico* 3 vols. Mexico: Publicaciones del Insitituto de historia, primera serie, num. 23. 1952-53.

Garcia Icazbalceta, Joaquin. *Bibiografia mexicana del siglo XVI.* Agustin Millares, Carlo, ed. Mexico: 1954.

Gardiner, C. Harvey. Martin Lopez, *Conquistador Citizen of Mexico.* Lexington, Kentucky: 1958.

——————-Naval Power in the Conquest of Mexico. Austin: 1956.

Gibson, Charles. *The Aztecs Under Spanish Rule.* Stanford: 1964.

——————-Tlaxcala in the Sixteenth Century. New Haven: 1952.

Gillmor, Frances. Flute of the Smoking Mirror. A Portrait of Nezahualcoyotl, Poet King of the Aztecs. Albuquerque: 1949.

Guzman, Eulalia. Relaciones de Hernan Cortes a Carlos V sobre la invasion de Anahuac. Vol.I. Mexico:1958.

Hanke, Lewis. The Spanish Struggle for Justice in the Conquest of America. Boston: 1965.

Herrera y Tordesillas, Antonio de. Historia general de las Indias occidentales. Title varies. 4 vols. 8 decades. Madrid: 1726-40.

Heyden, Doris. The Eagle, The Cactus, The Rock. The Roots of Mexico-Tenochtitlan Foundation Myth and Symbol. Bar International Series 484. Great Britain: 1989.

Historia tolteca-chichimeca. Anales de Quauhtinchan. Heinrich Berlin, Silvia Rendon, Paul Kirchoff, and Salvador Toscano, eds. Mexico: Fuentes para la historia de Mexico, I 1947.

Indice de documentos de Nueva Espana existentes en el Archivo de Indias de Sevilla. 4 vols. Monografias bibliografias mexicanas, 12, 14, 22, 23. Mexico:1928-31.

Indice de ramo de Indios del Archivo general de la nación. Luiz Chavez Orozco, ed. 2 vols. Mexico: 1951-53.

Ixtlilxochitl, Fernando de Alva. Ally of Cortes. Account 13: of the coming of the Spaniards and the beginning of evangelical law. Douglass K. Ballentine, trans. El Paso: 1969.

————————-Obras Historicas. Mexico: Universidad Nacional Autonoma de Mexico, 1975.

————————-Relaciones. Alfredo Chavero, ed. Obras Historicas, vol.I. Mexico: 1891.

————————-Historia de la nación chichimeca. Alfredo Chavero, ed. Obras Historicos vol II. Mexico: 1892.

Jimenez Moreno, Wigberto. "Sintesis de la historia precolonial del valle de Mexico." Revista mexcana de estudios antropologicos, XIV, Primera Parte, 219-36, 1954-55.

Kelley, Isabel, and Angel Palerm. The Tajin Totonac. Washington: Smithsonian Institution, Institute of Social Anthropology. Publication 13, 1952.

Landa, Fray Diego de. Yucatan, Before and After the Conquest, trans. William Gates. New York: 1978.

Las Casas, Bartolome de. Apologetica historia de las Indias. Serrano y Sanz, ed. Nueva Biblioteca de autores espanoles, XIII.Serrano y Sanz, ed. Madrid: 1909.

Leon Portillo, Miguel. Aztec Thought and Culture. Jack Emory Davis, trans. Norman: 1963.

————————La Filosofía Náhuatl. Universidad Nacional Autónoma de Mexico: 2001.

————————Trece Poetas del Mundo Azteca. Instituto de Investigaciones Historicos. Universidad Nacional Autónima de Mexico City, 1967.

Leon y Gama, Antonio de, "Descripcion de la ciudad de Mexico, antes y despues de la llegada de los conquistarores espanoles." Revista mexicana de estudios historicos, I Appendix, 8-58, 1927.

Lienzo de Tlaxcala, Artes de Mexico, nos. 51 and 52. Mexico: 1964.

López de Gómara, Francisco. Historia de la conquista de Mexico. Joaquin Ramirez Cabanas, ed. Mexico: 1943. Translated into English in an abridged edition by Lesley Byrd Simpson under the title, Cortés. The Life of the Conqueror by his Secretary. Berkeley and Los Angeles: 1966.

López de Menesis, Amada. "Dos nietas de Moctezuma, monjas de la Concepcion de Mexico." Revista de Indias, XII, 81-100.

1952.

————————-"El primer regreso de Hernan Cortes a Espana." Revista de Indias, XIV, 69-91, 1954.

————————-"Tecuichpochtzin, hija de Moctezuma (¿ 1510?-1550)" Revista de Indias. IX, 471-95. 1948.

Marquina, Ignacio. El Templo Mayor de Mexico. Mexico: Instituto Nacional de Antropologia y Historia, 1960.

Martyr, Peter (Pietro Marire de Angleria) De Orbo Novo. Decades del Nuevo Mundo. Buenos Aires: Editorial Bajel, 1944.

McAfee, Byron, and Robert H. Barlow. "Anales de la conquista de Tlatelolco en 1473 y en 1521." Memorias de la Academia mexicana de la historia, IV, 326-38.

Mendieta, Geronimo de. Historia eclesiastica indiana. Joaquin Garcia Icazbalceta, ed. Mexico: 1870.

Miranda, José. El tributo indigena en la Nueva Espania durante el siglo XIV. Mexico: 1952.

Molina, Alonso de Vocabulario in lengua castellano y mexicana. Madrid: Colección de incunables americanos, IV. 1944.

Molins, Fabrega N. "El codice mendecino y la economia de Tenochtitlán," Revista mexicana de estudios antropologicos. XIV, Primera Parte, 303-35. Mexico: 1954-55.

Monzon, Arturo. El calpulli en la organizacion social de los tenochca. Mexico: Publicaciones del Instituto de historia, primera serie, 14, 1949.

Moreno, Manuel M. La organizacion politica y social de los aztecas. Mexico: 1931.

Motolinia (Toribio de Benavente) History of the Indians of New Spain. Elizabeth Andros Foster, trans and ed. Berkeley: The Cortes Society, Documents and Narratives Concerning the Discovery and Conquest of Latin America. n.s. 4, 1950.

—————————Memoriales. Luis Garcia Pimentel. ed. Mexico, Paris, and Madrid: Documentos historicos de Mejico, I, 1903.

Muñoz Camargo, Diego. Historia de Tlaxcala. Alfredo Chavero, ed. Mexico: 1892.

Nahuatl Accounts of the Conquest of Mexico. James Lockhart, ed. and trans. Berkeley, Los Angeles, London: 1993.

Nueva Colección de documentos para la historia de Mexico. Joaquin Garcia Icazbalceta, ed. 5 vols. Mexico: 1886-92.

Nueva colección de documentos para la historia de Mexico. Joaquin Garcia Icazbalceta, ed. 3 vols. Mexico: 1941.

Orozco y Berra, Manuel. Historia antigua y de la conquista de Mexico. 4 vols. and atlas. Mexico, Editorial Porrua, 1960.

Ortega y Perez Gallardo, Ricardo. Historia genealogica de las familias mas antiguas de Mexico. 3 vols. Mexico:1908-10.

Oviedo y Valdes, Gonzalo Fernandez de. Historia general y natural de las Indias, islas y tierra-firme del mar oceano. 4 vols. Madrid: Biblioteca de Autores Espanoles, edicion y estudio de Juan Perez de Tudela Bueso.!959.

Padden, R.C. The Hummingbird and the Hawk. New York: 1970.

Papeles de Nueva Espana. Francisco del Paso y Troncosco, ed. 9 vols. Madrid and Mexico: 1905-48.

Pearce, Kenneth. The View from the Top of the Temple: Ancient Maya Civilization and Modern Maya Culture. Albuquerque: 1984.

————————- A Traveler's History of Mexico, London: 2002.

Powell, David Wayne. Soldiers, Indians, and Silver. Northward Advance of New Spain `1550-1600. Berkeley: 1952.

Prescott, William Hickling. History of the Conquest of Mexico. John Foster Kirk, ed. 3 vols. Philadelphia: 1873.

—————The Conquest of Mexico. The Conquest of Peru New York: Modern Library. n.d.

Quetazalcoatl and the Irony of Empire. Revised Edition. Boulder: 2000.

Radin, Paul. "The Sources and Authenticity of the History of the Ancient Mexicans." University of California Publications in American Archaeology and Ethnology, XVII, 1-150. Berkeley: 1920.

Ramirez Cabañas, Joaquin. "Los macehuales." Filosofia y letras, II, 119-24. 1941.

Rendon, Silvia, ed. "Ordenanza del Senor Cuauhtémoc" in Middle American Research Institute, Tulane University, Publication no. 12, 13-40. New Orleans: 1952.

Ricard, Robert. The spiritual conquest of Mexico; an essay on the apostolate and the evangelizing methods of the mendicant orders in New Spain, 1523-1572. Trans. Lesley Byrd Simpson. Berkeley and Los Angeles: 1966.

Romero de Terreros, Manuel. Bibliografia de cronistas mexicanas, num. 4, 1926.

Rounds, J. "Dynastic Succession and the Centralization of Power in Tenochtitlan." In Collier, Rosaldo, and Wirth, *The Inca and Aztec States, 1400-1800.* Academic Press, 1982.

Sahagun, Bernardino de. *General History of the Things of New Spain; Florentine Codex.* Arthur J.O. Anderson and Charles E. Dibble. trans. and eds. 13 parts. Santa Fe: Monographs of the School of American Research, No. 14, 1950 et seq.

—————-*Historia general de las cosas de Nueva Espania.* (Tolosana) Angel Maria Garibay, K. ed. Mexico: Editorial Porrua, 1969.

————————Relacion de la conquista, 1585. (Enmendada). Carlos M. Bustamante, ed. Published as La Aparicion de Ntr. Senora de Guadelupe de Mexico, comparada con la refutacion del argumento negativo que presenta D. Juan Bautista Munoz fundandose en el testimonio P. Fr. Bernardino de Sahagun; o sea historia original de este escritor, que altera la publicada en 1829 en el equivocado concepto de ser la unica y original de dicho autor. in 1840. In Historia universal de Nueva Espana. Mexico: Editorial Pedro Robredo. 1938.

————————*Conquest of New Spain: 1585 revision /by Bernardino de Sahagún;* reproductions of the Boston Public Library Manuscript and Carlos Maria Bustamante 1840 edition; translated by Howard F. Cline; edited with an introduction and notes by S.L.Cline. Sahagún, Bernardino de.

San Vincente, Juan Manuel de. "Exacta descripcion de la magnifica corte mexicana." *Anales de Museo nacional de arqueologia, historia y etnografia,* epoca 3, V, 3-40. 1913.

Saville, Marshal H. *Tizoc, Great Lord of the Aztecs,* 1481-86. New York: Contibutions, Museum of the American Indian, Heye Foundation, vol.7, no.4, 1929.

Sejourne, Laurette. *Burning Water.* Berkeley: Shambala, 1976.

Seler, Eduard. *Gesammte Abhandlungen zur Amerikanishen Sprach-und Altertumskunde.* 6 vols. Graz, Austria: Akademische Druck und Verlagsanstalt. 1960.

————————-"Mexican Picture Writing of Alexander von Humboldt." In Mexican and Central American Antiquities,

Calendar Systems, and History: Smithsonian Institution, Bureau of American Ethnology, Bulletin 28, 127-229. Washington: 1904.

Simeon, Remi. Dictionnaire de la Langue Nahuatl ou Mexicaine. Graz, Austria: 1960.

Siete Partidas; Las Siete Partidas de rey Don Alfonso el Sabio, cotejadas con varios codices antiguos por la Real Academia de la historia. 3 vols. Madrid: 1807.

Simpson, Lesley Byrd. *Many Mexicos*. Berkeley and Los Angeles: 1957.

————————-The Encomienda in New Spain. Berkeley and Los Angeles: 1950.

Solis, Antonio de. *Historia de la conquista de Mexico*. Mexico: Población y progresos de la America Septentrional conocide por el nombre de Nueva Espana. 2 vols. Imprenta de I. Paz. 1899-95.

Soustelle, Jaques. Daily Life of the Aztecs. Patrick O'Brian, trans. Stanford: 1970.

————————*Pensamiento cosmologico de los antiguos mexicanos*. Maria Elena Landa A., trans. Puebla; Federación Estudiantil Poblana. 1959.

Steck, Francisco Borgia. El primer colegio de America-Santa Cruz de Tlatelolco. Mexico: 1944.

Tapia, Ándres de. Relacion hecha por el Sr. Andres de Tapia sobre la conquista de Mexico. In Coleccion de documentos para la historia de Mexico. Joaquin Garcia Icazbalceta, ed. vol 2. 554-94. Mexico: 1858-66.

Ternaux Compans, Henri. Voyages, relations et memoires originaux por servir a l'histoire de la decouverte de l'Amerique. 20 vols. Paris: 1837-41.

Tezozomoc. See Alvarado Tezozomoc, Hernando.

The Broken Spears. The Aztec Account of the Conquest of Mexico. Miguel Leon-Portillo, ed. Lysander Kemp, trans. Boston: 1962.

The Tlaxcalan Actas. A Compendium of the Records of the Cabildo of Tlaxcala. 1545-1627. James Lockhart, Frances Berdan, Arthur J.O. Anderson. Salt Lake City: 1986.

Thomas, Hugh. *Conquest*. New York:1994.

Tira de la Peregrinación (Codex Boturini) Mexico: Libreria Anticuaria, 1944.

Torquemada, Juan de. *Los viente I un libros rituales i monarchia indiana.* Facsimile edition. 3 vols. Mexico: 1944.

——————————-*Monaquia Indiana.* 6 vols. Mexico: Universidad Nacional Autónoma Mexico: Investigaciones Historicas. 1975.

Tovar, Juan de. Relacion del origen de los yndios que havitan en esta Nueva Espana segun sus historias. Graz, Austria: 1972.

Ulloa Ortiz, Berta. "Catalogo de los fondos del Centro de documentación del Museo nacional de historia, castillo de Chapultepec." Anales del Insitituto nacional de antropolgia e historia. IV, 289-322. 1949-50.

"Unos anales coloniales de Tlatelolco, 1519-1633." *Memorias de la Academia mexicana d la historia.* VII, 152-87. 1948.

Vaillant, George C. Aztecs of Mexico. Origin, Rise, and Fall of the Aztec Nation. Baltimore: 1966.

——————————"The Death Throes of the Aztec Nation." *Natural History.* Vol. 43, 38-46.

——————————"The Twilight of Aztec Civilization." *Natural History.* Vol. 43, 38-46.

Vázquez de Tapia, Bernardino. *Relación de meritos y servicios del conquistador Bernardino de Tapia.* Antiguo Libreria Robredo. Mexico: 1953.

Vetancurt, Augustin de. Teatro mexicano. Descripción breve de los svcesos exemplares, historicos, politicos, militares, y religiosos del nuevo mundo occidental de las Indias. 2 vols. Mexico: 1953.

Veyita, Mariano. Historia antigua de Mejico. C.F. Ortega, ed. 3 vols. Mexico: 1836.

Wolf, Eric R. Sons of the Shaking Earth. Chicago: 1950.

Zantwijk, Rudolf van. "Principios organizadores de los Mexicas; Una introduccion al estudio de sistema interno del regimen Azteca." Estudios de Cultura Nahuatl. vol, 4. 176-85. 1966.

Zavala, Silvio. "Catalogo de los fondos del Centro de documentacion del Museo nacional de historia, en el castillo de

Chapultepec." Memorias de la Academia mexicana de la historia. X 459-95. 1951.

——————————-"Los esclavos indios de Nueva Espania." In Homenaje al doctor Alfonso Caso. 427-40. Mexico: 1951.

Zorita, Alonso de. Historia de la Nueva Espania. Madrid: Colección de libros y documentos referentes a la historia de America. IX. 1909.

Index

Printed in Great Britain
by Amazon

52858023R00272